WOMEN IN SOVIET SOCIETY

Tables

Women in Soviet Society

Equality, Development, and Social Change

Gail Warshofsky Lapidus

UNIVERSITY OF CALIFORNIA PRESS

BERKELEY • LOS ANGELES • LONDON

To my parents,
with gratitude and affection

UNIVERSITY OF CALIFORNIA PRESS
BERKELEY AND LOS ANGELES, CALIFORNIA
UNIVERSITY OF CALIFORNIA PRESS, LTD.
LONDON, ENGLAND
COPYRIGHT © 1978, BY
THE REGENTS OF THE UNIVERSITY OF CALIFORNIA
FIRST PAPERBACK PRINTING 1979
ISBN: 0-520-03938-6
LIBRARY OF CONGRESS CATALOG CARD NUMBER: 74-16710
PRINTED IN THE UNITED STATES OF AMERICA

1 2 3 4 5 6 7 8 9 0

Contents

Acknowledgments

THIS study grows out of a broader interest in the social consequences of modernization in Leninist systems. It focuses on a central feature of this process—the concern with the problem of equality, especially of sexual equality. It is based on the view that the explicit ideological commitment to social equality characteristic of Leninist systems is expressed in a distinctive pattern of institutional arrangements that can be examined most fruitfully in historical and comparative perspective. And it argues that these arrangements have important consequences both for the economic and political capacity of Leninist systems and for the scope and limits of participation within them.

One of the particular pleasures that accompanies the publication of a book is the opportunity it affords to offer public acknowledgment of the institutional and intellectual debts accumulated in the course of many years. To the late Merle Fainsod, whose unique gifts as a scholar and teacher first drew me into the study of Soviet politics, and who guided my early training with sensitive judgment and personal concern, I owe a special debt of gratitude. I should also like to express my appreciation to Barrington Moore, who kindled my interest in the relationship of social structure, politics, and human values, and whose intellectual influence left a lasting imprint on my scholarly concerns.

Three different academic communities have shaped the development of this study. The Department of Government and the Russian Research Center at Harvard University encouraged my earliest efforts and offered a continuing hospitality over the years. The University of California, Berkeley provided a stimulating intellectual environment in which to explore new questions. It is a special pleasure to express my gratitude to Carl Rosberg, who, as Chairman of the Political Science Department and Director of the Institute for International Studies, extended both personal encouragement and institutional support to my work. A study born at Harvard and nurtured at Berkeley came to fruition in the hospitable environment of Stanford University, and I am indebted to the Hoover Institution of War, Revolution and Peace and to its Director, Glenn Campbell, for the research support afforded by the National Fellows Program.

I should also like to thank the International Research and Exchanges Board and the Soviet Academy of Sciences for facilitating my work in the

USSR, and the American Council of Learned Societies and Social Science Research Council for speeding the completion of this project.

This study has been illuminated by the insights and sustained by the encouragement of several friends and intellectual companions whose contribution to its genesis and evolution was greater than they perhaps realize. Countless conversations and exchanges of manuscripts with George Breslauer, Natalie Davis, Carolyn Elliott, Arlie Hochschild, Kenneth Jowitt, Gregory Massell, and Myra Strober provoked, stimulated, and refined many of the ideas developed here. I have also benefited greatly from the work of a number of scholars—both in the USSR and in the West—and from their willingness to share both research materials and insights with me. While they bear no responsibility for the conclusions I have drawn from their work, I should like to thank them collectively here for making the ideal of a community of scholars a reality.

I owe a special debt of gratitude to Richard Abrams, Reinhard Bendix, Steve Cohen, Alexander Dallin, Murray Feshbach, Gregory Grossman, Jerry Hough, Jim Hughes, Gregory Massell, Joel Moses, William Rosenberg, Richard Stites, and Reginald Zelnik, who read sections of the manuscript at various stages of its development and who contributed much to whatever virtues it may have. Their specialized knowledge and experienced judgment guided me past innumerable pitfalls and enhanced my understanding of Soviet society in fundamental ways.

Some of the conclusions presented here were elaborated in earlier form as articles, and I am grateful to the *Journal of Industrial Relations* and to *Comparative Politics* for permission to draw on them.

Carol Eubanks Hayden, David Trollman, and Norman Baxter assisted in unearthing a vast array of materials, while the staffs of the Hoover Institution library and of the Cooperative Services Department of the library of the University of California at Berkeley were extraordinarily helpful in tracking down elusive sources. I am especially indebted to Paige Wickland, who brought a gift for language and a patience with technical detail to the editing of the manuscript, and to Bojana Ristich, who arranged the typing of its successive versions with a combination of efficiency and helpfulness.

Finally, but most importantly, I am grateful to Herbert Lehmann for gifts of insight that have enriched both work and life, and to my son Alex, who has patiently, and sometimes impatiently, shared me with this manuscript and added joy to the years of its preparation.

Gail Warshofsky Lapidus

Berkeley, California
1977

Introduction:
The Politics of Equality
and the Soviet Model

IN his preface to *Democracy in America*, Alexis de Tocqueville pointed to the spread of equality as the key to the transformation of Western social and political systems. "The gradual development of the principle of equality," he observed, "is a providential fact. . . . It is universal, it is lasting, it constantly eludes all human interference, and all events as well as all men contribute to its progress. . . . [It is] an irresistible revolution which has advanced for centuries in spite of every obstacle."[1]

It would indeed be tempting to write the history of the modern world as a study in the politics of equality. For a fundamental revolution in human values underlay the transition from a world view in which inequality was religiously sanctioned and hierarchy perceived as part of the natural order of the universe to a new world view in which equality came to be the norm from which inequality, however justified, nevertheless represented a deviation. An expanding conception of citizenship was the most direct expression of new values. The progressive elimination of ascriptive bases of political participation—birth, wealth, race, religion, and ultimately sex—redefined citizenship in universal terms, while its meaning gradually broadened to incorporate economic and social as well as political rights.[2]

The radical implications of the egalitarian impulse left no political order immune to its claims. But even as the democratic revolution established universal and equal citizenship as a guiding principle of political life, the extent of its realization in practice inevitably remained problematic. For, as Giovanni Sartori has rightly remarked, the ideal of equality is never fully realized. "The claim for equality is a protest against unjust, unde-

[1] Alexis de Tocqueville, *Democracy in America*, trans. Henry Reeve (London, 1946), p. 5.

[2] Suggestive theoretical treatments of the problem of equality include Ralf Dahrendorf, *Essays in the Theory of Society* (Stanford, 1968); Sanford Lakoff, *Equality in Political Philosophy* (Cambridge, Mass., 1964); John Rawls, *A Theory of Justice* (Cambridge, 1971); and T. H. Marshall, *Class, Citizenship and Social Development* (Garden City, 1964). Recent studies with an orientation toward policy include Christopher Jencks et al, *Inequality: A Reassessment of the Effect of Family and Schooling in America* (New York, 1972); Herbert Gans, *More Equality* (New York, 1973); and Nathan Glazer, *Affirmative Discrimination: Ethnic Inequality and Public Policy* (New York, 1975).

I

served, and unjustified inequalities. For hierarchies of worth and ability never satisfactorily correspond to effective hierarchies of power. . . . Equality is thus a protest-ideal, a symbol of man's revolt against chance, fortuitous disparity, unjust power, crystallized privilege."[3] Thus, in modernizing and industrial societies alike, changing circumstances as well as changing perceptions and values gave rise to a long sucession of social movements that called into question prevailing arrangements and pressed for the extension of the egalitarian principle into new arenas.

The emergence of European socialism represented just such a response. Whether in the utopian tradition of Fourier or Owen, or in the "scientific socialism" of Marx and Engels, the limitations of the democratic revolution were subjected to a trenchant critique. The erosion of ascribed bases of domination had not eliminated inequality, socialist critics contended, but merely shifted its locus to property relationships. In the absence of a fundamental transformation of economic arrangements, formal political equality merely served to mask the prevailing structure of domination.

The revolutionary leaders who proclaimed the establishment of the new Soviet state in October 1917 promised just such a radical reconstitution of society. A fundamental transformation of all economic and social institutions would finally destroy the very roots of inequality and permit the construction of a new and genuinely egalitarian social order.

A commitment to sexual equality was an important component of this broader egalitarian impulse. Class, ethnicity, and sex had long been identified as the major bases of discrimination and exclusion in capitalist society. By assimilating ethnic and sexual relationships to Marxist models of stratification, the Social Democratic movement insisted on their structural connection and proclaimed the achievement of ethnic and sexual equality to be inextricably entwined with the revolutionary reconstruction of society itself. Thus, the Soviet commitment to sexual equality had deep roots both in Marxist socialist theory and in the intellectual and political history of nineteenth-century Russia. The emergence of the "woman question" (*zhenskii vopros*) as a subject of controversy in the last decades of the century coincided with the rise of a radical intelligentsia that sought the transformation of a backward, agrarian society into an egalitarian and modern socialist community. Rejecting the path of legal political reform, and therefore the tactics and goals of bourgeois feminism, the revolutionary socialist movement insisted that the full liberation of women was inseparable from a larger social revolution.

With the establishment of Soviet power, the Bolshevik leaders confronted the problem of transforming broad revolutionary commitments

---

[3]Giovanni Sartori, *Democratic Theory* (New York, 1965), paperback ed., p. 327.

into concrete policies. Their efforts to draw women into new economic and political roles, to redefine the relationship between the family and the larger society, and above all to alter deeply ingrained cultural values, attitudes, and behavior represent the earliest and perhaps most far-reaching attempt ever undertaken to transform the status and role of women. This effort was in turn connected with a vast program of social mobilization that would have dramatic consequences for the economic and political capacity of the new regime and for the allocation of status and rewards within the political community.

Both the form of this experiment and its consequences deserve analysis. As an authoritarian regime with the commitment and the ability to mobilize extensive resources to achieve centrally determined objectives, the Soviet Union offers the opportunity to examine both the possibilities and the limitations of planned social change. As an avowed socialist society that insists on the connection between private ownership of the means of production and the subordination of women, it offers a setting in which to examine the effect of changes in the ownership and organization of production on patterns of social and sexual stratification. As a developing society that has rapidly moved from relative backwardness to industrial maturity, it offers evidence of the impact of modernization on sex roles. Finally, as a society that claims to have achieved, for the first time in history, full equality for women, the nature of its claim and the evidence on which it is based deserve close scrutiny.

SEXUAL EQUALITY AND SOVIET POLICY: THE PROBLEM

Socialists and feminists alike, critical of the position of women in Western capitalist societies, have long held up Soviet achievements as a model.[4] They have portrayed the Bolshevik revolution of 1917 as a milestone in the emancipation of women, the first occasion on which the complete economic, political, and sexual equality of women was explicitly proclaimed as a major political goal. They contend, moreover, that the Soviet Union is the first society in history to have actually achieved genuine equality. Soviet sources support this view, pointing with pride to Soviet efforts and citing a long list of achievements: the full political and legal equality of women; their extensive participation in the labor force; their equal access to educational and professional opportunities; liberal family legislation regulating marriage, divorce, and abortion; and extensive ma-

---

[4]See, for example, the accounts of travelers to the Soviet Union in the 1920s and 1930s: Jessica Smith, *Woman in Soviet Russia* (New York, 1928); Fannina Halle, *Women in Soviet Russia* (London, 1934); Ella Winter, *Red Virtue: Human Relationships in the New Russia* (New York, 1933). For two contemporary statements, see George St. George, *Our Soviet Sister* (Washington and New York, 1973) and William Mandel, *Soviet Women* (New York, 1975).

4 *Women in Soviet Society*

ternal protective legislation and public child-care facilities.[5] The emancipation of Soviet women is therefore directly attributed to the establishment of socialism. If no feminist movement exists today in the USSR, it is because the woman question is viewed as solved.

This perspective is not without its problems. By emphasizing the radical changes in the position of women that have come about as a consequence of the revolution of October 1917, it ignores the continuities that persist and the ways in which new forms of activity have been assimilated into older patterns and norms. As Kenneth Jowitt has pointed out more generally, "Marxist-Leninist regimes simultaneously achieve basic, far-reaching, and decisive change in certain areas, allow for the maintenance of pre-revolutionary behavioral and attitudinal political postures in others, and unintentionally strengthen many traditional postures in what for the regime are often priority areas."[6] In no area of Soviet life is this more true than in patterns of authority relationships in economic and political life. Revolutionary change in the USSR has not brought a total rupture with the past but a partial assimilation and even reintegration of prerevolutionary attitudes and patterns of behavior. These elements of traditional culture cannot be understood as mere "bourgeois remnants" destined to evaporate in the course of further development; they are defining features of a distinctive political culture.

Moreover, the narrow focus on elite orientations and power implicit in this perspective raises even more fundamental problems. In recent years, students of Soviet politics and society have increasingly come to question models of the Soviet system that exaggerate the omnipotence of the state and treat the process of social transformation as a simple revolution from above. The pervasive influence of deeply rooted cultural traditions and the role of diverse social forces and institutions have received increasing attention in recent work, and their impact on political structures, processes, and outcomes has been a central focus of current scholarship. If the Soviet state left a profound imprint on social structure and values, the state was itself transformed in the process.

[5]The official Soviet position was clearly stated by Lenin in 1919 in a speech to the Fourth Moscow City Conference of Non-Party Working Women, when he proclaimed that "apart from Soviet Russia there is not a country in the world where women enjoy full equality." V. I. Lenin, *Polnoe sobranie sochinenii* (henceforth *PSS*), 5th ed., 55 vols. (Moscow, 1958–1965) 39: 200. Article 122 of the Soviet Constitution reasserts that claim, as do more recent official Soviet sources. For three examples among many, see Tsentral'noe statisticheskoe upravlenie pri sovete ministrov SSSR, *Zhenshchiny i deti v SSSR* (Moscow, 1969), pp. 1–28; E. Bochkareva and S. Liubimova, *Women of a New World* (Moscow, 1969); and Valentina Nikolaeva-Tereshkova, "Zhenskii vopros v sovremennoi obshchestvennoi zhizni," *Pravda*, March 4, 1975, pp. 2–3.

[6]Kenneth Jowitt, "An Organizational Approach to the Study of Political Culture in Marxist-Leninist Systems," *The American Political Science Review* 68 (September 1974): 1176.

An excessive emphasis on revolution from above not only obscures the reciprocal relationship of regime and society but also assigns an intentional character to outcomes that were the secondary or even unintended consequences of other choices. Soviet efforts to emancipate women, for example, lacked the centrality, deliberateness, and coherence that is assumed by this perspective. Indeed, the position of women in Soviet society, particularly since the 1930s, has been shaped in crucial ways by the broader forces set in motion by the Soviet regime and by economic and political choices in which a concern for sexual equality played a negligible role.

Finally, to distinguish the impact of specific Soviet policies from the consequences of broader patterns of socioeconomic change poses a complex analytical problem. In some respects, changes in the role of women in the USSR parallel those occurring in other settings, under different political systems, which are generally associated with industrialization and urbanization;[7] in other respects, however, the distinctive orientations and priorities of the Soviet regime leave their imprint.

If an excessively narrow focus on Soviet policy is misguided, so too is an examination of Soviet achievements that neglects its costs. For the outcomes of Soviet policy are themselves ambiguous. The status and role of women in Soviet society today are far more problematic than their champions acknowledge, and a less sanguine evaluation of Soviet accomplishments may be warranted by the evidence. Indeed, some writers argue that many of the early hopes for women's liberation were disappointed as the Soviet regime consolidated its power.[8] They suggest that the massive participation of women in the labor force, far from liberating women and extending their freedom of choice, has occurred on terms that are in some respects quite oppressive.[9] While Soviet policies have opened new educational and professional opportunities for many women, they have also pressed others into heavy physical labor, often in harsh conditions, with harmful consequences for health and welfare. The liberal family legislation of the early revolutionary years, critics point out, was revoked in the authoritarian climate of the Stalin era with adverse effects on women. Moreover, economic priorities that resulted in the underdevelopment of the service sector and of consumer industries, as well as the failure to fully

---

[7]The classic treatment of the impact of modernization on women's roles is found in William J. Goode, *World Revolution and Family Patterns* (New York, 1963). A more pessimistic assessment of its consequences for women's economic roles is offered in Esther Boserup, *Woman's Role in Economic Development* (London, 1970).

[8]Kate Millett, *Sexual Politics* (Garden City, N. Y., 1970), Ch. 4; Sheila Rowbotham, *Women, Resistance, and Revolution* (New York, 1972), Ch. 5.

[9]Manya Gordon, *Workers Before and After Lenin* (New York, 1941), pp. 168–70; Solomon Schwarz, *Labor in the Soviet Union* (New York, 1951).

socialize child-care and household functions or to alter the allocation of roles within the family, meant that new economic and political obligations were superimposed on traditional feminine roles, creating for women a palpable "double burden" in daily life.

Analyses emphasizing the persistence of sexual inequality in Soviet Russia have offered a variety of explanations. Writers in the Marxist tradition point to the scarcity of resources as the fundamental constraint. According to this view, the material backwardness of Soviet society sharply limited the resources available for the communal facilities that might have lightened the burdens of women. Indeed, it was Trotskii who advanced this argument with particular acuity, treating the position of women as a function of society's level of productivity and not merely of its socioeconomic organization. "The actual liberation of women," he argued, "is unrealizable on the basis of 'general want.'"[10] But the limitation of resources does not in itself explain the ordering of priorities. Trotskii's own analysis went still further in arguing that the very poverty of Soviet society permitted the rise of a conservative bureaucracy, which saw in the restoration of the family a social support of its new position.

Other analyses of Soviet failures attach greater weight to the political and economic requisites of forced industrialization. They view the emphasis on productivity and power rather than welfare—an emphasis that reached its apogee under Stalin—as incompatible with the original goals of the revolution. Economic and social arrangements initially intended to serve human needs were transformed into mechanisms for subordinating them in a massive reversal of means and ends.[11]

Still other analyses focus on the relationship between family policy and broader patterns of sociopolitical change as the key to women's status. These analyses argue that the critical importance of the family—whether as a universal institution uniquely suited to meeting basic human needs (as functionalist sociological theorists would emphasize), as the central support of an increasingly authoritarian and patriarchal political system, or as a mechanism for social integration and stabilization at a time of rapid

---

[10]Leon Trotskii, *The Revolution Betrayed*, trans. Max Eastman (New York, 1937), p. 145.

[11]The classic statement of this general view is the study by Barrington Moore, *Soviet Politics: The Dilemmas of Power* (Cambridge, Mass., 1959). The basic conflict between egalitarian and developmental goals in the evolution of Communist systems is the central theme of Richard Lowenthal, "Development vs. Utopia in Communist Policy," in *Political Change in Communist Systems*, ed. Chalmers Johnson (Stanford, 1970). The view that sexual equality in particular was sacrificed to political and developmental priorities is argued in Janet Salaff and Judith Merkle, "Women in Revolution: The Lessons of the Soviet Union and China," *Berkeley Journal of Sociology*, 15 (1970): 169–91. For other critiques of the orthodox Communist position, see Dianne Feeley, "Women and the Russian Revolution," *The Militant* 35 (March 19, 1971): 18–19; Caroline Lund, "The Communist Party and Sexual Politics," *International Socialist Review* 32 (March 1971): 32–37.

social change—placed fundamental constraints on the pursuit of sexual equality and liberation.[12] Not only did a revolutionary transformation of the family prove incompatible with the revolutionary reorganization of economic and political life, thus contradicting a basic assumption of orthodox Marxism; but growing pressures for political conformity and economic productivity created such intense social strain as to require an actual *reduction* of tensions in communal, family, and sexual relations. In short, as Gregory Massell has recently put it, "a revolution in social relations and cultural patterns . . . could not be managed concurrently with large scale political, organizational, and economic changes."[13]

A final group of explanations assigns strategic importance to the psychological determinants of human behavior and insists on their partial independence of more general economic and political changes.[14] Both classical Marxist theory and Soviet revolutionary ideology, this perspective suggests, were relatively insensitive to the deeper psychological roots of family patterns and sex roles. By assimilating sexual relationships into Marxist models of stratification, Soviet ideology obscured the ways in which patterns of sexual inequality derived from irrational and indeed unconscious psychological processes,[15] and therefore differed from the forms of "instrumental" exploitation based on class. Soviet ideology thus concentrated on the more superficial economic aspects of women's roles, leaving intact the fundamental family structures, authority relations, and socialization patterns crucial to personality formation and sex-role differentiation. Only a genuine sexual revolution could have shattered these patterns and made possible the real emancipation of women.

Embedded in these divergent analyses of the Soviet experience are different assumptions about the locus of inequality itself. Marxist approaches

[12]Nicholas S. Timasheff, "The Attempt to Abolish the Family in Russia," in *A Modern Introduction to the Family*, eds. Norman W. Bell and Ezra F. Vogel (New York, 1961) pp. 55–63; Alex Inkeles, *Social Change in Soviet Russia* (Cambridge, Mass., 1968); Kent Geiger, *The Family in Soviet Russia* (Cambridge, Mass., 1968).

[13]Gregory Massell, *The Surrogate Proletariat: Moslem Women and Revolutionary Strategies in Soviet Central Asia, 1919–1929* (Princeton, 1974), p. 408.

[14]The limitations of classical Marxist approaches to the family form a common theme in critical theory and contemporary feminism. Both attempt to join Freudian and Marxist categories in order to develop a more comprehensive theory of the relationship of personality formation, family structure, and social change. The concerns of the Frankfurt School are reflected in Wilhelm Reich, *The Sexual Revolution*, trans. Theodore P. Wolfe, 4th ed. rev. (New York, 1969) and *The Mass Psychology of Fascism*, trans. Vincent Carfagno (New York, 1970), and in Herbert Marcuse, *Eros and Civilization* (New York, 1962). A parallel approach from an explicitly feminist perspective is developed in Millett, *Sexual Politics*, Ch. 4; Rowbotham, *Women, Resistance and Revolution*, Ch. 5, and *Man's World, Woman's Consciousness* (Baltimore, 1973); and Juliet Mitchell, *Psychoanalysis and Feminism* (New York, 1974).

[15]For this distinction, see George De Vos, "Conflict, Dominance, and Exploitation in Human Systems of Social Segregation," in *Conflict in Society*, eds. A. de Reuck et al. (Boston, 1966), pp. 60–82.

to the problem of equality tend to view the process of social change in evolutionary and systemic terms and to focus on the relations of production as the critical factor whose alteration gives the greatest impetus to broader social changes. Yet the very success of Leninism as a strategy for revolutionary transformation and rapid economic development presents a challenge to Marxist models by emphasizing political values and organization as an instrument of economic and social change. Indeed, the relative autonomy of the political system in Leninist theory and the crucial role of the Party as an "organizational weapon" constitute significant departures from the Marxist treatment of the relationship between base and superstructure. By emphasizing the segmentary rather than the systemic features of social organization, Leninist theory suggests that authority structures play a pre-eminent role in the patterning of social interaction.

Finally, the psychoanalytic tradition suggests yet another perspective from which to view the problem of equality, one that stresses the link between psychic and family structure and patterns of social organization and therefore treats sex roles not merely as dimensions of a social "superstructure" but as independent and causal factors in their own right.

If conventional treatments of Soviet policy have differed in their assessment of Soviet achievements, they have also relied on divergent criteria of evaluation. Analyses that use the position of women in prerevolutionary Russia or in other less developed societies as the basis for comparison emphasize the achievements of the Soviet regime. Those that compare present Soviet reality with the utopian vision of revolutionary ideology do so to draw attention to the discrepancy between promise and reality. The use of Western industrial societies as the relevant standard of comparison yields a more nuanced evaluation of Soviet accomplishments, one that compels serious consideraton of the very definition of equality itself.

The concept of equality is the subject of a vast and rich literature, although one that seldom addresses the problem of sexual equality in particular.[16] Insofar as the pursuit of sexual equality represents a further extension of the egalitarian principle, its definition raises a host of familiar issues: the tension between different and often conflicting aspects of equality; the relation of equality to other values, such as liberty or justice; the conflict between equality of opportunity and equality of result. Sexual equality poses in particularly acute form the contradiction between equal treatment and identical treatment, or, to use the formulation of Aristotle,

---

[16]A useful overview is provided by David Spitz, "A Grammar of Equality," *Dissent* 21 (Winter 1974): 1–16. See also Lyman Bryson et al., eds., *Aspects of Human Equality* (New York, 1956); J. R. Pennock and J. W. Chapman, eds., *Equality* (New York, 1967); and the works cited in footnote 2.

between numerical equality and equality proportionate to desert. But beyond these familiar problems, the definition of sexual equality has a unique dimension because it touches as well on the biologically rooted complementarity of male and female roles and on the nature of the family as a fundamental social institution. It therefore raises even more profound and sensitive issues than do other dimensions of social equality. Controversies surrounding the nature and consequences of masculinity and femininity, the degree of role differentiation based on sex that is essential to the functioning of any society, and the implications of role de-differentiation for the fate of the family itself,[17] offer testimony to the distinctive problems that any discussion of sexual equality must address. The attitudes and expectations with which these questions are approached cannot help but be reflected in any evaluation of the Soviet experience.

THE CONCERNS OF THIS STUDY

While the use of more systematic definitions and criteria of evaluation would greatly facilitate the tasks of cross-national comparison, it is the purpose of the present study to shift the terms of the discussion itself. The continuing controversy over the "achievements" and the "defeats" of Soviet policy reflects a basic failure to appreciate their relationship in the broader context of Leninist politics. It may prove more illuminating to move beyond this level of discussion to a new perspective—a developmental one—that views the Soviet effort to alter women's roles as one dimension of a larger pattern of political and social change. Indeed, this study argues that the Soviet approach to the liberation of women was ultimately shaped less by the individualistic and libertarian concerns of nineteenth-century feminism or Marxism than by a unique awareness of its potential for facilitating the seizure and consolidation of power by a

[17]The view that the increasing differentiation of sex roles is a consequence of modernization, and that a sex-based division of labor within the family along instrumental-expressive lines is functionally necessary to a modern, industrial society finds its classic statement in Talcott Parsons and Robert Bales et al., *Family, Socialization, and Interaction Process* (Glencoe, Ill., 1955), particularly in Morris Zelditch, "Role Differentiation in the Nuclear Family: A Comparative Study," pp. 307–49. This view has been challenged on a number of grounds, most notably by writers who argue that a sharp differentiation of sex roles inhibits the flexibility and role-substitutability increasingly demanded of the family in modern conditions. It is further argued that the differentiation of instrumental and expressive roles on the basis of sex has adverse effects on the early socialization of children and creates obstacles to the appropriate internalization of norms. For an elaboration of the argument in favor of diminished sex-role stereotyping, see Alice Rossi, "Equality Between the Sexes: An Immodest Proposal," *Daedalus* 93 (Spring 1964): 607–52, and Eugene Litwak, "Technological Innovation and Ideal Forms of Family Structure in an Industrial Democratic Society," in *Families in East and West*, eds. Reuben Hill and Rene König (The Hague, 1970), pp. 348–96.

revolutionary movement and for enhancing the economic and political capacity of the new regime. The pursuit of sexual equality, and indeed of social equality more broadly, was therefore both compelled and constrained by a distinctive set of imperatives that created new possibilities for human self-realization while simultaneously establishing sharp limits.

By approaching the position and role of women in contemporary Soviet society from a developmental perspective, a double purpose is served. On the one hand, such a perspective offers a more comprehensive framework for understanding both the extent and the limit of changes in the economic, political, and family roles of Soviet women over several decades. It enables us to build a more coherent balance sheet of Soviet actions and societal reactions, thus helping to explain why the long-term Soviet record presents such a complex—and controversial—mix: some persistent disagreements over tactical means and ultimate objectives; some dramatic vacillations in specific social policies; some very considerable achievements in many important spheres; and a pronounced unevenness in overall outcomes.

At the same time, such a perspective illuminates a critical, unique, and neglected aspect of Soviet economic and political development. Studies of modernization, whether or not they deal with the process of modernization in Leninist systems in particular, are essentially concerned with the "modernization of man," to borrow a current title. The implications of different patterns of development for the role of women, and the role of women in the development process, have been largely neglected in both empirical and conceptual treatments until recently.[18] This neglect is all the more striking in Western studies of Soviet development in view of the serious attention that the woman question has received within the USSR. From the earliest years of the Soviet regime, a concern with the economic and political integration of women has reflected an explicit and unique recognition of the pivotal importance not only of family structures but specifically of women's roles in the process of modernization. Deliberate and long-term efforts to draw women into political and economic life in large numbers, to alter family roles and demographic patterns, and to inculcate new cultural norms in support of new roles expressed an in-

[18]A pioneering study by Norton Dodge in 1966, *Women in the Soviet Economy*, pointed out the importance of "womanpower" in Soviet economic development. The relationship between political development and the transformation of women's roles is the subject of Gregory Massell's more recent and innovative study, *The Surrogate Proletariat*. While Massell's subject is historically and regionally delimited, his treatment addresses itself to some of the same issues as the present study and places the Soviet materials in a broad theoretical and comparative framework.

novative attempt on the part of a new state to incorporate the mobilization of women into a larger strategy of development. An examination of Soviet efforts to transform women's roles not only sheds light on the position of women in Soviet society today but also illuminates a distinctive approach to economic and political modernization, which has served as a model for other revolutionary regimes, including China. The full implications of this approach have yet to be assimilated into Western studies of development in Leninist systems.

From this perspective, the elaboration of an ideology of sexual equality in the Russian revolutionary movement in the nineteenth century offered a basis for solidarity between privileged and alienated men and women seeking to impose modern ideas and institutions on a backward agrarian society. A libertarian and egalitarian ideology incorporating a new definition of citizenship inspired and legitimized this effort and gathered support for an attack on existing social, economic, and political institutions. With the initial seizure of power accomplished in October 1917, efforts to mobilize women and to increase the level and intensity of female political participation formed part of a larger attempt to consolidate the new regime by creating new bases of support among previously disadvantaged strata of the population. The pivotal importance of family structure and roles as potential constraints on social change underlay initial Soviet assaults on the family and efforts to free women and children from its confines. These efforts reflected a sensitivity to the ways in which new values and patterns of behavior fostered by the modern sector of the economy and polity could be subverted by the perpetuation of traditional attitudes within the household. With the inauguration of the First Five Year Plan in 1928, the entry of women into the labor force on a large scale reflected not the implementation of Marxist theory but a response to the pressures of rapid industrialization. And in recent years, in the context of a new stage of Soviet development in which the optimal use of human resources has become a major political issue, women's roles have once again come to the center of attention.

In the course of these decades, the definition of equality was itself transformed. The libertarian strains in the revolutionary intellectual tradition succumbed to new economic and political priorities that altered roles and reallocated status, wealth, and power in ways that were not anticipated in revolutionary ideology. A fundamental redefinition of the rights and responsibilities of citizenship occurred that distinguished Leninist regimes from their Western counterparts. Equality came to mean an equal liability to mobilization.

This book therefore approaches the problem of sexual equality in Soviet

policy as a case study in the politics of equality in Leninist systems. Drawing on Franz Schurmann's treatment of ideology as "a manner of thinking
characteristic of an organization,"[19] it investigates the meaning of equality
by focusing on its institutional expression. The study explores the scope
and limits of egalitarianism in the Soviet system; analyzes the imperatives
that both compel and constrain it; and examines its consequences for political and economic capacity as well as for the allocation of social roles.

The first three chapters are organized chronologically and examine the
ideological and developmental imperatives that defined the scope and limits of equality in the Soviet system. Chapter I traces the emergence of
Bolshevik attitudes and policies toward the woman question against the
backdrop of nineteenth-century feminism and Marxism, exploring the
way in which a commitment to sexual equality took shape in prerevolutionary Russia, the intellectual currents and political forces that shaped
it, and the emergence of an uneasy marriage of Bolshevism and feminism
on the eve of the revolution of 1917.

Chapter II examines the evolution of Soviet approaches to sexual equality in the postrevolutionary period as initial egalitarian commitments confronted new problems and priorities. In the first decade of Soviet power
new political and legal norms established the juridical foundations of sexual equality, while new institutional arrangements slowly began to alter
the structure of pressures, opportunities, and rewards in the surrounding
environment. At the same time, the fundamental limitations of Soviet
egalitarianism revealed themselves in a number of areas, and nowhere
more acutely than in the tortuous history of the Zhenotdel, the Party
Department for Work Among Women.

Chapter III explores the basic shift in the orientation of Soviet policy
toward women, already foreshadowed in the first decade of Soviet power,
that was completed under Stalin. The pattern of rapid industrialization
inaugurated by the First Five Year Plan and the collectivization of agriculture that accompanied it had a profound impact on the economic, political, and social roles accessible to women, creating new pressures as
well as new possibilities. Both the developmental priorities and the political institutions and values associated with Stalinism had important implications for sexual equality, transforming the structure of opportunities
while at the same time establishing new constraints. It was accompanied
by a redefinition of female emancipation itself. A new image of femininity
emerged in the official culture of the Stalin period, one that joined new

[19]Franz Schurmann, *Ideology and Organization in Communist China* (Berkeley and Los Angeles, 1970), p. 18.

economic roles to the glorification of maternity and the reaffirmation of women's traditional domestic and familial responsibilities.

In its effort to transform women's roles, the Soviet regime relied on three mechanisms, which, taken together, may be said to have constituted a strategy of "affirmative action," Soviet-style. Protective labor legislation was promulgated. A network of public child-care institutions was created to assure the compatibility of women's family responsibilities with their employment in the labor force. At the same time, a vast expansion of educational opportunities enabled women to acquire new skills with which to enter new occupational roles. These programs, as well as the assumptions about sexual equality embedded in them, are explored in Chapter IV.

Three chapters that follow examine the outcomes of Soviet development for women's roles in contemporary Soviet society. Chapter V explores the level and patterns of female participation in the labor force and professions; Chapter VI deals with women's roles in the political system; and Chapter VII examines the changing role of women in the family and its implications for both social structure and public policy. The reassessment of traditional perspectives and priorities in the context of current policy debates is analyzed in Chapter VIII. A concluding chapter discusses the broader implications of Soviet development patterns for women's roles and attempts to locate the Soviet experience in a larger theoretical and comparative context.

CONCEPTUAL AND METHODOLOGICAL LIMITATIONS

A number of conceptual and methodological problems attend a study of this kind, and it may prove useful at the outset to point to several fundamental ones. Clearly, the treatment of "Soviet women" as a single analytical category subsumes other distinctions of fundamental importance. Basic differences in economic activities, family patterns, and life styles among urban and rural women create very different possibilities and constraints for the two groups. The ethnic and cultural diversity of the Soviet population and the adaptation of policy to local needs and values produce a complex array of social outcomes that make it difficult, if not impossible, to generalize about the consequences of particular measures for women collectively. The process of social change in rural Russia and among the non-Russian nationalities that constitute almost half the Soviet population is only touched on here, but cries out for serious study by Western scholars.[20]

[20]*The Study of the Soviet Family in the USSR and in the West*, a bibliographical essay prepared by Stephen and Ethel Dunn (American Association for the Advancement of Slavic Studies, Columbus, 1977), offers a useful starting point for further investigations.

Even more fundamental is the fact that the economic, political, and family roles of women are functions not merely of sex but also of socio-economic position. The relative weight to be assigned to class by comparison with sex as a determinant of female status, identity, and roles poses basic issues for sociological and feminist theory.[21] The fact that women share certain attributes in common by virtue of their sex does not necessarily mean that sex plays so critical a role in the allocation of status and rewards that it ought to be considered an independent dimension of stratification. And indeed, the opportunities and problems that women confront in their daily lives are not only different from those of men; they are also profoundly different for different social classes. Thus, it may be legitimate to use the family rather than the individual as the appropriate unit of analysis in many cases.

Nevertheless, the tendency to equate family status exclusively with the position of the male head of the household raises serious problems, particularly when studying industrial societies with high levels of female education and labor-force participation. Because the sociology of stratification has largely ignored the implications of women's occupational status for social structure, it is especially ill-equipped to deal with Soviet society. The preponderance of dual-worker families in the USSR and the high concentration of women in professional occupations limit the utility of conventional approaches to stratification and invite the elaboration of a new conceptual framework.

There is, however, still further justification for the treatment of Soviet women as a single analytical category: women are treated as a collectivity by Soviet analysts themselves. Despite the formal denial until recent years of the existence of distinctive group interests in the Soviet Union, and the insistence that Party and state institutions express the national interests

[21]In his classic study of stratification, Gerhard Lenski points to the lack of consideration of sexual stratification in contemporary sociological theory. Changes in the status of women as a result of industrialization, he argues, make it increasingly less feasible to treat women's status as derivative and dependent on that of the male head of household (*Power and Privilege* [New York, 1966], pp. 402–5). This view is challenged by Frank Parkin, who insists that inequalities associated with sex differences ought not be treated as components of stratification insofar as the disabilities attaching to female status are not sufficiently significant as to override the importance of women's vertical placement in the class hierarchy by virtue of family position. For a majority of women, claims over resources are determined by fathers and husbands, and it is therefore appropriate to regard the family rather than the individual as the basic unit of stratification (Parkin, *Class Inequality and Political Order* [New York, 1971], pp. 14–15). A sensitive appreciation of the effects of class position on women's family life in American society is Lillian Breslow Rubin's *Worlds of Pain: Life in the Working Class Family* (New York, 1976). For a thoughtful discussion of the possible consequences of an increase in dual-career families for the stratification system, see Constantine Safilios-Rothschild, "Family and Stratification: Some Macro-Sociological Observations and Hypotheses," *Journal of Marriage and the Family* 37 (November 1975): 855–60.

of an essentially solidary society, Soviet sources are almost obsessive in their preoccupation with group representation. A number of groups are specifically designated as collective entities in official Soviet writings. These include not only socioeconomic classes—workers, peasants, and intelligentsia—but also nationality groups and women. As Western scholars are all too well aware, a vast array of Soviet statistical data records the precise representation of these designated groups in various social and political institutions. The widespread use of such data to demonstrate the representative and responsive character of Soviet institutions involves the implicit acceptance of a microcosmic definition of representation whose implications deserve to be explored.

A second category of problems stems from the focus of this study itself. In examining the consequences of Soviet development for the status and roles of women relative to those of men, it necessarily neglects a comprehensive treatment of the larger issue, of the opportunities that a given society affords for the self-realization of all its members. Ultimately, sexual equality is only one among a number of human values, and it may be realized to a greater degree in circumstances that otherwise offer very limited opportunities for human fulfillment. While no study of the Soviet experience can ignore this issue, it will not be the central focus of our concern here.

If the exploration of women's roles in a single society raises difficult conceptual problems, the pitfalls of comparative analysis loom larger still. Similar patterns may be the product of very different historical and cultural forces, and the identification of similarities or differences is only a first step in the process of such analysis. Moreover, comparisons typically focus on institutions rather than functions or processes, thus obscuring the extent to which similar activities may be carried on in very different ways in different societies. To cite but one example, activities that in the Soviet Union are carried out by Party or governmental agencies are often performed in the United States by private or voluntary associations, and comparisons of the political role of women that are confined to public institutions may thus neglect an important dimension of political reality. Cross-cultural comparisons also tend to focus on identifiable structures and quantifiable relationships, thus neglecting such subjective elements of women's roles as their relative status, self-esteem, and ego-strength, or the congruence between aspirations and opportunities. In the Soviet Union such investigations unfortunately remain beyond our reach.

A final problem confronted in a study of this kind involves the unavoidable limitations of the data on which it is based. Constraints on empirical investigation of policy making and social processes and outcomes in the Soviet Union pose enormous problems for serious scholarship. The bulk of this study is based on published Soviet materials. Inevitably, if regrettably, it relies heavily on fragmentary and inadequate statistics and on sociological survey data that are limited both in conception and in execution, drawing from the Western conceptual literature in a number of disciplines, including economics, sociology, demography, anthropology, and literature, to interpret the Soviet data. The absence of important data in many areas, the total inaccessibility of the policy process, and the dearth of serious and comprehensive studies—either Soviet or Western —of this entire issue make any effort at synthesis premature. This study is offered in the hope that it may nevertheless provide a foundation for further research in Soviet social history and public policy, suggest a tentative framework for much-needed comparative studies of women's roles in modernizing and industrial societies, and link such studies to broader problems in the politics of equality.

ONE

The Woman Question in Prerevolutionary Russia: Changing Perceptions and Changing Realities

> The profound difference between us and the European West in the history of the long struggle for political freedom, the vast chronological distance between the beginning of this struggle there and here, and the unavoidable consequence of this difference [resulted in] the merging, in Russia, of the political overthrow with the social one.
>
> Paul Miliukov

No discussion of the problem of sexual equality in Soviet society can take the Bolshevik revolution of 1917 as its starting point. The uneasy marriage of Bolshevism and feminism had deep roots in the social and political history of prerevolutionary Russia, for it was during the decades following the Crimean War, in the context of broader discussions of Russia's future development, that the woman question emerged as a serious political concern.

Controversy over the proper role of women in modern society was by no means confined to nineteenth-century Russia. The process of modernization involved fundamental changes in the nature of political authority, in economic organization, and in family structure that called into question traditional values and patterns of behavior throughout the Western world. New conceptions of polity, economy, and family resting on individualistic and egalitarian premises raised new questions about the role of women not only in Russia but in all Western societies.

In Western Europe and in the United States, emerging feminist movements adopted reformist strategies that emphasized political and legal emancipation. The transmission of Western ideals of sexual equality to the very different social and political environment of nineteenth-century Russia altered the terms of discussion. In Western Europe a slowly expanding definition of citizenship resulted in the gradual extension of civil, political, and social rights to women.[1] In Russia, the weight of autocratic rule inhibited the development of a participant political culture and perpetuated the enormous gap between state and society. The result, as Paul Miliukov reflected in his history of Russia, was the compression of successive stages of development in the abrupt and telescoped transformation of 1917, or, as he put it, the merging of the political revolution with the social one.[2] While Western feminism did indeed have its Russian counterpart, the woman question in Russia was ultimately joined to the quest for a total social reconstruction by a radical intelligentsia that came to view the liberation of women not as a goal in itself but as one dimension of a broader transformation of all economic, social, and political institutions. Thus, a unique conjunction of feminism and revolutionary socialism occurred in Russia—a conjunction that eventually engulfed the liberal feminist movement, reshaped the terms of discussion of the woman question, and proposed a new framework for its solution.

MODERNIZATION AND EGALITARIANISM IN WESTERN EUROPE

The emergence of controversy in the mid-nineteenth century over the proper sphere of women's activity was a consequence of the vast social changes that had altered the nature of European society in the course of several centuries. The process of nation-building in early modern Europe had wrought profound transformations in the structure of political authority and in the property relationships and family structures with which it was entwined. As the diffuse pluralism of medieval society succumbed to new patterns of social organization in which authority was concentrated in fewer and more clearly differentiated institutions, the nature of polity, economy, and family were transformed together, and new conceptions of all three developed side by side.[3]

---

[1] For a more comprehensive analysis, see T. H. Marshall, *Class, Citizenship and Social Development* (Garden City, N. Y., 1964), and Reinhard Bendix, *Nation-Building and Citizenship* (New York, 1964), pt. 1. Marshall formulates a threefold typology of rights: *civil* rights, such as "liberty of person, freedom of speech, thought and faith, the right to own property and to conclude valid contracts, and the right to justice"; *political* rights, such as the franchise and the right of access to public office; *social* rights, ranging from "the right to a modicum of economic welfare and security to the right to share to the full in the social heritage and to live the life of a civilized being according to the standards of living prevailing in the society." I am grateful to Reinhard Bendix for pointing out the relevance of this formulation to the emergence of movements for sexual equality.

[2] Paul Miliukov, *Istoriia vtoroi russkoi revoliutsii* (Sofia, 1921), Vol. I, pp. 12–14.

[3] These changes in structure and values are explored in Peter Laslett, *The World We Have Lost* (New York, 1965); Philippe Aries, *Centuries of Childhood* trans. Robert Baldick (New

The history of Western political thought is replete with metaphors likening kingship to paternal authority. The analogy of family and polity is a recurrent theme in political writings, and a wide variety of theorists treat the family as both the source and the model of political authority. While these metaphors served a normative rather than a descriptive function, their changing content reveals a slow transformation of values and expectations in early modern Europe. Political tracts and marriage manuals alike shifted from organicist metaphors, based on the imagery of a great chain of being, toward images of family and polity as political rather than natural communities. As the rise of a powerful secular authority freed individuals from the bonds of corporate medieval structures, images of sovereignty and paternal authority reinforced and legitimized each other.[4]

The rise of the modern state entailed a centralization of political authority that encroached on the powers and functions of intermediary associations of all kinds. It was paralleled by a redefinition of family roles that enhanced the formal and legal authority of the male head of the household. The elaboration of a definition of treason in political life accompanied the emergence of the concept of "petty treason" to describe a wife's defiance of her husband, at the same time that the development of statutory law increasingly subsumed the person and property of married women under that of their husbands.[5]

But even as the idea of sovereignty reinforced the image of a single decision-maker, both in political life and within the family, it paradoxically also implied equality, a radical individualism in which the citizen rather than the household was conceived as the fundamental social unit. In classical liberalism economic dependence continued to justify political exclusion, as in the insistence in Lockean natural rights theory that "the fathers of families, or freemen at their own dispose, were really . . . all

York, 1962); Bendix, *Nation-Building*, pt. 1; Michael Walzer, *The Revolution of the Saints* (Cambridge, 1965), Ch. 5.

[4]Sir Robert Filmer's *Patriarcha* (1680) offers a classic illustration of the integration of new conceptions of sovereignty with older familial conceptions of the state: familial imagery legitimizes royal absolutism, but the view of the family remains traditional. For a discussion of the patriarchal context of seventeenth-century political thought, see Peter Laslett, ed., *Patriarcha and Other Political Works of Sir Robert Filmer* (Oxford, 1949); and R. W. K. Hinton, "Husbands, Fathers and Conquerors," *Political Studies* 15–16 (October1967–February 1968): 291–300, 55–67. For the argument that Hobbes' view of the family subverts patriarchal attitudes, see Richard Allen Chapman, "*Leviathan* Writ Small: Thomas Hobbes on the Family," *American Political Science Review* 69 (March 1975): 76–90.

[5]The doctrine of coverture was elaborated explicitly in Blackstone's famous formulation of 1765: "By marriage, the husband and wife are one person in law, that is, the very being or legal existence of the woman is suspended during marriage, or at least is incorporated and consolidated into that of the husband, under whose wing, protection, and cover, she performs everything."

the people that needed to have votes."[6] Yet the universalistic and egalitarian implications of democratic theory entailed an expanded definition
of citizenship founded on the inseparability of legitimacy from consent.
These implications were given an early statement by the Levellers, when
John Lilburne proclaimed in 1646: "All and every particular and individual man and woman, that ever breathed in the world, are by nature all
equal and alike in their power, dignity, authority and majesty, none of
them having (by nature) any authority, dominion or magisterial power
one over or above another."[7]

The corrosive implications of new values for older definitions of male-
female relationships were profound. Traditional treatments of inequality
rested on the assumption that the inferiority and subordination of women
had its origins in the hierarchy of nature itself.[8] Once this hierarchy was
called into question and inequalities were seen as the product of convention rather than nature, the way was open for questioning the rationale
of female subordination as well.

The political implications of new values were only slowly realized in
practice. By the end of the eighteenth century, the extension of full citizenship to women had found a distinguished array of champions. Mary
Wollstonecraft in England, Condorcet and Olympe de Gouges in France,
and Abigail Adams in the United States were outspoken in their insistence
that democratic political values were incompatible with the exclusion of
women from direct political participation. But despite the egalitarian language of both American and French revolutionary ideology, universality
of citizenship in theory was combined with its narrow restriction in practice.[9] For more than another century the political role of women was confined to raising citizens. By the mid-nineteenth century, however, the

---

[6]The close connection between political rights and the capacity to exercise them emerges
in the remainder of this passage whose author was James Tyrrell, a contemporary of Locke's:
"There never was any government where all the promiscuous rabble of women and children
had votes, as not being capable of it, yet it does not for all.that prove that all legal civil
government does not owe its original to the consent of the people, since *the fathers of families,
or freemen at their own dispose, were really and indeed are all the people that needed to have
votes.* . . . Children in their father's families being under the notion of servants, and without
any property in goods or land, have no reason to have votes in the institution of government." Quoted in Laslett, *The World We Have Lost*, pp. 180–81 (italics added).

[7]Laslett, *The World We Have Lost*, p. 179.

[8]As Ralf Dahrendorf has argued (in *Essays on the Theory of Society* [Stanford, 1968], p.
153), the Aristotelian view can be taken as a model for conventional treatments of equality
prior to the eighteenth century: "It is thus clear that there are *by nature* free men and slaves,
and that servitude is agreeable and just for the latter. . . . Equally, the relation of the male
to the female is *by nature* such that one is superior and the other inferior, one dominates and
the other is dominated."

[9]Sheila Rowbotham, *Women, Resistance and Revolution* (New York, 1972), offers a percep-
tive review of the development of modern feminism. The restriction of political rights in

demand for the extension of full political and civil rights to women was common to a wide variety of movements for political reform.

The transformation of medieval society and the development of new images of authority based on equality and consent affected the structure and image of the family as well as the state. The family was more and more frequently portrayed, like the state, as a political rather than a natural union, the product of convention rather than nature, conjugal rather than extended and patriarchal. Marriage was increasingly viewed as a voluntary association rather than a sacrament, a union based on mutual consent which assumed the equality of the two partners.[10] In family law, as in political life, the implications of new values came into conflict with existing legal arrangements, and pressures for reform of marriage and divorce laws merged with movements for political change.

The economic role of the family, as well as its political environment and structure, was also undergoing profound transformation. The household of preindustrial Europe was a tightly knit community, a unit of both production and consumption, which integrated family and work in the lives of its male and female members alike. The rise of capitalist agriculture weakened this unity, and the industrial revolution shattered it. The separation of household from employment entailed the separation of the family from economic life, while the development of more differentiated and complex economic institutions altered the structure of the household economy itself.[11] The bourgeois family, increasingly divested of its once important educational and placement functions and extended kinship solidarities, was reduced to a more specialized nuclear unit devoted increasingly to emotional gratification, reproduction, and the early socialization of children. At the same time, the industrial revolution drew growing numbers of women and children of the lower classes into the factory system, where they provided an inexpensive supply of unskilled labor. For

---

the French revolution is analyzed in Jane Abray, "Feminism in the French Revolution," *American Historical Review* 80 (February 1975): 43–62.

Some authors (for example, Gunnar Myrdal, *An American Dilemma* [New York and London, 1942]) have argued that ideological egalitarianism serves as a lever to bring about progressive social changes. Seymour Lipset and Reinhard Bendix, in *Social Mobility in Industrial Society* (Berkeley, 1959), argue that, on the contrary, the theory and practice of "equalitarianism" among the white majority has been aided by the continued presence of large ethnically segregated castes (p. 180).

[10]The shift was explicit in Reformation thought. While Catholicism continued to treat marriage as a sacrament and therefore indissoluble, Protestantism denied this view, treating marriage as a voluntary association and making provisions for divorce. This position is taken up explicitly by Milton; see the discussion in Walzer, *Revolution*, pp. 196–98.

[11]See in particular Neil Smelser, *Social Change in the Industrial Revolution* (Chicago, 1959), and Joan W. Scott and Louise A. Tilly, "Women's Work and the Family in 19th Century Europe," *Comparative Studies in Society and History* 17 (January 1975): 36–64.

a variety of social groups these changes called into question older definitions of women's roles based on the productive role of the household and the integration of family and work. Thus, the gradual decline of the family as a productive economic unit exposed its members to new opportunities and experiences that slowly altered the very basis of family relationships and encouraged new perceptions and values.

In both political and economic life, then, the process of modernization altered the role of women in important ways. In the segmented societies of an earlier epoch, the differentiation of functions between men and women occurred within a wider context of universal and religiously sanctioned inequality. The rise of the modern bureaucratic state and of the industrial economy accompanied the emergence of new values, opportunities, roles, and aspirations. The differentiation of functions along new lines and the reintegration of key political and economic activities in hierarchical and bureaucratic structures created new public arenas. The effect of the new forms of division of labor was to increase the differentiation between "public" and "private" spheres of activity—and to relegate the latter to an inferior position. The particularistic and increasingly private realm of family and household became the characteristic domain of women, inferior in status and power to the universalistic, competitive, and public domain in which men played a dominant, if not exclusive, role.[12]

If the process of modernization entailed profound alterations in political, economic, and social institutions, it involved an equally dramatic transformation of values. It encouraged a new conception of human nature and, along with this, new norms for personal behavior. Personal freedom, achievement, and equality were among the new values. Despite the universalistic language in which they were couched, however, these values were in practice largely confined to the new public sphere of male activity. The roles and attributes held up as desirable for women were complementary to those assigned to men and emphasized nurturance rather than self-assertion and achievement. Rousseau's *Émile* provides a striking illustration of the extreme differentiation of male and female roles advocated by some writers. Having devoted an entire treatise to the education of

---

[12]Recent historical researches into medieval records have illuminated the degree to which the extensive legal and property rights of medieval women were whittled away by later developments in theology and in statute law which accompanied the rise of the modern state and which are expressed in the codifications of Blackstone and Coke. See, for example, Barbara Westman's "The Attrition of Women's Rights in the Middle Ages" (Paper presented at the Center for the Study of Democratic Institutions, Santa Barbara, January 1974). The research of Natalie Zemon Davis in early modern European history supports a similar perspective. Analogous tendencies flowing from the imposition of European political and bureaucratic institutions on developing societies are traced in Judith Van Allen, "Sitting on a Man: Colonialism and the Lost Political Institutions of Ibo Women," *Canadian Journal of African Studies* 6 (1972): 165–81.

Émile for citizenship, Rousseau would educate Sophie for exclusively domestic functions: "A woman's education must be planned in relation to man. To be pleasing in his sight, to win his respect and love, to train him in childhood, to tend him in manhood, to counsel and console, to make his life pleasant and happy, these are the duties of women for all time."[13] Images of male-female complementarity therefore conflicted with universal norms and masked an inequality of status, power, and rewards.

This discrepancy between norms and social practice did not go unrecognized. Leading apostles of women's emancipation—from Condorcet and Fourier to John Stuart Mill and Harriet Taylor—insisted that the position of women in a society was a natural measure of its level of civilization and that the progress of women toward freedom was both an expression and a condition of more general social progress. In their view, social progress demanded the extension of egalitarian norms to women and the assimilation of women into the new political community. The implications of democratic theory should be realized in practice by opening public roles to women and giving them identical legal, civil, and political rights and responsibilities. The impulse to erase the pervasive "double standard" went beyond the realm of politics, inspiring pressures for the reform of marriage and for the re-evaluation of norms of personal behavior in all its dimensions, extending even to the claim for equal sexual freedom.

But this approach encountered fierce opposition. Far from wishing to extend further the implications of political radicalism and industrial progress, other social critics, such as Jules Michelet and Pierre-Joseph Proudhon, sought to limit their effects. A more general revulsion against the alienating impact of modern civilization on human relations, a revulsion shared by conservatives and utopian socialists alike, manifested itself in their views of the role of women.[14] A romantic reaction against the consequences of modern life, particularly against the social disintegration that it brought in its wake, resurrected a cult of domesticity in which antifeminism joined a sentimental glorification of a mythical medieval hearth.

Thus, the emergence of the woman question as a source of controversy in Western Europe in the mid-nineteenth century expressed the ambivalent response of social critics to modernization and industrialization more generally. Vigorous controversy over the proper role of women in polit-

[13]Jean-Jacques Rousseau, *Émile* (London, 1911), p. 328. Rousseau further argues: "When the Greek women married, they disappeared from public life; within the four walls of their home they devoted themselves to the care of their household and family. This is the mode of life prescribed for women alike by nature and reason" (p. 330).

[14]A suggestive discussion of the ambivalent response of Western intellectuals to industrialization is offered in Reinhard Bendix, "Tradition and Modernity Reconsidered," *Comparative Studies in Society and History* 4 (April 1967): 266–73. See Rousseau's *La Nouvelle Heloise* and the writings of Jules Michelet and Pierre-Joseph Proudhon for examples of the romanticist reaction.

ical, economic, and family life expressed wider disagreements about the direction and consequences of social change. Questions of political rights and legal equality, of economic opportunity and education, and of the reform of marriage and family life came together in a debate over the proper role of women, which in turn formed part of a larger debate over the proper constitution of society. The contours of this debate first emerged in clear form in France in the 1830s, where utopian socialists and radical St.-Simonians crossed swords with anti-feminist writers like Michelet and Proudhon. The debate spread to England in the 1840s, and was taken up by Russian intellectual circles in the late 1850s, when Russia's catastrophic defeat in the Crimean War raised new questions about the organization of Russian society.

The new currents of thought about women's roles, which demanded the extension of civil, political, and social rights to women and inspired the development of liberal feminism, were given their most coherent and eloquent expression in the writings of John Stuart Mill and his wife Harriet Taylor.[15] Their essays directly confront the contradiction between the egalitarian and libertarian premises of republican political institutions and the inferior status of women. If history entailed progress toward self-realization and the full development of human faculties—and this was emphatically Mill's view—then it required above all the progressive elimination of ascribed status. Inequality and subjection based on birth, religion, and race had already come under attack. Ascription based on sex remained, the last bastion to be assaulted by the forces of reason. "Every step in the progress of civilization has . . . been marked by a nearer approach to equality in the condition of the sexes," Mill insisted, "and if they are still far from being equal the hindrance is . . . in artificial feelings and prejudices."[16] For Mill, the principles of liberty, equality, and self-fulfillment at the heart of republican government were contradicted by the exclusion of half the population from citizenship. For women as for men, personal independence and freedom of action were preferable to even the most enlightened and benevolent of despotisms, for they provided the essential conditions for human development.

For Mill, there was an intimate connection between the purposes of the polity and those of the family. It was the family that provided the earliest socialization into political capacities and behavior; and the family must therefore cultivate the values and qualities desired in social and political life. Like the polity, marriage should be founded on equality and mutual consent. In a formal protest against existing marriage laws, which were

[15]Alice S. Rossi, ed. *John Stuart Mill and Harriet Taylor Mill: Essays on Sex Equality* (Chicago, 1970).
[16]*Ibid.*, p. 73.

based on the inequality of the partners and which gave the husband legal power over the property and person of the wife irrespective of her wishes, Mill renounced their terms in his own marriage and wrote a personal declaration in their place.

While Mill's image of the marriage relationship was modeled on classical liberal theories of political authority, it was also influenced by the form of the business partnership. Repudiating the imagery of paternal authority as a description of conjugal relationships, Mill envisioned the ideal marriage as a partnership of equals. Shared values and purposes were to be combined with a division of powers, with functions assigned on the basis of actual qualifications and each partner absolute in the executive branch of his or her department.

In both the political and the economic metaphors, equality presupposed financial independence. Just as a property qualification was a prerequisite for the independence required for political participation, so in marriage economic independence was a condition of equality and voluntary consent. The power to earn a living was therefore essential to a woman, unless she was provided by her family with independent property. Mill did not wish to require that married women be employed, but it was vital that women be educated in ways that would permit them to be self-supporting if the need arose. The equal education of women was therefore a precondition of their full participation in economic and political life, and it was essential to equality in marriage.

Mill devoted particular attention to the ways in which women's roles were the product of the differing socialization of men and women rather than nature. He called for the elimination of all legal and cultural restrictions on the full participation of women in public life: "We deny the right of any portion of the species to decide for another portion . . . what is and what is not their 'proper sphere.' The proper sphere for all human beings is the largest and highest which they are able to attain to. What this is, cannot be ascertained without complete liberty of choice."[17]

Extending the principles of free trade from economic life to the realm of sex roles would result in the greatest good for the greatest number:

What women by nature cannot do, it is quite superfluous to forbid them from doing. What they can do, but not so well as the men who are their competitors, competition suffices to exclude them from; since nobody asks for protective duties and bounties in favor of women, it is only asked that the present bounties and protective duties in favor of men should be recalled. If women have a greater natural inclination for some things than for others, there is no need of laws or social inculcation to make the majority of them do the former in preference to the latter.[18]

[17]*Ibid.*, p. 100.
[18]*Ibid.*, p. 154.

Mill proposed, then, to extend a negative definition of liberty to the realm of sex roles. Liberty was the absence of all legal prohibitions and social sanctions on freedom of competition and choice.

Mill's emphasis on equality of opportunity became the theoretical cornerstone of liberal feminism. Missing from Mill's writings, as from the preoccupations of the mainstream of British and American feminism, was the concern with social class, sexual emancipation, and the communal reorganization of family life that was embedded in French utopian socialism and that became an important theme in Russian radicalism as well.[19] Mill's strategy was essentially assimilationist. It defined sexual equality as equality of opportunity. Within the existing framework of bourgeois society and liberal politics, the elimination of the disabilities that impeded women's development would lead to their full participation as citizens. Political and civil rights and education were the essential conditions of equality. The elimination of obstacles to freedom of choice and competition would make it possible for women's roles to become more like those of men. A residual differentiation would remain within the family, where Mill envisioned the wife not sustaining life but "adorning and beautifying" it. Harriet Taylor's vision was far more radical, for she insisted that women needed not only the capacity to become self-supporting but also the opportunity to exercise it. For Mill, the future remained open; only experience would demonstrate what capacities and preferences women would reveal in a society that permitted them full development.

THE WOMAN QUESTION AND THE EMERGENCE OF RUSSIAN FEMINISM

The debates over the proper role of women in modern society that raged in Paris and London were soon transplanted to Moscow and St. Petersburg. The novels of George Sand, with their image of the "free heart," had a striking if brief influence on a small circle of educated readers, inspiring some to seek personal and sexual liberation by repudiating traditional family bonds. "Zhorzhsandizm," however, was an individual solution, not a response to the problems of women as a social group. The reform of marriage and the general emancipation of women were also embraced in a very tentative way by such early radical writers as Vissarion Belinskii and Alexander Herzen, who were influenced by French utopian socialist ideas and, in the case of Herzen and Belinskii, by Sand as well.[20]

But a more comprehensive discussion of the woman question awaited

---

[19]The emphasis on class in French social criticism tended to impede the emergence of specifically "feminist strategies," as in England and the United States; the situation of women was more frequently treated from the perspective of class rather than sex.

[20]For an excellent account of Herzen's views, see Martin Malia, *Alexander Herzen and the Birth of Russian Socialism: 1812–1855* (Cambridge, 1961).

the aftermath of the Crimean War, when Russia's crushing defeat and the nearly simultaneous death of Nicholas I created a new environment more hospitable to discussions of social reform. Once again in Russia's history, military defeat proved a catalyst to social change. In this new atmosphere, it was the Russian journalist and radical M. L. Mikhailov, a man acquainted with Parisian St.-Simonian circles and a friend and admirer of the French feminist Eugenie d'Héricourt, who played a central role in introducing the discussion of female emancipation to Russian intellectual circles.[21]

The view that women might constitute a single and distinct social group was in some respects a particularly anomalous one in the stratified and hierarchical society of nineteenth-century Russia. A vast gulf separated aristocratic and educated women from those of the middle classes, and an even wider gulf separated both from the world of the village. In the mid-nineteenth century, discussion of the woman question centered almost exclusively on the fate of the small stratum of women of the educated elite. Only in the last decades of the century did the emancipation of the serfs and the growth of industry turn attention to the plight of peasant and working-class women. A new preoccupation with their distinctive needs took shape in the context of movements in which the question of women's roles was subordinated to larger social goals.

The environment of nineteenth-century Russia affected the discussion of women's roles in yet another way. In a setting so inhospitable to egalitarian premises, where even male suffrage was a radical demand, society would have to be reconstituted politically before a concern with full citizenship could be meaningful. Advocacy of political rights for women, so central to the preoccupations of Mill and of the Western feminist movements, could find no soil in which to flourish.

Indeed, the libertarian individualism on which Western feminism was premised had little direct relevance to the problems of the overwhelming majority of Russian women, whose lives were circumscribed by the economic and social structure of rural Russia. The household formed the center of the social existence of the peasant community. The family was the crucial unit of organization, and the interdependence of its members was expressed in its collective ownership of property. As Teodor Shanin put it, "the individual, the family and the farm appear as an indivisible whole. . . . Peasant property is, at least *de facto*, family property. The head of the family appears as the manager rather than the proprietor of

---

[21]For a detailed and illuminating discussion, see Richard Stites, "M. L. Mikhailov and the Emergence of the Woman Question in Russia," *Canadian Slavic Studies* 3 (Summer 1969): 178–99.

family land."[22] Russian feminism, therefore, did not really confront the issues raised by the structure and values of the rural community; it was largely directed toward the needs of the small minority of women whose education and social position made them receptive to new currents of thought.

Even within the upper strata of nineteenth-century Russian society, however, the role of women was severely circumscribed. Universities and professional schools were essentially closed to women until at least the 1870s, while secondary education was extremely limited in scope and content. The education of a woman was designed to prepare her for a vocation as wife and mother in an aristocratic household, and marriage was the only avenue through which most women might hope to raise their social status. Ecclesiastical control of marriage, unequal inheritance laws, and legal arrangements that reinforced the authority of a husband all combined to deny a married woman a separate legal identity, mobility, and the skills and freedom to seek desirable employment.

Yet in some respects the position of privileged women in nineteenth-century Russia compared favorably with that of their West European counterparts. The legal and property rights enjoyed by women of the upper classes in particular offered them an unusual degree of independence. In contrast to what prevailed in most continental countries, and in Britain until 1882, Russian wives were legally entitled to own property, and daughters to inherit it, although not on an equal footing with sons.[23] The rising dissatisfactions that fed the development of both feminism and radicalism were a function of changing perceptions and values and not merely of a uniquely oppressive objective reality.

The early discussions of the woman question in Russia focused most directly on questions of educational opportunity and its relation to the wider role of women in society. By the middle of the century a number of educational reformers were calling for an extension of educational opportunities for women as part of a more general reorganization and democratization of the educational system; new educational opportunities

[22]Teodor Shanin, "The Peasantry as a Political Factor," in *Peasants and Peasant Societies: Selected Readings*, ed. Teodor Shanin (Harmondsworth, England, 1971), pp. 241–44. The notion of family ownership, however, was contradicted by the exclusion of women from its provisions. Although the dowry and personal earnings of the women could be passed from mother to daughter, women had no share in the partitioning of household property. See Teodor Shanin, *The Awkward Class* (Oxford, 1972), p. 222, and William T. Shinn, "The Law of the Russian Peasant Household," *Slavic Review* 20 (December 1961): 601–21.

[23]V. I. Sergeevich, *Lektsii po istorii russkogo prava* (St. Petersburg, 1890), p. 574. For a comprehensive review of the evolution of women's status and rights in Russia, see Dorothy Atkinson, "Society and the Sexes in the Russian Past," in *Women in Russia*, eds. Dorothy Atkinson, Alexander Dallin, and Gail Warshofsky Lapidus (Stanford, 1977).

implicitly suggested that new social roles would follow. A more comprehensive discussion of educational reform as it related to the nature of women and women's future social role was inaugurated by a series of articles that Mikhailov published between 1858 and 1861, articles that echoed many of the themes of the discussions in Western Europe.

In a series of essays that evoke the writings of Mill, Mikhailov attacked the Russian antifeminists for their insistence on the biological infirmity and moral inferiority of women and their glorification of motherhood as the only destiny of womankind. He argued that cultural conditioning rather than natural inferiority explained the subordinate position of women. Equal educational opportunities, Mikhailov affirmed, were the key to the emancipation of women. Such opportunities would develop a wide variety of latent capacities, make it possible for women to fulfill "the vocation of humanity," and encourage women to take up new private and public roles according to their individual inclinations and abilities.

Mikhailov's goal was to deemphasize sexual differences and affirm human capacities. As he put it: "There should be nothing feminine in women except their sex. All other traits should be neither masculine nor feminine, but purely human."[24] The diminution of excessive sexual differentiation would in turn reshape and indeed strengthen family ties by uniting two partners equal in status and sharing similar interests and concerns. In contrast to those who would repudiate marriage as an obstacle to human fulfillment, his ideal, like Mill's was a marriage based on comradeship.

The discussion of educational reform led inevitably to a wider discussion of the role of women in society. Mikhailov's views influenced a variety of writers who came to share his goal: the fullest development of women's capacities so that they too might contribute, in some still undefined way, to the common striving of educated Russia. His ideas shaped the strategy of liberal feminism in Russia for several decades, with its emphasis on creating wider educational and professional opportunities for women and on using these opportunities to serve a larger social cause.[25] The contributions of female medical personnel during the Crimean War had vindicated those who argued that women's capacities could be put to a useful social purpose. In the next decades the pressure of Russian feminists succeeded in opening higher educational institutions to women, in expanding secondary education, and in facilitating the entry of women into the professions of teaching and medicine in significant numbers.

[24]Cited in Stites, *Mikhailov*, p. 198.
[25]For an excellent discussion of Russian feminism, see Richard Stites, "Women's Liberation Movements in Russia, 1900–1980," *Canadian-American Slavic Studies* 7 (Winter 1973): 460–74.

State education for women had a uniquely long history in Russia. As early as 1784 Catherine the Great had issued a statute providing for "the education of youth of both sexes" and had established the first boarding schools for girls in Europe—the Smolny Institute for the daughters of the nobility in St. Petersburg and the Novodevichy Convent Institute in Moscow for girls of lower social classes. The subsequent spread of secondary and higher education for women followed an uneven course, paralleling the fate of educational reform more generally. A succession of educational reformers sought to expand the scope of education to reach larger segments of the population. During periods of political reaction, however, the autocracy, fearing the spread of subversive ideas, sought to limit educational opportunities and bring them under close central control. The fate of women's education fluctuated with these wider political currents.

In the immediate aftermath of the Crimean War, liberal educational reformers began to give increased attention to the question of women's education, and influential writers such as N. I. Pirogov explicitly linked the emancipation of women to an expansion of educational opportunities. Pressures from educational reformers and feminists alike for women's access to higher education mounted, and in the liberal political climate of 1861 the universities were opened to them. St. Petersburg was the first to formally admit women students, and its example was followed by a number of other universities. The admission of women was halted by the government in 1863 in a new wave of political repression, impelling large numbers of women to go abroad to continue their education. The universities of Zurich and Paris attracted the bulk of Russian women. Of the 152 women students at the Sorbonne in 1889, two-thirds were Russian.

The subsequent development of higher education for women in Russia involved the creation of separate women's courses and institutions rather than the integration of existing ones. The fate of these programs fluctuated with government policy and with the availability of financial resources. The first such courses were in the fields of pedagogy and medicine, inspired partly by the wish of the government to expand the supply of teachers and medical personnel and partly by the tendency of women to gravitate toward the free professions. The establishment of a limited form of local self-government gave added impetus to these trends. The close connection between the *zemstvo* movement, with its concern for public health and education, and the professionalization of teaching and medicine, as well as the flow of women into these fields, deserves separate study. By the early part of the twentieth century a large number of higher institutes for women had come into being, including some offering engineering and agricultural specialties as well as programs in the arts and sciences, law, and economics. By 1916 a total of thirty thousand women attended institutions of higher education in Russia, constituting almost a quarter of the total enrollment.[26]

Pressures for reform extended to secondary education as well. The statutes prepared by the Ministry of Education in 1858 to encourage secondary education for women left the bulk of their financing to local communities and private benefactors. Yet the very combination of low cost and closeness to the community acted as a stimulus to rapid growth. By the end of the nineteenth century, the number if not the quality of both schools and students was greater than that of the more completely financed men's schools.[27] By 1909, according to one account, the availability of general secondary education for women exceeded that for men. There were a total of 958 girls' schools in the country and 756 boys' schools, and the ratio of students to population was 1:423 for males and 1:319 for females.[28]

The rapid development of secondary education for women was given particular impetus by the growing demand for trained teachers.[29] The emancipation of the serfs and the development of a limited form of local self-government brought increasing pressures for the spread of public education, particularly at the primary level. Efforts to replace makeshift arrangements for training teachers with special preparatory programs accompanied a realization that women might also be trained in large numbers to meet the shortage of qualified teachers. In 1870 a supplementary course in pedagogy was added to the curriculum of the gymnasium to prepare women to enter teaching, and by 1911 primary school teaching was already a predominantly female profession.[30]

The expansion of the network of women's secondary schools was accompanied by a democratization of their clienteles. In 1880 about 40 percent of these students were daughters of the gentry and official classes. By 1914 these groups comprised only 20 percent of the total, while the proportion of women of peasant background had grown from 7 percent to 25 percent, and of worker, craftsmen, and merchant families from 22.8 percent to 35.2 percent.[31]

The expansion of opportunities for women also extended to primary

---

[26]Nicholas Hans, *History of Russian Educational Policy* (New York, 1964), p. 236.

[27]Patrick Alston, *Education and the State in Tsarist Russia* (Stanford, 1969), p. 204.

[28]*Ibid.*, pp. 204, 286–87; see also William H. E. Johnson, *Russia's Educational Heritage* (Pittsburgh, 1950), p. 146.

[29]See Allen Sinel, "Count Dmitrii Tolstoi and the Preparation of Russian School Teachers," *Canadian Slavic Studies* 3 (Summer 1969): 246–62.

[30]Johnson, *Russia's Educational Heritage*, p. 298. Of a total of 154,177 teachers, 83,311 were women.

[31]Hans, *History of Russian Educational Policy*, p. 236.

education. The enrollment of girls rose rapidly in the last decades of the nineteenth century and the early years of the twentieth century, increasing from 121,000 in 1871 to 2,700,000 in 1914. Female students constituted one-third of the total enrollment of eight million and an extraordinary two-fifths of the age cohort.[32] Even prior to the revolution of 1917, the opportunity for a primary education was available to roughly one of four female children. In short, by the outbreak of World War I, Russia already possessed a broad network of educational institutions in which women formed a high proportion of the total student body.

If an expansion of educational and professional opportunities for women was the focus of early feminist efforts, new causes were later added to feminist concerns. The emancipation of the serfs and the development of industry brought large numbers of destitute women to the cities in search of employment. Philanthropic activities were the feminists' response, and their energies were devoted—in Russia as elsewhere—to developing a network of charitable institutions to alleviate the misery of the urban poor.

The organizational experience gained in philanthropic activities was put to new use when, in the early twentieth century, the political democratization of Russia appeared to become a real possibility. The liberal feminists now turned to political organization in an effort to assure the inclusion of women in the new suffrage.[33] Their ranks had meanwhile been swelled by a younger generation of feminists, many the beneficiaries of expanded educational and professional opportunities and more militant in their pursuit of full political rights. The most active and successful of these new groups was the Union for Women's Equality (Soiuz ravnopraviia zhenshchin), formed in 1905 and supported by influential political figures, including Anna Miliukova, wife of the Kadet Party leader. The Union for Women's Equality and its successor, the All-Russian League for Women's Equality (Vserossiiskaia liga ravnopraviia zhenshchin), defended a classical democratic program, including universal suffrage, the convening of a constituent assembly, and major economic and social reforms. These demands were also shared by the Union of Liberation (Soiuz osvobozhdeniia), the clandestine political organization that attempted to unite a broad spectrum of opposition groups in the struggle for political liberty and a constitutional system.

The precarious unity of the opposition groups was shattered by the

[32]Calculated from figures given by Nicholas DeWitt, *Education and Professional Employment in the USSR* (Washington, D.C., 1961), p. 104.

[33]The Russian Women's Mutual Philanthropic Society (Russkoe zhenskoe vzaimoblagotvoritel'noe obshchestvo) was the best organized and most politically active of these groups; an account by its founder, Anna Shabanova, is found in *Ocherk zhenskogo dvizheniia v Rossii* (1912).

October Manifesto of 1905. In promising the creation of a parliamentary assembly, the Duma, to be elected by limited male suffrage, the Manifesto produced a serious split over the issue of female suffrage. Prior to 1905, the absence of political rights had encouraged solidarity in the struggle for reform. As Ariadne Tyrkova-Williams, a leading figure in the constitutional democratic movement, suggested, "Perhaps it was because of this that in the Russian educated class there was not the wall between the male and the female worlds that there was in Europe. Together we dreamed of freedom, of the rights and duties of a citizen, and together we would get them. How now, only halfway, could women be denied the long list of rights for all . . . ?"[34]

The resentment at exclusion from a new privilege, where formerly men and women had enjoyed equality in the absence of political rights, was not confined to the small elite of female activists. One of the many petitions from peasant women protesting their relegation to second-class citizenship and appealing for the right to vote eloquently conveys a more widespread dissatisfaction:

> We, peasant women of Tver gubernia, address ourselves to the honourable members of the State Duma elected from our gubernia. We are dissatisfied with our status. Our husbands and lads are glad to go out with us, but as far as the talk that is going on just now about the land and new laws is concerned, they simply will not talk sense to us. There was a time when, although our men might beat us now and then, we nevertheless decided our affairs together. Now they tell us: "You are not fit company for us. We shall go to the State Duma and take part in the government, perhaps not ourselves, but we will elect members. If the law had made us equal with you, then we would have asked your opinion." So now it happens that women and girls are pushed aside as people of no consequence, and are unable to decide anything about their own lives. This law is wrong; it leads to discord between women and men, and even enmity. . . . We lived in misery together, but when it got so far that everyone may live according to the law, we found we are not needed. . . . And they, the men, do not understand our women's needs. We are able to discuss things no worse than they. We have a common interest in all our affairs, so allow the women to take a hand in deciding them.[35]

The demand for female suffrage was sharply opposed by the Octobrists and by parties to their right. The Constitutional Democrats and liberals were divided. The first congress of the Kadet Party in October 1905 adopted female suffrage as part of the Party program, although initially

---

[34]Ariadne Tyrkova-Williams, *Na putiakh k svobode* (New York, 1952), p. 241.
[35]Quoted from archival sources by Vera Bilshai, *Reshenie zhenskogo voprosa v SSSR* (Moscow, 1956), p. 65.

not binding on its members, over the opposition of Paul Miliukov and others who stressed the lack of preparation of peasant women for political participation and who feared that the proposal would harm the party's appeal among the male peasantry. Tyrkova-Williams recalls in her memoirs her shock at Miliukov's opposition:

> At the time the question of women's equality was virtually decided in progressive social thought. And here he, a right-thinking radical, despite his habits, did not take the resultant position but occupied a sharply anti-feminist stance. . . . I listened to him with bewilderment which quickly became indignation . . . it didn't even occur to me that an educated person, an evident liberal, could deny my equality with him.[36]

She attributed Miliukov's opposition to personal as well as political considerations, suggesting that as a lover of women's society, he feared that political activity might "cloud their feminine charms."

The struggle for female suffrage continued for another decade. Although a coalition of liberals and socialists introduced a bill extending the suffrage to women in the first two Dumas, the issue failed to reach a vote. In 1912 a bill to enfranchise women was actually passed, but the government rejected it. The February revolution of 1917 finally ended the long struggle for political equality. The Provisional Government extended full civil and political rights to women and provided for universal suffrage in the election of the Constituent Assembly.[37]

RUSSIAN RADICALISM AND THE LIBERATION OF WOMEN

Neither the patient political tactics nor the limited objectives of the liberal feminists in the last decades of the nineteenth century satisfied the more radical wing of the Russian intelligentsia. For some members of the younger generation, hostile to traditional values in politics and art as in love, nihilism—to use the term made popular by Turgenev—expressed a credo of individual autonomy and liberation. The "emancipated woman" emerged as a dramatic figure in Russian literature, often as an object of ridicule, in the portrait of the *nigilistka* (nihilist), a mannishly dressed figure with close-cropped hair, eschewing all the appurtenances of traditional femininity and smoking an endless succession of *papirosy*.

But nihilism represented an essentially personal stance. For those who were concerned with social transformation as well as with individual self-assertion, the work of Chernyshevskii offered a more meaningful direc-

---

[36]Tyrkova-Williams, *Na putiakh k svobode*, p. 240.

[37]For a discussion of the election, see Oliver Radkey, *The Election to the Russian Constituent Assembly of 1917* (Cambridge, 1950), p. 1. A contemporary account insists that there was overwhelming support for female suffrage at the village level.

tion. Just as the writings of Mikhailov shaped the values and purposes of the moderate feminist movement for several decades, Chernyshevskii's famous novel *What Is to Be Done?* (1863), expressed much of the ethos of Russian radicalism, offering a very different solution to the woman question. It was a solution that had its roots in the ideas of George Sand as well as in those of John Stuart Mill.

Although Chernyshevskii had once objected that "the question of women is all very well when there are no other problems," he was unusually sensitive to the link between general currents of political and social change and the search for new standards of personal behavior.[38] The central preoccupation of his novel was to join the quest for personal autonomy with a strategy for social change in a highly structured society that offered neither encouragement nor institutional support to self-assertion in work or in love. Its heroine has antecedents as well as heirs in Russian fiction; from Pushkin's Tatiana through Turgenev, Goncharov, Dostoievskii, and ultimately Gorkii's Mother, the strong and decisive woman serves as a literary counterpoint to vacillating and unformed men, an instrument of their spiritual regeneration.

Chernyshevskii's novel offered a succession of formulas for resolving both the personal and the social problems encountered on the path to liberation. Confronted by parental tyranny that would force her into a hateful marriage, Chernyshevskii's heroine, Vera Pavlovna, escapes her family through a fictitious chaste marriage with a young student. The constraints of conventional marriage are in turn transcended when her husband sacrifices himself to her happiness so that she may join another man. Economic independence and work are the next problems to be resolved in a society that offered no ready institutional solutions for women. Vera Pavlovna creates both an outlet for her own skills and a model of socioeconomic organization by establishing a small workship on cooperative principles, thereby avoiding either enlarging the female industrial proletariat or engaging in merely charitable activities that would not alter the basis of the economic system itself. Finally, the creation of study circles circumvents the constraints on female access to formal educational institutions, and Vera Pavlovna eventually turns to the study of medicine to fulfill her vocation to humanity.

In its portrayal of the kinds of people and of the institutional arrangements needed to bring about social change, Chernyshevskii's novel borrowed from life while also reshaping it. Young Russian women of the 1860s modeled their lives after Vera Pavlovna's, moving to the cities in search of employment and personal freedom or abroad in search of edu-

---

[38]Franco Venturi, *Roots of Revolution* (London, 1960), pp. 244–45.

cational opportunities denied them within Russia. The organization of communes created new associational forms and new institutions to support young women (and men) who had cut themselves adrift from more stable social settings. In providing a model of personal liberation for young Russian women, the novel also had important implications for the redefinition of male roles. It held up equality, respect, and sexual self-denial as norms for male behavior toward women. It treated male attitudes toward women as a test of a man's own moral and spiritual regeneration. Jealousy was a demeaning and proprietary emotion, which had no place in the new morality; the ideal of ascetic comradeship replaced a bourgeois possessiveness in love. New forms of association between men and women based on new relationships were the prerequisites for the creation of a new society.

By the 1870s, radical movements for social change attracted women as well as men in growing numbers. In the large cities of European Russia to which they had moved in quest of autonomy, education, and work, or in emigration in Zurich and Paris, women came into contact with radical circles through brothers, friends, and lovers, and turned away from the personal liberation offered by nihilism to work for a more comprehensive social change.[39]

Despite their diverse orientations, the radical movements shared certain tendencies. The liberation of women was universally subordinated to the liberation of all oppressed and exploited groups. The goal of female emancipation through piecemeal reform was abandoned in favor of a more radical transformation of the entire social system. However differently that transformation might be envisioned by different groups—and the lines between them were at first extremely fluid—all were in search of a larger solution. Indeed, except for the Marxist Social Democrats, who were insignificant in Russia before the 1890s, none of the radical movements had any particular orientation toward the problems of women as such. As in populist movements everywhere, an agrarian orientation discouraged radical approaches to the future of the family that might alienate peasant supporters. Even within Social Democracy, where Marxist theory singled out women as particularly oppressed, the concern with class solidarity inhibited emphasis on sexual conflict. For all these radical movements, the solution of the woman question would await the success of the larger revolution.

All of the radical movements also exhibited an unusual solidarity of men and women in action. In contrast to feminist movements, both in

[39] A detailed study of the Russian colony in Zurich in which the populist movement took shape in 1870–1873 is offered in J. M. Meijer, *Knowledge and Revolution* (Assen, Netherlands, 1955).

Russia and elsewhere, which were overwhelmingly female in their membership, and even to other European radical movements, where women played a limited and subordinate role, Russian radicalism was distinguished by a high level of participation of women on terms of relative equality with men.

The very backwardness of Russian economic and political institutions was a contributing factor. One might speculate that the idealism and egalitarianism in Russian radical ideology combined with the extraordinary isolation of the intelligentsia from the larger society to produce this unique solidarity between men and women. The absence of political rights for men and women alike encouraged a joint struggle for social change. Moreover, for male members of the radical movement, women appeared to share to some degree the oppression and the exploitation common to the peasantry and proletariat. The guilt and responsibility so eloquently drawn in Herzen's novel, *Who Is Guilty* (1845), were the special burdens of privileged, alienated men. At the same time, radical women, unlike the peasantry and proletariat, shared the education and upbringing of their male comrades, which facilitated a common language and purpose.[40] The relationship between men and women within the revolutionary movement was, therefore, an opportunity for expiation and regeneration and a test of the ability to construct new social relationships in the socialist society to come.

Too little attention has been paid to the social history of the revolutionary movement and of the women in it.[41] It is virtually impossible to establish with any accuracy the proportion of women in the overall movement. Estimates based on police records and biographical directories suggest roughly 15 to 20 percent of the total, but this is a very rough guess.[42] In the early years, the small contingent of female radicals came primarily from the privileged classes—the nobility and the merchant class—but

[40]For a similar argument, see Robert H. McNeal, "Women in the Russian Radical Movement," *Journal of Social History* 5 (Winter 1971–1972): 143–63.

[41]Only recently have scholars begun to examine the social composition of the revolutionary parties in depth. David Lane's otherwise detailed study of Social Democracy, *The Roots of Russian Communism* (Assen, Netherlands, 1969), unfortunately does not offer any breakdowns by sex. Ralph Carter Elwood's *Russian Social Democracy in the Underground* (Assen, Netherlands, 1974) touches on the participation of women in the leadership of the movement, but does not investigate their place in the general membership. A useful study of the Socialist Revolutionary Party is Maureen Perrie, "The Social Composition and Structure of the Socialist Revolutionary Party Before 1917," *Soviet Studies* 24 (October 1972): 223 –50. However, the statistics on Party membership must be used with extreme caution, because they were compiled in the early 1920s and were therefore subject to substantial omissions and distortions.

[42]See the discussion of different estimates in McNeal, "Women in the Radical Movement," p. 144.

their social origins became increasingly mixed over time and as their numbers grew. A very high proportion of the women were also of Jewish origin, perhaps 15 to 20 percent. Within the Socialist Revolutionary Party, for example, for which the most comprehensive (but not altogether reliable) statistics can be found, 14.3 percent of the membership between 1901 and 1916 was reported to be female, including 13.3 percent of the Great Russians and 25 percent of the Jews.[43]

It would appear that women revolutionaries formed a smaller but more select group than their male comrades. They were, on the average, of higher social origin than the men, had higher occupational positions, and were better educated. Conversely, women who were not of privileged backgrounds with access to education were less likely than their male counterparts to join in radical movements, probably because they were also less likely to find themselves in settings conducive to the development of revolutionary consciousness. These patterns are congruent with the more general hypothesis that in revolutionary movements social and ethnic marginality merged.[44]

The participation of women tended to be greater in the populist and terrorist movements, with their emphasis on individual heroic actions, than in the more intellectual Marxist Social Democratic movement, which attached particularly high value to the exegesis of theoretical texts. Sofia Perovskaia, Vera Figner, and Catherine Breshkovskaia played central roles in the populist movement and inspired others by their example. Women were heavily involved in carrying out terrorist missions, where being female offered considerable tactical advantages. They also paid a high price for their activities: of forty-three sentences to life at hard labor for terrorist activities handed out between 1880 and 1890, twenty-one were given to women.[45]

In the Socialist Revolutionary Party, which was heir to populist traditions, women continued to play an important role in positions of leadership as well as in the larger membership. As Table 1 indicates, the proportion of women within the Party was roughly equal at different organizational levels.

The role of women in the Social Democratic Party, which became the major rival of the Socialist Revolutionary Party by the time of the revolution, awaits an investigator. The most recent and detailed study of its social composition offers no breakdowns by sex and therefore does not

[43]Perrie, "Social Composition," p. 237.

[44]Andrew Janos, "The One-Party State and Social Mobilization: East Europe Between the Wars," in *Authoritarian Politics in Modern Society*, eds. Samuel Huntington and Clement Moore (New York and London, 1970), pp. 221–22.

[45]McNeal, "Women in the Radical Movement," p. 155.

TABLE 1

WOMEN IN THE SOCIAL REVOLUTIONARY PARTY, BY LEVEL

	Sex			Women as percent
Level	M	F	Total	of total
Total sample	882	147	1,029	14.3
Local leaders	131	26	157	16.5
First Congress	81	10	91	10.9
Second Congress	105	12	117	10.2
First Conference	54	9	63	14.3
Top leadership	11	2	13	15.4

SOURCE: Maureen Perrie, "The Social Composition and Structure of the Socialist-Revolutionary Party before 1917," *Soviet Studies* 24 (1972): 235.

permit detailed comparisons of the role of women between the two parties. Nevertheless, the fragmentary data available suggest that women played a somewhat less significant role in Social Democracy.

Within the Social Democratic movement, it would appear that the Bolsheviks had a higher proportion of women members than did their Menshevik rivals, although here, too, the data are scanty.[46] The increasing proletarianization of the party after 1907 had a particularly adverse effect on its female membership, which was recruited disproportionately from the intelligentsia. This shift in Party composition may account for the fact that while nineteen women attended the Fifth Congress in 1907, none were present at the Prague Conference in 1912.[47] The revival of revolutionary activity, however, was accompanied by increased female political participation; 10 of the 171 delegates to the Sixth Party Congress (Bolshevik) in August 1917 who responded to a survey were women, roughly 6 percent of the total. The first comprehensive census of party members was not taken until 1922, and women then constituted just under 8 percent of the total membership of the Communist Party.[48]

A number of women were prominent in the Social Democratic leadership as well. At the turn of the century, Vera Zasulich and Ekaterina Kuskova were leading figures. Within the Menshevik movement, Eva Broido and S. M. Zaretskaia were both members of the Central Committee in 1917, and Aleksandra Kollontai, who joined the Bolsheviks in 1914, was an important theorist and organizer. Nadezhda Krupskaia,

[46]Of the female delegates at the Fifth Congress of the RSDLP the Bolsheviks outnumbered the Mensheviks five to one. Elwood, *Russian Social Democracy*, pp. 66–67.

[47]*Ibid.*, p. 66.

[48]Merle Fainsod, *How Russia Is Ruled*, 2nd ed. (Cambridge, Mass., 1963), p. 254.

Lenin's wife, who combined the functions of personal and Party secretary until 1917, was the best known of the women in the Bolshevik leadership. Elena Stasova, who succeeded her as Party secretary in 1917, was the only female member of the Bolshevik Central Committee until the brief addition of Kollontai and Vera Iakovleva in August 1917. E. F. Rozmirovich, secretary of the Duma faction, K. N. Samoilova, who served as Pravda's secretary in 1913, E. B. Bosh, and Inessa Armand complete the roster of eight women listed in a biographical directory of Bolshevik revolutionary leaders in 1926.[49] The omission of several additional names may have reflected editorial prejudice as well as relative importance, but even a generous interpretation would not bring the proportion of women in positions of leadership above 6 percent of the total.

It is all the more striking, then, that so small a number of women within the Party elite in the prerevolutionary period had so great an influence in shaping its strategy toward women and in adapting the writings of Marx and Engels about the woman question to the needs of Russian Social Democracy.

THE AWKWARD SEX: MARXISM, LENINISM, AND THE WOMAN QUESTION

As the industrial revolution swept over Russia with increasing force toward the end of the nineteenth century, it brought in its wake an array of new social problems that could not be adequately addressed within the original framework of Russian feminism or populism. Intensified urbanization, the entry of women into the industrial labor force in growing numbers and harsh conditions, the rise of prostitution, and the general social dislocation that accompanied such changes posed problems for which education and philanthropy offered inadequate solutions. Moreover, the appeal of populism was predicated on the belief that Russia could move toward an agrarian form of socialism without experiencing the dislocation of industrial capitalism. Only the Marxist Social Democrats insisted on the irreversibility of capitalist development while offering a comprehensive attack on its consequences.[50]

Liberal feminists had emphasized education and political rights as the key to women's status; the emerging socialist movement, influenced by the writings of Marx and Engels and by Bebel's application of them to the question of women's liberation, viewed economic participation as the

---

[49]*Deiateli SSSR i Oktiabr'skoi Revoliutsii: Avtobiografii i biografii*, 3 vols. (Moscow, 1926); tabulated by McNeal, "Women in the Radical Movement," p. 160. For short autobiographies of Krupskaia, Stasova, and Larisa Reisner, see Georges Haupt and Jean-Jacques Marie, eds., *Makers of the Russian Revolution* (Ithaca, 1974).

[50]The view that Marxism expresses an ambivalent response to industrialization is developed in Bendix, "Tradition and Modernity," and in Adam Ulam, *The Unfinished Revolution* (New York, 1960).

key to full citizenship. Liberal feminists sought to abolish restrictions on women's entry into the professions; Marx and Engels emphasized the connection between the more general economic organizaton of society and the exploitation of women workers.[51] Political and legal emancipation, while desirable and progressive in itself, could not fundamentally resolve the problem of women's oppression, which had its real roots in the capitalist economic system. The division of labor and the creation of private property were at the heart of the oppression of women, just as they were the source of class conflict. Indeed, proletarian women were victims of a double oppression by virtue of their class as well as their sex.

In their attack on capitalism, Marx and Engels joined a tradition of social criticism concerned with the dehumanizing consequences of industrialism. The weakening of the family was just one symptom of a larger social crisis in which genuinely human relationships had been supplanted by the "cash nexus." Not only in the relationships between social classes but also within the family, the accumulation and transmission of private property distorted emotional ties. Within the bourgeois family, women were themselves transformed into a species of property. Prostitution merely represented the other side of the same Victorian coin, for it was one more symbol of the reduction of human relationships to commodity exchanges. Ridiculing the fears of the bourgeoisie that communism would establish a community of women, Marx insisted that, on the contrary, its goal was to abolish the association of women and property altogether.

For Marx and Engels, however, the solution was not to return to some golden age of the past, when women were safely confined to the home, but to draw them ever more fully into the industrial system. In the proletarian family, Marx and Engels saw the rudimentary form of the future socialist marriage. The very absence of private property purified the quality of human ties by divesting them of extraneous economic calculations. Ironically, it was only in the proletariat that marriage could occur freely; only here was it based on personal ties rather than property considerations. Moreover, the employment of women in the industrial labor force provided the economic independence that alone could serve as the basis for full sexual equality. Like Mill, Marx and Engels viewed economic dependence as incompatible with equality in marriage. Where Mill had linked independence to ownership of property and education, Marx and Engels linked it to labor. At bottom, then, the further development of industry and the more intensive utilization of female labor power was a

---

[51]See in particular *The Communist Manifesto*, *The Holy Family*, and *The German Ideology* by Marx and Engels; Engels' *The Origin of the Family, Private Property, and the State* (New York, 1942); and August Bebel's *Woman Under Socialism* (New York, 1971), first published in 1883.

progressive tendency. Despite the extreme hardships faced by women workers, which Marx painted in agonizing detail in *Capital*, employment offered women a degree of freedom, independence, and equality inconceivable in preindustrial societies.

The equal participation of women in the industrial labor force required a major reorganization of the household. For the production of children was also valued: Marxian socialism was pronatalist and anti-Malthusian. Bebel even went so far as to portray maternity as a social service. "A woman who gives birth to children," he argued, "renders, at least, the same service to the commonwealth as the man who defends his country."[52] If women were simultaneously to bear children and to participate in productive labor, society itself would have to assume the responsibility for collective child-rearing and for performing the services formerly carried out by the individual household. The emancipation of women would occur as a consequence of the reallocation of functions between the family and the society at large.

Thus, Marxist theory postulated two conditions for the full liberation of women: access to productive employment outside the home, and the conversion of private, unpaid work performed within the household to work performed in the socialized sector and paid by public funds.[53] The transformation of the private household economy by industrialization and socialization and the abolition of private ownership over the means of production would provide the basis for complete sexual equality because men and women would then stand in an equal and identical relationship to the means of production.

In their concern with the oppression of women as a serious social problem and in their genuine commitment to sexual equality, Marx and Engels were among the more advanced and libertarian representatives of contemporary opinion. Yet their commitment to sexual equality remained abstract, and their writings contributed little in a concrete and direct way to a program for the actual liberation of women. The woman question remained a marginal one in the overall body of their writings, and its resolution was subsumed under the broader revolutionary transformation of society. Bebel's more elaborate treatment of the oppression and liberation of women, with its deeper sensitivity to the sexual and psychic implications of male domination, offered greater possibilities for a synthesis of feminist and socialist concerns, but Bebel never developed his ideas further.

The effort to link the liberation of women to the socialist revolution

---

[52]Bebel, *Woman Under Socialism*, p. 230.
[53]The structural implications of the Marxist analysis are explored in Margaret Benston, "The Political Economy of Women's Liberation," *Monthly Review* 21 (September 1969): 13–24.

raised difficult problems of theory and practice. First, Marxist theory left unclear the precise relationship of sex to class. If societies were stratified horizontally by class but vertically by sex, then the proletariat was divided by sex and women by class. As a practical strategy, how should revolutionary energies be allocated? If, as Bebel argued, women's dependence actually benefited men, then an emphasis on the woman question would undermine the Party's efforts to organize along class lines. Moreover, the working class, in Marxist theory, was to act as the agent of its own emancipation as well as the agent of all other social groups. But unless women organized against their own oppression, was there any reliable guarantee of ultimate liberation?

Second, the Marxian formulation—and its later elaboration by Engels —left unclear whether the family constituted base or superstructure in the Marxian hierarchy. Nor did it explain what changes the family would undergo in the future. Engels attempted to develop an anthropology that linked the stages of development of the family to successive stages in the development of modes of production. But if the original division of labor was a sexual one and was the origin of sexual oppression, how would the transformation of the economic system affect the relation of women to men? It is significant that Engels never returned to the sexual division of labor in analyzing capitalist or socialist society, nor was it listed among the specific types of social differentiation doomed to disappear in the Communist society of the future. The connection between production and reproduction remained ambiguous in Engels' reformulation, as in subsequent socialist theory, and the question of how changes in institutional structure would alter psychological and cultural patterns underlying male-female relations was never explicitly addressed.

Finally, the ambiguity of Marxist theory in its approach to sexuality left it open to divergent interpretations. The humanist strand of Marxism, with its emphasis on individual liberation and fulfillment, inspired many in the socialist movement, Bebel and Clara Zetkin among them, to view sexual freedom as a crucial dimension of liberation. Whether expressed in a romantic cult of self-expression or in a materialist treatment of sexuality as "a physiological phenomenon of nature," European socialism tended to be libertarian in its treatment of sexuality. Sexual repression was viewed as an undesirable aspect of bourgeois society. A number of socialist leaders, however—and Lenin was among them—were fearful that sexual liberation would divert energies away from social and political action. More wary of the enthusiasm for individual sexual expression, they advocated the sublimation of sexual energies in revolutionary work.[54]

---

[54]See, for example, Clara Zetkin's recollection of a conversation with Lenin concerning sexual issues in *Reminiscences of Lenin* (London, 1929), pp. 51–60.

The Party confronted more immediate difficulties in its effort to adapt Marxist theory to actual Russian conditions. Classical Marxism did not directly address itself to the problems of socialist revolution in a largely agrarian society that had yet to experience the leap from "feudal" autocracy to bourgeois democracy. Of what relevance were Marx's views on the woman question in a society that lacked a large proletariat—male or female—or the resources for the massive construction of urban communal facilities? Undaunted by these obstacles, Russian writers began to use Marxist categories in examining the woman question, seeing in the emergence of a female urban proletariat the germs of Russia's future. Its first mention in Lenin's writing occurred in a passage of *The Development of Capitalism in Russia*, written in the late 1890s, in which Lenin noted the increasing employment of women and children in Russian industry and defended the process—as Marx had done decades earlier in England—as being, at bottom, a progressive one. Despite the brutal conditions surrounding female industrial employment, Lenin viewed it as a higher stage of development that freed women from narrow isolation and dependence in the patriarchal household and promoted their independence and equality. At about the same time, and with Lenin's encouragement, Krupskaia wrote a short popular brochure entitled "The Woman Worker," which reiterated just this theme, explained that the complete liberation of women would come about with the victory of the proletariat, and urged women to join in the revolutionary struggle.

Little further thought was devoted to the woman question by the Russian Social Democratic Party leadership. The Party program of 1903 included standard democratic demands for equal rights for women as well as provisions for alleviating the hardship of working mothers in industrial enterprises. These proposals did not distinguish Social Democrats from other parties on the left of the political spectrum. The more elaborate provisions of the 1919 Bolshevik Party program and of early Soviet legislation demonstrate the extent to which Bolshevik thinking about the woman question evolved in subsequent years. For this evolution, the efforts of Aleksandra Kollontai and Inessa Armand were largely responsible.

BOLSHEVISM AND FEMINISM: THE ORGANIZATION OF WOMEN WORKERS

Aleksandra Kollontai was among the first within the Russian Social Democratic Party to concern herself seriously with the relationship of feminism to socialism. At the age of sixteen she had already taken the first step along the path toward personal autonomy and social commitment by refusing an arranged marriage and joining instead an improverished army officer with whom she was in love. After three years of marriage, Kollontai left husband and child to study in Switzerland; on her return in

1899 she joined the Russian Social Democratic Party as writer and propagandist. "The happy life of a housewife and spouse became for me a 'cage,'" she would later write.[55] A woman of enormous energy and enthusiasm, who attached great value to spontaneity in the development of revolutionary consciousness, her attention was early drawn to the special problems of women workers.

In her autobiography Kollontai dates this concern to the end of the year 1905, when the creation of the first Duma, with its promise of popular suffrage, awakened a campaign by Russian suffragettes for the inclusion of women in the new political constituency. As a committed Marxist, Kollontai was critical of liberal feminism. Its narrow political focus, its effort to unify women of all social classes, and its separation of women's needs from larger questions of social organization all expressed an orientation that she profoundly opposed. The real liberation of women, she insisted, depended on more than the achievement of political rights. It required a completely new social order constructed on new economic foundations.

For the next decade and more, within Russia and in exile, Kollontai's energies were devoted to attacks on the Russian suffragettes, both in theoretical works and in organizational activity. The woman question, she insisted, was not a matter of political rights for women of the privileged classes but of economic rights and social justice for proletarian women.

At the same time, Kollontai was both impressed and alarmed by the efforts of the feminists to organize political clubs among working women and to win their support in the campaign for female suffrage. Over forty thousand signatures were collected by feminist groups for petitions to the first and second Dumas requesting that the vote be extended to women. Kollontai concluded that, if working-class women were to be drawn into the wider struggle for a socialist society and not diverted and co-opted by bourgeois groups, it was imperative that the Russian Social Democrats begin to organize them more effectively. Kollontai herself played a major role in organizing a women's socialist club in St. Petersburg in 1907, and in the following year, to dramatize her efforts, she led a delegation of forty working-class women to the First General Congress of Russian Women in St. Petersburg to denounce the distinguished gathering of professional and intelligentsia feminists for their altogether misconceived purposes.

In the course of these efforts to organize women workers, Kollontai became ever more concerned with the lack of understanding of the woman

[55] Aleksandra Kollontai, *The Autobiography of a Sexually Emancipated Communist Woman*, ed. Irving Fetscher (New York, 1971), p. 1.

question within her own Party. As she records in her autobiography, "I realized for the first time how little our Party concerned itself with the fate of the women of the working class and how meager was its interest in women's liberation."[56] Her efforts to induce the Party to emphasize women's liberation as one of the aims of its struggle met with a combination of incomprehension and outright hostility. "I was completely isolated with my ideas and demands," she recalled. "My Party comrades accused me and those women-comrades who shared my views of being 'feminists' and of placing too much emphasis on matters of concern to women only."[57] Although the Central Committee of the Party had given formal approval to her effort to organize a workers' delegation to the All-Russian Women's Conference, some members, who were hostile to any cooperation with bourgeois reformists and who feared the development of separatist tendencies among women, opposed the effort. In this anxiety the Russian branch of Social Democracy was not unique. Not only did socialist theory assign a secondary and even marginal importance to questions of women's liberation, but the socialist movement had tactical as well as theoretical reservations. It was deeply suspicious of feminist activity as potentially bourgeois, separatist, even frivolous; moreover, it would divert energies from more pressing revolutionary priorities.

In 1909 Kollontai published a major theoretical work, *The Social Bases of the Woman Question*, which was simultaneously an attack on bourgeois feminism and a challenge to the Party to construct a real women-workers movement.[58] Invited by the Social Democratic (Menshevik) faction of the 1912 Duma to draft a bill on maternity welfare, she undertook a special study of the question from a comparative perspective, making a number of recommendations that were eventually incorporated in Soviet legislation in 1917. An adherent of the Menshevik branch of the Party after 1905, Kollontai was drawn toward the Bolshevik camp by Lenin's uncompromising opposition to World War I.[59] Her efforts to organize women against the war revived and intensified the struggle against liberal feminism, which had taken up the patriotic cause with enthusiasm in the

[56]*Ibid.*, p. 13.

[57]*Ibid.*, p. 14.

[58]Aleksandra Kollontai, *Sotsial'nye osnovy zhenskogo voprosa* (St. Petersburg, 1909). Other important writings by Kollontai include *Obshchestvo i materinstvo* (St. Petersburg, 1916); *Izbrannye stat'i i rechi* (Moscow, 1972), a collection that omits her major writings on sexual morality; and *Sexual Relations and the Class Struggle: Love and the New Morality*, trans. Alix Holt (Bristol, England, 1972).

[59]Kollontai's early Menshevik attachments stemmed from her support for participation in the first Duma, which the Bolsheviks initially boycotted. She was also critical of the Bolsheviks' elitism, deploring their failure to cultivate close ties with the working class. Her hostility to World War I pushed her into alliance with Lenin and full membership in the Bolshevik party.

hope that women would be rewarded for their contribution to the war effort with the right to vote. In 1917 she began more systematically to organize a movement of women workers and planned a major conference of women workers, whose first meeting coincided with the establishment of the Soviet republic. The new Soviet government rewarded Kollontai for her efforts and acknowledged her expertise by appointing her to head the new People's Commissariat of Social Welfare, where she turned her energies to drafting legislation for the protection of women and children.

Starting from a radically different background and orientation, Inessa Armand came to a political stance remarkably similar to that of Kollontai. Parisian-born and raised by a family of Russified French emigrés near Moscow, she spent her early adult years as the wife of a wealthy businessman and mother of four children, only to leave her husband for an affair with his younger brother. Described by one biographer as "an exceptional being who combined beauty with intelligence, femininity with energy, practical sense with revolutionary ardor," she was first drawn into political activity by her concern with the fate of prostitutes, the victims, in her view, of bourgeois hypocrisy and a double standard of morality.[60] She became an active revolutionary about 1901; was exiled by the police to Archangel, where her lover accompanied her; and eventually escaped to Paris in 1910, where she became a close personal friend of Lenin's and a collaborator in Leninist politics.

Like Kollontai, Armand insisted that the cause of women's liberation was inextricably tied to the success of socialism. There could be no real feminist movement outside the Party itself. But the concerns and needs of women were not exclusively bound up with the economic organization of society. The sexual emancipation of women and equal liberty in personal affairs were central preoccupations for Armand. Her concern with these issues met with misunderstanding and resistance among her Party colleagues. An exchange of letters between Armand and Lenin in 1915 reveals how divergent Armand's views were from even enlightened Party opinion. In a pamphlet intended for women workers, Armand included a passage in defense of "free love" and suggested that "even a fleeting passion and intimacy" were "more poetic" than the "kisses without love" of a vulgar married couple. After reading her draft, Lenin criticized the formulation as incompatible with a proletarian point of view and confusing to her working-class audience. Expressing anxiety that "free love" might be interpreted to mean "freedom from seriousness in love," "freedom from childbirth" and "freedom of adultery," he suggested that "for a popular pamphlet would it not be better to contrast the base and vile

[60]McNeal, *Bride of the Revolution* (Ann Arbor, 1972), p. 135.

marriage without love of the bourgeoisie—intelligentsia—peasantry . . . with a proletarian civil marriage with love."[61]

Kollontai and Armand were joined in their efforts to mobilize women workers, if not in their concern with sexual liberation, by other women activists. Krupskaia, Zinoviev's wife Lilina, and Lenin's sister Anna were involved in these efforts, and they were joined by other recruits from factory study circles. Their activities culminated in the publication, under the auspices of the Bolshevik Central Committee, of a new political journal for working women, *Rabotnitsa*, which appeared briefly in 1914 only to be silenced by government censorship. *Rabotnitsa* was intended as the theoretical organ and organizational center for a socialist women's movement, a device that would link female Party activists to women workers at the factory level. Its first issue appeared on February 23, 1914, in honor of International Women's Day, and it represented the first official commitment by the Party to confronting the special needs of working women. A series of articles in the first issues insisted that the interests of working women were identical with those of all workers and called for solidarity in action to win broader rights. The editorial in the first issue spelled out most clearly the official orientation of the Bolshevik party toward work among women. Contrasting the Bolshevik position to liberal feminism, it insisted on the common interests of working men and women:

> Politically conscious women see that contemporary society is divided into classes. . . . The bourgeoisie is one, the working class the other. Their interests are counterposed. The division into men and women in their eyes has no great significance. . . .
>
> The "women's question" for working men and women—this question is about how to involve the backward masses of working women in organization, how better to make clear to them their interests, how to make them comrades in the common struggle quickly. The solidarity between working men and women, the common cause, the common goals, and the common path to those goals. Such is the settlement of the "women's question" in the workers' midst. . . .
>
> *Rabotnitsa* will tirelessly repeat to [women] the necessity for organizing, entering into the workers' organizations. . . .
>
> In a word, our journal strives to help working women become conscious and organized.[62]

[61]V. I. Lenin, *Polnoe sobranie sochinenii* (henceforth *PSS*), 5th ed., 55 vols. (Moscow, 1958 –1965) 49: 51–52, 54–57.

[62]A. F. Bessonova, ed., "K istorii izdaniia zhurnala *Rabotnitsa*," *Istoricheskii arkhiv*, 1955, pp. 37–39. See also the letters of Lenin and Krupskaia to Lenin's sister Anna discussing the project in Lenin, *PSS*, 55: 446–449, and Anne Bobroff, "The Bolsheviks and Working Women, 1905–1920," *Soviet Studies* 26 (October 1974): 540–67.

This statement denied the existence of conflict between the interests of working women and working men, interpreted the woman question in the narrowest possible terms as the struggle to develop revolutionary consciousness among women workers, and offered the special backwardness of women rather than their double oppression as the rationale for the Party's efforts to organize them. Even such a circumscribed approach encountered opposition within the Party from those who denied the very existence of a distinct woman question and who insisted on exclusive and undivided attention to the class struggle. Even the most limited recognition that the political mobilization of women posed distinctive agitational and organizational problems and might require special institutions and tactics raised the specter of division in the workers' movement. Consequently, adherents of both positions shared a common hostility to a third orientation that was concerned with the special forms of oppression experienced by women as women and that sought to link this concern with socialist theory and practice.[63]

World War I gave further impetus to the political organization of women. The mobilization of millions of men resulted in a vast influx of women into industry. By the end of the war, women formed 40 percent of the labor force in large-scale industry and 60 percent of all textile workers in the Moscow region. Military defeats, economic breakdown, and soaring prices drew large numbers of women into sporadic strikes against deteriorating conditions. Indeed, it was a massive strike touched off by women textile workers on International Women's Day that culminated in the February Revolution of 1917 and the establishment of the Provisional Government.[64]

Subsequent months saw a feverish spurt of political activity. A wide variety of feminist groups renewed their struggle for political equality, seeking female suffrage as the reward for their contribution to the war effort. At the same time, the important role of women in strikes and demonstrations against the war and inflation was an indication of their growing assertiveness. The upsurge of political activity among women convinced the Petrograd Committee of the Bolsheviks that a special department for Party work among women was necessary. The arguments of Kollontai and of Vera Slutskaia reveal the impact of these new developments. Al-

[63]For a similar analysis of three distinct orientations toward the relation of Bolshevism and feminism in the context of the international socialist movement, see Alfred Meyer, "Marxism and the Women's Movement," in Atkinson, Dallin, and Lapidus, *Women in Russia*.

[64]Leon Trotskii's account of the outbreak of revolution emphasizes the independent initiative of women textile workers, many of them soldiers' wives, who launched the demonstrations despite the directives of the Bolshevik organizations. See Trotskii, *The History of the Russian Revolution* (New York, 1932), Vol, I, pp. 101–2.

though in 1908 she had opposed Kollontai's efforts, in a report now urging the creation of a Women's Bureau, Slutskaia insisted: "In view of the fact that at the present time an appreciable movement has come into existence among [working women], it is desirable to direct the said movement into the channels of political action, having first organized them into trade cells."[65] Kollontai drew an even more direct connection between the renewal of feminist agitation by liberal feminists and the need for a special Party organ, "especially seeing how the equal righters captured the minds of working women and got a following among soldiers' wives. The demonstration of soldiers' wives demanding an increase in grants . . . still more convinced me of the necessity of a specially planned party apparatus for work among women."[66]

By the time of the Sixth (Bolshevik) Party Congress in the summer of 1917, a second journal for women was being published in the Moscow region, and "women's sections," or *zhenotdely*, had been created informally in some district Party organizations. But the efforts of Bolshevik women activists to organize women workers had proven only partially successful. As one delegate to the Congress reported: "Our comrades are also conducting work in rallying women; they publish a special organ, *Zhizn' rabotnitsy*, but the women's organizations are weak, and the organ is poorly circulated. The exceptions are those organizations which are recruiting women in districts where women are working in the factories."[67] Even these limited efforts by female Party activists were hampered by the lack of substantial support from central Party organs.

The attempt by a small group of female Party activists to elaborate a theoretical stance toward the woman question and to organize women workers on behalf of revolutionary socialism culminated in the creation of the *Zhenotdel* (*Zhenskii otdel*), a special organization of the Party's Central Committee Secretariat responsible for Party work among women (discussed at length in Chapter II). But even in the prerevolutionary period, this effort was marked by certain features that later emerged as serious problems.

The first problem involved the definition of the Bolshevik constituency. While addressing itself to the woman question in universal terms, Bolshevism was, in fact, preoccupied almost exclusively with the problems of industrial workers. Marxist theory viewed the entry of women into the

---

[65]Bobroff, "The Bolsheviks and Working Women," p. 561.

[66]*Ibid.* Bobroff questions the official Bolshevik view that the backwardness of women workers inspired the Party's effort to organize them, arguing that on the contrary it was the growing militance and political consciousness of women workers that compelled the Bolsheviks to respond to their needs.

[67]Kommunisticheskaia Partiia Sovetskogo Soiuza, *Protokoly Shestogo S"ezda RSDRP(b) (August 1917)* (Moscow, 1934), p. 80.

industrial labor force as a necessary and desirable development that would establish the foundations for full sexual equality. Marx's views were echoed in the writings of Lenin and other Bolsheviks. Classical Marxism did not, however, speak to the problems that would confront an attempted revolution and social reconstruction in a largely agrarian society. In adapting Marxism to the inhospitable economic and social environment of Tsarist Russia, the Bolsheviks understandably focused their attention on the urban working class, viewing the peasantry as the residue of earlier stages of social development destined to die out in the course of industrialization. They never fully addressed the fundamental problems of the vast majority of Russian women, the rural peasants, to whom such notions as female economic independence, communal child care, and the destruction of the family would have seemed incomprehensible and even threatening.

A second problem involved the definition of goals. Like the Russian radical movement more generally, Bolshevism was committed to full sexual equality. It accepted without question the right of women to full civil and political rights in a democratic republic, while maintaining at the same time that political equality was not the ultimate goal but merely a stepping stone to full liberation. It rejected classical feminism by subordinating the woman question to the larger reconstruction of society and by insisting that class and not sex was the fundamental social division. The legitimacy of an appeal to women as women remained in question within the Party, accepted as a tactical necessity but viewed with enormous suspicion.

Lenin was particularly sensitive to the need for tactical flexibility in elaborating the Party's program. Liberal feminism threatened to draw women workers away from the socialist movement if the Bolsheviks did not respond to their special needs as women. He therefore insisted on the need to link the political goals of the Party—the conquest of power and the establishment of a proletarian dictatorship—with the needs and wishes of working women. The Party leadership consequently offered its encouragement to activities that would build support among women workers and demonstrate the connection between their interests and Party goals. But these efforts had low priority, and responsibility for them was relegated to Bolshevik women and wives. The precise relationship between the party organization as a whole and the women workers' movement was not fully clarified until after the revolution.

The official position of the Party leadership was not altogether satisfactory to the more radical and independent feminists within the Socialist movement, or indeed among the many attracted to the movement who subsequently left it. Kollontai and Inessa Armand in Russia and Clara Zetkin in Germany attached great importance to the particular and unique

ways in which women were oppressed as a sex. They were concerned
with the ways in which the relationships between men and women—both
within the family and outside it—perpetuated patterns of domination and
submission. A socialist transformation of economic life would contribute
to a solution of this problem, but for them a struggle to alter consciousness
was an important aspect of revolutionary activity.

Lenin was not unaware of this problem. He continually reproached his
Party comrades for their lack of attention to work among women and for
their view that it was a task that concerned only women comrades and
not the Party as a whole. He emphasized the necessity of altering male
attitudes as well, of rooting out the "old master right of the man." But
Lenin was less sympathetic to the concern with sexual freedom and
tended to view the preoccupation with questions of sex and marriage as
excessive, diverting energies away from more important and pressing
problems. Where the socialist feminists viewed the economic and sexual
emancipation of women as desirable for its own sake and central to the
meaning of liberation, the mainstream of Party leaders tended to treat
Party work among women as instrumental to the achievement of larger
goals.

Conflict over goals had organizational implications. The hostility of the
Bolshevik Party to autonomous group activity and the insistence on a
highly centralized organizational structure were obstacles to separate organizations to raise the consciousness of women as women. Yet for both
women and national minorities, some degree of organizational innovation
was vital. The Sixth Party Congress explicitly debated whether the Party
rules should permit national minorities to form separate, autonomous
Party sections, and the resulting disagreements had implications for the
organization of the women's movement as well. The combination of hostility in principle with flexibility in practice was epitomized in the speech
of a Petrograd delegate:

> I am speaking against such an addition to the Regulations. The formation of
> such sections in some districts under certain conditions is expedient, under
> others it's inexpedient. Since this is not forbidden, then consequently it is al-
> lowed, and therefore such an addition to the Regulations is completely super-
> fluous, since a principle of organization according to nationalities is unaccept-
> able, although in separate cases, called forth by the demands of expediency,
> it is allowed, just as sections of women, soldiers, etc. are allowed.[68]

Lenin defended precisely this approach in a conversation with Clara
Zetkin in 1920. In principle, he insisted, there could be no separate organization of women. "We derive our organizational ideas from our

[68]*Ibid.*, p. 175.

ideological conceptions. We want no separate organizations of Communist women. She who is a Communist belongs as a member to the Party, just as he who is a Communist. They have the same rights and duties."[69] At the same time, there were compelling practical needs for a flexible approach. "The Party must have organs—working groups, commissions, committees, sections, or whatever else they may be called—with the specific purpose of rousing the broad masses of women, bringing them into contact with the Party and keeping them under its influence. . . . We must have our own groups to work among them, special methods of agitation, and special forms of organization. This is not bourgeois 'feminism'; it is practical revolutionary expediency."[70]

Precisely what relationship would develop between the women's sections and the Party organization as a whole was still unclear on the eve of the 1917 revolution. A whole array of questions concerning the goals, organization, and strategy of women's liberation remained a continuing source of controversy right up to the revolution itself and, indeed, for years thereafter. Clearly, the marriage of Bolshevism and feminism was not without deep inner strains.

[69]Clara Zetkin, *Reminiscences of Lenin* (New York, International Publishers, 1934), p. 53.
[70]*Ibid.*, pp. 110–11.

TWO

Toward Sexual Equality:
Revolutionary Transformation
and its Limits, 1917–1930

Revolutions are the festivals of the oppressed and
the exploited. At no other time are the masses of
the people in a position to come forward so actively as creators of a new social order.

V. I. Lenin

THE collapse of the Tsarist autocracy under the pressures
of war and political opposition in 1917 and the emergence of the Bolsheviks as the rulers of the new Soviet state created sudden and vast opportunities for social transformation. The new Soviet regime would bring to
fruition a modernization of political institutions and values, economic
structures, and social relationships already underway in prerevolutionary
Russia, while at the same time giving a distinctive shape and direction to
the new society. It would build on the legacy of the past even while attempting to transform it.

Yet the leaders of the new Soviet state who came to power in 1917
lacked a well-defined plan for the reconstruction of Russian society. They
shared a vision rather than a blueprint, a broad set of aspirations rather
than a coherent economic and social program. Critical of a social order
based on economic exploitation, political exclusion, and social inequality,
they envisioned a new society in which socioeconomic, ethnic, and sexual
oppression would have no place. Its contours were only vaguely delineated. But in bold, if sparse, strokes, they had sketched the outlines of a
society in which the role of women in the economy, the polity, and the
family would be fundamentally altered.

Among those within the Party who had given some consideration to
the role of women under socialism—and these, as we have seen, were few

54

indeed—the alteration of women's roles appeared as a function of the economic and political reconstitution of the larger society. Public ownership and the rational organization of production would encourage the entry of women into the labor force in large numbers. Political democratization would make it possible for women to play a growing role in public affairs. Administrative functions would cease to be the exclusive prerogative of a select elite and would be shared more broadly among members of the society.

As women took on larger roles in economic and political life, they would be released from the petty and stultifying domestic chores to which they had traditionally been confined. This release would occur not through a redefinition of male and female roles but through a reallocation of familial and societal functions. In a socialist society, the burden of housework and child care would shift from the individual household to the social collective. Communal living arrangements would form the nucleus of the future socialist city, amply provided with public dining rooms, laundries, and sewing centers, while children would be raised from an early age in public institutions that would foster new collectivist values and behavior.

The emergence of women from the narrow confines of the household into the wider public arena and their entry into social production would have profound consequences for male-female relationships. The economic independence of women would ultimately guarantee their full equality, outside marriage as within it. Marriage would become a free association of equal and independent partners, while the socialist family, if it were to exist at all, would take on new and unanticipated forms.

Yet no coherent plan of action had been elaborated prior to the revolution of 1917 to guide the effort to transform vision into reality. A suspicion of utopian blueprints deeply ingrained in the Marxist tradition, a preoccupation with the critique of capitalism and the conquest of power, and a profound awareness of the theoretical and practical problems posed by Russia's backwardness all contributed to the Bolsheviks' reluctance to devote excessive energy to developing a coherent strategy of economic and social reconstruction prior to the revolution itself. Indeed, such an effort would have threatened the precarious unity of the Party. A radical vision of a reconstituted social and political community based on new cultural patterns and values—a goal culture, to use the terminology of Anthony Wallace—was widely shared. The methods by which traditional culture would be transformed and the nature of the "transfer culture" were the subject of heated disagreement and of successive redefinition in the course of Soviet development.[1]

---

[1] Anthony Wallace, *Culture and Personality*, 2nd ed. (New York, 1970), p. 192.

For even this broad vision was not widely shared within the Party leadership, to say nothing of the views of Party members as a whole. The revolutionary struggle had drawn together individuals and groups with widely differing perceptions, orientations, and priorities that began to assert themselves once power had been won. A concern with questions of female emancipation and sexual equality tended to be associated with the egalitarian and libertarian vision of socialism found predominantly within the Party left. The advocates of liberation were engaged in a constant struggle against the broader indifference, if not outright hostility, of the vast majority of Party activists, who considered these concerns frivolous, irrelevant, and potentially threatening to larger political goals. It involved a struggle against the weight of a traditional culture in which male chauvinism played a powerful role. And it involved such struggles in a political and socioeconomic context in which the desirability of all cultural changes would have to be measured against pressing economic needs.

A transformation of economic relationships was thought to be of decisive and defining significance for initiating wider patterns of social and cultural change. But the monopoly of political power by the Party made political organization a critical instrument in revolutionary transformation. In responding to criticisms of his seizure of power by more orthodox Marxists who viewed socialism as the culmination of a long process of economic, political, and cultural development, Lenin had argued that precisely because of Russia's backwardness political revolution was the precondition rather than the outcome of cultural change.[2] This Leninist reversal of the relation of base and superstructure was profoundly important in the evolution of Bolshevik approaches toward social and cultural change.

The role of the Party as an "organizational weapon," so critical in the prerevolutionary struggle for power, was now extended to the postrevolutionary reconstitution of political and social life. A whole series of new political and social institutions, hierarchically integrated through the Communist Party, would not only replace Tsarist bureaucratic agencies but would also dissolve traditional social networks rooted in religion and kinship and would provide a new mechanism for social coordination and control. Beyond these core assumptions of Leninist politics, the precise form that new institutions would take and the scope, sequence, and timing of transformation remained to be elaborated after 1917. The decade that followed was one of experimentation and improvisation, as the leaders of the new state sought to consolidate and extend their control over Russian

---

[2] V. I. Lenin, "O nashei revoliutsii," in *Polnoe sobranie sochinenii* (henceforth *PSS*), 5th ed., 55 vols. (Moscow, 1958–1965), 45: 381.

society and to define the new political community over which they ruled.

The political priorities of the new regime and the economic constraints it confronted profoundly affected the scope and thrust of measures adopted to transform women's roles. During the years of civil war, from 1918 to 1921, military concerns were uppermost. Economic dislocation and political turbulence sharply limited the resources available for vast experiments in social engineering and forced the postponement of many early commitments. The introduction of the New Economic Policy in 1921 signaled an economic retrenchment that adversely affected female employment and further curtailed social welfare programs. Under these circumstances, legal engineering and political mobilization came to the fore as central instruments of revolutionary change in the first decade of Soviet rule. The elaboration of new legislation extending the principles of sexual equality to political, economic, and family life was one important feature of this decade. The other was the attempt to mobilize women politically, which involved the creation of a special organization of the Communist Party—the Zhenotdel—to extend the Party's influence to the female population and to draw women into active participation in the construction of a new society.

Other measures, more costly of economic and political resources, were postponed or abandoned during this decade. The employment of women in industry on a large scale awaited the economic expansion inaugurated by the First Five Year Plan in 1928, as did the extension of educational opportunities and the creation of a network of child care facilities. But even the more limited programs undertaken in these early years brought to the surface the conflicting values and priorities of the new Soviet leaders. Diverse strains in the Marxist-Leninist heritage merged with the varied dispositions of individual Party leaders to generate disagreements over a wide range of economic, political, and social questions with important implications for the role and welfare of women. By the end of the decade, the improvisations and conflicts that marked the whole period had altered the very definition of the woman question. It remained for Stalin to give expression to these new concerns.

LEGAL ENGINEERING: THE ESTABLISHMENT OF NEW NORMS

The first measures of the new Soviet government expressed, often in dramatic imagery, its total repudiation of the old order. A series of decrees and proclamations attacked the economic, legal, political, and social bases of existing institutions at one stroke and promised the radical reconstruction of Russian society on new foundations.

A fundamental attack on sexual inequality required as a start the abrogation of all legislation and legal practices that assumed the subordi-

nation of women, as well as a more direct assault on the social customs
and behavior that perpetuated it. It was therefore essential to establish
comprehensive new legal norms and values that insisted on sexual equality. But a reliance on legal engineering as the basic mechanism for social
change was dictated by necessity as much as by choice. During these early
years, when economic and political resources were still severely limited,
"government by proclamation" was the least costly of mechanisms for
social change, but it symbolized the commitment of the new regime to
new values.

The promulgation of new political, civic, economic, and family codes
was intended as much to communicate new norms as it was to organize
and regulate the constitution of the new administration. The new decrees
and the hierarchical, centralized, uniform legal system established to en-
force them served an important symbolic function by providing a "he-
retical model" against which traditional values and attitudes could be
measured and subjected to criticism, even while the regime was in no
position to eradicate them.[3] Over time, it was expected that the existence
of such norms would influence behavior and attitudes in the desired direction and that the new Soviet culture would erode and ultimately replace the values and behavioral patterns of traditional Russian life.

The new decrees were also useful for deflecting criticism of the new regime for its undemocratic behavior. As Lenin proudly announced on the
second anniversary of the Bolshevik revolution: "In the course of two
years of Soviet power in one of the most backward countries of Europe
more has been done to emancipate woman, to make her the equal of the
'strong' sex, than has been done during the past 130 years by all the advanced, enlightened, 'democratic' republics of the world taken together."[4]
Lenin's statement reflected more than the ritual self-congratulation that
was to become a hallmark of the new regime. By emphasizing the commitment of the new Soviet government to sexual equality, Lenin sought
to defend its legitimacy in democratic terms. Responding to criticism of
Soviet violations of democratic procedures, Lenin turned on his accusers
the argument that, despite formal proclamations of political equality, no
bourgeois governments had actually granted full citizenship to women.
"Not a single state and no democratic legislation," he remarked on another
occasion, "has done even half of what the Soviet Government did for
women in the very first months of its existence."[5]

---

[3]For a more elaborate discussion of the revolutionary use of legal engineering, see the
excellent study by Gregory Massell, *The Surrogate Proletariat: Moslem Women and Revolutionary Strategies in Soviet Central Asia: 1919–1929* (Princeton, 1974).
   [4]Lenin, "Sovetskaia vlast' i polozhenie zhenshchiny," in *PSS*, 39: 287.
   [5]Lenin, "O zadachakh zhenskogo dvizheniia v sovetskoi respublike," in *PSS*, 39: 201.

The decrees and codes promulgated in the first years of the Soviet regime expressed a new conception of women's position in the larger society.[6] The extension of full citizenship to women and the elimination of their remaining legal, civil, and political disabilities in early Soviet legislation were part of a larger effort to create a new political community defined in egalitarian, if not universal, terms. The criteria for inclusion would no longer discriminate by sex but by social class and social contribution, and women would henceforth share equally with men the rights and responsibilities that their social position and efforts conferred.

In some respects the Soviet conception of citizenship marked a retreat from the program of prerevolutionary opposition parties, since it effectively disenfranchised large numbers of educated and politically active women. Yet it was a more embracing conception as well, going beyond the elimination of legal impediments to sexual equality and the mere proclamation of equal rights to measures that would guarantee their exercise in practice. In addition, the definition of rights and responsibilities was not confined exclusively to political and legal realms, but extended to economic and social activities as well. For example, the right to work and its corresponding obligation were defined as conditions of citizenship that in principle extended to women as well as to men, and in theory, if not always in practice, women were equally subject to labor conscription.[7]

A variety of measures was intended to provide a juridical foundation for women's economic independence. All restrictions on women's freedom of movement were abolished; no longer was a wife obliged to reside with her husband or accompany him in changes of domicile. Far-reaching changes in property relationships and inheritance laws weakened the family as an economic unit and the dominant position of the father within it. Other laws gave women equal rights to hold land, to act as heads of house-

[6]The Provisional Government had granted women full civil and political rights, implementing a program supported by a broad democratic opposition in the last decade of Tsarist rule. The sweeping character of early Soviet measures, however, went beyond the precedents of not only the Provisional Government but also of other contemporary states. For the decrees of the Provisional Government concerning the civil status of women, see Robert Browder and Alexander Kerensky, eds., *The Russian Provisional Government, 1917*, 3 vols. (Stanford, 1961). At the time of the Bolshevik revolution, Norway and Denmark were the only European countries to have extended the suffrage to women. Women were granted the right to vote in England in 1918, in the United States in 1920, and in Sweden in 1921. France and Italy did not introduce female suffrage for another 30 years.

[7]The Labor Code of 1918 treated labor as a form of service to society; capitalist conceptions of contractual relationships were repudiated. By a subsequent decree, labor service, including compulsory conscription, was extended in principle to women as well as men. Similarly, the 1918 Constitution of the RSFSR defined work as an obligation of citizenship that in principle extended to women as well as to men, a view reaffirmed in the 1936 Constitution of the USSR. In practice, the insistence on the obligation of women to work has remained an effort to alter attitudes and expectations; it is not enforced by coercive sanctions. See E. H. Carr, *The Bolshevik Revolution, 1917–1923* (London, 1952), Vol. 25, pp. 199–200.

holds, to participate as full members in rural communes, and, later, to be paid as individuals rather than as part of a household for collective farm labor. Efforts to encourage the entry of women into the labor force were buttressed by protective labor legislation based on or exceeding the most progressive European models.[8] Equal pay for equal work was established as a fundamental principle.

In the realm of family law, early Soviet legislation was equally revolutionary. Changes in property relationships and inheritance laws weakened the family as an economic unit and reduced the dominance of the male household head, while new family codes undermined the legal and religious basis of marriage and removed restrictions on divorce.[9] Ecclesiastical control was replaced by civil registration that gave equal rights to husband and wife, as well as to legitimate and illegitimate children. The Family Code of 1926 went even further in giving legal recognition to de facto, unregistered marriages, and indeed avoided any definition of the family itself. Abortion was also legalized in 1920, though as a health measure, quite independent of family legislation, whose main purpose was not so much to enhance women's freedom of choice as to reduce the high mortality rates associated with illegal abortions. It was therefore viewed as a necessary, but temporary, evil, rather than a positive contribution to female emancipation.[10]

[8]A decree of the Council of People's Commissars of November 11, 1917, for example, limited the working day to eight hours for all workers, and in addition banned night work, overtime, and underground assignments for women. The enforcement of these provisions proved to be extremely erratic, and with the increasingly rapid tempo of industrialization in the 1930s, labor protection tended to break down completely. For a more extensive treatment, see Chapter IV, and also Margaret Dewar, *Labor Policy in the USSR, 1917–1928* (London and New York, 1956); Solomon Schwarz, *Labor in the Soviet Union* (New York, 1931) Ch. 6; Norton Dodge, *Women in the Soviet Economy*, (Baltimore, 1966), pp. 57–75; Gaston Rimlinger, *Welfare Policy and Industrialization in Europe, America, and Russia* (New York, 1971), pp. 265–300; Bernice Madison, *Social Welfare in the Soviet Union* (Stanford, 1968), and "Soviet Income Maintenance Policy for the 1970's," *Journal of Social Policy* 2 (April 1973): 97–117; V. N. Tolkunova, *Pravo zhenshchin na trud i ego garantii* (Moscow, 1967).

[9]Shortly after the revolution, in December 1917, two decrees provided for the civil registration of marriage and the right of divorce on appeal by either partner. Registrar's Offices were established to implement the new legislation. A year later, on October 17, 1918, a more comprehensive Code of Laws on the Registration of Deaths, Births, and Marriages was enacted. These laws were further supplemented in 1922, and a revision and complete codification of family law was enacted in 1926. See the more extensive discussion in Chapter VII in Rudolph Schlesinger, comp., *Changing Attitudes in Soviet Russia—The Family in the USSR* (London, 1949), and Beatrice Farnsworth, "Bolshevik Alternatives and the Soviet Family: The 1926 Marriage Law Debate," in *Women in Russia*, eds. Dorothy Atkinson, Alexander Dallin, and Gail Warshofsky Lapidus (Stanford, 1977).

[10]The Decree on the Legalization of Abortions of November 18, 1920, asserted that the government viewed abortion as a "serious evil to the community," which would be fought with propaganda among working women. While working to eliminate it in the future, the authorities would permit abortions to be performed freely in Soviet hospitals. Nurses and

The traditional practices that maintained the inferiority of women in the Moslem communities of Central Asia posed special problems for Soviet legislation. Abduction, forced marriage, the payment of *kalym* (bride price), and polygamy were singled out as particular targets, and although some concessions were made to local custom—as, for example, by exempting the Central Asian republics from the more radical marriage laws—these practices were outlawed and subjected to criminal sanctions.

If early Soviet legislation was designed to secure the full political and civil equality of women, it was not intended to divert them from childbearing roles. Indeed, motherhood itself was treated as a social obligation in early Soviet legislation. Echoing Bebel's view of maternity as a social service, a decree of December 28, 1917, described procreation as a social function of women; this decree was followed by a series of measures for the protection of mothers and children. Aleksandra Kollontai had long criticized bourgeois feminism for its failure to deal with the protection of motherhood. In her view it was precisely the contribution that procreation made to social welfare that justified the special measures taken by the state to safeguard it:

> Motherhood must be safeguarded not only in the interest of women, but even more so to meet the difficulties of the national economy in its transformation into a workers system: it is necessary to save women's strength from being wasted on the family in order to employ it more reasonably for the benefit of the collective; it is necessary to preserve their health in order to guarantee a steady stream of fit workers for the Workers' Republic in the future.[11]

A similar view of maternity as a social contribution was defended by another Party activist, Vera Lebedeva, in November 1919.

> When a woman gives life to a child, she performs work every bit as important as that of the engineer who constructs roads—for the child she bears may later become a civil engineer and build roads. The state needs children, and therefore it must make provision for them. Do not, therefore, suppose that when the state takes thought for mothers in childbirth and for the newly born child, and when it combats infant mortality, it performs a charitable action. Oh no; in so doing the state takes thought for itself too and pays only a very small part of its debt to you.[12]

While the specific content of such statements reflected the mobilization mentality of war communism, as well as the somewhat idiosyncratic views

---

midwives were expressly forbidden to practice abortions and were threatened with prosecution. Schlesinger, *Changing Attitudes*, p. 44.

[11]Schlesinger, *Changing Attitudes*, p. 52.

[12]Fannina Halle, *Women in Soviet Russia* (London, 1934), p. 149.

of their authors, the treatment of reproduction as a contribution to social welfare would take on increasing significance in the evolution of Soviet policy.

As Minister of Social Welfare in the new Soviet republic, Kollontai insisted that equal rights for women were not incompatible with special treatment for mothers. Moreover, if the participation of women in social production were not to occur at the expense of a desirable population increase, special measures were necessary to encourage fertility. Family allowances would redistribute income in favor of large families, while new legislation would guarantee paid maternity leave before and after childbirth. The development of a broad network of public child-care institutions would make it possible for women to combine work and family obligations. The assumption of state responsibility for the welfare of mothers and children was, from this perspective, an investment in human capital, the corollary of the treatment of childbearing as a social service.

The promulgation of new legal norms that asserted the full equality of women in political, economic, and family life was the necessary but hardly sufficient condition of liquidating the past. It reflected as well an effort to define a new political community marked by a direct relationship between citizen and state. For women as well as for men, it would be a relationship uncontaminated and unencumbered by commitments to intermediary associations. The measures providing the juridical foundations for the independence of women had as their larger goal the destruction of the network of economic, religious, and familial ties that bound women to traditional social solidarities and inhibited their direct and unmediated participation in the larger political and economic arena. It was, therefore, a provision of the new marriage law that ended women's obligation to accompany a husband in a change of domicile that most dramatically underlined the larger thrust of early Soviet legislation: its effort to sever the constraints of traditional social solidarities on individual freedom of movement.[13]

But the promulgation of new laws was not sufficient to create and legitimize a new political community. The ability and willingness of women to exercise their new rights and to take advantage of new opportunities would depend not only on legal protection but on the far more subtle network of social pressures and sanctions and rewards. To alter that net-

[13]For a more comprehensive theoretical treatment of the relationship of personal mobility to economic and political modernization, see S. N. Eisenstadt, *Essays on Sociological Aspects of Political and Economic Development* (The Hague, 1961), p. 38; Chalmers Johnson, "Comparing Communist Nations," in *Political Change in Communist Systems*, ed. Chalmers Johnson (Stanford, 1970); and Samuel Huntington and Clement Moore, eds., *Authoritarian Politics in Modern Society* (New York, 1970).

work required a massive transformation of popular attitudes, values, and behavior. This was the special task of the Zhenotdel, the Women's Department of the Communist Party.

POLITICAL MOBILIZATION: THE ZHENOTDEL AND THE PARTY

The proclamation of the new rights and responsibilities of women was only a first step in their real emancipation. The need to inform women of their new position and to draw them into active participation in public life was even more fundamental and posed far greater problems of innovation and leadership. The same small group of female activists who had been prominent in prewar efforts to organize women workers—particularly Kollontai, Armand, Krupskaia, and Nikolaeva—now played a decisive role in winning official assent to the creation of new organizational mechanisms for the mobilization of women. A series of small conferences of women in the immediate postrevolutionary months preceded the convocation in November 1918 of the First All-Russian Congress of Working Women.

The Congress offered a dramatic contrast to the feminist general meeting held a long decade earlier. One thousand women gathered in the Kremlin Hall of Unions, including workers and peasant women from distant regions of the country brightly dressed in local costume, to be addressed by the leader of the new Soviet regime, Lenin himself. Lenin was greeted with wild enthusiasm. After outlining the measures already taken by the Soviet government to improve the position of women, Lenin called on women to play a more active political role. "The experience of all liberation movements," he informed them, "has shown that the success of a revolution depends on how much the women take part in it."[14]

The Congress led to the creation of Commissions for Agitation and Propaganda among Working Women, which were in turn reorganized in 1919 to form the Women's Department (*zhenskii otdel*, abbreviated as *Zhenotdel*) of the Central Committee Secretariat, under the leadership of Inessa Armand.[15] Local branches of the Zhenotdel were attached to Party committees at every level of the hierarchy, staffed by volunteers recruited among Party women, and charged with spreading the message of the Party to the unorganized women in factories and villages and drawing them into public affairs. Its existence was a stormy one; the Zhenotdel encountered widespread popular hostility as well as controversy within

[14]Lenin, "Rech' na I vserossiiskom s"ezde rabotnits," in *PSS*, 37: 86.

[15]Inessa Armand died of cholera in 1920 and was succeeded by Aleksandra Kollontai. Kollontai was removed in 1922 as a consequence of her oppositional activities and was succeeded in turn by Sophia Nikolaevna Smidovich (1922–1924), Klavdiia Nikolaeva (1924–1927), and Aleksandra Vasil'evna Artiukhina (1927–1930).

the Party itself over the legitimacy of its existence in principle and the scope and methods of its activity. Nevertheless, during the decade of its existence it played a central role in the political mobilization of women.[16]

The problems it confronted were vast. As late as 1922 only 8 percent of the total Party membership was female.[17] Even in the more urbanized and developed regions of European Russia, women played a very minimal public role. In rural areas, and particularly in the Moslem regions of Soviet Central Asia where female seclusion was practiced, women were not only absent from public view but were inaccessible to Party and government agencies.

The Zhenotdel was concerned with the whole range of obstacles to the political mobilization of women. In order to reach women at all, to inform women of the new rights and responsibilities conferred on them by the government, it was necessary to create a wide variety of new associational forms capable of penetrating the rural and traditional milieus in which most women were found and to invent new methods of agitation and recruitment. A network of communications was a prerequisite to forming a new political constituency.

Because effective political communications depended on the spread of literacy, the Zhenotdel was quickly drawn into that effort. Literacy was viewed by the Bolshevik leaders as a requisite of participation in public affairs. "A person who can neither read nor write," Lenin insisted, "is outside politics; he must first learn the ABC's, without which there can be no such thing as politics, but merely rumors, gossip, fairy tales, and prejudices."[18]

---

[16]No comprehensive study of the Zhenotdel has yet been published; two recent treatments in English include Richard Stites, "Zhenotdel 1917–1930: Bolshevism and Women's Liberation," *Russian History* (in press), and Carol Eubank Hayden, "The Bolshevik Party and Work Among Women, 1917–1925," *Russian History*, in press. This portrait of its activities relies on materials from its theoretical journal, *Kommunistka*, 1921–1930; on decrees and instructions reported in *Izvestiia Tsentral'nogo Komiteta*, 1919–1929, and *Spravochnik partiinogo rabotnika*, Vols. 1–8; on the memoir of two important activists, E. Bochkareva and S. Liubimova, *Svetlyi put': Kommunisticheskaia Partiia Sovetskogo Soiuza–borets za svobodu, ravnopravie, i schast'e zhenshchiny* (Moscow, 1967); on biographies and fictional accounts of the 1920s; and on the fragmentary descriptions of Western visitors: Thomas Woody, *New Minds: New Men?* (New York, 1932); Samuel Harper, *Civic Training in Soviet Russia* (Chicago, 1929); Jessica Smith, *Woman in Soviet Russia* (New York, 1927); Fannina Halle, *Women in Soviet Russia*, and *Women in the Soviet East* (New York, 1938). It also relies on Massell's treatment of Soviet policy in Central Asia, *The Surrogate Proletariat*.

[17]The Party itself constituted only a small stratum of the Soviet population at this time, with 514,529 members in a total population of over 130,000,000. It had only barely begun to penetrate rural Russia.

[18]Lenin, "Novaia ekonomicheskaia politika i zadachi politprosovetov," in *PSS*, 44: 174–75.

Increased female literacy would make it possible for the Zhenotdel, and through it the Party, to reach a widening circle of women through Party journals. A growing array of periodicals designed specifically for a female audience emerged in the course of the 1920s, relying on a network of worker and peasant correspondents. *Rabotnitsa,* the prewar Party journal for women workers, resumed publication under Soviet auspices, and *Kommunistka* was launched, under the editorship of Krupskaia, to serve as the theoretical organ of the Zhenotdel. By 1927 some eighteen women's journals were being published with a reported circulation of 386,000.

The major function of such journals was to emphasize the link between the emancipation of women and the establishment of socialism. The ultimate political objective, however, was to encourage women's entry into political affairs and to develop a growing pool of experienced female cadres for Party and government work. An ingenious mechanism was devised to help accomplish these goals. Conferences of Worker and Peasant Women, or Delegates' Assemblies, modeled after the system of soviets, were created to facilitate the political education, training, and recruitment of women and to initiate them into public roles. Elections were organized among women workers and peasants to select "delegates"—one for every five workers or twenty-five peasants—who would attend meetings and courses of instruction under Party guidance and then be assigned as apprentices to a variety of state, Party, trade union, or cooperative agencies. In this way widening circles of women would gain the experience and, equally importantly, the confidence to take up public roles independently.

The entire network of delegates—a voluntary, non-Party, mass organization—represented an innovative approach to the political education, training, and recruitment of women. But the actual extent of participation in its activities is difficult to ascertain with any precision. Stalin's organizational report of the Central Committee to the Thirteenth Party Congress in 1924 gives the figures of 46,000 women delegates in cities and 100,000 in villages. Figures available for 1926 report that some 620,000 women participated in 6,000 conferences held in urban areas and 12,000 in rural areas, and by 1928 it was claimed that 2,500,000 women were participating in the delegates' assemblies.[19]

In the early years of Soviet rule, the Zhenotdel was also encouraged by the Party to devote its energies to the task of organizing and constructing the communal institutions for dining and child care that would liberate women from the petty cares of individual households and lay the

[19]J. V. Stalin, *Sochineniia,* 13 vols. (Moscow, 1946–1952), 2:194; for 1928, Tolkunova, *Pravo zhenshchin,* p. 43.

foundation for the ultimate socialization of housework. Lenin was particularly emphatic in stressing the importance of these activities to the emancipation of women and in criticizing the Party for its failure to devote sufficient attention to this question. "Public catering establishments, nurseries, kindergartens . . . here we have examples of these shoots [of communism] . . . which can really emancipate women, really lessen and abolish their inequality with men as regards their role in social production and public life."[20]

In many respects the Zhenotdel functioned as a female auxiliary of the Party, perpetuating a sexual division of labor in new circumstances. During the civil war women were recruited for paramilitary service and nursing roles. The famine drew them into the distribution of food supplies. War and civil war and revolutionary upheaval had created large numbers of homeless and orphaned children whose care was also taken up by the Zhenotdel. Indeed, Kollontai herself encouraged this sexual division of labor, sharing with Lenin the view that the creation of new conditions of daily life was the task of women in particular:

> Men are quickly building soviet apparatuses of government, production, regulation; they are creating the Red Army. Before women workers and peasants arises the task of creating new forms of daily life, setting up dining halls, communal houses, social education, protection of motherhood. The October Revolution gave women rights. Life authoritatively pushes the broad female masses to use them, both for their own benefit and for the benefit of the Soviet republic.[21]

The dangers inherent in this approach were recognized by Krupskaia in particular, who complained on a number of occasions that women were all too frequently commandeered for work in social welfare, education, public health, and nurseries instead of being encouraged to participate fully in all fields of Soviet life and especially in economic and political construction.

The assimilation of the Moslem societies of Central Asia into the new Soviet state presented special difficulties. The failure of the regime to penetrate or destroy traditional associational networks by a direct assault on local elites led to a new strategy in which sex replaced social class as the decisive lever for effecting social change. Women came to be viewed, in the evocative terms of Massell, as a "surrogate proletariat," the most exploited stratum of Moslem society. The task of the Zhenotdel was to use women to gain access to the Moslem community, to bring to Moslem

[20]Lenin, "Velikii pochin," in *PSS*, 39: 24.
[21]Aleksandra Kollontai, "Kak my sozyvali pervyi vserossiiskii s"ezd rabotnits i krest'ianok," *Kommunistka* 11 (November 1923): 4–5.

women a vision of the new possibilities opened to them by the establishment of Soviet power, and to crystallize discontent and channel it in new
social and political directions.

Moreover, by identifying potential female cadres and training them to
staff new social and political institutions, the regime would gain entry
into a milieu heretofore closed to it. The recruitment of native cadres
would in turn enhance the legitimacy of Soviet power among the local
population by reducing the appearance of Russian domination. The mobilization of native women for social and political work was therefore an
important component of efforts at *korenizatsiia*, the effort to root the Soviet
apparatus among ethnic minorities.

In Soviet Central Asia the Zhenotdel launched its most sweeping attack
on the structure of traditional society. To dramatize challenges to Moslem
norms and authorities and to intensify social strain within the traditional
culture, the Zhenotdel encouraged women to initiate divorce actions, to
participate in mass public unveilings, and to enter new roles in direct
competition with men. The new civil and property rights granted to
women, and enforced through the Soviet legal system, were used to undermine traditional Moslem law and legal institutions and break their hold
over local life. The recruitment of women into the labor force and into
new semiprofessional, professional, and administrative roles was of particular importance in Central Asia, challenging the dominance of males
who previously mediated the relationship of women to the outside world
and obliging them to compete in new economic and political arenas.

These policies could backfire with serious repercussions. By encouraging women to assert their independence of local norms and kinship networks at a time when viable substitutes had not yet been created, the
Zhenotdel exposed them to severe hardship. Marriage and divorce laws
that might have liberating consequences in the urban areas of European
Russia had very different effects in Central Asia, where they encouraged
men to repudiate the oldest and least attractive of their wives, leaving
them without economic or institutional support. Numerous women found
themselves adrift, freed from stable if repressive family roles with no alternatives to prostitution and crime. Moreover, the creation of segregated
organizational forms to penetrate segregated societies also had its negative
side, perpetuating the differentiation of male and female roles in new
conditions.

The impact of the Zhenotdel is difficult to assess in quantitative terms.
In rural areas, the presence of the Party in general was still very marginal
by the end of the decade. Three-fourths of all villages had experienced
no Party activity at all, according to a 1927 account, and although rural
Party membership had increased from 200,000 to 300,000 between 1922

and 1927, there were still only 25 Party members for every 10,000 peasants.[22] For many peasants, men and women alike, Bolshevism was synonymous with atheism, sexual license, and the destruction of the family. The Zhenotdel in this respect represented official Soviet culture confronting a deeply conservative rural society suspicious of, if not hostile to, the intentions of the new ruling elite.[23]

The political mobilization of urban women, particularly in the Slavic regions, confronted fewer obstacles. The widening circulation of women's journals gives some evidence of growing familiarity and contact. Rising rates of female participation in elections, local soviets, in the Komsomol (Communist youth organization), and in the Party—discussed at greater length in Chapter VI—offer further indications of the growing impact of new values and opportunities. Small but increasing numbers of women were being appointed to responsible positions in the state and Party apparatus, in response to the steady prodding of a stream of Party directives, even if the functions and authority of women remained in many cases more nominal than real.[24] The influence of the Zhenotdel was also evident in the more militant forms of self-assertion by women, whether in mass demonstrations and conferences or in the more quiet utilization of legal institutions to initiate divorce proceedings or defend newly acquired rights.

The impact of the Zhenotdel on public consciousness was even more significant, if its prominence in the literature of the 1920s is any indica-

[22]Stephen Cohen, *Bukharin and the Bolshevik Revolution* (New York, 1973), p. 443. The correlation of census data and Party membership is based on figures given in Merle Fainsod, *How Russia Is Ruled*, 2nd ed. (Cambridge, Mass., 1963), p. 253. Efforts to recruit women into positions of rural leadership encountered severe obstacles and resulted in painfully slow change. The proportion of women in village soviets in the Russian Republic increased from 1 percent to 2.9 percent between 1923 and 1924, in *volost'* executive committees from .3 percent to .5 percent, in *guberniia* executive committees from 2 percent to 3 percent, and among candidates for Party membership from 9 percent to 11 percent (Stalin, "Organizational Report of the Central Committee to the Thirteenth Party Congress, May 1924," in *Sochineniia*, 2: 195). Fragmentary accounts of the slow penetration of Party activity into rural milieus with references to the recruitment of women are also found in Moshe Lewin, *Russian Peasants and Soviet Power: A Study of Collectivization* (London, 1968), p. 121; D. J. Male, *Russian Peasant Organization Before Collectivization* (Cambridge, England, 1971), p. 70; Teodor Shanin, *The Awkward Class* (Oxford, 1972), p. 176; Sula Benet, ed. and trans., *The Village of Viriatino* (New York, 1970), pp. 278–79.

[23]For a suggestive discussion of the coexistence of two cultures, see Robert Tucker, "The Image of Dual Russia," in *The Soviet Political Mind*, ed. Robert Tucker, rev. ed. (London, 1972).

[24]A particularly strong directive of the Party Central Committee in September 1929 requested the promotion of a fixed number of Communist working women to managerial positions in the Party, soviets, and other organs. It criticized the failure to promote the growing number of women in middle-level positions to higher levels and urged that the purge be used as an opportunity to increase the representation of women. *Izvestiia Tsentral'nogo Komiteta*, September 20, 1929, p. 24.

tion. It had clearly contributed to a revolution in the status of women, yet like all revolutions this one provoked hostility as well as enthusiasm. Writing in *Pravda* in 1923, Trotskii portrayed with special vividness one of the countless domestic tragedies that resulted from collisions between the old and the new consciousness, dividing families and setting them against each other.

> An old family. Ten to fifteen years of life together. The husband is a good worker, devoted to his family; the wife lives also for her home, giving it all her energy. But just by chance she comes in touch with a Communist women's organization. A new world opens before her eyes. The family is neglected. The husband is irritated. The wife is hurt in her newly awakened civic consciousness. The family is broken up.[25]

The Zhenotdel was more the symbol than the cause of social strain. The social dislocation resulting from war, revolution, civil war, and nationalization had as much to do with family instability as the new family legislation and the activities of the Zhenotdel. But its very visibility made it a tempting target in the rising anxiety over social disintegration.

The conflicts raged within Party circles as well as outside them. An extensive literature documents the resistance of Party activists to pressures from above and the ingenious mechanisms of evasion and selective accommodation that emerged. Lenin himself had many occasions to deplore the attitude of Party activists who gave lip service to the emancipation of women while refusing their wives the opportunity to participate in Zhenotdel work. The problems were especially acute, but not unique, in Central Asia. As one native female Communist delicately put it, even the most sincere, emancipated, and principled Communists among her male comrades retained a peculiar "psychological aberration" in their attitude toward women who had unveiled themselves. Even in the highest echelons, male Communists were unable "to suppress a reaction which in its immediacy is tantamount to a conditioned reflex; even they, although unconsciously, tend to assume that peculiar freedom of manner which men allow themselves in the presence of women of 'questionable character.'"[26]

Indeed, Zhenotdel activists encountered not merely hostility but far harsher treatment at the hands of their enemies. In Uzbekistan in 1928, some 203 cases of antifeminist murder were reported,[27] and in 1930 the

---

[25]Leon Trotskii, *Pravda*, July 13, 1923. Translated in Leon Trotskii, "From the Old Family to the New," in *Problems of Everyday Life* (New York, 1973), p. 40.

[26]Massell, *The Surrogate Proletariat*, pp. 302–3.

[27]Cases of antifeminist violence are described by S. Yakopov, "The Struggle Against Offenses Rooted in the Traditional Way of Life," in Schlesinger, *Changing Attitudes*, pp. 198–99.

Presidium of the Central Executive Committee, alarmed by the increasing
number of such crimes, sanctioned their classification as counterrevolutionary and therefore subject to the death penalty. So violent was the male
backlash that it became a serious threat to larger political priorities.

Nor did many of the activities of the Zhenotdel meet with whole-
hearted approval within the Party itself. Numerous conflicts over the
proper allocation of authority between the Zhenotdel organizers and Party
and trade union officials developed. Within factories employing large
numbers of women, efforts to divide responsibility between Zhenotdel
organizers and trade union leaders segregated workers by sex and heightened friction, until undivided responsibility was ultimately restored to the
factory committees.

Even at the very apex of the Party, the Zhenotdel was not accorded influence or respect. A telling indication of its political marginality was reflected in criticism of the "abnormal" treatment of the Zhenotdel and its
leadership by V. P. Nogin, reporter for the Auditing Commission at the
Eleventh Party Congress in 1922. Nogin pointed out that representatives
of all Central Committee departments except the Zhenotdel participated
in Organizational Bureau (Orgburo) meetings, and went on to paint a
vivid portrait of the insensitive and bureaucratic treatment of Zhenotdel
leaders. "When it is necessary for the Zhenotdel representative to come to
the Orgburo on some business, and if [the Orgburo] has a number of
questions . . . to consider . . . they hear her problem, they summon her
in, but when the discussion of her question is finished they say to her:
'And now wait.' She goes out to the waiting room and waits for a long
time, frequently for hours, until they summon her again."[28]

Disinterest in and outright hostility toward the activities of the Zhenotdel were even greater at lower levels of the Party apparatus. Local Party
organs frequently refused to supply the necessary personnel for work
among women, failed to carry out Zhenotdel programs, and in some instances actually liquidated local women's sections, ordering Zhenotdel
activists to carry out other assignments. Zhenotdel activists were therefore
subjected to a variety of pressures as they attempted to interpret broad
objectives in the light of local needs, to respond to the problems of local
women, and to transmit these appreciations back to the center. Neither
monolithic nor highly centralized, and receiving only minimal support
from central Party organs and leaders, the Zhenotdel was divided and
buffeted by the interplay of complex pressures.

But the vulnerability of the Zhenotdel had deeper causes, related to

[28]Kommunisticheskaia Partiia Sovetskogo Soiuza (KPSS), *Odinnadtsatyi S"ezd RKP (b),
1922, Stenograficheskii otchet* (Moscow, 1961), p. 67.

structural factors that established both the possibilities and the limits of a women's organization within the Party. Useful as a transmission belt for Party policy and as a mechanism for extending Party influence to an otherwise inaccessible female constituency, the Zhenotdel, as we have seen, functioned as a female auxiliary of the Party. Staffed by the wives and female relatives of Bolshevik leaders, as well as by recruits from factory circles, it was accorded organizational recognition but marginal status.

Yet this definition of its role strained against the commitments and goals that derived from its organizational mission. The creation of a new constituency involved, at least to some degree, the effort to define women as a particular social group with distinctive interests that cut across other identifications, such as family, region, nationality, religion, and even social class. The Zhenotdel tended to heighten the consciousness of women as women, to encourage them to take an active part in their own liberation, and to defend the interests of a female constituency even as it sought to integrate women into the larger political community.

The tension between these two fundamentally different orientations had already emerged in the prerevolutionary period in controversies over the legitimacy of a separate women's organization. It became even more acute in the increasingly monolithic political climate of the 1920s. As the remaining elements of fluidity and pluralism in Soviet political life were eroded, the Zhenotdel was increasingly vulnerable to accusations that its activities threatened the organizational unity of the Party. At the Twelfth Party Congress in 1923, a resolution was adopted that warned of the danger of "feminist tendencies," which "under the banner of improving the women's way of life, actually could lead to the female contingent of labor breaking away from the common class struggle."[29] Resolutions at the Thirteenth and Fourteenth Congresses expressed a similar alarm, stressing the danger of viewing the woman question in isolation from the common tasks of the working class.[30] The Zhenotdel was further accused of a one-sided emphasis on agitation, propaganda, and educational and cultural tasks that we might define as "consciousness raising" and criticized for its neglect of practical tasks.

The consolidation of power within the Party apparatus by Stalin and the inauguration of a crash program of industrialization and collectivization were accompanied by a redefinition of organizational and political needs. In 1930, as part of a general reorganization of the Central Com-

[29]Institut Marksizma Leninizma pri TsK KPSS, *KPSS v rezoliutsiiakh i resheniiakh*, 4 vols. (Moscow, 1954–1960), 1: 754–55.
[30]*Ibid.*, 2: 88–89.

mittee Secretariat, the Zhenotdel was formally abolished. Its activities were assigned to regular Party organizations and to the Commissions for the Improvement of the Working and Living Conditions of Women attached to local, provincial, and republic executive committees. Its abolition was defended as an effort to intensify work among women by regular Party and trade union organizations.[31] Yet, from an organizational perspective, the very existence of a functionally distinct body with a specific mission and the authority of the Party behind it compelled attention to the sphere of its activities. A recent index of Party resolutions and decrees includes some 301 entries on the subject of "women" for the period from 1917 to 1930 and only 3 entries for the three subsequent decades. From 1930 on, policies toward women were no longer the special competence of a distinct organization but a function of broader priorities and patterns of economic and social change that affected the society as a whole.

The rise and fall of the Zhenotdel had a counterpart in the stormy existence of the Evsektsiia, or Jewish section, the only other major Party organ of its kind.[32] In composition and goals, both organizations breached the sexual, ethnic, and organizational unity of the Party in an effort to reach and mobilize an otherwise inaccessible constitutency. Both were torn between the two functions of acting as transmission belts for Party policy while simultaneously defending the distinctive identities and interests of their constituents within Party networks. Both organizations flourished in the relative institutional fluidity and pluralism of the 1920s but came under increasing pressure as Party control tightened. Both were abolished in 1930 with the consolidation of Stalin's power.

The fate of the Zhenotdel was thus a particular manifestation of broader trends in the evolution of the Soviet regime. Its creation reflected an awareness of the need to draw women into the new political community and to mobilize them for new forms of political participation. The limited resources assigned to this task and the conflicts it provoked indicated its low priority and potentially disruptive consequences. And the abolition of the Zhenotdel, like that of the Evsektsiia, confirmed that the libertarian implications of a real transformation of sexual and ethnic relationships were incompatible with the political structure and values of the Stalin regime. The stormy history of the Zhenotdel expressed in microcosm the scope and limits of sexual equality in the early Soviet period, offering

---

[31]*Pravda*, January 17, 1930. Women's Departments were preserved in the Central Asian Party organization until the mid-1950s. They were also recreated after World War II in the newly incorporated Baltic republics and in the Western Ukraine and Belorussia.

[32]See Zvi Gitelman, *Jewish Nationality and Soviet Politics: The Jewish Sections of the CPSU, 1917–1930* (Princeton, 1972).

striking testimony of the uneasy relationship of Bolshevism and feminism in the first decade of Soviet power.

REVOLUTIONARY STRATEGIES AND ELITE PERSPECTIVES

The controversy surrounding the Zhenotdel was but one expression of a larger conflict within Bolshevism over the goals and strategies of revolutionary transformation. In the prerevolutionary period, as we have seen, disagreements had centered on questions of revolutionary strategy in which organizational issues were uppermost. Thus, Kollontai's efforts to win support for the creation of a special Party apparatus to organize women workers had raised anxieties within the Party about the possibility of a feminist deviation that might dilute the class basis of revolutionary activity. But implicit in even this conflict over organizational form was a larger tension between two political orientations, one viewing the liberation of women as a desirable objective in itself, to be realized through the socialist revolution, and the other treating the mobilization of women in more instrumental terms as a potential contribution to the larger revolutionary struggle. The tension between these approaches became more acute with the establishment of Soviet power.

The classic works of Marx, Engels, Lenin, and Bebel clearly shared the first orientation. Marx and Engels had depicted in agonizing detail the oppression and humiliation of women in bourgeois society and had held out the hope of liberation and equality under socialism. The oppression of women under capitalism was a double one, Lenin had pointed out in *Pravda* in 1921.[33] As workers and peasants, women were exposed to harsh conditions of employment in societies that denied them full equality as citizens. The foundations of economic and political oppression would be destroyed by the socialist revolution. The abolition of private ownership over the means of production and the expropriation of the exploiters would give control over production to the workers themselves. All working people would be assured of full economic and political participation in the new society.

But the second form of oppression described by Lenin, the oppression of women as women, would not be automatically eliminated by the socialist revolution itself. Further measures would be needed to eliminate the sexual division of labor that kept women in "household bondage," "overburdened with the drudgery of the most squalid, backbreaking, and stultifying toil in the kitchen and the family household."[34] The unproductive character of housework and the narrow and restricted lives that

[33]Lenin, "Mezhdunarodnyi den' rabotnits," in *PSS*, 42: 368–70.
[34]*Ibid.*, p. 368.

women led within the walls of the private household evoked Lenin's particular concern. "Women grow worn out in the petty, monotonous household work, their strength and time dissipated and wasted, their minds growing narrow and stale, their hearts beating slowly, their will weakened."[35]

To Marx's portrayal of the grim exploitation of women workers in the industrial factories of England, Lenin added a vivid and poignant portrait of the fate of Russian peasant women chained to the narrow confines of the traditional household. The virtues of Russian communal life, which figured so prominently in the antiindustrialism of the populist tradition, received no echo in Lenin. "As long as women are engaged in housework," he insisted, "their position is still a restricted one. In order to achieve the complete emancipation of women and to make them really equal with men, we must have social economy, and the participation of women in general productive labor. Then women will occupy the same position as men."[36]

Women were not the only victims of their backwardness. Lenin was particularly sensitive to the larger social and political consequences of women's restricted roles. The backwardness of women would limit their ability to share the new values and commitments that would develop among men and weaken the foundations of a new social order: "The backwardness of women, their lack of understanding for the revolutionary ideals of the man, decrease his joy and determination in fighting. They are little worms which, unseen, slowly but surely rot and corrode."[37]

If the maintenance of the traditional household could have a corrosive effect on efforts at social change, then any far-reaching modernization of Russian life required a transformation of the family and, with it, the position of women. The full integration of women into economic and political life was essential to comprehensive social change. The new Soviet regime must therefore strike directly at the role of women if it were to begin building in earnest a modern and socialist society. Yet Lenin's unique appreciation of the pivotal importance of women's roles in any larger strategy of revolutionary modernization was joined to a real concern over the desirable effects of such progress on women themselves. His approach was sensitive to the instrumental utility of female mobilization while retaining a humanitarian and libertarian concern with the fate of women themselves.

A similar mixture of normative and instrumental orientations charac-

---

[35]Clara Zetkin, *Reminiscences of Lenin* (New York, International Publishers, 1934), pp. 56 –57.

[36]Lenin, "O zadachakh zhenskogo dvizheniia v sovetskoi respublike," in *PSS*, 39: 201.

[37]Zetkin, *Reminiscences of Lenin*, p. 57.

terized the writings of many Zhenotdel activists. The humanitarian and libertarian strains of Marxism-Leninism found particularly strong echo in the articles and pamphlets of the female Party activists assigned to work among women in remote regions of the country. In Central Asia the catalog of oppression took new form, shaped by the distinctive features of Moslem life that demeaned and indeed mutilated women. A mixture of shock and outrage at the circumstances of women's lives and missionary zeal for reform informed the writings of a whole generation of Communist organizers, who struggled to keep these humanistic and libertarian concerns from being submerged by other priorities.

Far more characteristic and widespread within the Party, however, was a second orientation, an instrumental approach to the emancipation of women. The views of some leading figures, preoccupied with the rationalization of Soviet life, gave special weight to considerations of economic efficiency in redefining women's roles. Preobrazhenskii, for example, emphasized the economic advantages of collective child-rearing, pointing out: "If in the individual family one mother raises 3-5 of her own children, then with communal child-rearing one woman on the average will be able to raise 5-10 children of others."[38]

Economies of scale were an important preoccupation in Bolshevik economic doctrine, producing an emphasis on efficiency rather than equality in the allocation of sex roles. The endless and unproductive labor of millions of women in private households was a recurring theme in early writings. A stream of publications counted the millions of woman-hours wasted on cooking and child care and described with enthusiasm the social gains to be realized by redirecting this labor into social production. The superior efficiency of large-scale social organization provided an essentially technocratic rationale for the communal reorganization of social life.

Yet the dimensions of unpaid labor performed within the household were far too vast to contemplate its immediate replacement by socialized services. A major investigation of time budgets of worker families in 1922 conducted by S. G. Strumilin, a pioneer of new scientific methods for the study of Soviet society, discovered that for every 100 hours of paid employment, the families he studied spent an additional 142 hours on unpaid labor within the household itself. He went on to calculate the total number of paid workers who would be needed to perform all the services provided free within the household: 1,186,000 cooks and assistants; 1,490,000 nursemaids; 980,000 cleaning women; 783,000 shoppers; a grand total of 7,235,000 domestic workers for every 20,000,000 people. To pay for this entire mass of services, he estimated, would take some

[38]*Kommunistka*, 7 (1921): 20.

1,302,000,000 rubles annually.[39] The prohibitive costs associated with the transfer of household services to the public sector relegated Strumilin's concerns to a distant Communist future, if not to the realm of pure fantasy. But his work established an important precedent for the treatment of domestic labor as socially valued work to which an economic value could be attached, and this precedent would become important at a later stage of Soviet development when new social problems would bring the issue to the fore once again.

The writings of Stalin express yet a third orientation to the problem of social transformation. This orientation is political rather than technocratic, and a normative concern is altogether absent. Stalin's emphasis is on the utility of women as an economic resource, useful in the service of larger national goals. Even his early pronouncements on the woman question are permeated by an emphasis on the particular backwardness of women rather than their special oppression. For Stalin, women epitomized the ignorance and conservatism of Russian life. Left to themselves, they would constitute a drag on further social progress, an obstacle to political and economic development. As he explained in a major article:

> If our country has begun the construction of the new Soviet life in earnest, then surely it is clear that the women of this country, constituting half its population, would act as a drag on any advance if they remained backward, downtrodden, and politically undeveloped in the future also.
>
> The woman worker . . . can help the common cause if she is politically conscious and politically educated. But she can ruin the common cause if she is downtrodden and backward, not, of course, as a result of her ill-will, but because of her backwardness. The peasant woman stands shoulder to shoulder with the peasant man. She advances, together with him, the common cause of the development of our agriculture, its successes, and its flourishing. She can make an enormous contribution in this cause if she frees herself of backwardness and ignorance. And the contrary is also the case: she could act as a brake on the whole cause if she remains a slave to ignorance in the future also.[40]

The political enlightenment of women was essential not only for the sake of their own potential contribution to social progress but above all because of their role as mothers. As Stalin put it, "working and peasant women are mothers who raise our youth—the future of our country. They can cripple the soul of youth. The healthy soul of our youth and the advancement of our country depends on whether the mother sympathizes with Soviet order or trails along behind the priest, kulak, and bourgeois."[41]

    [39]S. G. Strumilin, "K izucheniiu byta trudiashchikhsia v SSSR," in *Izbrannye proizvedeniia* (Moscow, 1964), Vol. 3, pp. 190–200.
    [40]J. V. Stalin, "K piatoi godovshchine pervogo s"ezda rabotnits i krestianok" (November 1923), in *Sochineniia*, 5: 349–51.
    [41]*Ibid.*

This orientation was obviously not unique to Stalin alone. An emphasis on the special backwardness of women had characterized even prerevolutionary Party writings and indeed had been used to justify the special efforts needed to organize among them. The increasing emphasis on this theme in the 1920s, however, and the less and less frequent discussion of the special oppression of women expressed a more fundamental transformation of political values. Its effect was to shift the focus of discussion still further away from the question of female emancipation and to emphasize women's responsibilities rather than their burdens. The liberation of women was confined, in Stalin's view, to their liberation from ignorance, not from oppression, and its instrument was political education. Stalin's extreme emphasis on the need for solidarity between men and women was consonant with a concern for the potential contribution of women to national development and for the ways in which the energies of men and women together could be harnessed to the economic and political tasks laid out by the Party.

Evoking the military imagery of the civil war period, Stalin described working and peasant women as "an enormous army of labor," the "labor reserves" of the proletariat, on whose support the revolution depended for its success. The crucial task of the Party was to transform this reserve into an "active army" in socialist construction.[42] The few scattered references to women in his voluminous selected writings emphasized the need to make use of the great economic and political force that women, as half the population, constituted; the concern found in the works of Marx and Engels, Bebel, Trotskii, and Kollontai with the humiliation and oppression of women within the family finds no echo in Stalin's treatment of their role.

Stalin's failure to address himself to the problem of women's oppression had deeper roots and broader significance. As Robert Tucker has pointed out in his very suggestive study of Stalin's personality, Stalin selected out of Leninism its martial, elitist, and authoritarian strains.[43] His image of the Party was not of a "hospitable patriarchal family ready to take in all who sympathize," but of a fortress, an army, locked in perpetual combat, which demanded preeminently male qualities of toughness and ruthlessness.[44] This vision of the Party found eloquent expression in his speech at Lenin's death: "Comrades, we Communists are people of a special cut. . . . We are those who form the army of the great proletarian strategist, the army of Comrade Lenin. . . . It is sons of the working class, sons of

[42]Stalin, *Sochineniia*, 7: 49; 8: 339.
[43]Robert Tucker, *Stalin as Revolutionary, 1879–1929* (New York, 1973), Ch. 4.
[44]Stalin, *Sochineniia*, 1: 64, 65–67, 70, 73.

want and struggle, sons of incredible privation and heroic effort, who above all should be members of such a party."[45]

The contempt for weakness, which stamped his entire political outlook, offers a further clue to Stalin's orientation; it is no accident that he chose as his revolutionary pseudonym a name denoting "man of steel." Here, the intimate connection between ethnic and sexual equality and their attitudinal and psychological requisites assumes profound significance. In reclaiming the Tsarist patrimony through a combination of political interventions and military conquest, the Bolsheviks inherited also the legacy of local hostility to rule from the Russian heartland. Although he was willing to offer only the most circumscribed endorsement of national self-determinism by non-Russian minorities, Lenin remained a steadfast critic of all manifestations of Great Russian chauvinism. In his last writings on the national question, Lenin warned against the dangers of allowing Party agents to ride roughshod over native sensibilities. Insisting that it was better to stretch too far than too little in the direction of concessions and gentleness toward national minorities, Lenin went even further in suggesting that they be indemnified for past injustices:

> . . . we, the members of a great [Russian] nation . . . are guilty . . . of an infinite amount of coercion and insults [with respect to the smaller peoples within our borders]. . . . It behooves us [therefore] to indemnify [our] minorities . . . in one or another way—in the way we behave and in what we concede—for the mistrust, for the suspicion, for the insults which the ruling "great" nation has brought them in the past.[46]

For Lenin, the elimination of national oppression was to be one of the great achievements of Soviet power. On a number of occasions, the brutal and contemptuous treatment of national minorities by Party activists provoked him to complain: "Scratch certain Communists and you find a Great Russian chauvinist. . . . He sits in many of us and we have to fight him."[47] These comments by Lenin bear a striking resemblance to those recorded by Clara Zetkin in a conversation concerning the woman question. "Yes indeed," Lenin reportedly remarked on that occasion, "unfor-

---

[45]*Ibid.*, 6: 46.

[46] Lenin, "K voprosu o natsional'nostiakh," in *Lenin o natsional'nom, i natsional'no-kolonial'nom voprose* (Moscow, 1956), pp. 548–50. See also the discussion in Massell, *The Surrogate Proletariat*, pp. 52–54.

[47]Tucker, *Stalin*, p. 245. In a similar vein, Massell describes Lenin's concern that the ruthless self-assertion of his own lieutenants and their emissaries in Central Asia would crush and ultimately alienate even the most dedicated local cadres, because they—like local Russian officials and workers—treated minority populations with abuse, brutality, and contempt. It was therefore likely that the new native political leadership in Central Asia would "drown in the sea of Great Russian chauvinist riffraff like a fly in milk"; Massell, *The Surrogate Proletariat*, p. 50.

tunately it is still true to say of many of our comrades, scratch a Communist and find a philistine. Of course, you must scratch the sensitive spot. Their mentality as regards women. . . . The old master-right of man still lives in secret."[48] Such chauvinistic attitudes, expressed in relation to both women and national minorities, were a legacy of the past whose eradication, in Lenin's view, required a determined struggle.

Moreover, there was, in Lenin's orientation toward both ethnic and sexual issues, an awareness of the profound importance of the principle of self-determination. The durability of both national and marital unions would be enhanced, rather than reduced, by founding them on the ultimate right of secession.This analogy too is explicit in Lenin's writing: "To accuse the supporters of freedom of self-determination, i.e., freedom to secede, of encouraging separatism, is as foolish and as hypocritical as accusing the advocates of divorce of encouraging the destruction of family ties."[49] The conditions of both national and sexual emancipation were intimately connected, both psychologically and politically.

Lenin's concern with the oppression of national minorities, like his concern for the oppression of women, found no echo in Stalin. An arrogant contempt of minority cultures and the backwardness and weakness they represented accompanied a strong personal identification with Russian nationalism. In repudiating his Georgian background, Stalin chose a new national identity, which to him represented power as well as progress. He could not, therefore, share Lenin's anxieties about the danger of Great Russian chauvinism. On the contrary, he focused his own criticism on the nationalist deviations of formerly oppressed minorities. Speaking to a conference of Turkic Communists in 1921, he remarked that it was precisely those peoples who had suffered in the past from Russian oppression who had a particular problem in overcoming their own nationalist prejudices. The Russian nation, never having experienced external rule, was spared the problem of nationalist deviations in its midst. Despite a perfunctory reference to Great Russian chauvinism, which Lenin had seen as a serious problem, Stalin largely ignored the issue.[50] In contrast to

---

[48]Zetkin, *Reminiscences of Lenin*, p. 56.

[49]Lenin, "O prave natsii na samoopredelenie," in *PSS*, 25: 286.

[50]This episode is recounted in Tucker, *Stalin*, p. 250. It was, of course, Stalin's approach rather than Lenin's that was ultimately enshrined in official Party policy. At the 17th Party Congress in 1934 Great Russian chauvinism was no longer singled out as the main danger. In his official report to the Congress, Stalin—echoing the views expressed over a decade earlier—introduced local nationalism as an equally great danger, depending on the circumstances. Needless to say, this provided the political rationale for the sweeping purge of national cadres that followed. Donald S. Carlisle, "Modernization, Generations, and the Uzbek Soviet Intelligentsia," in *The Dynamics of Soviet Politics*, eds. Paul Cocks, Robert V. Daniels, and Nancy Whittier Heer (Cambridge, Mass., 1976), p. 403.

Lenin, Stalin was preoccuppied with deviance rather than with oppression, in both ethnic and sexual politics. His strategy called not for indemnification but for repression, suggesting yet a deeper connection between the twin fates of Zhenotdel and Evsektsiia.

If different orientations within the Party leadership emerged in the process of defining the objectives of liberation, conflicting views were also evident in the choice of means. From the very origins of the Bolshevik Party, both its ideology and its organization were predicated on the conviction that particular aspects of economic and sociopolitical organization played a decisive and defining role in the broader process of social and cultural change. Within this general Leninist framework, differences of emphasis and orientation emerged. At one end of the spectrum were those who emphasized the primacy of economic changes. The forms of production and the relationships that emerged from them were of decisive importance; changes in the position of women would occur naturally, if slowly, as a consequence of the larger development of Soviet society. As one early Soviet theorist explained: "Communists see the only lever to a real transformation of human relations in a change of the productive base, of the economic foundation of social life, over which various ideological forms constitute multiform superstructures in which are clothed human consciousness, morals, and customs." [51]

Other Party theorists, rejecting the extreme reductionism of this view, assigned greater weight to the influence of superstructure and urged a far more active intervention to bring about social change. Rather than waiting for larger economic changes to affect social relationships, they argued that to some degree the liberation of women was a condition and not exclusively a consequence of real economic development.

Kollontai and Trotskii were particularly attentive to the attitudinal and psychological roots of inequality. They emphasized the need to alter social attitudes and behavior through Party work among women and through a more direct assault on the family structures and sexual patterns that were responsible for inequality. Until inequality had been eliminated within the family, Trotskii maintained, there could be no equality in social production. [52] Refusing to accept the scarcity of resources as the basic constraint, Trotskii criticized an overly simple correlation of base and superstructure. He used the potential contradiction between material pos-

[51] Vadim A. Bystrianski, *Kommunizm, brak i sem'ia* (Petersburg, 1921), p. 66.

[52] The close connection that Trotskii saw between the problem of liberating women and that of transforming the family is described in a message to a rally of women workers in Moscow that appears in *Pravda*, November 28, 1923, translated in Leon Trotskii, *Women and the Family* (New York, 1970), pp. 29–30. The view that equality in the family is a precondition of equality in social life is elaborated in Trotskii's *Problems of Everyday Life* (1924; reprinted New York, 1973), p. 1.

sibilities and real social life as the justification for a more direct attack on prevailing values:

> Any social structure, including a socialist one, can find itself faced with the phenomenon that the material possibilities for a given improvement and alteration of life are present, but sluggishness, lazy habits of thought, servile traditions, conservative stupidity may be met even in the socialist structure, as a link with the past, as an absence of initiative and boldness in destroying the old forms of life. And the task of our party and the series of social organizations led by it . . . consists in pressing forward customs, everyday habits, and psychology, and preventing the conditions of everyday life from falling behind the socioeconomic possibilities. . . . Everyday life is fearfully conservative, incomparably more conservative than technology.[53]

A more active intervention to bring about social change could nevertheless take a variety of forms, and throughout the 1920s a muted struggle took place between the advocates of different approaches.

The introduction of the New Economic Policy in 1921 entailed a major shift in priorities—the temporary replacement of revolutionary assault as a central mechanism of social change by an evolutionary transformation of Russian society. A partial accommodation of the preexisting social and economic system would be accompanied by a long and gradual process of education, a protracted cultural revolution that would gradually reshape society along new lines.

Although Lenin's last writings contain an elaborate exposition of this gradualist approach, there is ample precedent in his earlier writings for a more militant and coercive strategy of revolutionary change, a strategy that would strike more directly and sharply at the economic, political, and cultural foundations of the old social order. This strategy continued to have its vocal adherents throughout the 1920s, particularly within the Komsomol and among Party activists at the local level whose outlook was shaped by the heroic traditions of war communism and whose authority was endangered by the gradualist and conciliatory elements of central policy after 1921.

The tensions between the two different approaches to revolutionary change, with their different implications for female emancipation, emerged most sharply in the conflicts over Soviet policy toward women in Central Asia. Militant Zhenotdel activists called for a direct attack on traditional Moslem society, an immediate, all-out assault on "feudal" and "tribal-patriarchal residues," on "everything that was old and obsolete" and that

---

[53]Leon Trotskii, "Address to the Third All-Union Conference on Protection of Mothers and Children," *Pravda*, December 7, 1925, translated in Trotskii, *Women and the Family*, pp. 34–36.

"stood in direct contradiction to . . . and impeded socialist construction."[54] These advocates of intense and dramatic intervention chose a narrow focus for their efforts. The mass unveiling of women formed the core of their revolutionary strategy. It was designed to have a dramatic psychological effect, which would, they believed, undermine traditional assumptions, values, and behavior in many areas of life at once. The opponents of this strategy urged instead an emphasis on broadly-based, systematic work. Advocating a retreat from the cultural offensive, which threatened to backfire in serious ways, they argued that it was "naive to think that, merely by issuing [a few] laws, we shall be in a position to change prevailing relationships immediately and totally."[55] Only patient, systematic, and long-term efforts would create the new economic, educational, cultural, and associational forms and opportunities that would eventually transform women's roles in the Soviet East.[56]

The relationship between local advocates of conflicting revolutionary strategies in Central Asia and the factional conflicts at the Party center that they echoed cannot be clearly established on the basis of the available evidence. The victory of Stalin in the succession struggle, however, coincided with a repudiation of revolutionary assault and a shift in official policy toward Soviet Central Asia, even as it inaugurated a revolutionary assault far wider in scope, though different in focus, in European Russia.

SEXUAL LIBERATION AND THE FAMILY

Conflicting orientations to the problem of sexual equality in early Soviet policy were most obvious in the controversy over sexual liberation and the future of the family. The Marxist intellectual tradition provided the theoretical rationale for treating the family not as a permanent entity rooted in immutable biological needs but rather as a social institution whose form and function changed in response to changes in economic and social organization. The precise relationship between family change and broader socioeconomic transformation remained undefined, as did the consequences of socialism for the future of the family itself.

The critical stance toward the family embodied in early Soviet legislation was grounded in several perceptions. The family was seen not as a bulwark of freedom and self-fulfillment but as a significant locus of exploitation, oppression, and humiliation. The peasant household was the very embodiment of tradition and backwardness, the bearer of counterrevolutionary values. It was, as Bukharin put it, "the most conservative

[54]Massell, *Surrogate Proletariat*, p. 215.
[55]*Ibid.*, p. 333.
[56]*Ibid.*, p. 343.

stronghold of the old regime."[57] As the most conservative of all social institutions, it was a serious barrier to wider social change.

That the family served as a barrier to change was particularly true for women. Insofar as the family served as a focus of female energies and loyalties, it diverted them from larger social and political concerns. A shift from familistic to individualistic values was vital to the social mobilization of women. Moreover, the family was the locus of traditional authority structures and relationships. In reinforcing ascriptive bases of social status and in emphasizing hierarchy, subordination, and patriarchy the traditional family posed formidable obstacles to the achievement of sexual equality.

The transformation of the family was therefore closely linked to the liberation of women. In the socialist society of the future, it was widely believed, the family, along with other features of the bourgeois superstructure, would undergo profound alterations. Indeed, some insisted, the family would simply "wither away" as human relationships took new and unprecedented forms. Early Soviet policies were designed to hasten this process by weakening the religious, economic, and legal ties that sustained the patterns of traditional family life.[58]

Soviet legislation attempted to alter both the role of the family and women's place within it. First, it attempted to reshape the relationship between the family and the wider society. The process of industrialization was itself, in the Soviet view, whittling away the critical economic and educative functions of the family. The erosion of its economic base would be hastened by measures that deprived the household of productive economic roles and the family of its importance in transmitting private property. The socialization of household services would complete the transfer of economic activities from the family to the wider society. At the same time, the expansion of public education and the development of institutional child care would diminish the family's importance in the socialization of children. This entire transfer of household functions would in turn free women for participation in the labor force, thus assuring that women's roles would increasingly resemble those of men.

A second object of early Soviet legislation was to alter the distribution of roles and power within the family itself. By granting new economic rights and responsibilities to women and by creating new social conditions to facilitate their exercise, the foundations of female subordination were challenged. No longer would women be economically dependent on their

---

[57]Kent Geiger, *The Family in Soviet Russia* (Cambridge, Mass., 1968), p. 52.
[58]For a discussion of early Soviet family policy, see Geiger, *The Family*; John Hazard, *Law and Social Change in the USSR* (Toronto, 1953); Schlesinger, *Changing Attitudes*; and Roger Pethybridge, *The Social Prelude to Stalinism* (London, 1974).

husbands, nor would marriage serve as a device for women's economic support. The freedom to love, unfettered by religious and economic constraints, would make possible the creation of a new family structure based on the full equality of the partners.

Equality within the family was also upheld by new legal codes that insisted on the identical rights and responsibilities of both partners. All ties that bound husband and wife other than emotional ones were to be destroyed. The economic foundations of the prerevolutionary family were assaulted in a series of decrees abolishing the right of inheritance and transferring the property of the deceased to the state, while the abolition of community property was designed to eliminate marriages based on economic calculation. Practices that implied that marriage was an economic transaction—such as the payment of bride price—were outlawed. The religious ties associated with marriage were also attacked by granting legal recognition only to civil marriages and by granting the right of divorce to either spouse.

Egalitarian values received further expression in a provision of the new family codes that allowed couples to adopt the surname of either spouse or a joint surname. Some even proposed the residential separation of husband and wife as the ultimate step toward full equality. The patriarchal family, with its hierarchical structure and authoritarian values, came under attack as well. Campaigns against wife-beating and the physical punishment of children attempted to inhibit extreme exercises of paternal authority, while experiments with progressive educational methods sought to replace authoritarian with egalitarian norms in larger social settings.

A new definition of femininity was implied in revolutionary culture, and repudiating Victorian and romantic images of feminine fragility and middle-class domesticity—alien in any case to Russian peasant culture—early Soviet writers drew on proletarian traditions to paint a new heroine, a forceful and independent *femme engagée*, who subordinated personal concerns to active participation in economic and social life. Dasha Chumalova, the heroine of Gladkov's revolutionary epic, *Cement* (1925), is the very epitome of this "new Communist woman." Drawn into Zhenotdel activities in her husband's absence during the civil war, Dasha sacrifices both her marriage and ultimately the life of her child in the name of public duty.[59]

For a number of female activists, the goal of sexual equality implied

---

[59]For a discussion of the treatment of female emancipation in early Soviet literature, see Louise E. Luke, "Marxian Woman: Soviet Variants," in *Through the Looking Glass of Soviet Literature*, ed. Ernest Simmons (New York, 1953), Xenia Gasiorowska, *Women in Soviet Fiction* (Madison, 1968), and Vera Dunham, *In Stalin's Time: Middle Class Values in Soviet Fiction* (New York, 1976), ch. 4.

identity of male and female roles. Proposals for the collective rearing of children and for the "separation of the kitchen from marriage," which one enthusiast described as a more significant historical event than the separation of church from state, would simply eliminate those aspects of family life that had traditionally been the concerns of women. Apart from the task of childbearing itself, women's roles and activities would essentially duplicate men's. Indeed, the impossibility of abolishing childbearing called for the introduction, as one writer put it, of a "social correction factor for the biological inequality of the sexes."[60] The voluntarism of another young Komsomolka went even further in insisting that "it is not fitting for revolutionaries and communists to do unconditional homage before the forces of nature. Not to subject oneself to nature but to subject nature to oneself—this is the worthy slogan of socialism. Nature is obsolete and in addition poorly organized. Nature is in very definite need of fundamental corrections."[61]

The widespread advocacy of such radical views posed a sharp challenge to official policy, which sought to weaken traditional family structure without encouraging sexual promiscuity. Others, however, like Aleksandra Kollontai, were groping for a new definition of femininity and for new moral standards. Sexual liberation for them was an essential feature of the revolutionary process, and a healthy sexuality an attribute of the new Communist woman. In the literature of the revolutionary period, and in Kollontai's novels in particular, there is an effort to explore the implications of new forms of social organization for human relationships and to develop, however tentatively, a new definition of feminine identity that incorporated both sexuality and work.[62] Kollontai's novels, like Gladkov's *Cement*, portray relationships between men and women that carry to their logical conclusion the underlying implications of libertarian strains in Bolshevism. They depict free-floating and independent women who inhabit a universe in which the work collective has replaced the family as a fundamental social unit. One episode in which mother and daughter share the same lover accentuates the irrelevance of family ties. In another, the heroine decides to bear her child at just the moment she leaves her lover, and to turn the child over to the collective to be raised.

Kollontai values the independence, strength, equality, and separate identity of man and woman in episodes that both recall the spiritual ca-

---

[60]Geiger, *The Family*, p. 56.

[61]Nina Vel't, "Otkrytoe pis'mo Tovarishchu Smidovich," in *Komsomol'skii byt*, ed. I. Razin (Moscow-Leningrad, 1927), p. 181.

[62]See, for example, the stories included in Kollontai's *Liubov' pchel trudovykh* (Moscow, 1923), and *Bol'shaia liubov'* (Moscow, 1926), as well as the recently translated Alix Holt, ed., *Sexual Relations and the Class Struggle: Love and the New Morality* (Bristol, England, 1972).

maraderie of which Mikhailov wrote decades earlier and foreshadow the androgynous conceptions of masculinity and femininity in modern feminist theory. Her heroes and heroines are without specifically "masculine" or "feminine" traits, and their individual identities are submerged not so much in a common humanity as in the single identity of the Party activist.

The attacks on Kollontai for her advocacy of sexual promiscuity were misguided, if not intentionally misleading. In her view, shared values and concerns were central features of an enduring and satisfying relationship. Romantic infatuation proves ephemeral without them, nor is mere sexual passion more than a passing temptation. Moreover, for Kollontai, the fate of personal relationships was entwined with the fate of the wider society. The extreme demands of the civil war period placed constraints on the possibilities of stable relationships among young Communists, just as the mixture of prosperity and philistinism of the New Economic Policy period had its own corrosive effects on the form of ties between men and women. Yet in searching for new standards of sexual morality congruent with changes in the larger social environment, Kollontai maintained the view that sexual behavior was an essentially private matter. The destruction of the family as an institution and the communal rearing of children would make unnecessary any regulation of personal relationships in the social interest. And, of course, superabundance of population never loomed as a problem.

Kollontai's novels attempt to portray "ideal types" rather than to describe what was happening in Soviet society more widely. Only among a very small circle of Party activists did reality approximate the ideal. Yet the novels are suggestive of the implications of new values and norms. The new Communist woman required freedom and mobility in interpersonal relationships, although these relationships might take a variety of forms. Kollontai's image of a socialist society was one in which every individual led an independent and self-sustaining existence, with society as a whole undertaking the support of its unemployed or dependent members through a general insurance fund. No longer would marriage serve as a device for the economic support of women, nor would women be demeaned by their dependence on alimony. In contrast to Trotskii, who supported the revised Family Code of 1926 as a form of protection for women, Kollontai criticized it as a retreat from collective responsibility.

Kollontai's effort to incorporate sexual liberation into a socialist strategy for female emancipation was ultimately unsuccessful. Indeed, by the mid-1930s, as we shall see, a profound shift in Soviet conceptions of the family was reflected in new legislation that no longer viewed the radical transformation of the family as either inevitable or desirable. The family came to be seen instead as the bulwark of the social system—indeed, as a microcosm of the new socialist society. But the shift in perception and policy under Stalin was not as abrupt and unprecedented as many scholars have suggested. Although it occurred in a new economic and social context and was precipitated by new needs, it was a shift already foreshadowed in the anxiety of the mid-1920s over unbridled sexuality, revolutionary degeneration, and social breakdown.

Both the social conditions of Soviet life in the early 1920s and the values and predispositions of the Bolshevik leadership made it difficult to criticize undesirable aspects of changes in family patterns while maintaining a general approval of sexual liberation. The social upheaval of revolution and civil war had shaken the foundations of Russian society. The disintegration of established social networks and norms and the increased flux in social relationships encouraged improvisation and mobility in personal life as well as in public affairs. Revolutionary critiques of the bourgeois family gave added impetus to the sexual revolution, a revolution that extended far beyond the borders of the Soviet Union. In these circumstances, greater freedom in sex and marriage could also entail the exploitation and abuse of women and children. Radical Soviet policies were less responsible for the social instability of the 1920s than the general dislocation that resulted from war, revolution, and nationalization. The breakup of extended families as a consequence of economic pressures and opportunities, the enormous increase in homeless and often delinquent children, the widespread sexual promiscuity—these were central features of Soviet social life in the 1920s that had little to do with the new family legislation. Family instability was certainly heightened by political changes, by the clash of old and new so eloquently described by Trotskii even as he attacked the alarm spreading in Party circles at the too-rapid loosening of family ties. But few were able to share Trotskii's confidence that out of the turmoil and instability of the 1920s new relationships would emerge on more solid foundations than those of the past.

The intellectual heritage of Bolshevism offered little guidance on these issues. The traditions of European social democracy contained no clear and consistent approach to questions of sexuality. A physiological naturalism that treated sex as the simple expression of natural instincts and an essentially private matter appeared to offer some theoretical justification for free behavior.[63] But it was sexual promiscuity masquerading as

[63]Bebel's *Woman and Socialism* stood in this tradition, with its statement that "of all the natural demands of man, sex—after eating and drinking—is the strongest" and its view that sexual satisfaction promotes physical and mental health for women as well as for men. Indeed, Bebel's treatment of the psychic consequences of sexual repression went far beyond Marx and Engels and anticipated Freudian analyses of the conflict between the needs of Eros and the demands of civilization.

the new Communist morality that attracted growing concern within Bolshevik circles. As one Zhenotdel journalist complained, free love was being interpreted as free vice.

In his wartime exchange of letters with Inessa Armand, Lenin had voiced his objections to a loosely defined advocacy of sexual liberation. For him, as for others attached to the traditions of the Russian intelligentsia and European social democracy, freedom of love meant the absence of economic, legal, and religious contraints, but not the absence of strong and stable attachments. A commitment to the right of divorce was not intended as an encouragement to its facile use. In his more elaborate remarks to Clara Zetkin in 1920, not published until after his death, Lenin expressed his deepening concern at the sexual excesses of the civil war period:

> You must be aware of the famous theory that in Communist society the satisfaction of sexual desires, of love, will be as simple and unimportant as drinking a glass of water. This glass of water theory has made our young people mad, quite mad. . . . I think this glass of water theory is completely un-Marxist. . . . Of course, thirst must be satisfied. But will the normal man in normal circumstances lie down in the gutter and drink out of a puddle, or out of a glass with a rim greasy from many lips?[64]

While his remarks contain a strong note of personal revulsion, they were motivated by a larger anxiety. Sexual promiscuity for Lenin carried with it the danger of revolutionary degeneration, the dissipation of revolutionary energies in unproductive activities that "wasted health and strength" among the younger generation. Voicing a hydraulic theory of sexual energy, Lenin advocated that this energy be sublimated and redirected into new constructive channels: "Young people particularly need the joy and force of life. . . . Healthy sport, swimming, racing, walking, bodily exercises of every kind, and many-sided intellectual interests. Learning, studying, enquiry, as far as possible in common."[65]

Lenin's remarks reveal a man seeking a middle ground between two equally unacceptable extremes, the excesses of sexual libertinism on the one hand and the hypocritical asceticism of bourgeois morality on the other. It was the first extreme, however, that increasingly compelled the attention of a growing circle of Party critics. Lenin's anxious concern with the excesses of sexual revolution was echoed with increasing frequency in a wide variety of Party forums and publications. Sexual conservatism found a particularly vulnerable target in Aleksandra Kollontai, who was

[64]Zetkin, *Reminiscences of Lenin*, p. 49.
[65]*Ibid.*, p. 50.

maliciously credited with the invention of the "glass of water" theory and attacked for its presumed social consequences.

The sublimation of sexuality on behalf of larger social commitments found its fullest expression in the writings of Aron Zalkind. A Bolshevik psychoneurologist, sexual conservative, and leading critic of Freudian theory in the mid-1920s, Zalkind's recommendations came to be known as his "Twelve Commandments."[66] His prescription for normalcy included complete sexual abstinence before marriage and extreme restraint within it, monogamy as the only natural form of human relationship, and reproduction as a major obligation to society. From this perspective, sexual liberation and revolutionary transformation were profoundly incompatible.

The controversy over sexual liberation and its limits was of more than theoretical concern in the mid-1920s; it involved very direct and pressing problems of social policy with respect to marriage, divorce, and abortion. Lenin himself had refused to treat sexual relationships as an exclusively private matter, insisting that "in love, two lives are concerned, and a third, a new life arises. It is that which gives it its social interest, which gives rise to a duty towards the community."[67] Lenin's statement pointed to a fundamental and little-discussed obstacle to the sexual liberation of women. The pronatalism of Bolshevism entailed a hostility to birth control that had far-reaching consequences for the definition of female roles.

The emergence of the new Communist woman was premised on the potential separation of sexuality from procreation. But even in the vision of Kollontai and of other advocates of sexual liberation, this separation would occur less through control over reproduction itself than through the creation of collective child-care institutions, which would make it possible to separate reproduction from the continuing responsibility of child-rearing. In the absence of a wide network of such institutions, however, the association of birth control with bourgeois selfishness and defeatism virtually precluded the possibility of defining femininity without reference to maternity. Kollontai's successor at the Zhenotdel, Sophia Smidovich, repeatedly admonished young women to avoid casual liaisons by warning of their dire consequences and refused even to discuss childless marriages in an exchange of letters with a young Komsomolka, remarking that it was unrealistic for a woman to think of love without considering her potential role as mother.[68]

---

[66]Aron Zalkind, *Revoliutsiia i molodezh'* (Moscow, 1925). The increasing conservatism in Soviet approaches to sexuality was also observed by Wilhelm Reich, who described his impressions of Soviet policy during a visit in 1928 in *The Sexual Revolution*, trans. Theodore P. Wolfe, 4th. ed. rev. (New York, 1969), pp. 186–89.

[67]Zetkin, *Reminiscences of Lenin*, p. 49.

[68]S. Smidovich, "Otvet na pis'mo Komsomolki," in Razin, *Komsomol'skii byt*, pp. 174–75.

Dissenting voices rose to challenge this approach. Nina Vel't, the young Komsomolka who had insisted that nature be made to serve human purposes, pointed out that motherhood should be the result of individual choice, not submission to nature.[69] Rejecting the view that biology should determine destiny, she insisted that the Party's hostility toward birth control resulted in the birth of unwanted children and the widespread resort to abortions. Implying that Smidovich was more interested in the supply of new citizens than in the welfare of women, Vel't insisted on women's right to choose an independent life without motherhood. In this respect, her views went beyond even those of Kollontai, who shared the general aversion to abortion and viewed its legalization in 1920 as a necessary evil. Vel't's dissent was echoed by others throughout the period. Amidst gathering medical opposition to legalized abortion in the late 1920s, for example, a conference of gynecologists dominated by advocates of increased restrictions on its availability was reminded by one speaker that women were entitled to control their own bodies:

> The woman's request is sufficient because no one is more capable than she herself of judging her social situation. No one of us men would accept a decision by some commission as to the social interest in his being married or not. Do not prevent women from deciding for themselves a fundamental issue of their lives. Woman has a right to a sexual life as freely realized as is that of a man. . . . Unquestionably, abortion is an evil; but as yet we have no substitute for it.[70]

What distinguished the position taken by Kollontai and Nina Vel't from that of Smidovich was the effort to incorporate sexuality into the image of the new Communist woman. Smidovich, by contrast, was closer to the sexual conservatism of the Stalin period. Her suspicious disapproval of sensuality and her concern for the stability of marriage as the key to social order and personal productivity accompanied a more limited definition of women's emancipation. Indeed, the insistence on the inseparability of femininity from maternity had become a weapon of sexual conservatism, rationalizing a rejection of sensuality and impeding a broader definition of female liberation.

Anxiety over the social consequences of sexual behavior was not unfounded. The social turmoil and instability of the early Soviet years had brought a vast increase in the breakdown of traditional marriages and in

---

[69] Vel't, "Otkrytoe pis'mo," pp. 181–82. The view that Smidovich held an image of woman as mother, which was offended by the sexuality of "kollontai-ism," and that she rejected the idea of female equality in favor of an image of women as victims is developed by Farnsworth, "Bolshevik Alternatives."

[70] Schlesinger, *Changing Attitudes*, pp. 186–87.

the number of women living in de facto, unregistered marriages. The economic consequences of the New Economic Policy—soaring unemployment combined with shrinking governmental resources available for child care and social welfare—left hundreds of thousands of women vulnerable to abandonment and without potential economic support. These circumstances made all the more urgent a reformulation of earlier Soviet family laws and a redefinition of marriage and the economic responsibilities it entailed.

In October 1925 the Sovnarkom (Council of People's Commissars) introduced to the Central Executive Committee new legislation designed to extend to the large numbers of women living in unregistered marriages the protection that earlier legislation afforded to legally registered wives. To prevent women and children from bearing the full brunt of the economic and social crises of the New Economic Policy, the sponsors of the legislation turned, understandably, to former husbands as an economic resource. The draft law included a community property arrangement that enabled a divorced woman to claim a share of property acquired during marriage, and it extended to de facto spouses the right to receive alimony during unemployment for a limited period of time. Linking as it did questions of morality with direct economic interest, the draft legislation touched off a protracted nationwide discussion, which delayed its implementation for a year and brought to the fore deep conflicts of values and interests between urban and rural populations, between different generations, and between men and women, exacerbating still further the existing conflicts over social policy.[71]

The concern that recognition of de facto marriages would undermine registered marriages and encourage promiscuity inspired many opponents of the new legislation. Among males there was a widespread further anxiety that women would exploit casual liaisons to extract alimony. Others, often women, expressed the hope that the material consequences attached to de facto marriages might in fact act as a deterrent to sexual promiscuity. The extraordinary complexities of defining the boundaries of unregistered marriages would have taxed the most Talmudic of legal scholars and led Kollontai to point out that if the effort to define "registered" and "unregistered" wives were successful, it would create a third category of "casual" women without any protection at all.

The most intractable problems, however, stemmed from the fact that legislation designed for an urban context evoked incomprehension and

---

[71]For a more elaborate treatment of the new legislation, see Farnsworth, "Bolshevik Alternatives." Schlesinger, *Changing Attitudes*, includes translations of the legislation itself as well as of the debates over its adoption.

hostility in a rural milieu that functioned on the basis of a different socioeconomic system and different values. The recognition of de facto marriage in particular aroused fierce opposition within the peasant community, which saw in such loose arrangements the epitome of urban degeneracy and resisted its intrusion into peasant life. In the rural community, the household remained a significant economic unit, and the village economy reinforced the mutual dependence of men and women. As one peasant woman put it:

> Yes, it's all very well to talk about divorce but how could I feed my children? Two's better than one when it comes to that. Alimony? Yes, I know about that—but what good would that do me when I know my husband has nothing in his pocket to pay me. And if my husband goes away, or if I get land somewhere else, how can I work the land alone? Together we can manage somehow.[72]

The image of marriage as a relationship between two autonomous partners, without economic or other constraints, had little meaning, given the economic functions of marriage for the 80 percent of the population that was still rural in the mid-1920s. As a fictional character in Yakovlev's *The Lot of a Peasant Woman* (1926) says: "A peasant family is like a cart: once you're harnessed, you've got to pull it for all you're worth, and no kicking either! It's not like in factory life here; we've got the land to consider."[73]

The new legislation regarding alimony also threatened the economic viability of the peasant household. The Land Code of 1922, in codifying revolutionary legislation, had reinforced the principle of communal ownership and assured women, at least in theory, of their right to a share of the possessions of the household in case of divorce. But this principle in turn implied the collective financial responsibility of the entire household, which was opposed as unfairly punitive. As one peasant delegate put it in discussing the draft legislation: "I divorce my wife. We have children. My wife immediately appeals to the court and I am ordered to pay for the children. Why should my whole family suffer on my account? As there was a common household, the court decides that the entire household must contribute . . . why should my brother suffer?"[74] The reassurance by the Public Prosecutor that the brother would not in fact be called on revealed a lack of appreciation of the complex economic network that bound the peasant *dvor*. As the speaker explained further: "If we live together the whole family suffers. If I am ordered to pay 100 rubles and

[72]Smith, *Woman in Soviet Russia*, p. 31.

[73]A. Yakovlev, *The Lot of a Peasant Woman* (1926), as translated in Gasiorowska, *Women in Soviet Fiction*, p. 28.

[74]Schlesinger, *Changing Attitudes*, p. 107.

the family owns two cows and one horse, we shall have to destroy the whole household."[75]

Because the most valuable possessions of the household were the means of production—land, livestock, and agricultural implements—the continuing economic viability of the *dvor* appeared threatened by the effort to guarantee support to women and children through alimony. On the other hand, as women delegates pointed out, peasant men were all too quick to claim that they had no possessions to sell.

> It sometimes takes a year and a half before a peasant woman manages to obtain the alimony awarded to her. The peasants at all their meetings clamor for a reform in the cruel exaction of alimony. . . . Although it is quite rightly said that the farms should not be ruined, but should, on the contrary, be fostered, we must think of safeguarding the children. We cannot wait until an extra lamb or an extra piglet is born on the defendant's farm. Even his cow should be sold and the proceeds devoted to the child's upkeep.[76]

A family code premised on the existence of a relatively isolated nuclear family, a high degree of personal mobility, and a relatively monetized economic system was altogether alien to the rural community where, in the words of Kurskii, the Minister of Justice, "we still have some 20,000,000 private households with the smoke daily rising from the family hearth and individual management still in charge,"[77] and where the harsh economic realities of daily life would continue to shape women's lives far more than the ideas of modernity and equality enshrined in early Soviet legislation. The enormous gap between the values and expectations of official Soviet culture and the economic and social realities of the countryside, so dramatically illuminated in the marriage code discussions, remained a fundamental problem for Soviet policy throughout this period.

The entire first decade of Soviet rule brought with it important progress toward sexual equality. The legal recognition of women's equal rights in economic and political life and in marriage had established new formal norms for social conduct that began to influence attitudes and behavior. Moreover, the organizational and educational activities of the Zhenotdel had encouraged a transformation of consciousness and had begun to offer women new possibilities and alternatives in both private and public life.

By the end of the decade, certain limitations in the definition and prospects of women's liberation had also emerged with some clarity. These limitations were intrinsic to the values, goals, and organizational structure of the Leninist system. The history of the Zhenotdel made it clear that

[75]*Ibid.*
[76]*Ibid.*, p. 147.
[77]*Ibid.*, p. 91.

whatever supportive role might be assigned to women's organizations, the liberation of women was not to be the result of action by women on their own behalf but a function of the policies and priorities of the male leadership of the Party. Within that leadership, moreover, conflicting orientations toward economic and social policy, as well as toward questions of women's roles, meant that the broader outlines of future policy would depend very heavily on the outcome of internal factional struggles. Finally, conflicts over family policy and sexual liberation brought into sharp focus the growing tension between libertarian and instrumental concerns within Bolshevism. The growing predominance of views hostile to any further strain in family and communal relations accompanied an increasing willingness to subordinate a broader definition of liberation to the need for social stability, control, and productivity—to the need, in sum, for harnessing the energies of men and women alike to the common cause of socialist construction.

With the triumph of Stalin, Soviet policy turned in new directions, and controversies over the role of women under socialism came to an end. The language of liberation was still widely used. But it had become a revolutionary myth, no longer informing policy but offering only retroactive legitimation for decisions which reflected very different concerns.

THREE

The Stalinist Synthesis: Economic Mobilization and New Patterns of Authority

Life was deviating from the blueprints, but the blueprints had been declared sacrosanct and it was forbidden to compare them with what was actually coming into being.   Nadezhda Mandelshtam

By the end of the first decade of Soviet rule, a gradual shift had occurred in the assumptions and orientations that guided Soviet policy. The egalitarian and libertarian strains of Bolshevism, limited and contradictory from the start, had been temporarily reinforced by the imperatives of insurgency. With the consolidation of the new regime, they were overwhelmed by new economic and political priorities.[1] Acute tensions arising from the rule of a modernizing, authoritarian elite over a largely peasant society compelled further adaptations of revolutionary aspirations to the realities of Russian life. Moreover, while the revolutionary generation of Old Bolsheviks steeped in the cosmopolitan intellectual traditions of European social democracy still dominated the Party's central organs, the vast expansion of the Party's membership in the 1920s altered its composition, center of gravity, and outlook. Lower levels of the Party apparatus were increasingly staffed by a new generation of Party recruits, who were of very different social origins and political orientations and who brought more traditional attitudes and patterns of behavior to political life.[2] Under these circumstances, a libertarian concern with the requisites

[1] For a suggestive treatment of the broader transformation of Soviet ideology see Barrington Moore, *Soviet Politics: The Dilemma of Power* (Cambridge, Mass., 1959).

[2] The rapid growth of the Party from a prerevolutionary membership of 8,500 in 1905 to 24,000 in early 1917 and to over 1,000,000 by 1925 offers some indication of the shrinking weight of the Old Bolshevik contingent. By the end of 1927 more than 60 percent of the secretaries of Party cells were persons who had joined the Party after 1921 (Leonard Schapiro, *The Communist Party of the Soviet Union* [New York, 1959], p. 311). See also Merle Fainsod, *How Russia is Ruled*, 2nd ed., (Cambridge, Mass., 1963), pp. 248–59. and T. H.

of female emancipation receded still further into the background, and more instrumental preoccupations came increasingly to the forefront of political life.

It was not, then, a revolutionary program of emancipation that brought about the profound changes in women's roles of subsequent decades. Nor was it the slow but cumulative effect of broader economic and social changes. The transformation of women's roles was, to a considerable degree, the indirect result of the inauguration of the First Five Year Plan in 1928, the collectivization of agriculture that accompanied it, and the emergence of new patterns of authority under Stalin.

The forced collectivization of agriculture, with its stunning impact on authority structures and social relationships in the rural milieu, and the massive entry of women into the industrial labor force during the 1930s, a process given still further impetus by the outbreak of World War II, were the central features of this social transformation. With them came a vast expansion of educational opportunities for women, the spread of a network of institutions for the education and care of children, and the enactment of protective labor legislation and social programs designed to ensure the compatibility of women's domestic responsibilities with industrial employment. These changes reverberated across the whole range of social institutions including, most importantly, the family itself.

Yet the context in which these changes occurred bore little resemblance to the visions surrounding initial discussions of the woman question. Where earlier advocates of drawing women into paid employment had seen it as a way of enhancing female status and independence, rising rates of female employment during the 1930s were a largely unplanned expression of a sustained economic and social crisis. The emergence of new institutional arrangements to support these new economic roles—communal child care facilities, communal dining, communal housing—occurred in a chaotic atmosphere, as a hastily improvised response to the pressures of rapid urbanization and rising female employment.

Nevertheless, the new roles assumed by women were neither accidental nor random. They were intimately linked to a strategy of industrial development in which women were not merely the beneficiaries but also the instruments and shock absorbers of a particular pattern of political, economic, and social modernization. Broadly speaking, the Stalinist strategy of industrialization—with its consequences for employment, urbanization, stratification, consumption, the supply of services, and the reproduction and socialization of children—necessarily entailed the performance of particular economic and social roles by women. Some aspects of these roles were dramatically new, and all involved an intensification of societal demands. In other respects, however, Stalinism perpetuated or even strengthened traditional norms and patterns of behavior and extended them to new contexts.

Indeed, it was the extraordinary scope and pace of social transformation and the unexpected emergence of what Moshe Lewin has aptly labeled a "quicksand society" that called forth Draconian measures to limit the scope of social dislocation and to create islands of stability in a sea of social chaos.[3] The family policies of the revolutionary era fell victim to new needs. Efforts to halt the further fragmentation of family life and to stem the alarming decline of birth rates occasioned by material hardship and social instability resulted in a partial reversal of earlier legislation. Measures originally designed to enhance the freedom and autonomy of women and to complement potential new economic roles were whittled away or abandoned in a desperate attempt to enhance the stability of the family and give greater official recogniton to its procreative and socializing functions.

A distinctive new social order gradually took shape under the force of these often contradictory pressures. New obligations, roles, and opportunities for women were assimilated into older values and patterns of behavior to create an amalgam of tradition and transformation that was the essence of the Stalin era.

SOCIAL PRODUCTION: FEMALE EMPLOYMENT
AND INDUSTRIALIZATION

The inauguration of the First Five Year Plan in 1928 and the forcible collectivization of agriculture that accompanied it brought profound changes in the economic and social roles of Soviet women. For rural Russia, Stalinism brought intense economic pressures and a new locus of authority while leaving intact many basic features of economic and social life. The extensive involvement of women in agricultural labor continued under collectivization; the intimate connection between household and productive activity in the rural milieu limited the direct impact of new economic and political conditions on patterns of female employment. The migration of large numbers of women to urban and industrial regions, where the separation of household from employment was sharp, had, by contrast, profound structural consequences.

Throughout the 1920s the conviction that women should be drawn into social production on a vast scale had remained a largely theoretical concern. The general contraction of the economy and the influx of rural migrants resulted in high rates of urban unemployment, which affected

[3]Moshe Lewin, "Class, State and Ideology in the Piatiletka," in *Cultural Revolution in Russia, 1928–1933*, ed. Sheila Fitzpatrick (Bloomington, forthcoming).

women with particular severity.[4] Similarly, the commitment to the creation of a network of public child-care institutions and communal services and to an expansion of educational opportunities for women was not translated into reality on any substantial scale during this first decade.

The rapid expansion of the economy after 1928 transformed a politically desirable objective into a pressing economic need. As late as 1929 the authors of the First Five Year Plan still looked at female labor primarily as it affected women's economic and political status. They recommended an intensified enrollment of women in new industrial areas, fearing that the planned expansion of basic industries, in which few women were employed, would lead to a decline in the overall ratio of women workers.[5] The Plan envisioned only a modest increase in the proportion of women employed in the public sector, from 27 percent of the socialized labor force in 1927–1928 to 32.5 percent in 1932–1933.[6]

These expectations were rapidly overtaken by the momentum of economic changes. In the winter of 1929–1930 unemployment began to decline, and by 1930 a combination of demographic and economic factors had created an acute manpower shortage. Party and governmental efforts to regulate the labor force were supplanted by measures to assure its supply and to allocate manpower to individual industries and plants. Growing concern with the fuller utilization of urban manpower resources focused increasingly on the need to draw women into industrial employment. A new perspective emerged in official documents, one that viewed the increased employment of women not in terms of its effects on women but as essential to the fulfillment of the economic plans.

A resolution of the Party Central Committee in September 1930 stated that, "to insure the fulfillment of the production program for the third year of the five-year period," it was necessary to "draw more juvenile workers as well as wives of workers and other toilers into production."[7] This Party directive was followed shortly by a government decree spelling out concrete measures to increase the employment of women. Quotas were established for the various industries, and educational institutions were required to admit fixed proportions of women for training in dif-

[4]The rise in unemployment between 1922 and 1929 and the particularly high incidence of female unemployment are documented in Solomon Schwarz, *Labor in the Soviet Union* (New York, 1931), pp. 38–39. The First Five Year Plan anticipated a gradual decline in unemployment between 1929 and 1933, not yet understanding the transformation of the entire labor market that was already under way and that would shortly result in acute labor shortages.

[5]"If the proportion of women employed in various occupational divisions remained unchanged, the different pace of developing the several sections of the national economy would result in a decline of the percentage of women among the total of wage earners . . . This would be quite unsound; we must make it our task to widen the scope of women's work everywhere." *Five Year Plan of Economic Construction of the USSR* (Moscow, 1929), Vol. 2, p. 180.

[6]*Ibid.* In the spring of 1930 the target was raised to 34 or 35 percent.

[7]*Pravda*, September 3, 1930.

ferent fields.[8] In January of 1931 the People's Commissariat of Labor issued two listings of occupations, one enumerating those to be reserved exclusively for women and one listing those to be reserved predominantly for women, a striking example of the tendency for traditional conceptions of "women's work" to be extended to a new context. While this particular measure was later superseded, the notion that certain occupations were particularly suitable for an expansion of female labor persisted and served both to enhance and to channel the entry of women into the modern sector of the labor force.

The years between 1930 and 1937 saw a massive influx of women into industry. By 1932 the number of women employed had risen from three million to six million, far exceeding all estimates, yet so dramatic was the increase in total employment during these years that the proportion of women remained at 27.4 percent, virtually unchanged from 1927–1928. The greatest gains were made in industry, and particularly in industries such as construction, were women had previously played a negligible role.

The reception of women workers in traditionally male fields was frequently hostile, according to many accounts, although this was less often the case in the eastern regions of the USSR, where the demand for new labor was particularly great and where the absence of entrenched male traditions permitted more flexible hiring practices. Most of these new women workers were young and unskilled, and lower levels of qualifications and experience combined with employers' discrimination to channel them into lower levels of the occupational hierarchy.

During the Second Five Year Plan period, between 1933 and 1937, an even more substantial rise took place in female industrial employment. A total of 3,350,000 women entered the labor force during these years, constituting some 82 percent of all newly employed workers. In 1937 almost 9.4 million women were employed, raising their proportion of the labor force to 34 percent.[9] By November 1939 the proportion of women in industry in general had reached 41.6 percent, and women constituted an even higher proportion of manual workers. Whole industries were now utilizing women on an unprecedented scale; women formed one-fourth of the manual workers in iron ore mining, coal mining, and the iron and steel industry. The First and Second Five Year Plans paved the way for the even greater reliance on women workers during World War II, when the massive mobilization of males for military service would otherwise have had adverse effects on productive capacity. As the war finally drew to a close in 1945, the proportion of women in the modern sector had reached an all-time high of 56 percent.

The massive entry of women into industrial production was interpreted by many in the language of an earlier epoch. The First Five Year Plan

[8]V. N. Tolkunova, *Pravo zhenshchin na trud i ego garantii* (Moscow, 1967), pp. 87–97.
[9]Schwarz, *Labor in the Soviet Union*, pp. 71–72.

period had evoked a revival of civil war militance and utopianism. In the enthusiasm of cultural revolution, the new role of women in economic life was seized on as additional evidence of the imminence of full socialism. A vast and vivid literature extolled the industrial millennium and linked the new economic role of women to sweeping plans for the communal reorganization of life. Elaborate economic calculations rationalized and buttressed visionary schemes.[10]

In the face of a growing labor shortage, the social costs of private household production appeared particularly wasteful. S. G. Strumilin, a prolific theorist of the future socialist society, and a key figure in the formulation of the First Five Year Plan, had computed that for every unit of population some seven hundred hours of precious time were lost in cooking, laundry, and the care of children. As a consequence, he estimated, some thirty million potential workers were required to devote full time to unproductive household labor.[11] Strumilin's concern was echoed in a study by the Workers and Peasants Inspection of the RSFSR:

> Every day 36 million hours are expended in the RSFSR for cooking alone. This means that on the basis of the eight-hour working day, four and one-half million workers or double the number that are employed in heavy industry are occupied in cooking. At the same time, collective cooking of the same amount of food would require one-sixth of this time, and would release over four million housewives for productive labor.[12]

The development of a wide network of communal institutions for child care, laundry, and cooking was now urged not merely to free women from the drudgery of household work but to release a vast pool of labor for the expanding Soviet economy.

The wider utilization of female labor offered still further advantages. The increased employment of urban women could substitute for an additional influx of labor from rural areas, thus substantially reducing the cost of the urban infrastructure needed to support a larger labor force. As another economist calculated:

> During the third and fourth year of the Five Year Plan we shall need at least one and a half million new employees in industry alone, and about four million

[10]For a fascinating discussion of these utopian visions, see S. Frederick Starr, "The Anti-Urban Utopias of Early Stalinist Russia," in Fitzpatrick, *Cultural Revolution*. A collection of proposals is included in B. Lunin, ed., *Goroda sotsializma i sotsialisticheskaia rekonstruktsiia byta* (Moscow, 1930). One approach called for the manufacture of portable dwellings in modular units to house one person each, encouraging geographical and social mobility for the "liberated" members of former households. Proposals for communal housing and services, utopian in appearance, were plausible in the context of the First Five Year Plan. As Starr points out, "collectivization was a fact wherever factories were built without first constructing adequate housing," while the shrinking allotment of space in both Moscow and in the newer cities meant that "communalization by necessity was already in practice."

[11]S. G. Strumilin, *Rabochii byt v tsifrakh* (Moscow, 1926).

[12]Susan Kingsbury and Mildred Fairchild, *Factory, Family, and Women in the Soviet Union* (New York, 1935), p. 202.

for the economic system as a whole. If we count even two members to a family, and if each family must have its own housewife engaged exclusively in unproductive labor, it would mean that we should have to bring in eight million people from the villages, in order to get four million workers—and this in turn would mean a building program quite beyond our means.[13]

Other Soviet writers were quick to point out that female employment would also facilitate a more efficient organization of urban life. The savings resulting from the reduction of the number of dependents per wage earner would become available for investment in communal facilities. This argument recurred frequently in the wave of pamphlets and books decribing the future socialist city that was inspired by the revival of utopian leftism between 1928 and 1932. As one prominent theorist suggested:

In individual households from 10 to 15 percent of the general cost of the establishment is spent on separate kitchens, laundries, and storerooms. When building centralized houses, all these auxiliary rooms will be unnecessary and our communal kitchens, dining-rooms, and laundries will not require so much expenditure. Construction of special buildings for the education and boarding of children may not be considered as an extra expense for this eliminates the need for living quarters for children in the adults' houses. We should also remember that the communal house emancipates women and thus decreases the number of dependents in the family. If, for instance, we need 10,000 workers for a new factory, we have to build a town for at least 40,000 people if we are going to have houses with individual apartments; but *if we build a socialist city, we shall need to accommodate only from 20,000 to 24,000 people, since the women will have free time for the factory and the only dependents will be children.* (Italics added.)[14]

Economic rationality appeared to buttress utopian fervor in the view that the employment of women would not only finance the development of new services but would result in higher levels of family income and therefore a real improvement in welfare: "It has already been planned to raise the workers' budget about 100 percent by the end of the five-year period, and the productive labor of the adult women members of the family will raise the income to a figure at least two and a half times greater than it is at present."[15]

To what extent these were conscious and explicit objectives directly affecting the planning process itself is difficult to answer on the basis of the available evidence. Influential economists and political figures were prominent among the authors of these proposals, and supported them with elaborate economic calculations. Yet the political conflicts surrounding the planning process, the atmosphere in which the First Five Year Plan was launched, and the chaotic conditions that followed suggest that

[13]*Ibid.*
[14]*Ibid.*, p. 203.
[15]*Ibid.*, p. 204.

events far outran the capacity of the leadership to direct and control them. It is, therefore, more likely that the rising participation of women in the labor force was a secondary consequence of labor shortages and falling real wages, retrospectively rationalized as a step toward liberaton.

Soviet planners clearly sought to limit the furious pace of urbanization.[16] Severe restrictions were placed on migration, internal passports were reintroduced in 1932, and *kolkhoz* (collective farm) members were required to obtain formal permission to leave the countryside. Still, the actual rate of migration vastly exceeded the planned rate. Also unplanned, but the inevitable outcome of economic decisions, was a sharp decline in real wages. An acute inflation was responsible for a dramatic increase in nominal wage levels, but this rise concealed a serious decline in purchasing power and living standards.

The decline in real wages made it virtually impossible to support an urban family with several dependents on the income of a single breadwinner. Large numbers of women were therefore obliged to seek employment to supplement family income. Indeed, the very fact that the decline in real wages did not preclude a rise in per capita urban consumption during these years was largely due to the entry of urban women into the labor force in large numbers.[17] As official statistics reveal, a steady decline occurred in the number of dependents per wage earner, from 2.46 in 1928 to 2.05 in 1930, 1.59 in 1935, and 1.28 in 1940.[18] While part of this decline was a consequence of falling urban birthrates, the figures also reflect the fact that rising female employment reduced the number of dependents supported by the income of the household head.

The massive entry of women into the labor force was given additional impetus by other features of Stalinist policy. The devastating impact of collectivization on rural economic and social life brought large numbers of women to cities in search of employment. The purges brought with them not merely political insecurity but deportations and deaths, which in turn obliged additional numbers of women to become self-supporting. Finally, the massive mobilization of men for military service during World War II required a vast influx of female replacements. The enormous loss of males transformed millions of widows into heads of households, and deprived a whole generation of women of the opportunity to marry at all. Throughout the Stalin era, then, an expanding demand for labor in the modern sector interacted with demographic imbalances and economic insecurity to increase the availability of women for such employment.

[16]The argument that socialist industrialization strategy involves an effort to economize on urbanization costs is developed in more general terms in Gur Ofer, "Industrial Structure, Urbanization, and Growth Strategy of Socialist Countries," Hebrew University of Jerusalem Research Report No. 53 (Jerusalem, 1974).

[17]Janet Chapman, *Real Wages in Soviet Russia* (Cambridge, Mass., 1963), p. 137.

[18]*Ibid.*, p. 167.

Whether the rise in female employment was anticipated or intended at the start of the First Five Year Plan or was initially an explicit feature of a larger strategy of industrial development, it was a consequence of both specific economic policies and of larger social changes associated with Stalinism. Moreover, the terms on which it occurred profoundly altered the definition of women's liberation. In earlier discussions, the entry of women into the labor force was viewed in political terms, as a dimension of emancipation. Economic independence was viewed as a prerequisite of genuine equality. Now, the employment of women in the industrial labor force was integral to a strategy of development that utilized female labor as a major economic resource, facilitating a rapid expansion of the labor force at relatively low cost.

Whether the massive entry of women into social production would in fact prove liberating depended on the wider social context in which it occurred. Educational opportunities and vocational training were essential if women were to occupy anything but the least skilled positions. Moreover, if the new economic roles of women were to place them on an equal footing with men, massive investments in public services were essential. An extensive network of preschool institutions and after-school programs was needed for the care of children of working mothers, while the development of communal laundries, dining rooms, and other social services to free women from household chores was vital if their employment was to constitute a form of liberation rather than an additional burden.

The development of these services, however, failed to keep pace with the entry of women into industry. Indeed, the whole pattern of Soviet industrialization explicitly depended on the low priority assigned to precisely those economic sectors that might have lightened the burdens of working women. Soviet development priorities not only failed to relieve the pressures on the individual household to any substantial degree; it actually increased them in ways that prevented women from profiting fully from new opportunities. Economic policies resting on the underdevelopment of the service sector and social policies designed to strengthen the family as a reproductive and socializing institution assigned a set of functions and roles to women that in some respects intensified the sexual division of labor both in public arenas and within the family itself.

DOMESTIC PRODUCTION: THE ROLE OF THE HOUSEHOLD IN SOVIET INDUSTRIALIZATION

The pattern of Soviet economic development inaugurated by Stalin in 1928—a pattern that dominates Soviet economic life to this day—was geared to the rapid expansion of heavy industry. The primacy of political and military needs dominated both the pattern and the pace of industrialization. The exploitation of agriculture to serve industrial expansion, the relative neglect of light industry and consumer goods, the under-development of the service sector, and the subordination of welfare to productivity were integral features of a pattern of economic growth designed to maximize the diversion of resources from present to future use in order to sustain high rates of investment in producer goods.

While the economic consequences of this pattern of growth have been explored at some length, its social implications have been relatively neglected in Western scholarship. Yet Stalinist industrialization patterns had far-reaching consequences for the role of the household in Soviet economic development and for the role of women within it. The effect of these patterns was to require the household to supply for itself a wide range of services that in other societies at comparable levels of development were usually provided by the market. For reasons we shall shortly explore, the burdens of supplying these services fell disproportionately on the shoulders of women, perpetuating and intensifying a sexual division of labor that ultimately limited the upward mobility of women in both economic and political life.

The forcible collectivization of agriculture constituted the economic and social foundation of the Stalinist approach. By controlling the procurement of agricultural produce rather than increasing productivity, and by treating the peasantry's claim on resources as residual, Stalinist policies retarded the modernization of agriculture as well as the social transformation of the rural milieu, thus reinforcing some features of traditional rural economic and social life even as they undermined others. As a result, Stalinist priorities not only sustained but sharpened the gap between the modern and the traditional sector, perpetuating a dual economy as well as a dual society, with a sharp bifurcation of opportunities and life styles along urban-rural lines that affected every aspect of social existence.

Different relationships to the means of production underlay the sharp distinction between "worker" and "peasant" in Soviet usage, but differences of legal status, social rights, educational opportunities, income, and life style made the urban-rural division especially acute.[19] The opportunities and resources available to urban industrial workers differed not only in scope but also in kind from those afforded to collective farm members, and the differences were particularly great for women. Women collective farmers, for example, faced greater obstacles to geographical mobility than their urban, industrial counterparts; the labor protection extended to them was more limited; and the degree of authority exercised by the collective farm over both employment and private life was far greater. Throughout the Stalin era, women collective farmers were largely excluded from the social insurance system; provisions for old-age pensions and for illness and maternity benefits were either absent or limited until

[19]For a more comprehensive treatment of these urban-rural differences, see Mervyn Matthews, *Class and Society in Soviet Russia* (New York, 1972).

1965, and the benefits remained less generous than those granted to industrial workers.

Moreover, the economic and cultural backwardness of rural areas, reflected in the limited number and poor quality of educational institutions, in the lack of cultural amenities, in the inadequate provision of consumer goods and services, and in the virtual absence of year-round day care for preschool children, perpetuated the patterns of traditional rural life and adversely affected women's opportunities for upward mobility.[20]

Finally, private subsidiary agriculture, with its almost exclusive dependence on female labor, continued to be crucially important to the individual household and to the national economy. The significant contribution of private plots to family consumption and income was a secondary and unintended consequence of an agricultural policy that ultimately depended on the productivity of the private sector for a wide range of agricultural products.[21] It was on the rural household, therefore, that the burdens of Soviet development fell most heavily.[22]

The rural milieu was not alone in suffering the consequences of Stalinist priorities. The neglect of urban housing in the allocation of Soviet investments and the inadequate provision of basic amenities created problems of their own for the urban population.[23] At the time of Stalin's death

[20]Rural underdevelopment persisted into the post-Stalin era. In 1964, for example, only 4 percent of all electricity consumed in the USSR went to rural areas. Or, to cite another illustration of rural deprivation, a total of three refrigerators, fifty washing machines, and four vacuum cleaners were present in 10,000 kolkhoz households in the Russian Republic in 1964. A more extensive account of the economic roles of rural women is found in Chapter V, of political roles in Chapter VI, and of family roles in Chapter VII.

[21]The private sector accounted for one-third or more of total farm employment between the mid-1930s and the mid-1960s. Estimates that household incomes from collective farming and from the private plots were roughly equal would indicate that the investment of a day's labor in the private sector was twice as valuable as the same labor in the socialized sector. The critical importance of private subsidiary agriculture in the output of key agricultural products is suggested by the fact that in 1959 private plots accounted for 64 percent of all potatoes produced, 41 percent of all meat, 47 percent of all milk production, and 81 percent of all eggs. Nancy Nimitz, "Farm Employment in the Soviet Union," in *Soviet and East European Agriculture*, ed. Jerzy F. Karcz (Berkeley and Los Angeles, 1967), pp. 191–93. See also Karl Wadekin, *The Private Sector in Soviet Agriculture* (Berkeley, 1973).

[22]A recent study concluded that the average rural woman spent twice as much time on housekeeping and domestic chores as her urban counterpart; T. Zaslavskaia, *Pravda*, May 19, 1975, translated in *Current Digest of the Soviet Press (CDSP)* 27 (June 11, 1975): 25. Moreover, the level of rural development had a real impact on such burdens. By comparison with more developed collective farms, an estimated additional forty minutes per work day is needed on backward farms due to the lesser availability of electricity, dining halls, childcare centers, and bakeries. Norton T. Dodge and Murray Feshbach, "The Role of Women in Soviet Agriculture," in Karcz, *Soviet and East European Agriculture*, p. 287.

[23]Average urban dwelling space in 1958 was 5.4 square meters, well below the 1928 figure. Although it has grown dramatically in the last two decades, over one-fourth of all urban families still inhabit communal apartments with shared kitchens and baths. Even if the goals of the Tenth Five Year Plan are met, per capita living space will not yet have reached the minimum standards for health and decency established by the Soviet govern-

in 1953, two-thirds of all urban families were still obliged to obtain water from a communal tap or pump, while in rural areas a household with running water was rare indeed. Hot water from a private tap was rarer still; it was available to less than 3 percent of the urban population.[24] The family laundry alone could therefore consume the equivalent of two working days a week.[25] As a consequence of the inadequate provision of such amenities, the household invested exceptionally large amounts of its own labor and time to meet internal needs.

Moreover, the problem was further intensified by the underdevelopment of the Soviet service sector. In the effort to economize on urbanization and to maximize the resources allocated to industrial production, Soviet economic growth involved a deliberate curtailment of investments connected with consumption and consumer services. Even today, retail trade and personal and public services account for only one-fifth of the total Soviet labor force, or 40 percent of what might be expected of a country with equivalent levels of gross national product and per capita income, and the number of retail stores in relation to population in the Soviet Union is only one-third as great as that found in other countries at comparable levels of development.[26]

As a result, economic activities that might have been shifted to the market were performed by the household instead. The Soviet population traveled further to shop, made a larger number of trips because of shortcomings in the supply network, made more stops per expedition because of the specialization of the retail network, and waited longer in line to be served than might otherwise have been necessary. Since retail trade offered fewer services with the goods it sold, the consumer was obliged to carry the extra service burden. Moreover, urban-rural differences were particularly acute in the service sector. One study estimated that urban women have access to six times as many social services as rural women and seventeen times as many as women in less developed republics such as Tadzhikistan.[27]

ment in 1928; Gertrude E. Schroeder and Barbara S. Severin, "Soviet Consumption and Income Policies in Perspective," *Soviet Economy in a New Perspective,* ed. U.S. Congress, Joint Economic Committee (Washington, D.C., 1976), pp. 625–26. For a more detailed discussion, see Willard S. Smith, "Housing in the Soviet Union: Big Plans, Little Action," in *Soviet Economic Prospects for the Seventies,* ed. U.S. Congress, Joint Economic Committee (Washington, D.C., 1973), and Henry Morton, "What Have the Soviet Leaders Done About the Housing Crisis?" in *Soviet Politics and Society in the 1970's,* eds. Henry Morton and Rudolf Tokes (New York, 1974).

[24]Smith, "Housing," in U.S. Congress, *Soviet Economic Prospects,* p. 408.

[25]By the mid-1970s approximately 20 percent of urban state housing was still not provided with running water and sewerage, and for all housing, rural and urban, the figure probably exceeded 50 percent; *ibid.*

[26]Gur Ofer, *The Service Sector in Soviet Economic Growth: A Comparative Study* (Cambridge, Mass., 1973), pp. 59, 107.

[27]Tolkunova, *Pravo zhenshchin,* p. 181; see also *Kommunist,* No. 3 (1965): 81. For proposals to correct this situation see U. Artamonova, *Trud,* September 2, 1965.

While the human costs of economic priorities are difficult to measure with any precision, Soviet studies of family time budgets offer some indication of the high demands that investment priorities made on individual households. In the mid-1960s, it was estimated, housework took up close to one billion man-and-woman hours, and only about 5 percent of the time needed for housework was assumed by service enterprises.[28]

The one area where economic priorities did in fact encourage a partial shift of activities from the household to the public sector was public catering. Rough estimates indicate that the number of workers in this sector was about one-third greater than would be found in other comparable countries.[29] Public catering first developed during the civil war, when food rationing was widespread, and received new impetus during the First Five Year Plan, particularly in industry and in schools, when it represented an inexpensive alternative to home-cooked meals. With the abolition of rationing in 1934 and a change in prices to reflect the effects of inflation, the public canteens priced themselves out of the reach of the majority of workers. As one report from Leningrad remarked, "The engineers' and technicians' canteen in the Stalin Machine Works in Leningrad charges 2 to 3 rubles for a mediocre lunch, and many married engineers and technicians who have thrifty and capable wives or domestics think it better nowadays to take their meals at home."[30] It went on to warn of the danger that "home cooking will replace public feeding, and housewives who have worked in factories in the past years will return to the kitchen stove."[31]

Moreover, poor quality and high prices limited the attractiveness of public canteens. A Soviet survey found that it was primarily the workers and employees in higher income brackets who purchased cooked meals, while workers in lower income brackets brought food with them to work or waited until returning home to eat.[32]

Finally, Soviet policies effectively precluded a significant reliance on an extrafamilial supply of labor for the performance of domestic chores. In most societies, the availability of domestic servants and household

[28]*Izvestiia*, April 14, 1974. Moreover, the average Soviet woman was obliged to walk 12 to 13 kilometers per day in the course of four hours of domestic chores, according to a study by the Institute of Economics of the Siberian Academy of Sciences, and this in addition to a full day at work; Tolkunova, *Pravo zhenshchin*, p. 168.

[29]Ofer, *Service Sector*, p. 125. Ofer calculates that the proportion of total retail sales made through catering and drinking establishments is 10 percent for the Soviet Union, 7 percent for the United States, and 5 percent for other countries at a comparable level of development. Of these establishments, 90 percent are self-service or cafeteria-style, and 50 percent of the food is taken out rather than consumed on the premises.

[30]Schwarz, *Labor in the Soviet Union*, p. 159.

[31]*Ibid.*

[32]According to Bolgov's study—*Vnerabochee vremia i uroven' zhizni trudiashchikhsia*—conducted in the early 1960s, 26.5 percent of workers and employees in the 20 to 35 ruble income group studied purchased cooked lunches, compared with 64 percent of those earning over 100 rubles. Cited in Matthews, *Class and Society*, p. 102.

workers has been a condition of freeing some number of women for demanding professional and public careers. The extreme devaluation of domestic labor in Soviet ideology, the hostility in principle toward personal services, and the expansion of employment opportunities for women in the labor force all combined to reduce the attractiveness of household work and the availability of women to perform it on a professional basis. Some affluent families were able nonetheless to employ household workers, and a number of Soviet sources indicate that were such help more readily available it would be warmly welcomed. The vast majority of working wives and mothers, however, relied on the assistance of other family members—the legendary *babushka* or other female relatives—to share the burden of domestic chores. The fact that the need for institutional child care vastly exceeded its availability for several decades made this dependence on unpaid female domestic labor an integral feature of the expansion of female employment in Soviet industry.

The extent of this dependence is difficult to estimate with any precision. At the time of the 1970 census, three-generation families constituted 22.9 percent of the total.[33] A special survey found that 21.9 percent of the Moscow families studied, and 14 percent of those investigated in Kaluga, had grandmothers in residence.[34] Even these figures are of limited utility because the availability of relatives for assistance with household and child care does not, of course, depend on joint residence. Three-generation families were more common among specialists and middle-level management, according to a Moldavian study, because of the extent to which the successful performance of professional responsibilities depended on assistance with household chores, but there is no evidence that would permit us to generalize this conclusion.[35] It seems clear, however, that such arrangements at least served to cushion the abruptness of the changes in roles and values resulting from the new relationship of the family to the industrial system.

It would be illuminating to be able to explore more fully, with appropriate techniques of analysis and from a comparative perspective, the changes that occur in the course of industrialization in the functions of the household as an economic and social institution and the shifting relationship between household and external institutions in performing a whole range of services. As we have seen, Marxist analysis of social

[33]G. M. Maksimova, *Vsesoiuznaia perepis' naseleniia 1970 goda: Sbornik statei* (Moscow, 1976), pp. 268–69.

[34]R. V. Kogan, "O potrebnosti materei-rabotnits promyshlennykh predpriiatii v detskikh uchrezhdeniiakh," cited by Stephen P. Dunn and Ethel Dunn, *The Study of the Soviet Family in the USSR and in the West* (American Association for the Advancement of Slavic Studies, Columbus, 1977), p. 46.

[35]A. V. Novitskaia, "Chislennost' i sostav sem'i v Moldavskoi SSR," cited in Dunn and Dunn, *The Soviet Family*, p. 46.

change assumed that the socialization of household functions would accompany economic development, thereby shifting the burden of housework from the household itself to the socialized sector. But the pattern of Soviet development precluded any such substantial shift, either to the socialized sector or to extrafamilial professionals. Consequently, the family was compelled to absorb the additional burden of female industrial employment itself through an internal intensification and redistribution of labor.

While the absence of systematic data and uniform procedures makes comparisons over time difficult, the evidence of family time budgets suggests that the amount of time spent on housework in the Soviet Union in the past five decades has not diminished as substantially as revolutionary theorists had anticipated.[36] According to recent calculations, almost half the Soviet population devotes two or more hours a day to housework, excluding the direct care of children. Although this figure represents a reduction of roughly 20 percent compared with thirty or forty years ago, the author of these calculations warns against taking great comfort from the figures: "The historical comparison should not deceive us. . . . The figures reflect only the extreme backwardness of the country in the past, but by no means the extreme height of the level now achieved."[37]

The allocation of roles within the household will be taken up at greater length in a discussion of sex roles and the family in Chapter VII. It is clear, however, that one of the consequences of Stalinist priorities for the economic role of the household as an institution was to give it major responsibility for the supply of services. A strategy of industrialization that recognized the potential contribution of women to economic growth was also one that imposed enormous burdens on women within the household, sharply limiting their mobility relative to men and producing distinctive patterns of occupational segregation and sexual stratification.

As this review has indicated, the expectation that domestic chores would be abolished by the socialization of housekeeping functions con-

---

[36]The investigation of family time budgets offers a potentially valuable tool for exploring the impact of economic changes on the household and the allocation of roles within it. It would facilitate the measurement and analysis of change over time within a given society as well as making possible a broad range of cross-national comparisons. Unfortunately, research in this area, as in the area of social indicators more generally, is still in its infancy, and the Soviet studies, though suggestive, are still too insufficiently developed in conception and too limited and fragmentary in their execution to permit many conclusions to be drawn with any confidence. For a more comprehensive treatment of Soviet findings, see Chapter VII.

[37]B. A. Grushin, *Svobodnoe vremia: Aktual'nye problemy* (Moscow, 1967), p. 51. A review of the defects as well as of the conclusions of a number of Soviet time budget studies is presented in Matthews, *Class and Society*, pp. 97–107; Dunn and Dunn, *The Soviet Family*, pp. 31–46; and Michael Paul Sacks, *Women's Work in Soviet Russia* (New York, 1976), pp. 100–140.

flicted with the implications of Soviet economic priorities, which depended on the continuing performance of important economic functions by the household. The backwardness of rural life, the inadequate provision of housing and related amenities, the low priority given to the production of consumer durables and labor-saving appliances, the underdevelopment of the service sector and particularly of the retail trade network, and the absence of paid domestic labor all obliged the Soviet household to perform services for itself that in other societies at comparable levels of development have been transferred to external agencies. The resulting volume of unpaid household labor has continued to fall disproportionately on the shoulders of women, as we shall see. It is in this sense that consumerism is a genuinely feminist issue in Soviet society, and that a reshaping of economic priorities is an important condition of women's improved welfare.

FAMILY POLICY AND THE REDEFINITION OF FEMALE ROLES

The economic pressures on the household associated with Stalinist industrialization were accompanied by new political demands as well. Since they contradicted the central assumptions on which early Soviet orientations toward the family rested, it is not surprising that a reassessment of family policy followed.

The new family legislation of the Stalin era was marked by certain conservative, even authoritarian, features that constituted a significant departure from earlier precedents. In the face of such massive social transformations as those brought about by industrialization and collectivization, and the new opportunities for social mobility these changes created for women, a focus on the conservative features of Stalinism may appear puzzling. Yet the central feature of Stalinism—the feature that distinguished it most sharply from the preceding regime—was precisely its amalgam of radical transformation and social conservatism. Massive social dislocation called forth efforts at stabilization and integration that drew heavily on the values, behavioral patterns, and organizational mechanisms of traditional Russian society while adapting them to new purposes.

The "revolution from above" of 1928–1932, which marked the first phase of Stalinism, was characterized by a militance and radicalism evocative of the civil war period.[38] Rapid industrialization and agricultural collectivization were its central features, but these were also years that saw a dramatic increase in the availability of institutional child care and in the scope of women's industrial employment, educational opportunities, and political participation. The first stage of Stalinism was, in short,

[38]For a collection of studies dealing with the effects of these events in different areas of Soviet politics and society, see Fitzpatrick, *Cultural Revolution in Russia.*

a period of rapid social change that left its imprint on a very wide range of social indicators.

The campaign for industrialization and collectivization absorbed the energies and enthusiasm of Party militants, temporarily eclipsing the burning social and sexual controversies of the 1920s. It simultaneously undermined the institutional and political bases of support of an older generation of revolutionary leaders and cultural authorities. By late 1931, in reaction to the social disorganization and breakdown that these radical changes had precipitated, a process of retrenchment was visible, and the contours of a new stage of development with new priorities began to emerge. By the mid-1930s—in education, law, and culture, as well as in family policy—a new orientation had taken shape.[39]

Interpretations of Stalinism that see only its archaic and Thermidorean features, on the one hand, or those that stress its functional necessity to the creation of a modern industrial society, on the other, overlook its adaptive and integrative aspects. A complex interplay of historical and cultural traditions, the socioeconomic environment, the emerging political system, and the personality and attitudes of Stalin himself shaped the transformation of Soviet political culture in the 1930s.

This transformation involved the final repudiation of the libertarian and egalitarian strains that had stamped the economic and social legislation as well as the political values of the 1920s. Stalin's attack on "petty-bourgeois egalitarianism" in 1931 signaled the reintroduction of substantial wage differentials as an incentive to economic productivity and an increasing differentiation of status and prestige to reinforce new authority relations. These broader changes in social and political values, which were themselves significant for the definition of women's roles, had particular ramifications for the role of the family.

The shift in Soviet policy toward the family in the mid-1930s was neither a conclusive demonstration of the family's functional necessity nor a complete reversion to the status quo ante. It occurred in the context of political and economic changes that transformed the environment in which the family was embedded. The nationalization of industry and the collectivization of agriculture had shattered the family's control over productive resources, while the expansion of public education reduced its influence over the socialization and placement of children. Moreover, as refugee interviews made clear, the conviction that the Soviet state controlled the future made the majority of families unwilling to jeopardize the future access of their children to education and employment by communicating their own hostility to the younger generation. In the light of

[39] These shifts are reviewed in N. Timasheff, *The Great Retreat* (New York, 1946); Leon Trotskii, *The Revolution Betrayed*, trans. Max Eastman (New York, 1937); and Fainsod, *How Russia is Ruled*, pp. 104–16.

these circumstances, a change in official policy could be based on the reasonable assurance that the new recognition now granted the family would
not seriously compromise the new social order.

The actual substance of the family legislation enacted in the mid-1930s
was relatively moderate in its provisions.[40] In a broader sense, however,
such legislation expressed a new orientation toward the family that constituted a dramatic departure from the values and expectations of elite culture in the earlier decade. No longer was the "withering away" of the family or, for that matter, of the state itself viewed as the inevitable and
desirable consequence of economic and political change; like the state, it
was argued, the family grows stronger as full socialism approaches. The
family was now said to be the bulwark of the social system, a microcosm
of the new socialist society. It was required to reproduce in miniature the
authoritarian and hierarchical features of the emerging political Leviathan. In *The Revolution Betrayed* (1936), Trotskii pointed to the shift in
family policy as an especially telling expression of a Thermidorean reaction, explaining that "the most compelling motive of the present cult of
the family is undoubtedly the need of the bureaucracy for a stable hierarchy of relations and for the disciplining of youth by means of 40 million
points of support for authority and power."[41]

The new orientation, far from devaluing the role of the family, now
treated it as a pivotal social institution performing vital functions. It was
to serve above all as a model of social order, and for this purpose marital
stability was essential. The independence, autonomy, and mobility encouraged by earlier legislation were henceforth to be restricted in the interests of preserving a stable and monogamous partnership. As *Pravda*
proclaimed, "so-called 'free love' and all disorderly sex life are bourgeois
through and through, and have nothing to do with either socialist principles or the ethics and standards of conduct of the Soviet citizen. . . . The
elite of our country . . . are as a rule also excellent family men who dearly
love their children. And vice versa: the man who does not take marriage
seriously . . . is usually also a bad worker and a poor member of society."[42]

The effort to promote the stabilization of the family was also linked to
a serious concern with the declining birthrate. A massive press campaign
linked the joys of motherhood with the benefits of Soviet power. "A
woman without children merits our pity, for she does not know the full

---

[40]For a translation of the text of such legislation, as well as some of the accompanying
official explanations of the new family policy, see Rudolf Schlesinger, comp., *Changing
Attitudes in Soviet Russia—The Family in the USSR* (London, 1949), pp. 251–347. See also
Alex Inkeles, *Social Change in Soviet Russia* (Cambridge, Mass., 1968), Ch. 11; Kent Geiger,
The Family in Soviet Russia (Cambridge, Mass., 1968), Ch. 4; and Wilhelm Reich, *The Sexual
Revolution*, trans. Theodore P. Wolfe, 4th ed. rev. (New York, 1969), Pt. II.

[41]Trotskii, *The Revolution Betrayed*, p. 153.

[42]Schlesinger, *Changing Attitudes*, p. 252.

joy of life. Our Soviet women, full-blooded citizens of the freest country in the world, have been given the bliss of motherhood."[43] The idealization of the family and of marital stability and the close association of femininity with maternity had as a counterpart the repression of sexual deviance as a social crime. Harsh measures were directed for the first time against both prostitution and homosexuality in the effort to extend order and discipline to personal life.

Yet the attempt to encourage reproduction by portraying motherhood as the supreme obligation of Soviet women cast some doubt on the simultaneous claim that it was the supreme joy. Indeed, the enormous hardships faced by women workers in the forced industrialization of the times were reflected in the decline of birthrates and in the large numbers of abortions. These conditions motivated the effort to offer enhanced protection and increased material incentives to potential mothers.[44] Special state allowances were granted to mothers of large families. Single-child families, insisted one distinguished educator, breed egotism and unhappiness, while large families—seven was his favorite number—make it possible to rear children in a proper collective spirit.[45]

But the effort to encourage reproduction did not rely on moral suasion and material incentives alone. The abolition of legal abortions was the most dramatic feature of the new family legislation of 1936. Abortions could henceforth be performed only when pregnancy endangered the life or health of the potential mother; criminal penalties were attached to violations.

This particular provision of the draft legislation did not go unchallenged. A number of critical letters were published in the press, along with elaborate justifications for the changes. Its objectionable features were spelled out in a letter from a young engineer, who wrote:

> The prohibition of abortion means the compulsory birth of a child to a woman who does not want children . . . The birth of a child ties married people to each other. . . . Where a child comes into the family against the will of the parents, a grim personal drama will be enacted which will undoubtedly lower the social value of the parents and leave its mark on the child. A categorical prohibition of abortion will confront young people with a dilemma: either complete sexual abstinence or the risk of jeopardizing their studies and disrupting their life. To my mind any prohibition of abortion is bound to mutilate many

---

[43]*Ibid.*, p. 254.

[44]The annual total fertility rate dropped from 4,826.1 in 1930 to 4,255 in 1931 and 3,575 in 1932; a low of 2,904.9 was reached in 1934. See D. Peter Mazur, "Reconstruction of Fertility Trends for the Female Population of the USSR," *Population Studies* 21 (July 1967): 38.

[45]Anton Makarenko, *The Collective Family: A Handbook for Russian Parents*, trans. Robert Daglish (New York, 1967), pp. 43–47.

a young life. Apart from this, the result of such a prohibition might be an increase in the death rate from abortions because they will then be performed illegally.[46]

Her anxieties, in retrospect, appear to have been well-founded. In evaluating the effects of Stalin's legislation, perhaps with an eye to current controversies, the author of a recent study concluded that its impact on birthrates was short-lived, and its larger consequences harmful: "The 1936 resolution forbidding abortion in point of fact did not and could not be any serious stimulant to raising the birth rate . . . it merely led many women having unwanted pregnancies to have illegal abortions, risking their health and sometimes their lives."[47]

If the stabilizing and reproductive functions of the Soviet family were reinforced by new legislation, the economic role of the household in providing a wide array of services was recognized in new attitudes. Even housework, once so harshly stigmatized by Lenin, was now considered "socially useful labor," while Soviet wives were assured that achieving a comfortable home life was a desirable goal. The ranks of proletarian heroines were now joined by the wives of the new Soviet elite of managers and engineers, praised not for heroic feats of production but for introducing civilization into the lives of their men by planting flowers outside power stations, sewing linen, and opening fashion studios.[48] The status and identity of a woman were no longer to be derived exclusively from her independent role in production but at least in part defined ascriptively, as functions of her performance in the roles of wife and mother. The full implications of this redefinition of femininity for the stratification system remained to be worked out.

The socializing functions of the family received particular emphasis in the new orientation of the Stalin period. Marital stability was itself a condition of the proper upbringing of children. But the view of the family as a central socializing agency represented a major shift of perspective. No longer was upbringing treated as properly a communal responsibility; the burden was shifted back to the family. But the function itself was redefined in the process, so that upbringing within the home was not merely a private matter but involved parental responsibility to the larger community. In the words of Anton Makarenko, a leading educational authority of the period: "In our country the duty of a father toward his children is a particular form of his duty toward society. . . . In handing over to you a certain measure of social authority, the Soviet state demands from you correct upbringing of future citizens."[49]

[46]Schlesinger, *Changing Attitudes*, p. 257.
[47]E. A. Sadvokasova, *Sotsial'no-gigienicheskie aspekty regulirovaniia razmerov sem'i* (Moscow, 1969), p. 210.
[48]Schlesinger, *Changing Attitudes*, pp. 235–50.
[49]Makarenko, *Collective Family*, p. xii.

Taken together, these aspects of Stalinism represent an effort to mobilize women intensively on behalf of a widening array of economic, social, and political objectives. Increasing demands on women were the accompaniment of expanding opportunities. Pressures toward female employment in industry, the demands on the household, and the treatment of marriage, reproduction, and socialization—all effectively broadened the definition of women's obligations to the larger community. The new image of feminine virtue incorporated wifely and maternal duties in addition to a contribution to the building of socialism.

The tension of contradictory norms and expectations in the new definition of femininity is splendidly conveyed in the speech of a Soviet fictional heroine on a visit to the Kremlin in 1937:

> "Our feminine hearts are overflowing with emotions," she said, "and of these love is paramount. Yet a wife should also be a happy mother and create a serene home atmosphere, without, however, abandoning work for the common welfare. She should know how to combine all these things while also matching her husband's performance on the job."
>
> "Right!" said Stalin.[50]

The new Soviet heroine was to join a highly competitive participation in the economic arena with nurturing family roles of a rather traditional kind. This portrait, however, offers striking contrast to the female political activists of revolutionary literature. In the first decade of Soviet development, the entry of women into public roles was inextricably associated with their liberation from family roles, and emancipation was defined as the opportunity for women to enter as fully into public roles—political and economic—as men. With the shift in policy toward the family, this unity was ruptured. It was now argued not only that women's public roles, largely confined to participation in production, were compatible with extensive family roles but also that the two reinforced each other and were both necessary to real womanhood. Where revolutionary feminism had anticipated the increasing identity of male and female roles, the values of the Stalin era stressed differentiation and complementarity.

The Stalin era was marked by a sharpening differentiation of male and female roles in political life as well. The growth of female political participation did not produce a corresponding increase in the role of women at the apex of the political hierarchy. In the increasingly hierarchical, elitist, authoritarian, and competitive political climate of Stalinism, women were virtually excluded from positions of real importance and were utilized—like Kollontai, Krupskaia, and Stasova—for largely symbolic purposes.

All these trends were further intensified by World War II. The massive mobilization of men for military service created extraordinary opportuni-

---

[50]F. Panferov, *Bruski*, cited in Xenia Gasiorowska, *Women in Soviet Fiction* (Madison, 1968), p. 53.

ties for women to rise to positions of real authority in economic and political life. Communal facilities were rapidly expanded to enable increasing numbers of mothers to join the labor force, while the higher educational institutions became almost entirely female. The heroic performance of Soviet women in wartime—whether on the military front or behind the lines—received elaborate recognition in wartime fiction and seemed to promise more genuine equality in the postwar era.

But the war years brought still further pressures, which sharpened the normative differentiation of masculinity and femininity, even as women took on previously male roles.[51] This differentiation extended even to the labor camps, where the sexual segregation of prisoners was introduced in 1944. It received its ultimate expression in the abolition of coeducation in many Soviet schools in 1943. While the separate education of boys and girls proved temporary, its justification went beyond the military needs that precipitated it. Underlying the measure was a definition of masculine and feminine roles of far wider significance, which survived the abolition of separate education to persist in more limited form to this day. A leading educational authority explained its underlying rationale:

> It is essential to introduce into girls' schools such additional subjects as pedagogics, needlework, courses in domestic science, personal hygiene and the care of children. . . . Those who attend boys' schools . . . must be able to cope with simple repairs to electrical installations and heating systems, and with the repair of household objects. . . . It is necessary that the future warrior and commander should be able to use a map. . . . In boy's schools the principal should as a rule be a man, and in girls' schools a woman.[52]

The trend toward increased differentiation of males and females in both family law and educational policy thus offers support for the hypothesis of Philip Slater that the sharper the differentiation of conjugal roles in a society, the greater the reliance that will be placed on sex segregation in the training of children for these roles.[53]

The Family Edict of July 1944 represented the capstone of this trend.[54] It introduced even more severe restrictions on divorce, requiring a two-stage legal proceeding and the payment of high fees. It went still further

[51]Jean Lipman-Blumen's treatment of role de-differentiation as a system response to crisis offers a useful perspective for interpreting the patterns of female employment in the USSR. When the specific crisis involves a major war, however, the result may be a sharpening of normative definitions of masculinity and femininity, as the Soviet experience suggests; "Role de-Differentiation as a System Response to Crisis: Occupational and Political Roles of Women," *Sociological Inquiry* 43 (April 1973): 105–30.
[52]Schlesinger, *Changing Attitudes*, pp. 364–65.
[53]Philip Slater, "Parental Role Differentiation," in *The Family: Its Structure and Functions*, ed. Rose Laub Coser (New York, 1964), p. 362.
[54]For its text, see Schlesinger, *Changing Attitudes*, pp. 367–76.

in protecting the sanctity of marriage by ending all recognition of unregistered marriages. The new edict thus recreated for the first time in postrevolutionary Russian history the distinction between legitimate and illegitimate children. Not only would a blank space now appear on the birth certificates of all children born outside registered marriages, but suits to establish paternity in such cases were also banned. At the same time, honorary titles and increased material incentives to motherhood, married or unmarried, offered additional protection and security to mothers as compensation for new burdens.

In its effort to encourage the postwar reestablishment of family life by protecting men from paternity suits, the new legislation obliged women to bear alone the consequences of extramarital relationships. But the official encouragement of a double standard of sexual morality and the sacrifice of women's and children's rights to the desire for a high birthrate further undermined the commitment to sexual equality enshrined in early Soviet legislation. In essence, in the words of a recent Soviet critic, it "encouraged a frivolous attitude toward women."[55]

In the aftermath of World War II, the high priority assigned to marital stability and the need to replenish the severe population losses of wartime further sharpened the tension between the political and economic priorities of the Stalin period and the commitment to female equality and independence. As demobilized veterans returned to reclaim positions of authority now occupied by women or to rebuild shattered families with the expectation of female support, comfort, and self-sacrifice as reward for wartime hardships, conflicting needs and contradictory norms emerged acutely. Bare statistics document the fall of women from positions of economic and political authority without conveying the extent of regret or relief. But the human strains and ambiguities that accompanied the difficult transition of a war-torn society to the new priorities of the postwar era and the tensions involved in the readjustment of male-female relationships to postwar life are best captured in the fiction of the postwar period.

In a poignant tale of rural life, a woman widowed by war who drowns her sorrows in work and rises to the chairmanship of the collective farm is suddenly confronted, after years of separation, by the unexpected return of her husband. The adjustment to new realities proves difficult for both. The husband, vacillating between pride and humiliation, muses:

> He was used to being boss in his house. He used to walk along the village with an unhurried step, holding his head high and proud. When he was on his way home from the army, he thought he would turn mountains over. But there are no mountains. . . . And Marya, she moves about, gives orders. And the more

[55]E. Z. Danilova, *Sotsial'nye problemy truda zhenshchiny-rabotnitsy* (Moscow, 1968), p. 64.

she gives orders, the more she grows even in his eyes. And the more she grows, the smaller he gets. . . . And it seems she needs her husband and then again it seems she does not.[56]

A struggle over power leads to growing estrangement, ended by the intervention of the local Party secretary, who, far from encouraging Marya's aspirations, criticizes her misuse of power.

In countless similar tales, postwar authors chide their too ambitious heroines for clinging to newly won independence and neglecting the psychic needs of their men. The dilemmas created for women by the conflict of public commitments and personal life are a recurrent theme of postwar literature, and the sacrifice of ambition to family life is the prescribed solution. The potential conflict over status and mobility that equality might create is conveniently forestalled, and domestic happiness is offered as a surrogate for competitive achievement.

A similar lesson emerges from the story of another marriage in which the heroine occupied a position of greater authority than her husband. Affirming her determination to compartmentalize roles, she announces: "'At work, I am your boss. Watch out and don't resent it. But at home, if you want to, I'll submit to you.' Having, however, thought it over, she refined her statement: 'But at home, we'll be equals.'"[57] But even this solution is insufficient to resolve the tension felt to be inherent in the reversal of traditional statuses. The heroine therefore urges her husband to continue his studies so that a more fitting balance can be restored, and as if further explanation is necessary, the author firmly drives the point home: "'Come on, do me the favor, catch up. . . . I can't be the boss forever. I'll be having children. . . .' In her speaks no longer a stubborn agronomist but a woman's ambition. That ambition consists not of a drive to surpass one's beloved, but, rather, in being able to consider him superior to anybody else, including herself."[58]

The submissive heroines of postwar Soviet fiction represent a response to strains resulting from the structural changes of the Stalin era as well as the social effects of the war years. The increasing education and employment of women, juxtaposed to pressures for the maintenance of stable family relationships, created disequilibrium and tension in male-female relationships based on relatively traditional cultural assumptions. Parsonian sociology has suggested that the precarious balance between family and occupational structure in industrial societies has generally been maintained by inhibiting dual linkages between the two, which would create

[56]Georgii Medynsky, "Marya," translated in Vera Dunham, *In Stalin's Time* (Cambridge, England, 1976), p. 216. For a suggestive general treatment of this issue, see Chapter 14 of Dunham.
[57]Yu. Kapusto, "Khleboroby," translated in Dunham, *In Stalin's Time*, p. 223.
[58]*Ibid.*

tension and competition between husband and wife and which would undermine the complementarity of roles it assumes to be essential to family stability.[59] By excluding married women from labor-force participation or confining them to secondary and residual occupational roles and by treating marriage as a mechanism for the economic support of women, equilibrium is maintained at the cost of full equality.

Because it was committed to and dependent on the participation of women in the labor force, Soviet policy rejected the use of marriage for the support of women and emphasized measures that would make it possible for women to combine work and family responsibilities. But, in the absence of an elaborate network of supporting services, and without a redefinition of cultural norms to support new roles within the family, some curtailment of female professional aspirations and mobility was necessary to preserve the equilibrium of the two-worker family. If the family was not to be sacrificed to the professional equality of women, equality itself would have to give way.

For the new Soviet heroine, therefore, economic independence had altered but not destroyed the traditional foundations of marriage. While productivity in economic life was valued and achievement rewarded, female occupational mobility was limited by the competing requirements of family life. The proud independence of the revolutionary heroine had faded from literature, along with images of the political activist whose dedication to building the new society overrode all other commitments and priorities. Male prerogatives in economic and political life received emphasis, while women were assigned as a high priority the task of producing citizens.

Thus, the acute role strain that was the legacy of the Stalin era was managed by women through the limitation of family size, on the one hand, or the limitation of professional commitments, on the other. The official insistence that Soviet policy had created optimal conditions for combining professional and family responsibilities could not be challenged, nor the problems it created directly confronted, so long as Stalinist priorities dominated Soviet life.

THE STALINIST LEGACY AND THE
REASSESSMENT OF STALINIST PRIORITIES

The death of Stalin in 1953 and the partial repudiation of the Stalinist legacy inaugurated by Khrushchev created new possibilities for Soviet

[59]Talcott Parsons, "The Social Structure of the Family," in *The Family: Its Function and Destiny*, ed. Ruth Anshen (New York, 1940), pp. 173–201; see also Constantina Safilios-Rothschild, "Dual Linkages Between the Occupational and Family System: A Macrosociological Analysis," in *Women and the Workplace*, eds. Martha Blaxall and Barbara Reagan (Chicago, 1976), pp. 51–60.

policy. By granting a degree of legitimacy to the questioning of Stalinist priorities and by encouraging a more direct confrontation with critical problems of political and economic life, de-Stalinization permitted new departures in Soviet politics and policy that had important implications for the definition of sexual equality.

The development of Soviet society itself—the construction of a modern industrial economy, the creation of a more highly educated population, and the emergence of a sophisticated and articulate professional elite—altered the economic and social foundations of the Stalinist system.[60] A redefinition of the relationship of regime and society was vital if Stalinist political values and institutions were not to stifle the creative potentialities of this new social community.

Fundamental to this redefinition was the attempt to overcome the isolation and exclusivity of the political elite by broadening its political base, widening the scope of participation in decision-making, and expanding the consultative role of professional elites in the policy process. New recruitment policies enlarged the size of the Communist Party while also enhancing the representation of previously underrepresented groups. Women were among the beneficiaries of these new trends in recruitment, as well as of deliberate efforts to draw women into positions of leadership.

In economic life, too, the past two decades have seen a cautious revision of Stalinist priorities. An exclusive preoccupation with quantitative targets, to the exclusion of considerations of quality and efficiency, was modified in favor of more modest but better coordinated progress. A slowdown in growth rates and a growing shortage of labor made the efficient utilization of human resources a central preoccupation. New attention was therefore directed to the role of women in the labor force and to optimal patterns of female education and employment. At the same time, a declining birthrate has caused particular anxiety, calling into question the compatibility of women's employment with family responsibilities as they are now defined. In an effort to simultaneously enhance the productivity of women workers and encourage larger families, more attention has been directed to the improvement of conditions of employment as well as the conditions of everyday life, including housing, child care, and the provision of consumer services. An increase in the resources allocated to light industry and consumer goods, the advocates of further reforms argue, has now become an important investment in future productivity.

In social policy as well as in political and economic life, some of the more objectionable features of the Stalinist legacy have been repudiated. Stalin's death unleashed a bitter attack on the principles of the 1944 family

[60]For a suggestive conceptualization of the current stage of Soviet development, see Kenneth Jowitt, "Inclusion and Mobilization in European Leninist Regimes," *World Politics* 28 (October 1975): 69–96.

legislation. The advocates of reform ultimately achieved a partial victory with the introduction of new codes that made divorce and abortion more accessible and that attempted to balance the regime's desire for family stability with greater recognition of individual needs for freedom and equality in marriage. The emergence of family sociology as a major focus of current research and the preoccupation with social planning and the "socialist way of life" reflect a more critical and less dogmatic approach to social realities as well as uncertainty and even anxiety about the direction of social change.

This new stage of Soviet development has therefore brought important changes in the nature of political authority, the pattern of economic development, and the direction of social policy in the USSR. As a consequence, it has reopened discussion of the role of women in Soviet society. A growing consciousness of pervasive inequalities on the part of various socioeconomic groups, ethnic minorities, and women has once again brought the problems of equality to the forefront of political concern. New claims on resources, status, and power pose new challenges to current priorities.

The crystallization of new expectations and demands, along with a more critical attitude toward the past, is dramatically conveyed in a journalist's account of the confrontation of two generations of women activists. A former Young Communist League militant named Klavdia, who played a heroic role in the first campaigns for industrialization and who faced extreme adversity without complaint, now heads a construction project where she is criticized by a younger group of women workers for tolerating objectionable conditions. "Why keep quiet about foul-ups?" they admonish her. "Were our young years made to be wasted standing in line for an apartment, or for a place for our children in a kindergarten? The apartments and kindergartens should be the first things built in Siberia, before the hydroelectric power stations and the plants, and not after them."[61] Klavdia insists that deprivations and sacrifice hastened the construction of Bratsk. But the author of the account suggests that one must evaluate Klavdia's experience critically. "No one has ever proven, and there are no calculations to show, that labor productivity would have dropped and construction times increased if better provision had been made for everyday life, trade, culture and medical services at the construction sites. Common sense and history," she concludes, "suggest the opposite."[62]

The questions that are now being raised and their potential impact on the future direction of Soviet policy are likely to reflect the nature of dis-

[61]*Izvestiia*, April 14, 1974, p. 6.
[62]*Ibid.*

satisfactions, the resources available to the actors, and the actors' perceptions and objectives in trying to induce certain types of change. Accordingly, an investigation of the educational attainments of Soviet women
and of the economic and political positions that they occupy should shed
additional light on the nature and the limits of sexual equality in Soviet
society as it emerged from the Stalin era.

FOUR

Enabling Conditions
of Sexual Equality:
Affirmative Action,
Soviet-Style

Women must be equal to men. But when a stick
has been bent too long in one direction, to
straighten it out it has to be bent a great deal in
the other.   Nikolai Chernyshevskii

THE ability of women to assume the new economic and
political roles that Soviet development opened to them, indeed pressed
on them, depended on the presence of what were, in effect, three enabling
conditions: the existence of protective labor legislation designed to maximize the compatibility of female employment with family responsibilities; the availability of child care for working mothers; and access to education and professional training commensurate with new needs. The
elaboration of the policies and institutional arrangements needed to sustain new roles constituted what might be considered a program of "affirmative action," Soviet-style.

The promulgation of protective measures regulating the terms of female
employment revealed the basic thrust of Soviet efforts. Rejecting the traditional argument that special treatment would limit women's access to
new economic opportunities, Soviet policy proceeded from the assumption that fundamental biological differences between males and females
required the adaptation of working conditions to women's distinctive
needs. This approach received additional impetus from the desire to encourage high birthrates. Special arrangements were therefore justified by
the desire to prevent rising rates of female labor-force participation from
compromising women's maternal and reproductive functions. Since the
protective measures were nationwide in application and their cost was

shared by the society as a whole, no individual enterprise was obliged to absorb by itself the full additional burden of female employment.

The creation of a network of child-care institutions heavily financed by public funds was the second feature of Soviet efforts to maximize female labor-force participation. Since roughly half the female labor force consisted of women with family responsibilities, the availability of institutional child care encouraged continuing employment or reentry of a substantial number of mothers of young children who might otherwise have been unable to accept jobs.

Finally, the expansion of educational opportunities for women was of crucial importance in shaping the patterns of female employment. A dramatic rise in female educational attainments resulted not only from the general expansion of the educational system itself but also from deliberate efforts to raise the relative proportion of women in educational institutions. Moreover, Soviet policy altered the content of education as well as its scope. The effort to link education to manpower planning oriented it toward technical and scientific training and created an unusually high concentration of women in such fields. Sex-stereotyped educational aspirations and valuations persisted, encouraged in some respects by the schools themselves. But the sharp line that divided humanistic from scientific orientations in other countries, and therefore the education of women and men, was blurred to a considerable degree in the USSR.

Protective labor legislation, publicly supported child care, and expanding educational opportunities thus provided the underpinning for a transformation of women's roles. They rested, in turn, on a wider system of values that viewed the additional costs of female employment to be offset by its economic and social benefits and on a pattern of economic and political organization that facilitated the shift of such costs from individual employers to the wider community. The perception of women as an important national resource for both production and reproduction and the high value attached to both functions sustained a high level of investment in the social infrastructure that supported both roles.

THE REGULATION OF WOMEN'S EMPLOYMENT: EQUALITY THROUGH PROTECTION

The development of protective measures regulating the conditions of female employment rested on the view that the equal treatment of women did not require the identical treatment of both sexes.[1] The provision of

[1] For a more extensive discussion of labor and welfare legislation affecting female workers, see V. N. Tolkunova, *Pravo zhenshchin i ego garantii* (Moscow, 1967), and her more recent *Trud zhenshchin* (Moscow, 1973); and E. Z. Danilova, *Sotsial'nye problemy truda zhenshchiny-rabotnitsy* (Moscow, 1968). Surveys in English include Norton T. Dodge, *Women in the Soviet Economy* (Baltimore, 1966), pp. 57–75; Gaston Rimlinger, *Welfare Policy and Industrialization*

special conditions for women workers rested on both a biological and a social rationale. The argument from biology pointed to the distinctive physiological and psychological features of the female organism to justify limitations on female employment. The argument from social function assumed the primary responsibility of women for the care of children and household. In theory, therefore, although not always in practice, female employment was adjusted to these special needs.

A wide array of special protective measures was designed to guarantee women's right to favorable working conditions. Broadly speaking, these measures fell into two categories. The first included measures that governed the working conditions of women as women; their main purpose was the prohibition of heavy work or work harmful to the female organism. The establishment of limits on the hours women might work or the weights they might be permitted to lift were examples of the effort to regulate the terms of female employment. An even greater degree of regulation was embodied in measures that explicitly excluded women from entire occupations.[2] A list of jobs forbidden women for medical reasons was first drawn up in 1932 and was further supplemented in 1938. While the principle behind such regulations appears to be widely accepted, their substance has come in for considerable criticism. A number of analysts have argued that technological changes have rendered some of the original prohibitions unnecessary while creating new occupational hazards not considered in the original regulations. Moreover, the basis of classification is itself unclear. The measures exclude many activities that women customarily carry on that may be as harmful as others prohibited for women. The rationale for the special treatment of women is especially weak, as some critics have pointed out, in the case of the many activities that are equally harmful to men.[3]

Moreover, infractions of the prohibitions have been widespread. Particularly during the Stalin period, the rapid tempo of industrial growth and the high priority assigned to crash programs to increase output eroded protective labor legislation in virtually every area. The pressure on women to perform hard physical labor was further intensified during World War II. Despite efforts in recent years to restrict or eliminate the reliance on female labor in dangerous or demanding occupations, such as mining, the

in Europe, America, and Russia (New York, 1971), pp. 265–300; and Bernice Madison, "Soviet Income Maintenance Policy for the 1970's," *Journal of Social Policy* 2 (April 1973): 97–117, and *Social Welfare in the Soviet Union* (Stanford, 1968).

[2]The original list was published by the People's Commissariat of Labor on May 17, 1930, and was supplemented by additional decrees on May 9, 1931, and April 10, 1932. For the complete text see *Izvestiia NKT SSSR*, 1932, Nos. 2–3.

[3]For an assessment of the defects in current practice and a variety of proposals for reform, see Tolkunova, *Pravo zhenshchin*, pp. 128–32; Danilova, *Sotsial'nye problemy*, pp. 26–33.

enormous and persistent gap between legislation and practice continues to be the subject of criticism by Soviet analysts.[4]

The special treatment of women extends beyond their years of gainful employment. As compensation for the dual burden of employment and family responsibilities, the retirement age for women is five years earlier than that for men—fifty-five for workers and employees (white-collar workers) and sixty for collective farm workers—with pension benefits granted after twenty years of service rather than twenty-five.

A second category of protective measures was directed toward mothers rather than toward women in general. Employers were forbidden to refuse jobs to pregnant and nursing women for those reasons or to reduce their pay or dismiss them on those grounds. Pregnant women were given the right to be transferred to lighter work in the later months of pregnancy and could not be required to work overtime or to travel on business without their agreement. A maternity leave of 112 days at full pay was guaranteed, along with the right to an additional three months of unpaid leave. Women who chose to remain at home with their infants had the right to return to work with no loss of seniority within a year of childbirth, although critics claim that presently women are not in fact saved the job they leave. Nursing mothers were entitled to a shortened work day; proposals have even been made to extend this provision to mothers of young children as well. Finally, family circumstances were taken into account in the assignment of new women graduates. A woman who was pregnant or who had children under one year of age was guaranteed work in her specialty at the place of family residence.

The protective measures that are now in force show the effects of a number of improvements in the past few years. More liberal provisions for maternity leave and for sick leave to care for family members offer some indication that the leadership has been responsive to the criticisms and recommendations that are most widely expressed. Widely voiced proposals for a further liberalization of these arrangements include further restriction of harmful and night work; extended leaves for mothers of young children, including a reduction of the working day without loss of salary; provisions for the time lost in the care of sick family members; and changes in the scheduling of vacations to enable mothers to be free in summer and families to vacation together.

The creation of special working conditions for women was an effort to ensure their full equality in economic life; it was not intended to infringe

[4]Government decrees restricting the employment of women in underground work and in the fishing fleet were issued in 1957 and 1960. For a review of the continuing struggle to ensure the observance of protective legislation, see Lotte Lennon, "Women in the USSR," *Problems of Communism* 20 (July-August 1971): 47–58.

on their rights as workers. Protective legislation was therefore supplemented by guarantees that the terms of women's employment be equal to those of men's.

The guarantee of women's right to work was the cornerstone of the entire edifice; this guarantee included freedom from unemployment, the right to work in positions suited to individual qualifications, and the right to equal pay for equal work.

Freedom from unemployment was essentially achieved by 1930, although it is recognized that even today there exist reserves of women in households who have not been drawn into social production. Until recently, the lack of suitable employment opportunities due to unbalanced patterns of industrial development and the unavailability of child care were two of the major obstacles to higher levels of female labor-force participation. In recent years a concerted effort to draw on these labor reserves has been linked to the expansion of child-care facilities. There is also evidence of growing interest in incorporating social planning into economic decision-making so that, for example, the construction of new industrial enterprises will take into account the need to offer employment to reserves of women in small and medium-sized cities.

The right to equal pay for work equal to that of men in quantity and quality is also enshrined in Soviet legislation. A single and uniform system of classification of skills, qualifications, and wages is designed to eliminate the discriminatory treatment of women. While there is evidence of the existence of a substantial difference between male and female incomes, which we shall take up at greater length in Chapter VI, the male-female income gap is more the result of the differential distribution of men and women in the occupational structure than of direct wage discrimination. However, the underclassification of women in job assignments and in failures to promote them to positions commensurate with their skills, and the tendency to assign lower value to women's work, all effectively undercut the principle of equal pay.

The mere proclamation of women's rights in employment does not of itself guarantee that these rights will be implemented in practice. In fact, Soviet sources provide ample evidence that infractions of these measures are frequent and widespread. A leading Soviet specialist on women's employment recently concluded:

An analysis of the practical application of jurisprudence to female labor reveals that there are many infractions of the laws which in good time are exposed and eliminated. But there are also infractions which are not disputed or not even noted by the proper organs and therefore last for years. Thus, for example, although labor legislation forbids women taking work harmful to their organism, some enterprises are still taking women on in such work, and the FZMK is not reacting to this as it should.[5]

Violations of the rights of pregnant women to employment and to job security appear to be especially common.

Soviet law holds employers accountable for violations of labor legislation. The actual responsibility for protecting these rights, however, is assigned to the trade unions, with factory committees and women's soviets also playing some role.

The failure of trade union organizations and factory committees to function as vigorous defenders of workers' rights is partly a consequence of their conflicting responsibilities. Although the unions are enjoined to struggle against violations of labor legislation and to defend the needs and rights of workers, they are simultaneously expected to cooperate with management in meeting production targets. In practice, the pressures to increase productivity tend to override all other considerations.

At the same time, there is ample evidence of violations reported and rectified through the efforts of trade unions, the press, and other social agencies, and of disciplinary action taken against those responsible. Systematic and extensive investigations of administrative procedures and of actual outcomes are necessary to permit a more comprehensive evaluation of the adequacy of these procedures.

The elaboration of Soviet legislation concerning female employment reflected the effort of the Soviet regime to join the equal rights of female workers to their differential treatment. The problems that such an approach generates in capitalist economies were partly offset in the Soviet case by the fact that the additional costs of female employment were borne by the society as a whole rather than by any individual employer. But if Western experience is any guide, the creation of special protective arrangements for women without their extension, insofar as possible, to men as well, tends to reinforce patterns of occupational segregation based on sex and to inhibit, rather than to promote, genuine sexual equality.

THE DEVELOPMENT OF INSTITUTIONAL CHILD CARE

In providing for the special needs of women workers, Soviet protective measures attempted to create working conditions compatible with women's domestic responsibilities. For this purpose, the availability of child care outside the home was vital. Connected as it was with the ability of women to combine family with employment, child care made a serious claim on the allocation of resources. In other sectors, low investment in services so characteristic of Soviet patterns of economic growth affected welfare

[5]Tolkunova, *Pravo zhenshchin*, p. 166.

more than productivity. In the area of child care, however, economic priorities dictated large investments to provide a vital social service. The commitment to extensive public child-care facilities was explicitly and firmly grounded in early Bolshevik programs and pronouncements.[6] It was a commitment that derived from three somewhat distinct objectives. First, communal child-care arrangements appeared to represent a higher degree of economic rationality than private upbringing of children, offering substantial efficiencies of scale by comparison with family-provided child care. Secondly, communal child care was absolutely essential in urban areas if married women were to participate in the industrial labor force in large numbers. Since agricultural employment was not as sharply separated from household functions as was industrial labor, and because the focus of Bolshevik thinking was directed toward the urban, proletarian family, the organization of peasant family life received less attention.

Finally, public child-rearing was considered advantageous for the children themselves. Particularly during the early decades of the Soviet regime, the family was not considered an altogether desirable environment in which to rear children. It was widely believed that the removal of children from family influence would facilitate the development of new attitudes and characteristics appropriate to citizenship in a new socialist society. Great value was attached to the socializing influence of a properly organized peer group in fostering the solidarity, cooperation, and discipline necessary to a genuinely socialist community. In the view of Soviet theorists, the process of child-rearing had to be established on a firm scientific foundation and carried out by specialists with professional training and skills. For the proper development of children's intellectual and social faculties, the nursery and preschool offered a setting superior to that of the family. Some theorists went even further, calling for the creation of boarding schools and children's homes so that children might be completely freed from family influences, but this was a more controversial point of view. General agreement, however, existed from the beginning on the necessity and desirability of arrangements for part-time, publicly provided care for younger children.

The development of a network of preschool institutions began immediately after the revolution. The decree of November 9, 1917, which established the Commissariat of Enlightenment (Narkompros), provided for a section for preschool education, thus affirming the view that child care was an integral aspect of the educational system. Despite the desire of a number of educational and political activists to incorporate the preschool

[6]It was, for example, explicitly included in the Party Program of 1903; Institut Marksizma Leninizma pri Ts.K. KPSS, *KPSS v rezoliutsiiakh i resheniiakh*, 4 vols. (Moscow, 1954–1960) 1: p. 41.

network into the public educational system, it remained distinct in both its administration and its financing, relying on private fees as well as on public funds. The refusal of the Central Committee in 1932 to adopt a proposal by Narkompros to institute universal preschool education confirmed the lower priority of preschool education and the expectation that it would embrace only a portion of the eligible age group for a number of decades.[7]

The system of child care that gradually developed was composed of three types of institutions which together embraced 12 million preschoolers in 1976: crèches or nurseries, enrolling 1 million infants and children under three; kindergartens, enrolling 2.5 million children aged three to seven; and combined nursery-kindergartens, introduced in 1959 to provide a more unified learning experience, and enrolling a total of 8.5 million children, of whom 2.2 million were under three.[8]

Despite an underlying political commitment to public child care, the actual tempo of growth of preschool institutions in the Soviet Union (Table 2) has closely paralleled the rhythms of female employment. Very few institutions were actually created in the first decade of Soviet power. A rapid period of growth began with the introduction of the First Five Year Plan and the recruitment of large numbers of women into industry. Between 1927 and 1932 the number of kindergartens rose from 2,155 to 19,611. After a slower period of expansion in the 1930s, another spurt occurred during World War II with the massive entry of women into the labor force, reaching a peak of 28,436 kindergartens enrolling almost 1,500,000 children by 1945. A postwar decline was halted by a renewed upturn in the 1950s, which surpassed the wartime level in 1954 and was given further impetus by the expanded construction program promised at the Twentieth and Twenty-First Party Congresses. Another period of extremely rapid growth occurred during the 1960s, in conjunction with another large effort to draw the remaining pool of unemployed women from households into the labor force and in response to studies that showed the shortage of child-care facilities to be the major obstacle. In 1960, permanent crèches and kindergartens accommodated 4.4 million children; by 1976 the figure had risen to 12 million. In addition to the

---

[7]"Development of the Soviet Preschool Education System," *Soviet Review*, 9 (Fall 1968): 6, translated from M. A. Prokof'ev, ed., *Narodnoe obrazovanie v SSSR, 1917–1967* (Moscow, 1967).

[8]The term "kindergarten," while a direct translation of the Russian *detskii sad*, is misleading because of its different connotation in the American setting and also because of the widespread existence of a Soviet version of the kindergarten in the 1920s and 30s. "Nursery school" is the proper functional equivalent, but this term is avoided because "nurseries" is used as a translation for "iasli" (crèches) in most English-language studies. For current enrollments see Tsentral'noe statisticheskoe upravlenie, *Narodnoe khoziaistvo SSSR za 60 let* (Moscow, 1977), p. 519.

TABLE 2

NUMBER OF PERMANENT KINDERGARTENS AND NURSERY-KINDERGARTENS, AND STAFF AND ENROLLMENT
IN THOUSANDS 1914–1980

Year	Total			Urban			Rural		
	Number	Staff	Enrollment	Number	Staff	Enrollment	Number	Staff	Enrollment
1914	150	—	4.0	150	—	4.0	—	—	—
1927	2,155	6.1	107	1,932	5.8	99.1	223	0.4	8.4
1928	2,537	—	130	2,222	—	119	315	—	11
1932	19,611	52	1,062	10,979	38	710	8,632	14	352
1937	24,535	71	1,045	12,505	47	697	12,030	24	348
1940	23,999	75	1,172	14,427	55	906	9,572	20	266
1945	28,436	101	1,471	17,932	78	1,114	10,504	24	357
1948	26,143	89	1,055	17,046	70	839	9,097	19	216
1951	26,337	98	1,257	17,638	79	1,037	8,699	19	220
1955	31,596	144	1,731	20,961	117	1,423	10,635	27	308
1958	36,800	192	2,354	24,300	157	1,946	12,500	35	408
1960	43,600	243	3,115	28,600	199	2,550	15,000	45	565
1963	57,600	350	4,813	36,700	283	3,902	20,900	67	911
1965	67,537	453	6,207	42,294	362	5,000	25,243	91	1,207
1970	83,134	576	8,100	49,008	451	6,396	34,126	125	1,704
1974	96,000	702	9,906	52,000	539	7,650	44,000	163	2,256
1975	99,400	731	10,470	53,000	558	8,067	46,000	173	2,403
1980 (planned)			14,500						

SOURCES: Tsentral'noe statisticheskoe upravlenie, *Narodnoe obrazovanie, nauka i kul'tura v SSSR* (Moscow, 1971) for institutions and enrollments. For staff, see "Development of The Soviet Preschool System," *The Soviet Review* 9 (Fall 1968). For 1965–1975, see Tsentral'noe statisticheskoe upravlenie, *Narodnoe khoziaistve SSSR v 1975 g.* (Moscow, 1976), pp. 674–75. For 1975, see "Zhenschchiny v SSSR," *Vestnik statistiki* 1 (January 1977):93. For 1980, see M. Prokof'ev, *Izvestiia*, July 8, 1976, p. 5. If enrollments in crèches were added to these figures, they would raise current enrollments by roughly one million children. Comparable figures for the United States are actually higher. In 1976, some 10,186,000 children between the ages of three and five were enrolled in public or private prekindergarten programs, roughly 50 percent of the age cohort; U.S. Bureau of the Census, *Statistical Abstract of the United States in 1976* (Washington D.C., 1977), p. 121. In addition, because the school-starting age is lower in the United States, a large number of children between the ages of five and seven who are enrolled in the preschool network in the USSR would be enrolled in the public educational system in the U.S. There are major differences in the number of hours children spend in such programs each day, however, as well as in the setting and financing.

regular, permanent child-care institutions, a large number of seasonal facilities were also created, primarily in rural areas and functioning mainly
during harvest time, accommodating an additional 5 million children.

Despite the enormous expansion of recent years, the network of permanent child-care institutions continues to fall short of the actual demand.
At the present time, according to Soviet sources, the facilities accommodate 37 percent of all preschoolers, compared to 23 percent in 1965.[9]
The shortages are greater outside the large population centers and are
particularly acute for the youngest age groups. The guidelines in the 1959
legislation provided that 36 out of every 100 places in the newly combined
nursery-kindergarten complex be reserved for the under-three age group.
In practice, however, only 25 percent of the younger age group has been
accepted and 10 percent of all children under a year old.[10] The higher
costs involved in the care of younger children and the shortage of nurses
with appropriate training account for the preferential acceptance of older
children. Moreover, within the younger group, priority that should have
been given to infants between two and ten months old in fact went to
older infants, so that only 171,400 children under the age of one remain
in the nursery-kindergartens, 2 percent of the total.[11]

If the availability of places falls short of actual demand, it also falls short
of planned targets. Even though funds are allocated in the state budget
for construction of additional facilities, both the regional authorities and
the ministries responsible continually underfulfill their plans.[12] The Ministry of Light Industry fulfilled its plans during the past five years by
only 52 percent, while for the Ministry of Food Industry the figure was
46 percent. The longest waiting list in 1972 for places in child-care facilities was in light industry, with 150,000 names. The availability of child
care thus tends to reflect priorities in economic life more generally. The
provision of state funding does not of itself guarantee that resources will
be available, for priorities of individual ministries and enterprises as well
as pressures to provide better facilities for their employees are crucial.

[9]Tsentral'noe statisticheskoe upravlenie pri sovete ministrov SSSR, *Zhenshchiny v SSSR:
Statisticheskii sbornik* (Moscow, 1975), p. 103. In 1970, according to the estimates of Bernice
Madison ("Social Services for Families and Children in the Soviet Union since 1967," *Slavic
Review* 31 [December 1972]: 831–52), the facilities accommodated about 50 percent of all
urban preschoolers and 30 percent of those in rural areas. It should also be noted that because
compulsory primary education in the USSR does not begin until age seven, a large number
of children in Soviet preschool facilities would in the United States be included in figures
for primary school attendance.

[10]D. Novoplianskii, "The Waiting List," *Current Digest of the Soviet Press (CDSP)* 23
(August 17, 1971): 8–9; L. Ovchinnikova, "Problems of Upbringing: Children from Birth
to Three," *Izvestiia* April 28, 1973 in *CDSP* 25(1973): 11.

[11]Novoplianskii, "The Waiting List." See also "Zhenshchiny v SSSR," *Vestnik statistiki*
1 (January 1977): p. 93.

[12]For a detailed account of one failure to fulfill the local plan for construction of preschool
facilities, see *Pravda*, April 5, 1974, p. 3.

State allocations, nevertheless, remain at a high level; the 10th Five Year Plan, recognizing continued shortcomings, projects a continuing growth of facilities and an expected enrollment of 14.5 million children by 1980. Even if this target is reached, only 40 percent of the age cohort will be embraced by child-care institutions.

It is difficult to estimate the ratio of availability to demand because the demand for child-care facilities is not in fact universal. The system is beset by a number of difficulties that limit its attractiveness to families with other alternatives. The quality of these institutions reportedly varies widely, and the staffing raises serious problems. The occupations of nursery school and kindergarten teaching are low in status and rewards, turnover is extremely high, and the level of training is inadequate. Some 40 percent of nurse counselors, one Soviet source claimed, had no particular training for their position; in the Russian Republic, 20 percent of the personnel lacked a complete secondary general education.[13] The positions in day nurseries are commonly filled by young girls who are described as unprepared for such work.

A variety of other complaints is also recorded in Soviet publications. The exposure of children to disease is somewhat higher in group situations, and there are no provisions for the care of sick children. A high rate of absenteeism in turn disrupts the work schedules of mothers. The fees for preschool care, while adjusted to family income and need, are substantial enough to create a large dent in the family budget: the cost per child ranges from 300 to 400 rubles a year, of which parents pay from 15 to 25 percent and the state subsidizes the remainder.[14]

The liveliness of current debates suggests that Soviet families are not uniformly enthusiastic about institutional care, particularly for very young children. In one recent survey, only a third of the respondents indicated that they considered public day care superior to upbringing at home. The absence of better alternatives was cited as the main reason for placing children in such institutions. According to another survey of different child-care arrangements, the level of satisfaction was 100 percent for child care performed by a domestic servant *(domrabotnitsa)*, 86 percent for grandparents, 80 percent for parents, and lower for other forms of care, while kindergartens reported 90 percent of respondents satisfied and crèches 70 percent.[15] Moreover, in recent years even Soviet researchers have begun to question the desirability of institutional care for infants.

---

[13]For descriptions of Soviet preschool institutions, see Uri Bronfenbrenner, *Two Worlds of Childhood: US and USSR* (New York, 1970), and Toni Blanken, "Preschool Collectives in the Soviet Union," in *Child Care—Who Cares?*, ed. Pamela Roby (New York, 1973), pp. 386–399.

[14]Danilova, *Sotsial'nye problemy*, p. 43.

[15]Ia. Andriushkiavichene, "Zhenskii trud i problema svobodnogo vremeni," in *Problemy byta, braka i sem'i*, eds. N. Solov'ev, Iu. Lazauskas, and Z. Iankova (Vilnius, 1970), p. 80.

One prominent demographer suggested that, while nurseries may have been a necessity at earlier stages of development, the Soviet Union was now "wealthy enough not to deprive a child of its mother's affection."[16] Claims for the beneficial effects of family nurturing on young children, combined with growing concern about a declining birthrate, have led to wide consideration of proposals that would reward mothers for remaining at home to care for young children (see Chapter VIII). Even economists have joined the controversy by demonstrating that the increasing costs of construction and staffing of the nurseries may make the home care proposal economically preferable.

Meanwhile, protective labor measures, combined with the limited availability of child care outside the home for infants, encourage mothers to remain at home for at least the first year of a child's life, and frequently longer. If a grandmother or other close female relative is available, the child may then be left in her care to permit the mother to return to work. However, the growing mobility of the younger generation, the greater availability of private apartments, and the increased opportunities for employment for pensioners are making the proverbial *babushka* a relic of the past. Group day care and private baby sitters provide an alternative for a very small number of Soviet families. Some writers have even suggested that a system of cooperative preschool institutions be developed that would offer more attractive facilities at higher fees, on the analogy of cooperative apartment construction, or even the creation of baby-sitting services. At the present time, however, radical departures from the present arrangements appear unlikely; current planning envisions a steady incremental expansion of existing facilities.

The most innovative departures in current Soviet programs involve the after-school care of older children. The numerous social and cultural activities and youth groups for school-age children are now being supplemented by the creation of extended-day schools, which offer a variety of supervised programs during the hours when parents are at work. Their enrollment has grown extremely rapidly in the past fifteen years, rising from 611,000 children in 1960 to 5,200,000 in 1970–1971.[17] This expansion is projected to continue in the next few years. Boarding schools, on the other hand, once widely heralded as the ideal solution to the problem of child upbringing and given renewed life by the enthusiasm of Khrushchev, are now receiving less attention. Their cost—five to six times as much as that of the extended-day school—makes them prohibitively expensive for mass purposes, and they are now used primarily for children who cannot be adequately cared for in their own families. By 1980, the

[16]B. Urlanis, "Babushka v sem'e," *Literaturnaia gazeta*, March 3, 1971, p. 11.
[17]Tsentral'noe statisticheskoe upravlenie, *Narodnoe obrazovanie, nauka i kul'tura v SSSR* (Moscow, 1971), p. 92.

combined enrollment in boarding schools and extended-day programs is expected to reach thirteen to fourteen million.

The elaboration of protective labor legislation and the development of a broad network of public child-care institutions were essential to the employment of married women on a large scale. It was, however, the expansion of educational opportunities and the content of new educational curricula that shaped the pattern that female employment assumed.

THE EXPANSION OF EDUCATIONAL OPPORTUNITIES

The expansion of educational opportunities for women was viewed from the start as the key to an alteration of their status and essential to their full integration into economic, political, and social life. New legal norms establishing full equality for women could gradually reshape popular attitudes, and political mobilization might draw women into public life, but education alone would provide a durable foundation for new social roles. As Lenin explained to the First Congress of Teachers in 1918: "The victory of the revolution can only be consolidated by the school— the training of future generations will anchor everything won by the revolution."[18]

Education was central to the "cultural revolution" that would create a new position for women. It would communicate the broad scientific knowledge and technological skills needed to transform Russia from a backward agrarian society to a modern industrial one and to enable women to escape the narrow confines of household and family and to enter productive economic activity. It would serve as a channel of social mobility for previously disadvantaged groups, undermining hierarchical and ascriptive patterns of social stratification and offering opportunities based on achievement to women as well as to men. Finally, it would help to transform the very character of the Russian population, imbuing it with new values, attitudes, and patterns of behavior appropriate to a modern socialist society. No longer would women remain the bearers of traditional cultural and religious values, a drag on cultural and political development. Education would transform them into the workers and citizens of the new society.

Basic literacy was viewed as the fundamental requirement for political communication and full participation in public affairs. For the adult female population already beyond the reach of formal educational institutions, the new government initiated a massive literacy campaign, reserving one-fifth of local educational budgets for this purpose. Through the use of simple textbooks, adult women were taught the fundamentals of "political grammar" along with reading and writing. A second campaign

[18]Cited by Manya Gordon, *Workers Before and After Lenin* (New York, 1941), p. 433.

for the liquidation of illiteracy was launched in 1928 in conjunction with
rapid industrialization. Special efforts were directed at women to narrow
the differential between male and female literacy rates. Between 1926 and
1939, the reported percentage of literate males between the ages of nine
and forty-nine rose from 71.5 percent to 93.5 percent, while for females
it rose from 42.7 percent to 81.6 percent.[19]

Although the campaigns for the liquidation of illiteracy did offer large
numbers of adult females at least a minimal amount of instruction and
political education, female literacy remained low in rural areas. Among
women over age fifty, only one in four could read. A large proportion of
the increase in literacy rates in the Soviet period, therefore, resulted from
the expansion of the formal education of the younger generation and the
diminution of the proportion of the older age groups in the total population over time. For this younger generation, the Soviet regime had great
ambitions. An ever-widening system of formal educational institutions
would socialize boys and girls together in common skills and values to
become the skilled workers and politically conscious citizens of the new
society.

The efforts of the Soviet regime to enhance the educational opportunities of women were in many respects unprecedented. Yet Soviet achievements must be seen against the backdrop of prerevolutionary educational
traditions and accomplishments in order to be properly evaluated. As we
have seen, the last decades of Tsarist rule saw an expansion of the educational network at all levels and a growing democratization of the student
body that increased the opportunities available to women as well as to
men. Soviet educational policy built on this foundation; only in the more
backward rural regions and in Soviet Central Asia was it obliged to construct from the ground up.

The expansion of educational opportunities for women was not the only
objective of early Soviet efforts. A change in educational orientations was
also essential if women were to participate more extensively in the economic life of the future socialist society. If women were not equipped with
new skills, they would remain confined to the lowest levels of the occupational ladder. Yet the skills required were preeminently of a technical and
scientific nature. Humanistic and literary accomplishments, so highly val-

[19]Tsentral'noe statisticheskoe upravlenie, *Narodnoe obrazovanie*, p. 21. In 1897, 16.6 percent of women were reported to be literate. However, the statistics must be read with extreme caution. The rise in literacy rates from 1897 to 1926 largely reflects the expansion of
formal educational opportunities in the last decades of Tsarist rule. The literacy rate declined
from 1914 to 1921 as a consequence of the disruptions of war and civil war. Moreover, the
absence of uniform definitions of literacy covering both prerevolutionary and Soviet Russia
renders the statistical comparison misleading. For purposes of the 1897 census, literacy was
defined as "the ability to read and write proficiently." In 1926 it was defined only as the
ability to read, and no standard test was required either in 1926 or 1939. Thus, many individuals reported as literate were probably functionally illiterate.

ued for women in aristocratic milieus of prerevolutionary Russia, were of lesser utility in a workers' state committed to rapid industrial development. Krupskaia stated the case for giving women a technical education with characteristic simplicity and bluntness:

> It is important that in the organization of vocational education the strength of old traditions [no longer have force] and that free access is opened to women into even those vocations which to this day have been closed to them, not because of any lack of capability but because of the legacy of old prejudices. . . . Young women need to study not the weaving of lace, not the embroidery of handkerchiefs, not the manufacture of ladies hats or flowers . . . but agronomy, animal husbandry, sanitation, technology, and so on. It is necessary for them to study those fields of production where a shortage of skilled workers threatens to have serious repercussions for the republic of workers and peasants.[20]

Soviet educational efforts therefore involved the transformation of a sexually segregated system into one in which both sexes would share a uniform educational experience and in which education and productive labor would be closely linked. With these aims in mind, the early decrees of Narkompros established a unified, coeducational ladder system intended to offer a universal and equal education to all children and to prepare them equally for full participation in economic, political, and social life.[21] Legal impediments to equal access were removed by the abolition of all restrictions based on religion, race, or sex. A uniform basic educational experience was to be offered to boys and girls alike by establishing a single type of institution, the Unified Labor School, with a nine-year educational program that would be free, coeducational, and universal.[22] Finally, a vast expansion of the entire educational system at all levels would make even higher education universally available to all who desired it. "In principle," insisted Lunacharskii, the first head of Narkompros, "every child of the Russian Republic enters a school of an identical type and has the same chances as every other to complete the higher education."[23] New institutions would be created to meet the anticipated demand, while existing facilities would be used more intensively.

[20]Krupskaia, *O rabote sredi zhenshchin* (Moscow, 1926), p. 54.

[21]For a compilation of official decrees, see *Direktivy VKP(b) i postanovleniia sovetskogo pravitel'stva o narodnom obrazovanii, 1917–1947* (Moscow 1947). An excellent study of the organization and activities of Narkompros in its early years is Sheila Fitzpatrick, *The Commissariat of Enlightenment: Soviet Organization of Education and the Arts under Lunacharsky* (Cambridge, England, 1970).

[22]Military schools remained the only exception to coeducation until 1943, when segregated education was introduced in a number of urban secondary schools to facilitate military training for boys. Although Nicholas DeWitt (*Education and Professional Employment in the USSR* [Washington, 1961]) emphasizes the very limited extent of separate education (p. 57), it had wider social implications, as we have noted.

[23]A. V. Lunacharskii, *O narodnom obrazovanii* (Moscow, 1958), p. 523.

The reform of educational structure could be accomplished largely by decree. The expansion of educational opportunities, however, required an enormous investment of resources. In the immediate postrevolutionary period, widespread popular enthusiasm for education and the pent-up demands of the wartime years resulted in a rapid proliferation of educational institutions at all levels. But the wish to make access to education universal proved utopian in the extreme. The scarcity of resources and the primacy of military and economic needs relegated educational claims on the central budget to low priority. The NEP brought massive economic retrenchment, and the severe contraction of the central budget shifted the burden of support for primary education back to the local communities. The commitment of the regime to free public education was eroded by the reintroduction of fees at all levels of the system. The contraction of educational opportunities meant that, for a number of years, these opportunities were reallocated rather than extended. In some ways, however, women were among the beneficiaries of this process.

The statistics on school attendance published by Narkompros for the Russian Republic in the late 1920s enable us to evaluate the outcomes of the first decade of Soviet educational efforts and to make some comparisons with the educational position of women in prerevolutionary Russia.[24] At the primary level of education, which encompassed four years of basic education, 85 percent of children in the Russian Republic were receiving some schooling in 1927. In urban areas, the ratio of female to male pupils in primary schools was almost equal. Disparities persisted, however, in rural areas, where the proportion of girls was one-third of the total enrollment and their average length of schooling 2.1 years compared to 2.4 years for boys.

Secondary education in these years was largely limited to urban areas, and the urban seven- and nine-year schools, which continued to serve as the main channel to higher education, were disproportionately composed of children of white-collar families. Urban female children were particularly advantaged by the redistribution of opportunities, remaining in school longer than their male counterparts and forming a higher proportion of the upper grades. The disparity between rural and urban areas, as well as the advantaged position of urban female children of white-collar and intelligentsia background, is apparent in the index of school attendance compiled by Narkompros for 1927 (Table 3).

Women were also well represented in specialized secondary educational institutions (technicums), where they comprised 41.9 percent of the stu-

[24]Narodnoe komissariat po prosveshcheniiu, *Kul'turnoe stroitel'stvo 1929* (Moscow, 1929). For a more extensive discussion, see Gail Warshofsky Lapidus, "Socialism and Modernity: Educational Policy and Social Change in the USSR, 1917–1932," in *The Dynamics of Soviet Politics*, eds. P. Cocks, B. Daniels, and N. Heer (Cambridge, Mass., 1976).

TABLE 3

INDEX OF URBAN AND RURAL SCHOOL ATTENDANCE BY SEX,

RUSSIAN REPUBLIC, 1927[a]

				Year of study					
	1	*2*	*3*	*4*	*5*	*6*	*7*	*8*	*9*
Urban									
Boys	100	99.8	97.9	94.1	78.2	53.4	33.9	13.1	8.9
Girls	100	96.6	99.4	90.5	74.8	57.6	41.5	18.0	12.8
Rural									
Boys	100	80.4	58.2	32.6	6.9	4.1	2.3	0.2	0.2
Girls	100	62.3	34.8	17.1	4.2	2.7	1.6	0.3	0.2

SOURCE: *Kul'turnoe stroitel'stvo* (Moscow, 1929), Diagram 8.
[a]The figures give the number of children of each sex enrolled in each grade as a percent of the total initial enrollment of each sex.

dent body, and they formed 29.3 percent of total enrollments in higher educational institutions. For the Soviet Union as a whole, the school census of December 1927 revealed the following numbers and proportion of women at each level of the educational ladder:[25]

Educational Level	*Female Students*	*Percent of Total*
Primary Schools	3,132,580	37.5
Seven-Year Schools	863,918	44.3
Nine-Year Schools	439,013	50.0
Higher Educational Institutions	44,726	28.2

As these figures suggest, the scope of educational opportunities remained limited and had undergone little expansion since the prewar period.

If the first decade of Soviet educational efforts laid the legal and institutional foundation for equal access by women, cultural development lagged far behind economic recovery. Beginning in 1928, however, a rapid expansion of the educational network at all levels was launched to accompany the drive for rapid industrialization. With universal compulsory primary education the goal, the level of enrollment in primary schools began to increase dramatically after 1930. By the late 1930s, enrollment encompassed almost the entire age cohort, for girls as well as for boys, except in the more remote rural areas and in the Central Asian republics, where

[25]*Bol'shaia Sovetskaia Entsiklopedia* (Moscow, 1932), Vol. 22, p. 260.

the persistence of traditional cultural values inhibited the school attendance of girls.[26]

Enrollments at the junior secondary level (grades five through seven)
also rose rapidly from the early 1930s. While under 10 percent of this age
cohort attended school in 1926, the proportion reached 65 percent in 1939,
97 percent in 1958, and almost 100 percent in 1975. Of the total enrollment, the proportion of female pupils—already 44.4 percent in 1927—
rose to almost half, and this apparently small change actually reflects a
massive extension of educational opportunities to rural girls.

Senior secondary enrollments (grades eight through ten) began their
expansion at a somewhat later date, in the late 1930s, and increased more
rapidly in the early 1950s. In 1926, only 1.3 percent of this age cohort
had access to senior secondary education. By 1958 the proportion had
risen to one-third, and by 1975 eight-year education was almost universal.
The achievement of universal complete secondary education, involving
a full ten years of schooling, was repeatedly postponed. The Twenty-
Fourth Party Congress delayed its introduction until 1975 and expressed
no intention of making it obligatory.

The enrollment of girls in secondary schools shows substantial regional
variations, reflecting the continuing influence of traditional cultural values
as well as low rates of urbanization of certain national minorities. The
1970 census revealed that for the USSR as a whole, 8 percent of girls
between the ages of sixteen and nineteen failed to complete eight years
of schooling. The highest proportions of girls dropping out were found
in Armenia, with 20 percent; Tadzhikistan, with 23 percent; and Azerbaidzhan, with 27 percent.[27] Early marriage and low rates of female employment sustained the lower value of female education in these regions.

Enrollments in the upper secondary grades are also highly correlated
with family status. Girls predominate in the upper grades, and they tend
to come from advantaged urban families in disproportionate numbers. A
Soviet study comparing the social composition of the fourth- with the
tenth- and eleventh-grade classes in Gorki *oblast* in 1965 found a high correlation between family status and school attendance in the latter years.[28]

[26]For an extensive discussion of enrollment trends from which these statistics are compiled, see DeWitt, *Education and Professional Employment*, pp. 133–44. Although wartime
losses created a substantial demographic imbalance, in the population under age nineteen
in 1959 the ratio of males to females was equal. The higher proportion of female enrollments
does not, therefore, reflect a demographic disparity.

[27]Tsentral'noe statisticheskoe upravlenie, *Itogi vsesoiuznoi perepisi naseleniia 1970 goda: Tom*
3 (Moscow, 1972), Table 1.

[28]G. V. Osipov, *Rabochii klass i tekhnicheskii progress* (Moscow, 1965), p. 127. For a more
general treatment, see Murray Yanowitch and Norton T. Dodge, "Social Class and Education: Soviet Findings and Reactions," *Comparative Education Review* 12 (October 1968), pp.
619–643, and Seymour Martin Lipset and Richard Dobson, "Social Stratification and Sociology in the Soviet Union," in *Social Stratification and Mobility in the USSR*, ed. Murray
Yanowitch and Wesley Fisher (White Plains, N.Y., 1973).

Children of lower socioeconomic backgrounds, particularly boys, tended to leave school at earlier ages. While 25.8 percent of fourth-grade children were the sons and daughters of specialists, they formed 42.8 percent of the tenth- and eleventh-grade pupils; the children of skilled workers made up 44 percent of fourth graders and only 23 percent of tenth and eleventh graders.

Female educational attainment is also highly correlated with ethnic identity, although the extent of differences between nationalities has been significantly reduced during the past four decades. According to the calculations of Brian Silver, a comparison of female-male education ratios for different nationalities in 1926, 1959, and 1970 reveals a progressive decrease in the absolute gap between women's and men's education and in the absolute and relative differences among nationalities.[29] The crude figures available for 1926 indicate that for every 1,000 literate men in the USSR there were 284 literate women, giving a female-male literacy ratio of .284. The highest ratio of female to male literacy was found among the Slavic nationalities—Russians, Ukrainians, and Belorussians—and among the Georgians and Armenians, while extremely low ratios were recorded for women of the Central Asian nationalities.

By 1959 female literacy had increased dramatically, the proportion of men and women with at least a partial secondary education had risen significantly and the gap between male and female educational attainment had narrowed (Table 4). As in 1926, female educational attainment remained higher among the Russian and Transcaucasian populations than in Central Asia, but the range of variation had significantly diminished. In the more recently annexed Baltic republics, female educational attainments were above the Soviet average, actually exceeding male ratios in Estonia and Lithuania.

Calculations based on the 1970 census data show a further rise in the ratio of female to male educational attainment. By 1970, for the USSR as a whole, 830 women had achieved at least an incomplete secondary education for every 1,000 males, and even the lowest figure, 710, for Tadzhik women, indicated a further narrowing of the gap. Both an expansion and an equalization of eduational opportunities has occurred, with the rates of increase in educational attainment at the primary and the secondary level greater for women than for men, and greatest among the Moslem communities of Soviet Central Asia.

SEX-LINKED DIFFERENCES IN EDUCATIONAL ORIENTATIONS

The widening scope of Soviet educational efforts has been accompanied by an increasing differentiation of institutions and programs. While this

[29]Brian Silver, "Levels of Sociocultural Development among Soviet Nationalities: A Partial Test of the Equalization Hypothesis," *American Political Science Review* 68 (December 1974): 1618–37.

TABLE 4
FEMALE-MALE EDUCATION RATIOS BY NATIONALITY, 1959 AND 1970

	1959			1970		
	Urban	*Rural*	*Total*	*Urban*	*Rural*	*Total*
Russians	.966	.839	.921	.934	.838	.908
Ukrainians	.860	.702	.772	.865	.724	.794
Belorussians	.935	.729	.816	.922	.737	.824
Moldavians	.760	.660	.673	.863	.789	.799
Estonians	.961	.966	.964	.973	.945	.968
Latvians	.917	.904	.919	.948	.915	.937
Lithuanians	.942	.959	.953	.952	.872	.925
Georgians	.955	.904	.923	.964	.891	.929
Armenians	.931	.794	.874	.953	.878	.928
Azerbaidzhanis	.660	.549	.589	.749	.645	.685
Kazakhs	.642	.534	.561	.819	.722	.748
Kirgiz	.684	.556	.566	.868	.717	.744
Tadzhiks	.530	.650	.619	.658	.748	.710
Turkmenians	.620	.752	.707	.731	.824	.786
Uzbeks	.679	.633	.640	.775	.773	.767
Mean for 11 Groups[a]	.769	.695	.726	.840	.772	.802
V for 11 Groups	.199	.169	.186	.112	.094	.102
Mean for 15 Groups	.803	.742	.766	.865	.801	.830
V for 15 Groups	.185	.192	.192	.110	.105	.109

SOURCE: Brian Silver, "Levels of Sociocultural Development Among Soviet Nationalities: A Partial Test of the Equalization Hypothesis," *American Political Science Review* 68 (December 1974): 1632.

[a]The figures are based only on the portion of each nationality that resides in its official national area, and represent the proportion of females (aged 10 and over) having incomplete secondary education or beyond divided by the proportion of males who have achieved such education.

differentiation derives from the complex and variegated skill requirements of an industrializing economy, it also intersects with patterns of socialization into sex roles to create a sex-based differentiation of educational orientations and attainments. Differential patterns of male-female educational enrollments are most visible at the secondary level. Soviet sources, in fact, take great pride in noting that in the senior secondary grades girls constitute over half the student body, or 56 percent of total enrollments.[30] Their proportion rises to 58 percent in urban areas and reaches almost 63 percent in the Baltic republics of Latvia, Lithuania, and Estonia. But the higher proportion of girls in the upper grades of general secondary schools reflects not only the higher level of academic performance by girls, so amply documented in Soviet educational research, but also a significant bifurcation of male and female educational and occupational choices. Boys tend to enter the labor force at earlier ages or to enroll in larger numbers in technical and vocational programs that train skilled workers, while girls acquire a more general educational preparation and apply to higher educational institutions in larger numbers. Since these differential outcomes at the secondary level have important implications for the patterning of subsequent occupational roles, it may prove useful to explore their roots in more detail.

Unfortunately, the absence of scholarly investigations of sex-role socialization in Soviet schools makes it necessary to venture some highly speculative hypotheses. A recent content analysis of samples of Soviet children's readers indicates that from a very early age children are exposed to different images of male and female roles.[31] Despite the high rates of female labor-force participation in Soviet economic life, women in these readers are overwhelmingly identified as mothers and grandmothers and are portrayed in situations that emphasize their maternal roles. Men, by contrast, are portrayed in a broad range of activities almost exclusively outside the home. The behavior characteristic of each sex is also sharply differentiated in these stories: males are depicted as active, confident, ambitious for advancement, and politically involved, while women are portrayed as passive, expressive, supportive, nurturant, unconcerned with advancement, and politically naive.

These stereotypes appear to have little direct relation to the reality of roles within the school itself, where girls demonstrate consistently higher levels of academic performance, are more active in extracurricular activities, and, to the dismay of some Soviet social scientists, predominate in positions of leadership both within the schools and in the youth organizations. The fact that girls tend to play a similarly dominant role in the American context is interpreted as evidence of their greater compliance vis-a-vis adults and their greater propensity to maintain order and stability in school, as later in life. Boys, by contrast, are more aggressive and dem-

---

[30] Tsentral'noe statisticheskoe upravlenie, *Narodnoe obrazovanie*, p. 90.

[31] Mollie Rosenhan, "Images of Male and Female in Soviet Children's Readers," in *Women in Russia*, eds. Dorothy Atkinson, Alexander Dallin, and Gail Warshofsky Lapidus (Stanford, 1977).

onstrate greater independence of social norms, characteristics that prove more advantageous at later stages of development.[32]

The differentiation of male and female roles in children's readers is echoed within the school itself. A recent American visitor observed that a required course in "labor" for seventh graders engaged boys in metal-working while assigning girls to study home economics.[33] When she commented that it seemed incongruous, in a society where almost all women worked, to pigeonhole boys and girls into such sex-stereotyped subjects, the principal replied: "Yes, yes, but the woman still has the responsibility for the home. She needs to learn something about cooking and sewing and caring for her family. The boys certainly wouldn't like to take these classes."

At least one prominent Soviet official, a deputy minister of the Lithuanian Republic and an active participant in International Women's Year conferences, L. Dirzhinskaite, has criticized the sex-stereotyping of roles in Soviet children's texts and emphasized the importance of upbringing in overcoming traditional preferences.[34] Her concern is not widely expressed in current Soviet writings, however. It would appear that although educational policy has attempted to influence the attitude of girls toward science and mathematics, there has been little effort to use the influence of the educational environment to alter the wider definition of sex roles presented to children.

The intricate process by which children develop orientations toward sex roles remains unclear, and the complex interplay of external pressures and internal preferences in channeling children's aspirations requires further investigation. Yet it would appear that the school environment itself is a socializing influence that, in at least some respects, supports a substantial degree of sex-stereotyping of roles. The differential socialization apparent in the lower grades subsequently extends to educational and occupational orientations as well. A number of Soviet studies have con-

[32]According to one recent study conducted in Moscow, boys made up 13 percent of pupils receiving excellent grades (*otlichniki*) but comprised 83 percent of all the unsatisfactory ones (*dvoechniki*) (V. D. Popov, "Nekotorye sotsiologopedagogicheskie problemy vtorogodnichestva i otseva," in *Sotsiologicheskie problemy obrazovaniia i vospitaniia*, ed. R. G. Gurova [Moscow, 1973], p. 35). Boys also constitute a high proportion of grade repeaters—roughly 70 percent of the total—between the third and sixth grades, according to the Minister of Education of the RSFSR (M. Kashin, "The Problem of Grade Repeating," translated in Fred Ablin, ed., *Contemporary Soviet Education* [White Plains, N. Y., 1969], p. 168). A similar pattern can be found in the American context, according to a variety of studies whose findings are summarized in Eleanor Maccoby and Carol Jacklin, *Psychology of Sex Differences* (Stanford, 1974). For a review of Soviet findings bearing on the differential behavior of boys and girls, and of Soviet interpretations of the differences, see Richard Dobson, "Educational Policies and Occupational Achievement: The Performance of Girls and Women in the Soviet Educational System," in Atkinsom, Dallin, and Lapidus, *Women in Russia*.
[33]Susan Jacoby *Inside Soviet Schools* (New York, 1974), pp. 102–103.
[34]L. Dirzhinskaite, *Sovetskaia Litva*, December 29, 1975, p. 2.

cluded that by the eighth grade, sex-based differences in the evaluation of occupations are already sharply defined, with boys expressing a preference for the natural and technical sciences, while girls reveal a stronger orientation toward the humanities. In planning their futures, over 25 percent of the girls expressed an interest in teaching, while the overwhelming proportion of boys selected technical occupations.[35]

By the time students graduate from secondary school, these general orientations have influenced their evaluation of specific occupations. A study conducted in Novosibirsk in the mid-1960s asked 3,000 graduating students to rank seventy-four occupations in terms of their general attractiveness.[36] Although the definition of this criterion raises certain methodological problems, a very distinct pattern of male-female preferences emerged from the study. Among male respondents, six of the ten most highly ranked occupations were in the field of engineering. Among the female respondents, only one engineering occupation was included in the top ten. Girls ranked occupations in health, education, and cultural fields most highly, while none of these positions received high rankings among male respondents. A more recent study along similar lines in Leningrad confirmed this pattern. Boys consistently assigned lower rankings to all teaching, medical, and cultural occupations than did girls (Table 5). The matter-of-fact tone in which these findings are described by Soviet scholars does not suggest that they are a cause for concern or that special efforts are being made to reduce these differential preferences and valuations.

These differential preferences in turn help explain differences in the pattern of male and female enrollments in educational institutions as well as in the distribution of men and women within the labor force. The enrollments of vocational-technical schools, for example, which prepare workers for semiskilled and skilled labor, are largely male. Although efforts have been made in recent years to recruit increasing numbers of women, they constitute under 30 percent of total enrollments and 10 percent in rural areas.[37] Moreover, vocational programs tend to be divided

[35]P. Petrov, "The Formation of Career Plans in School," in *The Career Plans of Youth*, ed. M. N. Rutkevich (White Plains, 1969), p. 42.

[36]V. V. Vodzinskaia, "Orientations toward Occupations," and L. F. Liss, "The Social Conditioning of Occupational Choice," in *Social Stratification and Mobility in the USSR*, ed. and trans. Murray Yanowitch and Wesley Fisher (White Plains, N.Y. 1973). See also Yanowitch and Dodge, "Social Class and Education."

[37]E. Voronin, "The Young Worker's Skills," *CDSP* 29 (February 23, 1977): 19. See also David W. Carey, "Developments in Soviet Education," in U. S. Congress, Joint Economic Committee, *Soviet Economic Prospects for the Seventies* (Washington, D.C., 1973), p. 635. The effort to attract women into vocational programs has encountered particular obstacles among the local nationalities in the Central Asian regions. As the chairman of the Tadzhik Gosplan observed: "Native girls are drawn into vocational schools quite feebly. Despite the keen shortage of workers in the textile industry, where, as is well known, female labor predominates, there are very few girls from the local nationality studying in the two vocational

TABLE 5
DISTRIBUTION OF OCCUPATIONS BY ATTRACTIVENESS
ACCORDING TO THE EVALUATIONS OF BOY AND GIRL GRADUATES
OF LENINGRAD'S SECONDARY SCHOOLS

Occupations	Ranks of 40 occupations according to the criteria of attractiveness	
	Boys	Girls
Physicist	1	2
Mathematician	2	6
Radio engineer	3	5
Radio technician	4	9
Scientific worker	5	3
Pilot	6	4
Chemical engineer	7	10
Mechanical engineer	8	14
Geologist	9	7
Physician	10	1
Higher-education teacher	11	12
Philosopher	12	18
Construction engineer	13	12
Metallurgical engineer	14	15
Philologist	15	11
Driver	16	20
Worker in literature and art	17	8
Locksmith	18	35
Shipbuilder	19	17
Automatic equipment setter	20	27
Automatic equipment operator	21	24
Mechanic	22	30
Secondary-school teacher	23	13
Steel founder	24	30
Chemical worker	25	28
Lathe operator	26	29
Railroad worker	27	28
Agronomist	28	27
Installation worker in construction	29	28
Tractor operator, combine operator	30	37
Culture and education worker	31	21
Cook, waiter	32	32
Kindergarten teacher	33	20
Livestock worker	34	31

TABLE 5 (Continued)

DISTRIBUTION OF OCCUPATIONS BY ATTRACTIVENESS
ACCORDING TO THE EVALUATIONS OF BOY AND GIRL GRADUATES
OF LENINGRAD'S SECONDARY SCHOOLS

Occupations	Ranks of 40 occupations according to the criteria of attractiveness	
	Boys	Girls
Housepainter	35	37
Field worker	36	35
Tailor, seamstress	37	32
Clerical worker	38	38
Housing-maintenance worker	39	40
Salesclerk	40	35

SOURCE: V. V. Vodzinskaia, "Orientations Toward Occupations," in *Social Stratification and Mobility in the USSR*, eds. M. Yanowitch and W. Fisher (White Plains, N.Y., 1973), pp. 169–70.

into "masculine" and "feminine" specialities, and those schools with substantial female enrollments train workers for the clothing industry and for a variety of crafts rather than for heavy industrial skills.

Differential enrollments of men and women are also conspicuous in specialized secondary schools. Women make up 54 percent of total enrollments, and they are heavily concentrated in the fields of education, health, and the humanities, where they constitute 80 percent of all students. Of the 607 students attending special boarding schools for math and physics in Novosibirsk, only 67 were girls.[38]

The available evidence is still too scanty to permit a judgment about the degree to which the organization of the school system itself or specific features of Soviet educational policy contribute to the pattern of sexual differentiation just described. It is, however, consistent with Soviet expectations in other areas to view these differences as natural ones and to avoid direct efforts to alter them in the absence of compelling economic or political reasons. There is some evidence, however, that the consequences of these patterns for higher educational enrollments are a cause of increasing concern.

---

schools preparing textile workers" (*Kommunist Tadzhikistana*, October 4, 1969, as cited in Grey Hodnett, "Technology and Social Change in Soviet Central Asia: The Politics of Cotton Growing," in *Soviet Politics and Society in the 1970's*, ed. Henry Morton and Rudolf Tokes, [New York, 1975] p. 98.)

[38]Ludwig Leigle, *The Family's Role in Soviet Education* (New York, 1975) p. 101.

WOMEN IN HIGHER AND PROFESSIONAL EDUCATION

In higher education, as in primary and secondary education, opportunities for women have expanded dramatically as a consequence of Soviet policy. But while primary and secondary education are universal in principle, access to full-time higher education is intentionally limited, and the pattern of enrollments and rate of growth have been shaped more by the requirements of the planned economy than by the preferences of secondary school graduates.

A period of relatively slow growth through the late 1930s was interrupted during World II. In the postwar period enrollments began to rise sharply. The rate of growth reached a high point in the early 1960s and has slowed in recent years. The total enrollment in 1972–1973 was 4.6 million students, roughly one-fourth the total age cohort, of whom half were enrolled in full-time day programs.[39]

In the first decade of the Soviet regime's existence, Narkompros expressed its commitment to increasing the enrollment of women in higher educational institutions. Special efforts to accomplish this goal really began with the inauguration of the First Five Year Plan. The most far-reaching of these efforts was introduced by a Central Committee decree of February 22, 1929, which sought to increase the proportion of women—especially women of peasant and worker background—by reserving a fixed share of total places specifically for them. A quota of 25 percent was established for chemical and textile institutions and from 6 to 10 percent in other industrial institutes, and party and trade union organizations were encouraged to "commandeer" women for educational purposes.[40] In June of 1930 the quotas were raised still further. Higher educational institutions were now required to admit at least 20 percent women in industrial specializations, 30 percent in agricultural faculties, and 35 percent in socioeconomic fields. Similar quotas were introduced for technicums.[41] Quotas were also used to draw more women into preparatory programs, such as *rabfaks* (workers' faculties), and were specifically designed to increase the enrollment of women in technical and scientific fields in which they were underrepresented.

Between 1927 and 1937, the proportion of women in higher educational institutions rose from 28 percent to 43 percent of total enrollments (Table 6). Fields like industrial engineering, which had a low ratio of women in 1927, grew even more rapidly. During the war years the mobilization of men for military service radically altered the student body of higher edu-

---

[39]Tsentral'noe statisticheskoe upravlenie, *Narodnoe khoziaistvo SSSR v 1972 g.* (Moscow, 1973), p. 637.
[40]*Izvestiia Tsentral'nogo komiteta*, No. 7, March 20, 1929, p. 15; see also "Zhenskoe obrazovanie," in *Bol'shaia Sovetskaia Éntsiklopedia*, Vol. 25, p. 261.
[41]Tolkunova, *Pravo zhenshchin*, pp. 87–88.

TABLE 6

PROPORTION OF WOMEN IN SOVIET HIGHER EDUCATIONAL INSTITUTIONS, BY FIELD, 1926–1976

	1926	1927	1932	1937	1940	1950	1958	1962	1970	1973/74	1975/76
Proportion of women students at higher educational institutions	31	28	33	43	58	53	47	42	49	50	50
By field:											
Industry, construction, transportation, and communications	7	13	20	28	40	30	32	28	38	39	40
Agriculture	16	17	31	30	46	39	31	25	30	32	33
Economics and law	17	21	35	41	63	57	—	49	60	61	62
Public health, physical culture, and sports	52	52	71	68	74	65	62	54	56	56	56
Education, art, and cinematography	48	49	49	48	67	71	65	62	66	68	68

SOURCES: Tsentral'noe statisticheskoe upravlenie, *Narodnoe khoziaistvo SSSR: 1922–1972* (Moscow, 1972), p. 445; "Zhenshchiny v SSSR," *Vestnik statistiki,* I (January, 1977): 89; Nicholas Dewitt, *Education and Professional Employment in the USSR* (Washington, D.C., 1961), p. 654.

cational institutions, the overall percentage of women reaching a high of 77 percent. Their proportion declined in the postwar period to a more even 52 percent by 1955, exactly reflecting the proportion of women in the total age group.

Between 1956 and 1962, however, the share of women in higher education declined by one-fifth, reaching a low of 42 percent in 1962. The evidence suggests that this reduction in the proportion of women was not merely an unintended consequence of the Khrushchev school reforms of 1958 but an explicit objective. The admissions policies introduced in 1958 adversely affected women by giving preference to applicants with previous work experience, and by reducing the weight of competitive examinations in the selection process. Soviet sources hint at the imposition of a quota system as well—this time one that discriminated against women rather than in their favor.[42] The removal of Khrushchev from office was followed by the partial repudiation of his educational policies and by a renewed emphasis on academic criteria. Beginning in 1965, the proportion of women in higher educational institutions began to rise once again, reaching 49 percent in 1971–1972 and 50 percent in 1972–1973, and 51 percent in 1976–1977.

Yet there is substantial evidence that discriminatory admissions policies persist. As one Soviet author reported, "for young women, it is harder to gain entrance to higher educational institutions, even though they study and pass examinations just as well as young men."[43] The imposition of higher standards of admission for women by medical institutes was explicitly admitted by another writer who defended the unequal treatment of male and female applicants in the following terms:

> Boys, and it is unfitting to conceal this, are accepted to medical institutions with a lower average than girls. . . . Girls occupy a more complex position in medicine than do boys: marriage, immobility for purposes of assignment, departures from work—temporary or permanent—when family interests outweigh professional considerations, especially when the family's material situation makes this possible. Boys may not always have deeper knowledge nor do they know how to apply it any better, but given time they become dependable workers.[44]

The writer, a professor of child surgery, went on to insist that special treatment not be given any groups, whether national minorities or less well-prepared rural students, and that the only criterion for admission to medical school be professionalism.

The conflict between a reliance on purely academic criteria for admis-

[42]Norton T. Dodge, *Women in the Soviet Economy* (Baltimore, 1966), p. 113.
[43]S. Berezovskaia, *Literaturnaia gazeta*, January 22, 1969.
[44]S. Doletskii, "Dva balla vysshe mechty," *Komsomol'skaia pravda*, December 22, 1970, p. 2.

sion and preferential treatment for particular groups has on the whole been resolved in favor of the former. Yet there appears to be some lingering doubt about the economic rationality of this approach when it results in the admission of high proportions of women for professional training. Recent statements deploring the excessive "feminization" of higher educational insitutions and of certain specific professions, such as medicine, suggest that the educational attainments of women exceed what some educational authorities consider an optimal allocation of opportunities.[45] Calculations of expected productivity appear to provide the economic rationale for the preferential selection of male over female candidates at the margin.

A second factor, deriving from the interaction of the admissions process itself with the sexual differentiation of fields, may also play a role in obstructing women's access to higher education. Since applications for admission to higher educational institutions in the Soviet Union are directed to a particular faculty as well as to a specific institution, the ratio of applicants to available places differs widely between institutions and specialties within them. At the same time, these applications are themselves highly differentiated between "masculine" and "feminine" fields. A study at the University of Novosibirsk, for example, found that males constituted 86 to 90 percent of the applicants in physics, 67 to 72 percent in geology, and 67 to 69 percent in applied mathematics, while the fields of chemistry, history, economics, cybernetics, and biology attracted a preponderance of females, including 89 to 94 percent in linguistics.[46] If the ratio of applicants to places is greater in fields and institutions in which women applicants predominate, a lower ratio of acceptance of female students would result even if the selection process was not explicitly discriminatory.

Indeed, a Soviet study offers some confirmation that this may in fact be the case. A survey of applicants to five major higher educational institutions in Leningrad in 1968 found that there were twice as many female as male applicants.[47] However, since only one-fifth of the women, as compared with one-half of the men, were actually admitted, men and women formed roughly equal proportions of entering students. The orientations of male and female applicants, however, were rather different. Some 60 percent of the women applicants, as compared to 30 percent of the men, sought to specialize in the humanities rather than in technical fields. The more limited number of places in these fields may therefore adversely af-

[45]See, for example, the discussion of education issues at a recent session of the Supreme Soviet in *Zasedanie verkhovnogo soveta SSSR, Vos'mogo sozyva, shestaia sessiia, 17–19 iiulia 1973 g.: stenograficheskii otchet* (Moscow 1973), pp. 87–88.

[46]L. R. Liss, "Social Conditioning," in Yanowitch and Fisher, *Social Stratification and Mobility*, p. 282.

[47]Cited by Richard Dobson, "Educational Policies," in Atkinson, Dallin, and Lapidus, *Women in Russia*.

fect the educational access of women, leading one Soviet author to conclude that "a certain portion of the places in special academic institutions
are intended for the study of specifically 'masculine' occupations. Regardless of the reasons for this, it is necessary to acknowledge the reality of the
fact that even though a woman in a large town realizes her equal right to
education, she achieves it through additional personal effort as compared
with a man." [48] Far more detailed information about the entire admissions
process is necessary to determine the extent to which the overall proportion of female students reflects the proportion of qualified female applicants.

The access of women to higher education and their distribution by field
is not uniform throughout the Soviet Union but varies by republic, by
nationality, and by social class. The proportion of women is highest in the
higher educational institutions of the Baltic republics and lowest in the
Central Asian regions. The Tadzhik republic is the most backward in this
respect: in the mid-1960s women comprised roughly one-third of enrollments in higher education there, and of these only one-third were of the
local nationality; but even in Turkmenistan in 1973 women constituted
only 37 percent of higher education enrollments. [49] In the Central Asian
republics, Russians are strongly overrepresented among women in higher
educational institutions. In Tadzhikistan, for example, where Slavic nationalities make up 14.7 percent of the population, they constitute 55.2
percent of all women in higher education.

Among certain non-European nationalities, the proportion of women in
higher education, as well as in secondary institutions, is roughly half the
national average. While 52 percent of all higher education students of Russian nationality in 1970–1971 were female, women constituted only 33
percent of the Uzbeks, 32 percent of Azerbaidzhanis, 24 percent of Tad-
zhiks, and 23 percent of the Turkmen (Table 7). Substantial progress has
been made in altering the aspirations and opportunities of Central Asian
women, yet the obstacles to full equality remain great. Indeed, although
Soviet writers claim that the lag in the education of non-European women
is being rapidly overcome, a comparison of the figures for 1960 with those
for 1970–1971 do not fully corroborate their assertion. While the male-
female educational gap has narrowed over time, the rate of change varied
among different nationalities. Where official policy coincides with cultural
patterns, high proportions of women enter higher education; among the
Turkmen and Tatar nationalities, by contrast, the figures remain low and
the rate of increase very slow.

[48]E. K. Vasil'eva, *Sotsial'no–professional'nyi uroven' gorodskoi molodezhi*, (Leningrad, 1973),
p. 73.
[49]Dodge, *Women in the Soviet Economy*, pp. 118–121; Tsentral'noe statisticheskoe upravlenie pri sovete ministrov Turkmenskoi SSR, *Zhenshchiny Sovetskogo Turkmenistana* (Ashkhabad, 1973), p. 103.

TABLE 7

NUMBER AND PROPORTION OF WOMEN IN HIGHER EDUCATIONAL INSTITUTIONS
BY NATIONALITY, 1970/71, AND PROPORTION OF WOMEN IN 1960

	Number of students	Number of women students	Women as percent of total	Women as percent of total in 1960
Total USSR	4,580,600	2,247,000	49	43
Russian	2,729,000	1,421,800	52	46
Ukrainian	621,200	296,000	48	42
Belorussian	130,200	64,400	49	40
Uzbek	150,700	49,500	33	25
Kazakh	100,300	45,100	45	32
Georgian	87,800	39,700	45	—
Azerbaidzhani	86,000	27,900	32	28
Lithuanian	49,800	26,300	53	47
Jewish	105,800	47,300	45	—
Latvian	21,800	11,600	53	48
Tadzhik	28,100	6,700	24	16
Armenian	81,500	35,600	44	—
Turkmen	22,000	5,000	23	21
Estonian	17,900	9,100	51	48
Tatar	87,000	42,000	49	44
Kirgiz	26,400	11,400	43	29

SOURCES: For 1960, *Vysshee obrazovanie v SSSR* (Moscow, 1961), pp. 87, 128–57; for 1970, Tsentral'noe statisticheskoe upravlenie, *Narodnoe obrazovanie, nauka i kul'tura v SSSR* (Moscow, 1971), p. 196.

Educational attainments are also highly correlated with social background, although the evidence bearing on this is very scanty. Without offering any breakdowns by sex, recent Soviet sociological studies have pointed to a high correlation between social background, educational aspirations, and educational success.[50] As Table 8 indicates, children of urban intelligentsia families have the highest aspirations for continuing full-time education beyond the secondary level and the greatest likelihood of

[50]The Soviet studies do not permit an adequate and sharp distinction between the effects of lower aspiration and those of poor preparation. The research of V. N. Shubkin in the 1960s explored differences in the educational aims of children of different social groups. While 71 percent of children of the intelligentsia aspired to intelligentsia occupations, only 36 percent of the children of workers in service industries, and none of the children of agricultural workers, revealed similar aspirations ("Molodezh' vstupaet v zhizn'," *Voprosy filosofii*, May 1965, p. 65.) Other studies show that children of lower socioeconomic groups tend to leave school at earlier ages, while an extremely high proportion of the children of

TABLE 8

EDUCATIONAL ASPIRATIONS OF SECONDARY SCHOOL GRADUATES
AND THEIR REALIZATIÓN, BY SOCIAL GROUP, NOVOSIBIRSK *OBLAST* 1963

| | *Percent of children:* | | | |
| | *Wishing to* | | *Actually going to* | |
Parents' occupations	*Work with or without part-time study*	*Study only*	*Work with or without part-time study*	*Study only*
Urban intelligentsia	7	93	18	82
Rural intelligentsia	24	76	42	58
Workers (industry and construction)	17	83	39	61
Workers (transport and communication)	18	82	55	45
Workers (service industries)	24	76	41	59
Agricultural workers	24	76	90	10
Other occupations	50	50	75	25
Average for the sample	17	83	39	61

SOURCE: V.N. Shubkin, "Molodezh' vstupaet v zhizn'," *Voprosy filosofii* 5 (1965), p. 65.

actually doing so. For children of peasant background, the gap between aspiration and opportunity is greatest, while children of workers fall in between. Thus, the children of the social group classified as employees formed the bulk of full-time students in higher educational institutions— 41 percent of the total in 1964—while worker and especially peasant children were underrepresented.[51] The underrepresentation of peasant children in particular reflects the poor quality of rural schools as well as the lower level of aspirations.

The very large proportion of women in higher educational institutions

---

higher social groups complete ten years of schooling. In addition, the poor quality of instruction in rural schools adversely affects the further educational opportunities of rural students. A survey conducted in Novosibirsk *oblast'* in 1963 by Shubkin revealed that only 28 percent of ten-year-school graduates from rural areas were admitted to full-time study at higher educational institutions, while the figure for towns was 46 percent (cited in Matthews, *Class and Society*, p. 263).

[51]Workers, forming 34.1 percent of the total population, constituted 39.4 percent of full-time students, while peasants, 24.8 percent of the population, constituted 19.6 percent of full-time students (E. L. Manevich, *Problemy obshchestvennogo truda v SSSR*, cited in Matthews, *Class and Society*, p. 297).

in the Soviet Union is the realization of a central aspiration of nineteenth-century feminism. Finland alone has a higher proportion of women, while only in the United States, France, and Sweden do women constitute 40 percent or more of all enrollments in higher education.[52] But the pattern of enrollments in the Soviet Union is perhaps more remarkable, reflecting an extraordinary decline in the sex-stereotyping of certain professional fields. Although education and health, in which women were heavily concentrated even in 1926, remain fields with a high proportion of women, the entry of women into scientific fields and into industrial engineering faculties represents a major transformation of values, distinguishing the pattern of women's educational enrollments in the Soviet Union, as well as in several East European countries, from those found in other Western societies.

At the same time, differential preferences and valuations of fields have by no means been eliminated by the expansion of educational opportunities. Indeed, Soviet researchers show growing interest in the historical and psychological roots of such sex-stereotyping, for the degree to which some preferences have been altered by explicit government policy serves to focus more attention on the persistence of traditional stereotypes in other areas.

At the level of graduate training, the pattern of opportunities for women is more complex. At the end of 1931, 23 percent of graduate students at higher educational institutions and research establishments were women. The proportion rose to a high of over 43 percent during World War II and subsequently declined, reaching 23 percent in 1960. Thus, the proportion of women in graduate training has not increased steadily over time, although in absolute terms their numbers have grown considerably. Moreover, women are heavily concentrated in relatively few fields; public health and education account for roughly 60 to 70 percent of women graduate students.

This growth in the number of women in graduate training has been particularly rapid since 1950. In 1950 some 11,400 women held the degree of Candidate of Science, a degree corresponding roughly to the American Ph.D. This figure increased to 28,800 in 1960, to 60,700 in 1970, to 79,600 in 1973, and to 97,000 by 1976 (Table 9). The number of women Doctors of Science, a degree that requires great scholarly accomplishment, almost doubled—from 600 to 1,100—between 1950 and 1960, and then quadrupled between 1960 and 1976 to reach a total of 4,800. Yet, despite the enormous increase in the numbers of women holding these advanced degrees, in 1976 they formed 28 percent of the total number of

[52]For a comprehensive survey of the position of women in American higher education, see Alice S. Rossi and Ann Calderwood, eds., *Academic Women on the Move* (New York, 1973).

TABLE 9

PROPORTION OF WOMEN AMONG SCIENTIFIC WORKERS AND DISTRIBUTION OF HIGHER DEGREES AND SCHOLARLY RANKS, 1950–1976

	1950	1960	1965	1970	1973	1974	1975	1976
No. of scientific workers	162,500	354,200	664,600	927,700	1,108,500	1,169,700	1,223,400	1,253,500
Number of women	59,000	128,000	254,000	359,900	439,500	464,644	488,300	497,900
Percent of women	36.3	36.3	38.2	38.8	39.6	39.7	39.9	39.7
Total of scientific workers with scholarly degree of Candidate of Science	45,000	98,300	134,400	224,500	288,300	309,500	326,800	345,400
Number of women	11,400	28,800	34,800	60,700	79,600	83,685	94,000	97,400
Percent of women	25.0	29.3	25.9	27.0	27.6	28.0	28.7	28.1
Total of scientific workers with scholarly degree of Doctor of Science	8,300	10,900	14,800	23,600	29,800	31,700	32,142	34,600
Number of women	600	1,100	1,400	3,100	4,000	4,398	4,500	4,800
Percent of women	7.2	10.0	9.4	13.0	13.4	14.0	14.0	13.8
Total with scholarly rank of Academician, Corresponding Member, Professor	8,900	7,954	12,500	18,100	21,600	22,500	22,900	24,000
Number of women	500	700	1,100	1,800	2,200	2,300	2,400	2,500
Percent of women	7.1	8.8	9.9	9.9	10.0	10.2	10.4	10.4

TABLE 9 (Continued)

PROPORTION OF WOMEN AMONG SCIENTIFIC WORKERS
AND DISTRIBUTION OF HIGHER DEGREES AND SCHOLARLY RANKS, 1950–1976

	1950	1960	1965	1970	1973	1974	1975	1976
Total with scholarly rank of Associate Professor	21,800	36,257	48,600	68,600	80,500	84,400	86,900	92,500
Number of women	3,200	6,200	9,500	14,400	17,800	18,800	18,800	21,200
Percent of women	14.7	17.1	19.6	24.5	22.1	22.3	22.3	22.9
Total with scholarly rank of Senior Research Associate	11,400	20,279	28,700	39,000	47,800	50,000	50,000	56,300
Number of women	3,500	5,800	8,300	9,800	11,500	12,100	12,100	13,100
Percent of women	30.7	28.6	28.9	21.3	24.0	23.9	23.9	23.2
Total with scholarly rank of Junior Research Associate and Assistant	19,600	26,719	48,900	48,800	48,800	47,100	46,400	44,300
Number of women	9,400	13,600	25,000	24,300	24,300	23,300	23,900	21,600
Percent of women	48.0	50.9	51.1	49.8	49.8	49.4	49.4	48.7

SOURCES: Calculated from figures given in Tsentral'noe statisticheskoe upravlenie SSSR, *Narodnoe obrazovanie, nauka i kul'tura v SSSR* (Moscow, 1971), pp. 246, 271; Tsentral'noe statisticheskoe upravlenie, *Narodnoe khoziaistvo SSSR v 1972 g.* (Moscow, 1973), p. 129; Tsentral'noe statisticheskoe upravlenie, *Narodnoe khoziaistvo SSSR v 1974 g.* (Moscow, 1975), pp. 143–144; "Zhenshchiny v SSSR," *Vestnik statistiki* 1 (January 1975):91; Tsentral'noe statisticheskoe upravlenie, *Zhenshchiny v SSSR* (Moscow, 1975), p. 81; "Zhenshchiny v SSSR," *Vestnik statistiki* 1 (January 1977):90; Tsentral'noe statisticheskoe upravlenie, *Narodnoe khoziaistvo SSSR za 60 let* (Moscow, 1977), p. 141.

candidates, a slight decline from the 1960 figure, and 14 percent of the total number of doctorates, an increase of 4 percent over 13 years. Although the Soviet degrees are not quite comparable to the American M.A. and Ph.D., as they involve a higher level of preparation, there is nonetheless a striking similarity in the proportion of women receiving higher degrees in the two countries. In the United States in 1974–1975, 45 percent of all M.A.'s were awarded to women and 21 percent of all Ph.D.'s.[53] In recent years, the rate of change in the United States has been far more dramatic than in the USSR, where a plateau appears to have been reached.

The lower proportion of women among holders of advanced degrees in the USSR and the slow growth of this proportion are not exclusively the results of lower individual aspirations. Female graduate students appear to experience serious obstacles in the course of their advanced training. The legal provisions for maternity leave with pay for women workers are not automatically applicable to graduate students; pregnant students must request additional leave to complete their programs of study. Complaints published in the Soviet press indicate that educational officials are frequently insensitive or even hostile to female students' special needs. One student publicly criticized the attitudes of high Ministry of Education officals who refused to grant such an extension of time, quoting one of them who remarked:

> We still have such, m-m-m, shall I say, unconscientious women. They stay on to do graduate work, and you know—This is how they behave. They want to arrange their affairs at the state's expense. Were it up to me, I would not extend the deadline on graduate study for anyone under any circumstances. And if I were Prosecutor, I would press charges against anyone who squanders state funds this way.[54]

But without more detailed information about graduate applications and admissions and about the degree to which the problems encountered by graduate students differ for men and women, it is impossible to weigh the relative role of different variables in the lower proportion of women at higher levels of training.

The Soviet regime has made great efforts to fulfill its promise of equal educational opportunities for women. This commitment to equality was linked with a view of women as an important capital resource and of education as a form of investment in human capital to provide the ideological foundation for massive educational investments. The expansion of the educational system has increased the average length of schooling, the pro-

[53]National Center for Educational Statistics, *Earned Degrees Conferred: Analysis of Trends, 1965/66–1974/75* (Washington D.C., 1977), p.10.
[54]*Izvestiia*, December 17, 1971.

portion of the age cohort receiving an education, and the proportion of women relative to men. Moreover, the enormous emphasis on scientific and technological training in Soviet education and the imposition of a uniform curriculum through the tenth grade have altered older stereotypes about occupational roles and eased the entry of women into scientific and technical fields in extremely large numbers.

At the lower levels of the educational system, access is virtually universal; with few exceptions access is available to women equally with men. At the secondary level, the proportion of women receiving specialized training has actually exceeded that of men since the late 1930s, while higher proportions of men are trained as skilled workers for industry and agriculture. In higher education, the share of women has also grown, but the structure of opportunities is shaped by a selection process that limits both the total number of admissions and the distribution by fields.

The principle of equality of access has been modified in practice by shifting criteria of admissions. In earlier years the criteria gave preferential treatment to women, but from 1955 to 1964 they tended to discriminate against them. More recently, a renewed emphasis on academic qualifications as the main criteria for admissions has raised the proportion of women in higher education to a figure just short of their proportion in the age group. The tension between equality based on achievement and the preferential treatment of special groups, whether for political or economic reasons, is a persistent one. While the preferential treatment of women at an earlier stage of development may have increased their access to educational opportunities, it would appear that deviations from achievement criteria at the present time are to their disadvantage.

The effects of Soviet educational policy are perhaps best summed up by the changing educational attainments of the Soviet population. For every 1,000 men aged ten or over in 1939, 127 had received higher or secondary education, while the figure for women was 90. By 1976 the proportion had reached 614 for men and 532 for women, multiplying 4.8 times in the first case and 5.9 in the second (Table 10). The increase in higher education is even more striking: the proportion of women rose ten times between 1939 and 1976, compared to 5.6 times for men.

It is possible that the long-term trend toward the equalization of male and female educational attainments is reaching its upper limit, particularly in those republics where women's educational level is already extremely high. The highest ratio in the Soviet period was reached in 1975: 519 of every 1,000 women aged ten or over had achieved at least an incomplete secondary education, compared to 594 of every 1,000 men (Table 10), yielding a ratio of 882 women for every 1,000 men. This trend reversed itself in 1976, with the ratio declining to 873. It is, of course, too soon to know whether this decline will prove to be a temporary one, but it reflects

160   *Women in Soviet Society*

TABLE 10

MALE AND FEMALE EDUCATIONAL ATTAINMENTS, USSR,

1939–1977

Of the population aged 10 and over:	Those with secondary education (per 1,000 of the corresponding sex)		Those with higher education (per 1,000 of the corresponding sex)		Total (per 1,000 of the corresponding sex)	
	Male	Female	Male	Female	Male	Female
1939	116	85	11	5	127	90
1959	365	318	27	20	392	338
1970	474	415	48	37	522	452
1975	534	471	60	48	594	519
1977	566	494	65	53	631	547

SOURCE: "Zhenshchiny v SSSR," *Vestnik statistiki* 1 (January 1977):84; Tsentral'noe statisticheskoe upravlenie, *Narodnoe khoziaistvo SSSR za 60 let* (Moscow, 1977), p. 56.

a trend (revealed in Table 4) that has been apparent in two of the most developed republics—Russia and Lithuania—since 1959. Viewed in conjunction with the stabilization or even the slight decline in the proportion of women receiving higher scholarly degrees and appointments in recent years (Table 9) it may foreshadow a more general diminution of both the pressures and the opportunities for female mobility as a result of the gradual return to demographic "normalcy" in the context of a relative saturation of elite positions.

The educational investments of the Soviet regime have provided a large body of women, particularly in the younger age groups, with the training that should enable them to enter a variety of positions in economic life and to rise to positions of importance in industrial and governmental agencies. Their ability to make use of these new opportunities has been further enhanced by the development of protective labor legislation and the creation of a network of child-care institutions designed to minimize the inhibiting effect of family responsibilities on employment. As we shall see, however, these efforts—creating what were in effect enabling conditions for the assertion of female roles in the society at large—did not necessarily or consistently go hand in hand with real opportunities for women to assume responsible positions in economic and political arenas on equal terms with men.

FIVE

Women and Work:*
Changing Economic Roles

The supply of female manpower is more elastic.
It depends to a greater degree on the extent to
which a family's requirements are satisfied by the
earnings of the head of the family (the male) and
by income from public consumption funds. The
lower the level at which these requirements are
being satisfied, the more the family needs earnings
from its women.

V. Guseinov and V. Korchagin

THE broad patterns of economic and social development
whose contours we have briefly traced created a distinctive role for
women in Soviet economic life. The complex pressures that drew women
into the labor force and the affirmative measures that affected the terms
on which they would be employed had important outcomes for the pattern of female employment. In the Soviet Union today, women constitute
51 percent of the labor force in the socialized sector of the economy. If
all agricultural employment is included, female participation rates approach the demographic maximum, with over 85 percent of able-bodied
women between the ages of twenty and fifty-five currently employed full
time. Just fifty years ago nine-tenths of all women in the Soviet labor
force were engaged in agriculture; today the agricultural sector accounts
for under one third of female employment.

Yet neither high participation rates nor the transition to non-agricultural employment are altogether unique to the Soviet Union. The proportion of women entering the nonagricultural labor force has been rising
in a number of industrial societies in recent decades, particularly in the
United States. The upward trend in female labor-force participation was

---

*The restrictive use of the term 'work' in the title of this chapter is not intended to equate
work exclusively with paid labor outside the home. A more detailed analysis of women's
role in domestic production is presented in Chapter VII.

first confined to single women. By the middle of the twentieth century, encouraged by postwar economic expansion and labor shortages, growing numbers of married women began to enter the labor force, and in recent years the proportion of married women with young children in the total has also begun to rise.[1] Close to 45 percent of American women are currently employed, comprising 39 percent of the labor force, and the proportions are mounting in Western Europe as well. Female participation rates are close to 40 percent in Belgium, West Germany, and Austria, almost 50 percent in Sweden, England, and Denmark, and close to 60 percent in Finland, compared with 65 percent for the USSR.[2] These trends have called into question the traditional assumption that women constitute a marginal and unstable labor force with a limited attachment to work.

In Western industrial societies, the entry of women into the modern sector of the labor force has occurred in ways that largely confine their contribution to the least rewarding positions. They typically occupy low-paid and often marginal positions, predominating as relatively unskilled laborers in industrial enterprises and in clerical positions or concentrated at the lower levels of administrative work and in the paraprofessions, holding jobs rather than pursuing careers. Few women are found in the more prestigious areas of the business world and the professions, while they tend to be overrepresented in traditionally feminine occupations that are low in status and rewards.[3] In the United States, for example, 72.6 per-

[1] Recent research has attributed this pattern to the interaction of structural and demographic changes. The expansion of education, white-collar work, and services has increased the demand for female labor. At the same time, a diminishing supply of the preferred types of women—young and unmarried—has resulted in an acceptance of such new categories as married women and women with young children. See, for example, Valerie Oppenheimer, "Demographic Influence on Female Employment," *American Journal of Sociology* 78 (1973): 946–61, and her larger study, *The Female Labor Force in the United States*, Population Monograph Series, No. 5 (Berkeley, 1970).

[2] The comparison overstates the actual differences because the Soviet figures are calculated as the proportion of working women aged sixteen to fifty-five while the Western figures include those up to age sixty-five, an age cohort with considerably lower participation rates. Unpaid family workers are excluded from the Western figures. For the United States, see *Economic Report of the President* (Washington, D.C., 1973), p. 91. For Western Europe, see Robert Gubbels, "The Female Labor Force in Western Europe," in *Women in the World: A Comparative Study*, eds. Lynne Iglitzin and Ruth Ross (Santa Barbara, 1975); Marjorie Galenson, *Women and Work* (Ithaca, N. Y., 1973), pp. 18–19; and Judith Blake, "The Changing Status of Women in Developed Countries," *Scientific American* 3 (September 1974):140–41. In the past, women workers have functioned in part as a reserve labor force, a cushion to facilitate economic expansion and absorb the shock of contraction. In recent years, however, a number of trends, including the increase in single-parent families, have made work an economic necessity for large numbers of women who are the sole support of their families. In the United States, for example, some six million families, or roughly 12 percent of the total, are headed by women, and one-third of these are below the low-income level (*Economic Report of the President*, p. 108).

[3] In the United States, roughly one-third of working women are employed as clerical workers, almost a fifth are in services, 15 percent are professional and technical personnel,

cent of all women are employed in occupations in which women are grossly overrepresented, and 59 percent are found in occupations that are 70 percent or more female.[4]

Several studies have contended that this pattern of occupational segregation is extremely stable over time. While one might anticipate a correlation between occupational distribution and developmental level, in fact a recent effort to calculate changes in the sexual structure of occupations in the United States between 1900 and 1960 concludes that the degree of sexual segregation has been relatively constant, seemingly unaffected by the vast changes that have altered the American labor market in so many other ways.[5] The great expansion in female employment has not diminished the degree of occupational segregation. It has occurred, rather, through the expansion of occupations already heavily female, and the emergence of new occupations defined as female from the start, as well as through the takeover by women of occupations defined previously as male. New opportunities have developed, but in a persistently segregated context. In the United States in 1960, according to these calculations, 68.4 percent of females would have had to change occupations to achieve an equal distribution of sexes.

Although there is increasingly widespread acceptance of the principle of equal pay for equal work, its application in practice is vitiated by the sexual segregation of the labor force.[6] Educational disparities and lesser work experience are additional obstacles to improved employment opportunities and higher wages. But it has been demonstrated that even with comparable educational attainments women are systematically underclas-

---

and 14 percent are factory operatives. For more extensive treatment of the sexual structure of occupations, see Valerie Oppenheimer, "The Sex-labeling of Jobs," *Industrial Relations* 7 (May 1968): 219–34; Edward Gross, "Plus ça change? The Sexual Structure of Occupations Over Time," *Social Problems* 16 (Fall 1968): 198–208; Harold Wilensky, "Women's Work: Economic Growth, Ideology, Structure," *Industrial Relations* 7 (May 1968): 235–48. For a comprehensive survey of the economics of sexual discrimination, see Cynthia B. Lloyd, ed., *Sex, Discrimination, and the Division of Labor* (New York, 1975), and Martha Blaxall and Barbara Reagan, eds., *Women and the Workplace: The Implications of Occupational Segregation* (Chicago, 1976).

[4]Barbara R. Bergmann and Irma Adelman, "The 1973 Report of the President's Council of Economic Advisors: The Economic Role of Women," *The American Economic Review* 63 (September 1973): 511; Oppenheimer, *The Female Labor Force,* p. 75, utilizing 1960 census data.

[5]Gross, "Plus ça change"; see also Bergmann and Adelman, "Economic Role of Women," pp. 510–11.

[6]Studies of the structure of employment in countries belonging to the Common Market have discovered the same tendency. Although the convention of the International Labor Office and Article 112 of the Treaty of Rome both require the payment of equal wages for equal work, the sexual segregation of the labor force undermines its application in practice (unpublished results of six-nation survey conducted in 1971 by the Institute of Sociology, Free University of Brussels; personal communication to the author by Elaine Vogel-Polsky, Institute of Sociology, Free University of Brussels). See also Alice Cook, "Equal Pay: Where Is It?" *Industrial Relations* 14 (May 1975): 158–77.

sified and underpaid by comparison with men. Thus, the sexual segregation of the industrial labor force, both vertically and horizontally, contributes to a pattern of remuneration in which the average wages of the female labor force are about two-thirds those of men, and the average woman college graduate who works full time all year ends up with about the same income as the average male high school dropout.[7]

To what extent are such patterns found in the Soviet Union as well, despite a more explicit commitment to the full participation and equality of women in economic life? What forces have shaped the entry of women into modern sectors of production and their patterns of participation? How are women distributed within the labor force both horizontally, by economic sector, and vertically, by levels of skill and authority? How do the average wages of employed women compare with those of their male counterparts? In what respect are these patterns similar to those found in Western industrial societies and in what respects do they differ?

PARTICIPATION IN THE LABOR FORCE

Long before the Bolshevik revolution, women in Russia were engaged in productive economic activity. Agriculture was the central economic activity, although women had already begun to enter the industrial labor force and the professions in substantial numbers by the turn of the century. The 1897 census recorded three million women workers, of whom roughly 50 percent were employed as domestic servants, 25 percent as agricultural laborers, 13 percent in industry, and 4 percent in education and health.[8] Although a relatively low proportion of all employed women worked in industry, women comprised over one-third of the industrial labor force of Russia in 1913 and close to one-half during World War I.[9]

[7]The *Economic Report of the President* calculates that the ratio of female to male earnings, adjusted for age and education, ranges from 72 percent for professional and technical workers to 47.8 percent for sales personnel. Other studies calculate the differential to be between 35 and 57 percent, depending on the data base used. The authors of the Presidential *Report*, after adjusting for every possible factor including experience, found a residual differential of about 20 percent, but stopped just short of attributing it to direct discrimination (pp. 103–6). Six recent econometric studies, reviewed in Bergmann and Adelman, "Economic Role of Women," variously calculated the differential due to discrimination to be between 29 and 43 percent. See, for example, Larry Suter and Herman Miller, "Income Differences Between Men and Career Women," in *Changing Women in a Changing Society*, ed. Joan Huber (1973), pp. 210–12, for a demonstration that women receive lower increments of income for equal increases in educational level and occupational status. A study of university faculty salaries by the Carnegie Commission on Higher Education, *Opportunities for Women in Higher Education* (New York, 1973), reveals a similar pattern and concludes that women faculty members earn an average of $1,500 to $2,000 less a year than men in comparable positions with comparable qualifications. See also Myra Strober, "Lower Pay for Women: A Case of Economic Discrimination," *Industrial Relations* 11 (May 1972): 279–84.
[8]Tsentral'noe statisticheskoe upravlenie, *Zhenshchiny i deti v SSSR* (Moscow, 1969), p. 9.
[9]Of a total of 1,951,955 workers in industry in 1911, some 606,588 were women. Their proportion rose to almost 50 percent during World War I and declined with demobilization. A. Riazanova, *Zhenskii trud* (Moscow and Leningrad, 1926), pp. 35–39.

Women were heavily concentrated in the textile industry, where they formed over half the labor force, but were also found in substantial numbers in chemical and paper factories and in food industries.

If agricultural as well as urban industrial employment is included, the overall participation rate of women has always been relatively high in modern Russia.[10] But while the proportion of economically productive women has undergone little change over several decades, there has been a massive shift of women from agricultural into nonagricultural occupations in the Soviet period. In 1926, nine-tenths of all women in the labor force were working in agriculture. By 1959, agriculture occupied about half of all working women, and by 1975 the proportion had declined to under a third.[11]

The new Soviet regime explicitly undertook to increase the number of women in the industrial labor force, for reasons that were at first more ideological and political than economic. Nevertheless, the economic dislocation of the postrevolutionary years prevented any real progress. Indeed, widespread unemployment struck female workers with particular severity, and the resultant decline in their proportion of the total number of workers and employees from 25 percent to 23 percent was noted with alarm at the Party Congress of 1924. A resolution insisted that "the preservation of female labor power in industry is of political significance" and directed Party organs "to intensify the work of improving the qualification of female labor, and, where possible, to draw women into industries where they have either never been employed or have been employed in inadequate numbers."[12] By 1928 their proportion had risen to 24 percent of the total.

[10]A slight *decline* in participation rates actually occurred between 1926 and 1959 as a consequence of urbanization and industrialization: see Norton T. Dodge, *Women in the Soviet Economy* (Baltimore, 1966), pp. 32–33; Alex Inkeles and Raymond Bauer, *The Soviet Citizen: Daily Life in a Totalitarian Society* (Cambridge, Mass., 1961), pp. 496–97; and the debate between Warren Eason and Frank Lorimer in *Soviet Economic Growth*, ed. Abram Bergson (Evanston, 1953), pp. 109, 124. Agricultural employment was a seasonal activity, however, particularly for women. Soviet economists estimated the contribution of adult women to agricultural production in the mid-1920s to be 30 percent less than that of men; Dodge, *Women in the Soviet Economy*, p. 33.

[11]Norton T. Dodge, "Recruitment and the Quality of the Soviet Agricultural Labor Force," in *The Soviet Rural Community*, ed., James Millar (Urbana, 1971), p. 182; Tsentral'noe statisticheskoe upravlenie pri sovete ministrov SSSR, *Narodnoe khoziaistvo SSSR v 1975 g.* (Moscow, 1976), p. 440.

[12]Institut Marksizma Leninizma pri TsK KPSS, *KPSS v rezoliutsiiakh i resheniiakh*, 4 vols. (Moscow, 1954–1960), 2: 89. The postwar demobilization and rising unemployment led to widespread dismissals of women employed in heavy industry after World War I. As a statement by the Petrograd Council of Trade Unions warned: "The question of how to combat unemployment has come sharply before the unions. In many factories and shops the question is being solved very simply . . . fire the women and put men in their place." The Council warned that this was an unsatisfactory solution, and that until expanded productivity could eliminate unemployment altogether it was necessary to base dismissals entirely on the needs of each individual worker regardless of sex. "Only such an attitude will make it possible for us to retain women in our organizations and prevent a split in the army of workers." Cited in Jessica Smith, *Woman in Soviet Russia* (New York, 1927), p. 16.

The vast economic expansion touched off by the First Five Year Plan in 1928 and the all-out commitment to rapid industrialization in the following decade required an enormous increase in the size of the labor force. Both the absolute number of women in the industrial labor force and their proportion of the total increased rapidly. The expansion of the female labor force occurred in three successive waves that were closely associated with increased demand for labor. The first wave occurred between 1928 and 1940, coinciding with the first two Five Year Plans. The absolute number of women among workers and employees grew almost fivefold between 1928 and 1940, and their proportion of the total rose from 24 to 39 percent (Table 11).

An additional influx of women entered the labor force during World

TABLE 11

FEMALE WORKERS AND
EMPLOYEES IN THE NATIONAL ECONOMY,
1922–1976

Year	Number of female workers and employees	Percent of total
1922	1,560,000	25
1926	2,265,000	23
1928	2,795,000	24
1932	6,000,000	27.4
1940	13,190,000	39
1945	15,920,000	56
1950	19,180,000	47
1955	23,040,000	46
1960[a]	29,250,000	47
1965	37,680,000	49
1968	42,680,000	50
1970	45,800,000	51
1972	48,707,000	51
1974	51,297,000	51
1976	53,700,000	51.5

SOURCES: Tsentral'noe statisticheskoe upravlenie, *Narodnoe khoziaistvo SSSR: 1922–1972* (Moscow, 1972), p. 348; for 1932, Solomon Schwarz, *Labor in the Soviet Union* (New York, 1951), p. 72; for 1972–1976, "Zhenshchiny v SSSR," *Vestnik statistiki* 1 (January 1977): 86.

[a]Note that women constituted 54.9 percent of the total population in 1959 and 63.4 percent of the age cohort 35 and over.

War II to replace the millions of men mobilized for military service. Between 1940 and 1950 women constituted 92 percent of all new entrants, and this fact, in addition to the exodus of males, resulted in a labor force that was 56 percent female in 1945. The return of surviving males to civilian life in the postwar years reduced the proportion of women to 47 percent in 1950, but the absolute number of women continued to increase.

A final, intensive effort to recruit women for the economy was launched in the early 1960s in response to extreme labor shortages caused by the stabilization of the population and the declining manpower reserves available from rural migration. The only major untapped source of labor was the still-large pool of women remaining in households. According to the 1959 census, of the nearly 13 million able-bodied adults not productively employed, 89 percent were women, most of whom lived in smaller urban areas where employment opportunities were limited and child-care facilities largely unavailable.[13] Between 1960 and 1971 a vast recruitment drive brought almost 18 million more women into the labor force, roughly 14 million of them from households, virtually exhausting this source (except among the Moslem population) and bringing the total number of women workers and employees in the socialized sector to over 47 million, or 51 percent of the total. According to the current plan, fewer than one million more women can be drawn from households. A few further gains may be realized by drawing pensioners and invalids into part-time employment, but current rates of participation are close to the demographic maximum and are likely to remain stable through the 1970s. (Table 12).[14]

The major reserves of untapped female labor today are found in the Central Asian and Transcaucasian republics, where female participation rates in nonagricultural employment fall considerably below the national average. In Turkmenistan in 1973, for example, only 54 percent of able-bodied women were workers or employees, and of these fewer than a third were Turkmen.[15] The recruitment of native women into industry has encountered great difficulties; a high proportion of the women workers and employees in these regions are Russian or Ukrainian.

The entry of women into the modern sector of the labor force repre-

[13]Murray Feshbach and Stephen Rapawy, in "Labor Constraints in the Five Year Plan," U.S. Congress Joint Economic Committee, *Soviet Economic Prospects for the Seventies* (Washington, D.C., 1973), p. 494.

[14]*Ibid.*, p. 495. While households supplied 41.5 percent of the total growth of employment between 1959 and 1965, most of this was in the European regions of the USSR. In Kazakhstan and Azerbaidzhan, by contrast, they accounted for only .8 and 1.8 percent of the growth.

[15]Calculated from figures in Tsentral'noe statisticheskoe upravlenie pri sovete ministrov Turkmenskoi SSR, *Zhenshchiny Sovetskogo Turkmenistana* (Ashkhabad, 1973), pp. 70, 78, 79, 81. Of a total female population of 1,161,000, including 713,000 of Turkmen nationality, there were 210,700 women workers and employees of whom 63,400 were Turkmen. Fewer than one-fourth of these were employed in industry and construction, while over one-half were found in education, health and the services. Female participation rates were lower still in Tadzhikistan.

TABLE 12

ESTIMATES AND PROJECTIONS OF
FEMALE LABOR-FORCE PARTICIPATION RATES,
BY AGE COHORT, 1959–1990

Age Cohort	1959	1970	1980	1990
16–19[a]	71.0	47.8	40.8	35.0
20–29	80.4	86.3	86.1	86.1
30–39	77.7	92.7	92.7	92.7
40–49	75.4	90.6	90.6	90.6
50–54	67.7	77.3	77.3	77.3
55–59	48.5	44.4	45.4	46.4
60 +	33.8	25.0	26.0	27.0

SOURCE: Murray Feshbach and Stephen Rapawy, "Soviet Population and Manpower Trends and Policies," in *Soviet Economy in a New Perspective*, U.S. Congress Joint Economic Committee, (Washington D.C., 1976), p. 152.
[a]The falling rate reflects increased school attendance.

sents a social change of considerable magnitude. Between 1922 and 1974 the total number of women workers and employees rose from 1.5 million to over 51 million, and their proportion increased from one-fourth to over one-half of the total. To be sure, ideological and political considerations were foremost in the early years. Early Soviet policies rested on the assumption that genuine equality and independence for women depended on full economic participation. Moreover, in the social instability of the early 1920s, female unemployment brought with it rising prostitution, and increased employment was viewed as the only real solution.

But it is clear from the patterns of recruitment of women that after 1928 the interaction of demographic and economic factors was the real determinant of female employment. The periods in which women entered the labor force in the largest numbers were periods of severe manpower shortages. In the effort to mobilize all available resources for economic development and to encourage capital savings through labor-intensive methods of production and the neglect of the consumer sector, female labor was an important addition to the pool of manpower. Role change could be viewed as an important economic, political, and social resource, and the mobilization of women into new roles could be seen as a way to enhance the economic capacity of the Soviet system. Far from competing with men for scarce jobs, women were a welcome addition to the labor supply.[16]

Demographic pressures intensified economic needs to provide an ad-

[16]This is not to suggest that the employment of women in traditionally male occupations encountered no resistance on other grounds. A great array of accounts documents the hostile attitudes that greeted new women workers and testifies to the barriers women had to overcome to gain acceptance.

ditional impetus to the mobilization of women. As a consequence of war and civil war, a deficit of males had already developed by 1926. The cumulative casualties of collectivization, purges, deportations to forced labor camps, and ultimately of World War II created a severe imbalance in the structure of the Soviet population. In 1946, there were only 59.1 males for every 100 females in the thirty-five to fifty-nine age group (Table 13). By the time of the 1959 census, 54.9 percent of the total population was female, with the figure reaching 63.4 percent of the age cohort thirty-five and over.[17] As the supply of labor became tighter, and with males fully employed, it was natural that attention turned to women as a potential addition to labor resources.

The absence of males also affected the supply of female labor by obliging large numbers of women to become self-supporting. Political deportations and military service transformed wives as well as widows into heads of households, while the scarcity of men deprived a large proportion of women of the opportunity to marry. Almost 30 percent of the total number of Soviet households in 1959 were headed by women. As one Soviet economist noted, "women could not but work, because their earnings are the basic source of income for the family."[18] A substantial part

TABLE 13

THE RATIO OF MALES TO FEMALES, 1897–1975

Age Group	1897	1926	1939	1946	1959	1970	1975
All ages	98.9	93.5	91.9	74.3	81.9	85.5	86.4
Under 16	100.1	101.2	101.3	99.5	103.6	103.8	103.6
16–34	96.9	89.8	96.1	72.0	93.8	101.1	101.6
35–59	100.7	90.4	80.1	59.1	60.6	74.1	81.3
60 and over	95.5	78.8	66.1	51.9	50.8	47.7	38.8

SOURCES: Norton T. Dodge, *Women in the Soviet Economy* (Baltimore, 1966), p. 6; Tsentral'noe statisticheskoe upravlenie, *Narodnoe khoziaistvo SSSR v 1972 g.* (Moscow, 1973), p. 34. Ratios for 1975 computed from unpublished figures provided by the Foreign Demographic Analysis Division, U.S. Department of Commerce.

[17] For an analysis of demographic patterns revealed by the Soviet population census of January 15, 1970, see Frederick Leedy, "Demographic Trends in the USSR," in U.S. Congress, *Soviet Economic Prospects*, pp. 428–84. See also Tsentral'noe statisticheskoe upravlenie, *Itogi vsesoiuznoi perepisi naseleniia 1970 goda: Tom 2* (Moscow, 1972) for more detailed breakdowns.

[18] Cited in Murray Feshbach, "Manpower Trends in the USSR: 1950–1980," (Foreign Demographic Analysis Division, Bureau of the Census U.S. Department of Commerce, n.d.) p. 9. Mimeographed. The massive impact of war losses of males is further indicated by the fact that only 62.3 percent of women aged forty to forty-four and 54.9 percent of women aged forty-five to forty-nine were married in 1959 (Leedy, "Demographic Trends," in U.S. Congress, *Soviet Economic Prospects*, p. 441).

of regional variations in the proportion of economically active women is therefore attributable to marital status.[19]

But even in families that did have a male wage earner, the low level of wages also encouraged female employment. Official sources cite a figure of 620 rubles per year as the minimum per capita income necessary for "material well-being." A family of four, then, would need 2,480 rubles annually or 206.6 rubles per month.[20] The average monthly wage in 1972, however, was 130.3 rubles, or less than two-thirds of what would be required to support such a family. As the author of a recent study of female employment concluded:

> The participation of women in social production is, under the conditions of socialism, dictated to a significant extent by economic necessity. . . . In an overwhelming majority of cases, the participation of women in social production is connected with strivings to raise the family income in conjunction with the growth of the cultural and material needs of family members.[21]

It is clear, then, that the economic requirements of Stalinist development policies and the economic pressures faced by Soviet women as a consequence of larger societal changes combined to increase both the demand for and the supply of female labor, creating a situation in which women entered the industrial labor force in extremely high numbers.

These trends were strongly supported by an official ideology that insisted on the value of work in fostering the independence, personal growth, and social status of women. A woman who restricted her activities to the household was considered dependent, incomplete, and even unpatriotic. Although allowances were made for the persistence of traditional cultural constraints among some of the minority nationalities or of certain obstacles, such as the unavailability of child care, the official expectation was that, in the absence of such inhibiting factors, women would seek employment.

It is difficult to determine the extent to which these expectations have been internalized; in even the most recent opinion surveys, working women cited material need as a more central motivation in their employment than "broadening of horizons" or "civic satisfaction."[22] Nevertheless, other motivations, such as the desire to participate in a group, or the wish to be financially independent, also play a significant role.

[19]Denis Peter Mazur "Fertility and Economic Dependency of Soviet Women," *Demography* 10 (February 1973): 37–52.
[20]G. S. Sarkisian and N. Kuznetsova, *Potrebnosti i dokhod sem'i* (Moscow, 1968), p. 66.
[21]V. B. Mikhailiuk, *Ispol'zovanie zhenskogo truda v narodnom khoziaistve* (Moscow, 1970), p. 24.
[22]G. V. Osipov and J. Shchepan'skii, eds., *Sotsial'nye problemy truda i proizvodstva* (Moscow, 1969), pp. 444, 456. For another detailed discussion of the motives for female employment, see A. G. Kharchev and S. I. Golod, *Professional'naia rabota zhenshchin i sem'ia* (Leningrad, 1971), pp. 38–69.

SECTORAL PATTERNS OF EMPLOYMENT

As we have seen, sexual segregration is universal in Western economic systems. Women tend to cluster in what have traditionally been "women's fields," such as nursing and teaching, or in semiskilled and clerical occupations that are low in status and pay, and they are correspondingly underrepresented in the more prestigious professions and in managerial and executive ranks. While industrialization has expanded the range of opportunities available by developing entirely new fields and occupations, there is a tendency for occupations that were female at an earlier time to remain so.[23]

Similar patterns of female employment characterize the Soviet economy. Women predominate in economic sectors and occupations found at the lower end of Soviet wage scales and are underrepresented in more highly rewarded positions. In all areas of the economy, the proportion of women declines as one moves up the hierarchy of status and authority. As a consequence of both horizontal segregation and vertical stratifications, the average earnings of female workers and employees in the Soviet Union are substantially lower than those of men.

Nevertheless, the economic roles of Soviet women differ from those of their American and West European counterparts in a number of important ways. The very magnitude of female labor-force participation, its timing in relation to stages of industrialization, the economic framework within which it occurred, and its articulation with changing patterns of education all had a distinctive impact on the structure of the female labor force and account for a number of variations from the Western pattern.

The distribution of women by economic sector reveals a high degree of continuity in the patterns of employment from 1940 to 1974; increases in the proportion of women in different economic sectors followed very closely their ratio within the total labor force (Table 14).

Moreover, the gap between those sectors in which women are overrepresented and those in which they are underrepresented has actually widened in the intervening years. In transport and construction, where they constituted 21 and 24 percent, respectively, of the total employment in 1940, in 1974 they made up 24 and 29 percent, an increase that is smaller than their rate of growth in the labor force overall. In two fields—public health and education—the proportion of women was high in 1940 and has risen even further since, from 76 to 85 percent in public health and from 59 to 73 percent in education.

Finally, there are three exceptions to the relative stability in patterns of sectoral employment, three fields in which the proportion of women

[23]See Wilensky, "Women's Work," and Oppenheimer, "Sex-Labeling."

TABLE 14
CHANGES IN THE DISTRIBUTION OF FEMALE EMPLOYMENT
BY ECONOMIC SECTOR, 1940–1974

	Percent of women workers by economic sector					Ratio of women in given sector to their proportion of total labor force	
	1940	1950	1960	1970	1974	1940	1974
Percent of women in total labor force	39	47	47	51	51		
By economic sector:							
Industry	38	46	45	48	49	.97	.96
Agriculture (socialized sector)	30	42	41	44	44	.77	.86
Transportation	21	28	24	24	24	.54	.47
Communications	48	59	64	68	68	1.23	1.33
Construction	24	32	30	29	29	.62	.57
Trade, public catering, material-technical supplies and marketing, and procurement	44	57	66	75	76	1.12	1.49
Municipal housing and consumer services	43	54	53	51	53	1.10	1.04
Public health, physical culture, and social culture	76	84	85	85	85	1.94	1.66
Education and culture	59	69	70	72	73	1.51	1.43
Art	39	37	36	44	45	1.00	.88
Science and scientific services	42	43	42	47	49	1.07	.96
Banking and state ins.	41	58	68	78	81	1.05	1.59
Apparatus of organs of state and economic administration, of cooperatives and of social organizations	34	43	51	61	63	.87	1.23

SOURCES: Tsentral'noe statisticheskoe upravlenie, *Narodnoe khoziaistvo SSSR: 1922–1972* (Moscow, 1972), p. 348; "Zhenshchiny v SSSR," *Vestnik statistiki* 1 (January 1975): 86.

has increased even more rapidly than their proportion in the labor force overall.

The first is in the area of trade, procurement, supply, and public catering, reflecting the rapid growth of the service sector in recent years; it is now largely dominated by women. The second area that has experienced considerable growth is that of credit and state insurance, a field that employs large numbers of white-collar personnel performing secretarial and bookkeeping tasks. The third field, which also employs a large number of clerical workers, is that of governmental and economic administration. In these three fields the proportion of women has risen to 76, 81, and 63 percent, respectively. Indeed, these three rapidly growing sectors have absorbed much of the large wave of women drawn into the economy in recent years.

A closer examination of occupational structure based on the 1970 census data reveals the existence of substantial sex-stereotyping of occupations in patterns that resemble those found outside the Soviet Union.[24] A number of occupations listed in the all-Union tabulations have no counterpart in the tables dealing with female employment. Mechanical engineering and metallurgy, for example, are occupations that are overwhelmingly male, and a number of other occupations also have extremely small proportions of women. The garment industry and textiles, at the other extreme, are largely female. Women are also heavily concentrated in trade and public catering (91 percent of all employees) and in nursing (98 percent), and women constitute 75 percent of all teachers, 98 percent of nursery school personnel, 95 percent of librarians, 96 percent of telephone operators, and 99 percent of typists and stenographers. What is distinctive in the Soviet pattern of employment is the high concentration of women in agriculture, on the one hand, and in scientific and technical occupations, on the other. Women form 56 percent of the agricultural labor force, excluding private subsidiary agriculture, while at the same time they constitute 44 percent of engineers and technicians and 75 percent of doctors and dentists. They occupy, therefore, a wide range of economic roles from heavy and unskilled agricultural labor to modern scientific research.

The occupational breakdowns presented in the 1970 census data are too heterogeneous to permit a comprehensive analysis. Yet they do allow us to examine not only the pattern of female employment but also the changes in the distribution of the female labor force that have occurred since the 1959 census. Between 1959 and 1970, the number of women employed rose from 47,604,000 to 57,375,622, an increase of 21 percent.

[24]Tsentral'noe statisticheskoe upravlenie, *Itogi vsesoiuznoi perepisi naseleniia 1970 goda: Tom 6* (Moscow, 1973), especially pp. 14–23 and 165–69.

During this same period, female agricultural employment declined by roughly 7,000,000. The largest influx of women occurred in engineering and technical operations, which recorded an additional 2,000,000 women, including almost 1,000,000 new engineers. Other occupations that experienced a large influx of women workers include planning, bookkeeping, and accounting (1,700,000); food supply and public catering (1,600,000); scientific workers, teachers, and nursery personnel (1,500,000); workers in machinery and metallurgy (1,000,000); and medical workers (900,000, of whom almost 600,000 were nurses). With the exception of engineering and metallurgy, these were all occupations in which women were already heavily overrepresented.

The effect of this influx of female labor on patterns of occupational segregation can be measured crudely by comparing the proportions of the total female labor force employed in predominately female occupations in 1959 with 1970. In 1959, just under 16 million women, or 33 percent of the total, were employed in occupations in which women formed 70 percent or more of the labor force. In 1970, over 30 million women, or 55 percent of the new total, fell into this category, a substantial increase over 1959. In 1959, just under 10 million women, or 20.9 percent of the total, were employed in occupations that were at least 85 percent female; in 1970, 18.5 million women fell into this category, almost 33 percent of the total.

One way of measuring the degree of occupational segregation in any labor force is to calculate the percentage of any given group that would have to change occupations in order to have its distribution within each occupation exactly reflect its proportion in the labor force overall. While the broad categories utilized in Soviet census data tend to mask the amount of segregation that actually exists, a rough calculation suggests that 40 to 50 percent of all workers would have to change places for the distribution of men and women within each occupation to reflect their proportion in the Soviet labor force more generally.[25]

[25]These calculations rely on a method for measuring occupational stratification developed by Otis Dudley Duncan and Beverly Duncan, "Residential Distribution and Occupational Stratification," *American Journal of Sociology* 60 (March 1955), and adapted for the study of sexual segregation by Edward Gross. For a full description of the methodology utilized, see Gross, "Plus ça change," pp. 201–202. The heterogeneity of Soviet occupational categories will result in the underestimation of the degree of occupational segregation by sex. A more detailed analysis of one category for which subclassifications are available, engineering-technical workers, indicates the potential scope of the downward bias. Taken as a whole, the category yields a male-female disparity of 15.7 percent. Breaking the category into nine component parts and totaling them separately yields a differential of 22.5 percent. The lack of comparable classifications therefore stands in the way of cross-national comparisons.

For a more elaborate analysis of trends over time utilizing 1939 and 1959 data as well, see Michael Paul Sacks, "The Growth of the Female Labor Force in Soviet Russia" in *Women in Russia: Changing Realities and Changing Perceptions*, eds. Dorothy Atkinson, Alexander Dallin, and Gail Warshofsky Lapidus (Stanford, forthcoming). Separating the labor force into

It would appear that, at an earlier stage of economic development, the rapid growth of the industrial sector drew women into industry and into previously male occupations on a large scale. The growth of the service sector in recent years has tended to absorb a very high proportion of new female entrants; this situation, combined with the heavy influx of women into professional and paraprofessional fields, has resulted in the observed increase in occupational segregation. The relative weight of different factors in patterning the sexual structure of occupations remains the subject of considerable controversy. But if, as has been suggested,[26] women first entering the labor force chose fields in which they felt most at home, or which were most closely associated with their traditional roles, this pattern has not been substantially reversed at later stages of development. While industrialization in the Soviet Union has clearly created a new range of economic opportunities for women, in some respects the polarization of certain sectors into male-dominated or female-dominated sectors has actually intensified with economic development.

THE VERTICAL STRUCTURE OF OCCUPATIONS

The patterns of female employment by economic sector, however, tell us little about the vertical structure of occupations within each sector, nor do they provide an indication of the extent to which women have moved from relatively unskilled and low-paid jobs to jobs requiring professional skills and executive responsibility commensurate with their training and ability. Thus, a more complete picture would be revealed by comparing the structure of the employment pyramid for women with that for men. While such a broad comparison is beyond the scope of this study and would require more comprehensive data than are presently available, the analysis of several fields in some detail may illuminate aspects of the larger picture. For this purpose, we shall focus on the hierarchy of responsibility and skill in four areas involving four different levels and types of skills: agriculture, industrial engineering, education and medicine, and advanced scientific work.

If we examine the structure of employment in agriculture, perhaps the most striking feature of the Soviet scene is the very high proportion of women engaged in it. According to the calculations of Norton Dodge and Murray Feshbach, at the time of the 1959 census some 55 percent of all working women were engaged in agriculture.[27] The largest group was

three component parts, Sacks calculates the degree of occupational segregation in 1970 to have been 50.7 percent for the nonagrarian labor force, 42.4 percent for the professional and semiprofessional group, and 52.5 percent for nonprofessional workers.

[26]William Mandel, "Soviet Women in the Work Force and Professions," *American Behavioral Scientist* 15 (November–December 1971): 255–80.

[27]Norton T. Dodge and Murray Feshbach, "The Role of Women in Soviet Agriculture," *Soviet and East European Agriculture*, ed. Jerry F. Karcz (Berkeley and Los Angeles, 1967),

composed of collective farmers, some 17.6 million women, who formed 57 percent of all collective farmers. A second group of women, numbering about 2.7 million, worked on state farms, and some 9 million were engaged in private subsidiary agriculture—91 percent of all such workers —cultivating private garden plots for home consumption and the local market. By the time of the 1970 census, a lower but still substantial proportion of the female labor force was engaged in agricultural occupations. A total of 12.6 million women formed 56 percent of agricultural laborers, roughly 8 million on collective farms and 4 million on state farms, in addition to an estimated 7 to 9 million engaged in private subsidiary agriculture. A further decline reduced female agricultural employment to roughly 18 million women by 1976, half of them working on collective farms, a fourth on state farms, and the remaining fourth engaged in private subsidiary agriculture.[28]

This female agriculture labor force is aging, unskilled, and engaged in physically demanding labor, particularly on the collective farms.[29] A pattern common to other less developed societies has emerged in the Soviet Union as well, with men moving into more skilled and better-paid positions, often involving mechanized operations, while women are left to perform heavy manual labor.[30] Soviet commentators have themselves drawn attention to this situation, noting that "a peculiar division of labor has arisen between men and women: the sphere of mechanized work is a male privilege and that of manual labor is reserved to women."[31]

Despite official encouragement given to the wider enlistment of women

---

pp. 265–305; Dodge, "Recruitment and Quality," in Millar, *Soviet Rural Community*, pp. 180–213; Dodge, *Women in Soviet Economy*, pp. 160–75.

[28]The figures for 1970 were derived from *Narodnoe khoziaistvo SSSR: 1922–1972*, p. 283, and B. Urlanis, *Literaturnaia gazeta*, April 28, 1972, p. 10. Using the figure 26.6 million for the total agricultural labor force in 1971, of which 16.5 million workers are in the collective farm sector and 10 million on state farms, the number of women was computed by using the 1959 ratios. The figure arrived at is almost identical with the 12,632,741 reported in the 1970 census data, Tsentral'noe statisticheskoe upravlenie, *Itogi vsesoiuznoi perepisi: Tom 6*, p. 166. The additional 7 to 8 million women engaged in private subsidiary agriculture is based on estimates of the Foreign Demographic Analysis Division of the U.S. Department of Commerce. For 1975, see *Narodnoe khoziaistvo SSSR v 1975 g.* (Moscow, 1976), pp. 440, 542. This calculation assumes that slightly over 50 percent of kolkhoz workers, and 90 percent of all persons exclusively engaged in private subsidiary agriculture, are female.

[29]Of the 34 million agricultural workers reported in the 1959 census, some 24 million were recorded as unskilled, of which an estimated 80 percent were female, The 1970 data give this figure as 12.8 million of a total of 22.7 million, implying that almost all of the decline in agricultural employment between 1959 and 1970 was accounted for by this category. Indirect evidence that an extremely high proportion of women fall into this category is also found in the 1970 census data. While 12.6 million women are recorded as employed in agriculture, the enumerated specialties account for only 3.5 million workers. It may be inferred that the residual 9 million workers are largely unskilled.

[30]Esther Boserup, *Woman's Role in Economic Development* (London, 1970).

[31]Zinaida Monich, *Intelligentsiia v strukture sel'skogo naseleniia* (Minsk, 1971), as translated in *Soviet Sociology* 12 (Fall 1973): 12–13.

in skilled agricultural labor, particularly to training women as equipment operators, the distribution of women workers among various agricultural activities reveals the persistence of the traditional and sharply defined sexual division of labor that prevailed in prerevolutionary peasant communities. The portrait of the village of Viriatino painted in the famous ethnographic study reappears in the bare statistics of the 1970 census volumes.[32]

In the peasant communities this study described, women had the primary responsibility for household chores, for feeding livestock and tending poultry, and for work in vegetable and fruit gardens, while field work was divided, with men performing the more skilled tasks. As the figures for 1959 in Table 15 suggest, the sexual division of labor on the Soviet *kolkhoz* (collective farm) and *sovkhoz* (state farm) reflects the perpetuation of these older patterns. The overwhelming proportion of collective farm women were engaged in seasonal field work involving planting, cultivating, and harvesting crops. They constituted over 90 percent of milking personnel, swineherds, and poultry workers and 80 percent of vegetable growers, while forming under 10 percent of the workers in traditionally male agricultural activities and in the more mechanized modern sectors.

Over a decade later, the position of women in agriculture had not improved appreciably. Analyzing the structure of the female agricultural labor force in 1972 a Soviet economist concluded:

> Of all women employed in field work and animal husbandry on state farms, only 11.3 percent (25 percent in agriculture as a whole) worked with machinery or agricultural equipment. Among field workers—some two-thirds of all women farm workers—only 1.9 percent were engaged in mechanized labor, while for those employed in animal husbandry, the figure was 28 percent. Three percent worked basically by hand but used some mechanical equipment, while 85.7 percent worked completely by hand. In some republics the proportion working by hand was higher still, reaching 90 percent to 98 percent in some cases. The percentage of women tractor drivers and machine and combine operators on collective and state farms is no more than 0.5 percent to 0.6 percent.[33]

Part of the problem, in the view of this author, was the failure to train women in new skills precisely because traditional views about "male" and "female" labor persisted unchallenged. Although agricultural technical-vocational schools were required to teach men and women on an equal basis, the share of women among the students of such schools was in fact under 10 percent. Summing up the situation, she concluded sharply: "no

---

[32]A description of the sexual division of labor in prerevolutionary and postrevolutionary rural Russia is found in Sula Benet, ed. and trans,. *The Village of Viriatino* (New York, 1970), pp. 95–96, 225–56.

[33]M. Fedorova, "The Use of Women's Labor in Agriculture" *Voprosy èkonomiki*, translated in *Current Digest of the Soviet Press (CDSP)* 28, no. 18 (1976): 14–15.

TABLE 15

PERCENTAGE OF WOMEN AMONG COLLECTIVE AND STATE FARMERS
ENGAGED IN PREDOMINANTLY PHYSICAL LABOR, BY OCCUPATION, 1959

Occupation	Collective farmers (percent)	State farm and other workers (percent)
Administrative and supervisory personnel:		
Heads of livestock and poultry subfarms	15.0	25.2
Brigadiers of field brigades	8.3	12.9
Brigadiers of livestock brigades	12.8	18.0
Other brigadiers	5.2	9.3
Skilled workers and junior supervisory personnel:		
Bookkeepers	18.6	27.5
Tractor and combine drivers	0.8	0.7
Implement handlers and workers on agricultural machinery	1.4	5.1
Field-team leaders	87.3	85.5
Specialized agricultural workers:		
Workers in plant breeding and feed production	71.3	67.3
Cattle farm workers	60.4	47.0
Milking personnel	98.8	99.1
Stablemen and grooms	7.1	11.6
Swineherds	90.6	93.0
Herdsmen, drovers, shepherds	17.5	22.0
Other livestock workers	21.0	52.0
Poultry workers	93.4	94.3
Beekeepers	15.2	23.5
Orchard and vineyard workers	41.1	62.0
Vegetable and melon growers	80.6	78.2
Irrigators	10.8	18.5
Nonspecialized agricultural workers	66.0	63.4
Total employed in physical labor	60.1	44.6

SOURCE: Norton T. Dodge, "Recruitment and The Quality of The Soviet Agricultural Labor Force," in *The Soviet Rural Community*, ed. James R. Millar (Urbana, 1971), p. 183.

rural women are trained for skilled jobs in the nonproduction sector."[34]

Among those women engaged in agricultural labor, the cultivation of private plots occupies considerable time and energy. Because women's contribution to collective farming is more irregular and involves lower levels of skill, women collective farmers accumulate fewer work-days (credit for time worked) than their male counterparts.[35] However, they devote triple the amount of time men do to private plots.[36] The important contribution that women make to family income is not, therefore, measured only in wages from work on the collective farm. Indeed, the high return on labor devoted to private subsidiary agriculture makes this a rational expenditure of time.

Despite their heavy concentration in agriculture, few women occupy high administrative positions there. As a Soviet analyst commented, "a clear underestimation of the capacities and potentials of women as executive personnel is evident . . . When candidates are advanced for posts of leadership, men are a majority, although there are no adequate grounds for this."[37] Consequently, the proportion of women in lower level administrative and managerial roles has been relatively large for a long period of time, but upward mobility has been extremely limited. Only during World War II did the proportion of women holding chairmanships of collective farms or directorships of state farms become substantial, rising from 2.6 percent in 1940 to 14.2 percent in 1943 (and to as much as 27.2 percent near the front or in German-occupied areas).[38] However, such women were replaced by returning men in the postwar years. By 1961 women occupied fewer than 2 percent of these positions, and in 1975 they accounted for 1.5 percent of collective farm chairman and state farm directors.[39] As Khrushchev once remarked at an agricultural conference, "It turns out that it is men who do the administrating and the women who do the work."[40]

Upward mobility for rural women, therefore, tends to involve the de-

[34]*Ibid.*, p. 14. Similar views are expressed by Monich, *Intelligentsiia v strukture*, and by L. V. Ostapenko, "Vliianie novoi proizvodstvennoi roli zhenshchiny na ee polozhenie v sem'e," *Sovetskaia ètnografiia* 5 (1971): 95–102.

[35]In the Russian Republic, according to Fedorova, women devote 30 percent less time to social production than do men; "The Use of Women's Labor," p. 15.

[36]Ethel Dunn, "The Status of Rural Women in the Soviet Union" (Paper delivered at Conference on Women in Russia, Stanford University, May 1975). If, however, the time that women spend on private plots is counted into their working day, then women are occupied a total of 292 days a year, compared to 268 days for men.

[37]Monich, *Intelligentsiia v strukture*, p. 14.

[38]Jerry F. Hough, "The Changing Nature of the Kolkhoz Chairman," in Millar, *Soviet Rural Community*, p. 106. Statistics on the proportion of women in middle-level collective farm management are found in Robert C. Stuart, "Structural Change and the Quality of Soviet Collective Farm Management, 1952–1966," in Millar, *Soviet Rural Community*, p. 130.

[39]Fedorova, "The Use of Women's Labor," p. 14. Of a total of 29,033 collective farm chairmen, 524 were women; *Narodnoe khoziaistvo SSSR v 1974 g.*, p. 451.

[40]Dodge, "Recruitment and Quality," in Millar, *Soviet Rural Community*, p. 187.

parture from agricultural occupations. The proportion of women in agricultural higher educational institutions has been increasing only slightly in recent years, from 27 percent in 1960 to 32 percent in 1974, while the proportion of women in agricultural specialties at the secondary level has actually declined.[41] A few fields, such as agronomy and animal husbandry, have attracted increasing numbers of women at higher levels of skill. But, on the whole, upward mobility for rural women tends to mean careers in education, health, and other non-agricultural occupations rather than more skilled and responsible work in agriculture.[42]

Deploring this tendency for women to be concentrated in the "nonproductive" sphere while males dominated the production of tangibles, Zinaida Monich warned:

> One can hardly regard as a positive phenomenon the squeezing out of men from the sphere of education, culture and public health on such a scale. . . . The numerical predominance of female labor in the sphere not producing tangibles serves as a peculiar sort of psychological barrier to men's working in it . . . . Women are most common among agronomists, animal husbandry experts, economists and accountants, and virtually none are found among technicians and engineers. These occupations are associated with the servicing of equipment and for the most part remain male. For women, however, because of the nature of the work, they remain rather complicated to engage in, and not entirely convenient for combination with conducting a household.[43]

The low status of agricultural work, the limited opportunities for creativity, and the lack of physical and cultural amenities in rural areas motivate young women as well as men to leave the countryside. The rural exodus has taken on massive proportions in recent years, with an annual average net migration of 1.9 million.[44] If "the countryside is moving to the city," as a leading Soviet demographer recently remarked, the reasons are not difficult to comprehend. Young people find agricultural work extremely unattractive and are eager to avoid agricultural occupations, as numerous Soviet surveys have discovered.[45] Over 85 percent of Soviet

[41]"Zhenshchiny v SSSR," *Vestnik statistiki* 1 (January 1975): 90.

[42]A study of professional and paraprofessional workers in sixty-one Belorussian *kolkhozy* in 1967 found that women constituted 74.7 percent of those engaged in the "nonproductive" sphere and only 30.5 percent of those involved in the production of tangibles. Of 2,530 tractor and truck drivers, 5 were women. Monich, *Intelligentsiia v strukture*, pp. 12–13.

[43]Monich, *Intelligentsiia v strukture*, as translated in *Soviet Sociology* 12 (Winter 1973–74): 58.

[44]For a more comprehensive discussion, see David E. Powell, "The Rural Exodus," *Problems of Communism* 23 (November–December 1974).

[45]See in particular the Novosibirsk study by V. N. Shubkin in *Kolichestvennye metody v sotsiologicheskikh issledovaniiakh*, eds. A. G. Aganbegian, et al. (Novosibirsk, 1964), and the reviews of a series of Soviet studies in David Powell, "The Rural Exodus"; Dodge, "Recruitment and Quality," in Millar, *Soviet Rural Community*, pp. 205–9; and Stephen P. Dunn and Ethel Dunn, *The Peasants of Central Russia* (New York, 1967), pp. 85–88.

secondary school graduates who were asked about their career plans aspired to nonagricultural occupations, and rural young people even preferred to become industrial workers rather than join the rural intelligentsia. Although men have left the countryside in larger numbers than women, girls predominate among the youngest migrants, those between age sixteen and nineteen. Enhanced educational opportunities in the cities are a major attraction, and rural families appear to share the aspiration of their daughters for the increased mobility that education will bring, as the reflections of a collective farm chairman in a recent novel suggest:

> The elderly kolkhoz women on whose shoulders had rested all the hardships of the postwar confusion had now faded away: the hands of one were deformed by rheumatism; another had developed a hernia, a third—some other ailment. Yes, and how could you achieve a sharp increase in farm output with these half-literate women: all they knew was how to pitch hay, in the ancient way, for the cattle. So you had to round up the senior schoolgirls and keep them at it for weeks and months on end. If a girl herself was willing, her mother would be up in arms. What? Have my daughter raking manure? Was it for this that the old man and me broke our backs so she could get an education?[46]

Young rural women graduating from pedagogical institutes or medical facilities go to great lengths to avoid assignment to rural regions. As one study complained, "many of the young women who were graduating began to arrange weddings with eligible city bachelors, while the men suddenly began to suffer from heart disease and terrible headaches."[47] Current efforts to raise living standards and enhance the attractiveness of rural life by improving cultural amenities and providing a wider range of services may slow the rural exodus, but those young people who leave are often precisely those with education, skills, and ambition, whose continued presence would enhance the quality of rural life.

In contrast to agricultural work, industrial occupations offer women wider opportunities for advancement and upward mobility. Indeed, the basic changes in occupational structure that accompanied the early stages of industrialization encouraged women to enter new fields in industry. The first wave of women to enter industry in the early 1930s consisted of unskilled workers with little education. The number of women with specialized training in industrial fields was extremely low at first, but with extensive governmental encouragement, the number and proportion grew

[46]Fedor Abramov, *The New Life* (New York, 1963), pp. 25–26. The poor educational opportunities available in the countryside for oneself or one's children was cited as a major motive for leaving by almost one-fourth of the adults questioned in a survey by T. I. Zaslavskaia, *Migratsiia sel'skogo naseleniia*, cited by Powell, "The Rural Exodus," p. 5.

[47]*Pravda*, July 16, 1972. See also A. Andreev, "When Will the Teacher Arrive?" *Izvestiia*, April 23, 1972, p. 3, and the discussion by Christian Duevel, "Two Ways to Activate the Soviet Rural Intelligentsia," *Radio Liberty Dispatch*, April 8, 1968, p. 5.

rapidly between 1930 and 1950. There was little change from 1950 to 1960, but since then the proportion has risen further. Soviet sources provide little information about the proportions of women workers at different levels of skill in industry. But the fragmentary data available suggest that although they have begun to enter the middle and higher levels, they predominate in low-level unmechanized and unskilled jobs. Several small-scale studies found that women constituted 70 to 80 percent of all workers in the two lowest skill classifications and 5 to 10 percent of those in the two highest. In one case, 94.5 percent of all female workers, compared to 47.8 percent of the males, were classified in the three lowest grades. At a majority of factories surveyed in one study, there were no women in the higher skilled groups at all.[48]

A more detailed sketch of the pattern of female industrial employment was offered by a study conducted in Moscow. The study found that in the first and second skill categories, the lowest on the scale, women outnumbered men by five to one, while in the three highest skill groups, men outnumbered women by five to one. Only 8.5 percent of the women, but 43 percent of the men, were located in the higher earnings brackets.[49] This pattern was not confined exclusively to an older generation of women with lower levels of education and skills. In twenty-five industrial enterprises in Leningrad that were the subject of another study, 11 percent of those engaged in hard physical labor were women under age thirty, while this age group formed only 2.3 percent of highly qualified professionals.[50] A Soviet specialist on female employment concluded that, on the basis of the available evidence, there has been no appreciable growth in recent years in the proportion of highly qualified and highly paid women workers.[51]

In white-collar positions in industry, the proportion of women is significantly greater than among skilled workers. Engineering in particular is a field that women have entered in large numbers. The number of female engineers increased tenfold between 1941 and 1964, from 44,000 to 460,000, and another large increase brought the total to over 1,000,000 in 1970. Engineering appears to be a profession in which women are underrepresented; women engineers constitute only 40 percent of the total number.[52] However, the absolute number of women engineers is twice

---

[48]V. K. Mikhailiuk, *Ispol'zovanie zhenskogo truda*, pp. 73–77; N. M. Shishkan, *Trud zhen-shchin v usloviiakh razvitogo sotsializma* (Kishinev, 1976), p. 137; A. E. Kotliar and S. Ia. Tur-chaninova, *Zaniatost' zhenshchin v proizvodstve* (Moscow, 1975), pp. 67–68.

[49]*Trud*, December 19, 1973, p. 2.

[50]E. Z. Danilova, *Sotsial'nye problemy truda zhenshchiny-rabotnitsy* (Moscow, 1968), p. 21.

[51]*Ibid.*, p. 23.

[52]Tsentral'noe statisticheskoe upravlenie, *Itogi vsesoiuznoi perepisi: Tom 6*, p. 169. Outside the Soviet Union, the highest percentage of women engineers is found in Finland, where they form 3.6 percent of the total. In Great Britain they form 0.4 percent of the total, and in Norway 0.6 percent (Marjorie Galenson, *Women and Work* [Ithaca, N. Y., 1973], p. 26).

as large as the number of women physicians, a field in which women predominate. Engineering is thus an example of a field in which Soviet development priorities, including an emphasis on the training of large numbers of industrial technicians and specialists, both male and female, have resulted in patterns of female employment substantially at variance with those of other industrial societies.

A background in engineering is almost a prerequisite for advancement to positions of responsibility in Soviet industry, and it is possible that the concentration of women at lower levels of the hierarchy of authority in industry may be partly explained by the lateness of their entry into this field in large numbers. Scattered evidence suggests that there has been some progress in recent years in bringing more women into high-level managerial positions. The proportion of women enterprise directors, for example, rose from an infinitesimal 1 percent of the total in 1956 to 6 percent in 1963 and to 13 percent in 1970. Excluding *sovkhoz* directors, and looking only at industrial enterprises, women constituted 9 percent of all directors in 1975 and almost one-fourth of all heads of production-technical sections and subgroups.[53] Yet although women do seem to hold a rather respectable proportion of responsible positions in economic life, by comparison with other industrial societies, they have not moved into such positions in the proportions that one might expect on the basis of their training, work experience, and the existence of large industries, such as textiles, which are largely female in composition (Table 16). When we bear in mind that women constitute almost 65 percent of the key administrative age cohort, their absence in managerial roles is striking indeed.

Complaints that insufficient attention is paid to recruiting women to leading positions recur with predictable regularity in official pronouncements. Expressing doubts that exhortations produce real results, a Soviet specialist proposed a more radical solution: the adoption, in effect, of sexual quotas along the lines that have been proposed for national minorities, with the number of women in managerial positions to be proportional to the number of women working under their management.[54]

The predominance of women in white-collar occupations, particularly of a nonprofessional kind, is associated with the erosion of the boundaries that formerly separated them from skilled manual work.[55] The increasing complexity of occupational structure has tended to undermine the blue-collar–white-collar distinction in all industrial societies, but the trend has

[53]Tsentral'noe statisticheskoe upravlenie, *Zhenshchiny i deti v SSSR*, p. 102; *Itogi vsesoiuznoi perepisi: Tom 6*, p. 165; for 1975, "Zhenshchiny v SSSR," p. 80.
[54]Tolkunova, *Pravo zhenshchin*, p. 103.
[55]Frank Parkin, *Class Inequality and Political Order* (New York, 1971); David Lane, *The End of Inequality: Stratification Under State Socialism* (London, 1971); Walter Connor, "Blue Collars, White Collars and Inequality" (Paper presented at 8th World Congress of Sociology, Toronto, Canada, August, 1974).

Women in Soviet Society

TABLE 16
WOMEN IN RESPONSIBLE POSITIONS IN ECONOMIC ENTERPRISES, 1959 AND 1970

Position	Number of women 1959	Number of women 1970	Percent of total 1959	Percent of total 1970
Enterprise management (including industry, construction, agriculture, forestry, transport, communications and their structural subdivisions)	140,567	255,732	13	16
Of which:				
Directors of enterprises (including *sovkhoz* directors)	35,637	41,968	12	13
Heads of production—technical departments, sectors, groups, offices	26,489	94,489	20	24
Heads of shops, sections, departments, and foremen	54,220	98,175	15	15
Managers of livestock departments of collective and state farms	22,273	18,394	16	22

SOURCE: Tsentral'noe statisticheskoe upravlenie, *Itogi vsesoiuznoi perepisi naseleniia 1970 goda: Tom 6* (Moscow, 1973), p. 167. According to figures for 1973, women were 9 percent of all directors of industrial enterprises; Tsentral'noe statisticheskoe upravlenie, *Zhenshchiny v SSSR* (Moscow, 1975), p. 80.

been more dramatic in socialist countries, where the traditional status of nonmanual labor was particularly great. The relative status and income level of skilled workers has been raised, while that of routine white-collar work has diminished. The two groups continue to differ in many aspects of their life styles. But for women it is particularly important that at a time of rising female educational attainments the close association of education, income, and status is being eroded.

A number of Soviet studies of occupational structure illuminate the implications of this trend, although they do not touch on the sexual aspects of occupational structure directly. For example, an investigation of a Soviet factory conducted in Sverdlovsk in 1969 found that only modest differences in the educational level of workers and employees were accompanied by wide differences in monthly wages.[56] Just 6 percent of workers but 27.7 percent of employees fell into the lowest wage category (66 to 80 rubles per month) while, at the upper end of the wage scale, 41.1 per-

[56]L. G. Kamovich and O. V. Kozlovskaia, "Sotsial'nye razlichiia sredi rabotnikov umstvennogo truda na promyshlennom predpriatii," cited by Connor, "Blue Collars," p. 15.

cent of workers and only 0.6 percent of employees earned over 160 rubles per month. This pattern of occupational stratification is inseparable from sexual differentiation: 95.5 percent of the employees were women. Thus, the tendency for women to occupy routine, nonmanual positions is also associated with the lower pay characteristic of these occupations, by comparison with skilled manual work in which women are underrepresented.

An even more detailed insight into the social structure of Soviet industry is offered by a study of machine-building enterprises in Leningrad conducted by O. I. Shkaratan.[57] The labor force at these enterprises was broken down into eight categories: (1) managers and organizers of production; (2) skilled scientific and technical personnel; (3) skilled nonmanual workers; (4) skilled workers combining manual and nonmanual functions; (5) skilled manual workers; (6) skilled machine tenders; (7) other nonmanual workers; and (8) unskilled manual workers. A number of indicators of social position were then given for each category, including average educational level, income, and Party membership. The 1970 census data for the Russian Republic can be used to make a very approximate estimate of the proportion of women in each category, permitting us to make some very interesting observations. (Table 17). The group in which the highest proportion of women is found is at the bottom of the scale in income, though at the middle range in educational level. Unskilled manual workers show the lowest level of educational achievement, but rank higher in income. Skilled nonmanual workers, another category in which women are strongly represented, rank near the top of the educational scale but below the income level of most categories of skilled workers. Only among the skilled scientific and technical personnel, where women form almost half the total, are education and wages roughly correlated. The implications of this pattern of stratification for average male and female incomes will be explored shortly. As for the relationship of education and status, the pattern of stratification that characterizes Soviet industry suggests that the higher proportion of women in general secondary schools is of marginal utility in occupational terms, while the characteristic educational and career choices of boys are more highly rewarded in the occupational structure.

It is primarily in professional careers, then, that women's increasing educational attainments find their reward. An extremely high proportion of women is found among professional workers with higher education —52 percent of the total. Teachers constitute the largest group, followed by engineers and then physicians. But in the professions, as in agriculture and in industry, the proportion of women declines as the level of responsibility rises.

[57]O. I. Shkaratan, "Sotsial'naia struktura sovetskogo rabochego klassa," *Voprosy filosofii* 1 (1967): 28–39.

TABLE 17

THE SOCIAL STRUCTURE OF A SAMPLE OF MACHINE-BUILDING

ENTERPRISES BY INCOME, EDUCATION, AND SEX (LENINGRAD, 1965)

Occupational Classification	Income (Unskilled worker =100)	Education (in years)	Party membership (percent)	Proportion female (percent)
Managers and organizers of production	177	13.6	54.4	16
Skilled scientific and technical personnel	130	14.0	19.8	46
Skilled mental workers (technologists, bookkeepers)	113	12.5	19.6	87
Skilled workers combining mental and manual functions— (mechanics—adjusters)	132	8.8	23.4	8
Skilled manual workers (metal workers, fitters, mounters, welders)	123	8.3	16.2	10
Skilled machine-tenders (machine operators, punchers)	110	8.2	12.2	30
Mental workers of middle-level skills (inspectors, sorters, accounting personnel)	86	9.1	7.8	90
Unskilled manual workers	100	6.5	3.7	34

SOURCES: O. I. Shkaratan, "Sotsial'naia struktura sovetskogo rabochego klassa," *Voprosy filosofii*, No. 1 (1967): 36, and Tsentral'noe statisticheskoe upravlenie, *Itogi vsesoiuznoi perepisi naseleniia 1970 goda: Tom 6* (Moscow, 1973), pp. 170–74.

This tendency can be seen most clearly in the two professions dominated by women, education and medicine. While women represented 79 percent of the teachers of grades one through eleven in 1975–1976 and 83 percent of the directors of primary schools, they constituted 33 percent of the directors of eight-year schools and 29 percent of the directors of secondary schools. (Table 18).[58] As Table 18 indicates, these figures have

[58]"Zhenshchiny v SSSR," p. 89. For purposes of comparison, women constitute about 50 percent of elementary teachers in Denmark, Norway, and the Federal Republic of Germany; 66 percent in France; 75 percent in Sweden and Great Britain; and 85 percent in the United States. (Galenson, *Women and Work*, p. 27). The low status of teaching is the subject

TABLE 18

PROPORTION OF WOMEN EMPLOYED IN PRIMARY AND
SECONDARY EDUCATION, 1955/56, 1960/61, AND 1975/76

	Percent women		
Position	1955/56	1960/61	1975/76
Directors of secondary schools	21	20	29
Directors of 8-year schools	22	23	33
Deputy directors of secondary schools	—	53	65
Deputy directors of 8-year schools	—	54	61
Directors of primary schools	67	69	83
Teachers: Total	70	70	}71
Grades 5–11		—	
Grades 1–4		87	}79

SOURCES: Tsentral'noe statisticheskoe upravlenie, *Zhenshchiny i deti v SSSR* (Moscow, 1963), p. 127; "Zhenshchiny v SSSR," *Vestnik statistiki* 1 (January 1977), p. 89.

been rising steadily. However, the proportion of women among administrators and other specialists at higher levels of the educational system is substantially lower.

The all-Union figures do not convey the wide scope of regional variations in this profession. The highest ratio of women teachers is found in the Baltic republics, with women constituting 83 percent of all teachers in Estonia, 81 percent in Latvia, and 80 percent for Lithuania.[59] In the Russian Republic, women constitute 78 percent; in the Ukraine, 73 percent; and in Belorussia, 71 percent. In the three Central Asian republics and in Azerbaidzhan, by contrast, women teachers are in the minority —34 percent in Tadzhikistan, 39 percent in Turkmenistan, and 43 percent in Uzbekistan. The correlation between female educational attainment and entry of women into the teaching profession is very great. Other variables, however, linked to cultural traditions, appear to affect the mobility of women in terms of administrative positions. The highest proportion (by a substantial margin) of women school directors is found in Latvia, and the lowest is found in Armenia.

The structure of the medical profession reflects a similar tendency for

---

of numerous articles in the Soviet press commenting on the difficulty of developing adequate training programs in pedagogical institutes and of assuring the placement of teachers in rural schools. One recent article criticized the disparaging attitude toward teaching held by instructors at pedagogical institutes. The graduates of such programs frequently do not take up the teaching positions to which they are assigned, "trying instead to get a job anywhere but in a school" ("In Order to Train a Teacher," *Pravda*, June 4, 1971, p. 3).

[59]Tsentral'noe statisticheskoe upravlenie, *Narodnoe obrazovanie, nauka i kultura v SSSR* (Moscow, 1971), p. 122.

the proportion of women to decline as the level of training, responsibility, status, and income rises. Nursing is almost completely female. Similarly, women constitute the overwhelming majority of physicians assigned to practice in rural areas. Women also tend to be concentrated in internal medicine and constitute over 90 percent of pediatricians but only 6 percent of surgeons (compared to 5 percent in the United States). The more prestigious medical assignments, especially in urban areas, and those that involve administrative responsibilities, have higher proportions of males. Thus, while seven out of ten physicians are women, half of the chief physicians and supervisory personnel are male.[60] This situation has been noted even in Soviet writings, one observer commenting: "Even given an equal level of professional preparation representatives of the stronger sex as a rule hold the managerial posts. How does one explain that while men comprise 15 percent of all medical personnel, they are 50 percent of all chief physicians and executives of medical institutions. . . . In the overwhelming majority of cases, it is men who head departments, enterprises, and administrative agencies."[61]

Moreover, the effort to improve the quality of training and medical care in recent years and the increase in pay have been associated with a decline in the proportion of women in the profession. The share of women admitted to medical schooling was reportedly reduced by decree in the mid-1960s, from 85 to 65 percent,[62] and current medical enrollments are 54 percent female. This trend has resulted in a fall in the proportion of female physicians, from 77 percent in 1950, to 74 percent in 1965, to 69 percent in 1976. A recent Western visitor was told that the Soviet goal was a profession evenly divided between males and females.

The same considerations that motivated the preferential admission of males to higher medical institutions may account for the disproportionately heavy enrollment of women in health-related fields at the secondary level. An official Soviet source estimates that the annual cost of training a student at a technicum is roughly 500 rubles, while at institutions of higher education the cost is 900 rubles and the length of training is more

[60]Tsentral'noe statisticheskoe upravlenie, *Itogi vsesoiuznoi perepisi: Tom 6*, p. 168. In Europe, medicine, along with dentistry and pharmacy, has traditionally been regarded as an occupation suitable for women. While the proportion of women physicans is particularly high in the Soviet Union, the low proportion of women in the American medical profession is also exceptional. Women constituted 6.7 percent of physicians in the United States in 1960 and 9 percent in 1970. In Western Europe in the mid-1960s, the proportions were 12.8 percent in France, 17.4 percent in Sweden, 18 percent in Great Britain and Italy, 20 percent in the Federal Republic of Germany, and 23.4 percent in Finland. (Galenson, *Women and Work*, p. 24).
[61]M. Sonin, *Literaturnaia gazeta*, April 16, 1969.
[62]John C. Bowers, "Special Problems of Women Medical Students," *Journal of Medical Education* 4 (May 1968): 532–37.

extended.[63] But the educational level attained at an earlier stage of the life cycle is more decisive for women than for men because of the constraints of family responsibilities. More limited opportunities for upgrading professional skills at later stages of their careers may compound women's disadvantaged position in seeking professional advancement. Thus, the argument that the low proportion of women in positions at the top of their professions more generally reflects the time lag necessary to overcome earlier educational disadvantages would not seem valid for these two professions, where the proportion of women with specialized secondary or higher education was already high in the 1930s and 1940s.

A final area of our investigation involves the role of women at the apex of the scholarly and scientific world. As we noted in Chapter IV (Table 9), there has been a very rapid rate of growth in the total number of women scientific workers in the two decades since 1950. However, their proportion of the total has remained rather stable: 36 percent in 1950, 36 percent in 1960, 38 percent in 1965, and 40 percent in 1975. Moreover, women tend to be more heavily concentrated at lower levels of the profession. Women constitute 50 percent of junior research associates and assistants, 24 percent of senior research associates, 22 percent of associate professors, and only 10 percent of academicians, corresponding members, and professors. As of 1977, there were 14 women among the 749 members of the prestigious and powerful USSR Academy of Sciences; 3 were full members and 11 were corresponding members.[64] In academic and scientific life, as in other areas we have examined, women play an important role in the profession as a whole, have advanced to positions of some responsibility, but are largely absent at the apex of the profession. In scientific work as in other fields, the proportion of women is inversely related to rank.

Thus, patterns of female employment in the Soviet Union are not altogether unlike those that prevail in the United States and in Western Europe. The large proportion of women performing heavy, unskilled physical labor, in industry as well as in agriculture, is perhaps the most striking difference, although the high proportion of women in technical fields and in the professions is equally noteworthy. Extensive opportunities for women in an educational system that puts great emphasis on scientific and technical training has facilitated the entry of women into scientific and technical occupations, such as medicine and engineering, on an unprecedented scale. But in the middle ranges of the occupational hierarchy, occupational segregation remains great, with men predomi-

---

[63]Tsentral'noe statisticheskoe upravlenie, *Zhenshchiny i deti v SSSR*, p. 22.
[64]Central Intelligence Agency Reference Aid, *Membership, USSR Academy of Sciences* (Washington, D.C., 1977). No women were members of the Presidium.

nating in skilled labor while large numbers of women are engaged in clerical work, in the paraprofessions, and in the service sector of the economy.
Upper levels of management remain a male preserve.

THE IMPACT OF OCCUPATIONAL STRATIFICATION ON EARNINGS

The combination of horizontal and vertical segregation of the labor
market in the Soviet Union must inevitably result in a considerable gap
between average male and female incomes. Unfortunately, the absence
of Soviet data permitting a direct and accurate comparison of the average
annual earnings of women with those of men at comparable levels of educational achievement renders any effort at analysis extremely speculative,
but there are several reasons to suspect that substantial disparities exist.

First, the Soviet wage structure explicitly reflects larger political and
economic priorities. The division of branches of industry into groups of
widely differing political and economic importance has a direct effect on
wage levels. The preferred economic sectors are precisely those in which
women are underrepresented—heavy industry and construction—while
light industry and the service sector, which have high concentrations of
women, are at the low end of the scale of priorities. Although a uniform
scale for classifying skills, and therefore wages, ensures a certain unifor-
mity within categories, the base rates for each sector differ, as do the
range of wage differentials and the scope of bonuses. In light industry,
for example, starting wage rates are lower and the range of wages narrower than in heavy industry.

The effect of this pattern on incomes can be illustrated by looking at
the income of a chief engineer. The monthly wage of a chief engineer in
the coal industry is 380 rubles. In ferrous metallurgy, an engineer with
identical training and functions would earn 270 to 320 rubles; in machine-
building, 260 to 300; in light industry, 200 to 210; and in the food industry, 180 to 200 rubles.[65] Similar differences exist at all levels of the
occupational structure. Both the economic sectors and the professions in
which women predominate—light industry, trade, communications, health
and culture, communal services and housing, clerical work, medicine, and
teaching—are among the most poorly paid. Wage increases in these areas
lag behind the national average. In education, for example, over a period
of twenty years, wages increased only two-thirds as much as they did for
the economy as a whole (Table 19). In such professions as teaching and

[65] Andreas Tenson, "Wage and Salary Rates in the Production Sphere of the Soviet
Economy," *Radio Liberty Dispatch*, June 15, 1973, pp. 11–12; Tsentral'noe statisticheskoe
upravlenie, *Narodnoe khoziaistvo SSSR v 1970 g.* (Moscow, 1971), p. 516; U.S. Department
of Commerce, Foreign Demographic Analysis Division, *Wages in the USSR, 1950–1967:
Education* (Washington, D.C., 1969), p. 19; *Health Services* (April 1968), pp. 18–19. See also
Janet Chapman, "Equal Pay for Equal Work?" in Atkinson, Dallin, and Lapidus, *Women
in Russia.*

TABLE 19

AVERAGE ANNUAL WAGES IN THE EDUCATION
SECTOR AND THE NATIONAL AVERAGE, 1950 TO 1972

Year	Education Wages (in rubles)	Index	National average Wages (in rubles)	Index
1950	800	100	767	100
1955	844	106	858	112
1960	839	105	961	125
1963	904	113	1051	137
1965	1123	140	1147	150
1967	1157	145	1241	162
1968	1233	154	1352	176
1970	1270	159	1464	191
1971	1289	161	1511	197
1972	1352	169	1562	204

SOURCES: George Hoffberg, *Wages in the USSR, 1950–1967: Education* (Foreign Demographic Analysis Division, Bureau of the Census, U.S. Department of Commerce, 1969), p. 19; personal communication from Murray Feshbach, Chief, USSR/East Europe branch, Foreign Demographic Analysis Division, U.S. Department of Commerce.

medicine, however, a shorter workday may partially compensate for lower wages. As Table 20 indicates, a ranking of economic sectors by their average monthly salaries demonstrates a high correlation between female participation and wage levels.

Second, the effects of horizontal stratification further compound this basic disadvantage. The virtual absence of women in the highly skilled categories of the labor force, combined with their lower seniority and limited mobility,[66] also exerts downward pressure on wages, while the paucity of women in managerial positions deprives them of the valuable opportunity to earn the larger bonuses as a supplement to basic salary.

Finally, although Soviet law requires that equal work receive equal pay, there is no way to ensure that women are placed in positions commensurate with their training and skills. A number of Soviet writers have noted that women's employment differs substantially from men's in that women have fewer jobs to choose from. Thus, more than twice as many women as men reported in surveys that they were holding their present jobs because no other, more suitable ones, were available to them. Married women experience additional difficulty in finding suitable employment because the family's place of residence is usually determined by the

[66]A study of women in Odessa enterprises indicated their work seniority was 1.5 to 2.0 times lower than that of men. Mikhailiuk, *Ispol'zovanie zhenskogo truda*, pp. 79–81.

Women in Soviet Society

TABLE 20

DISTRIBUTION OF WOMEN WORKERS AND EMPLOYEES AND AVERAGE MONTHLY
EARNINGS, BY ECONOMIC SECTOR, 1975

Economic sector	Number of women workers and employees	Women as percent of labor force	Average monthly earnings (rubles)
Construction	3,002,000	28	176.8
Transport	2,211,000	24	173.5
Industry (production personnel)	1,662,000	49	162.0
Science and scientific services	2,015,000	50	155.4
Nationwide average	*52,539,000*	*51*	*145.8*
Credit and state insurance	423,000	82	133.8
Apparatus of government and economic administration	1,457,000	65	130.6
Education	5,904,000	73	126.9
Agriculture	4,530,000	44	126.8
Communications	1,042,000	68	123.6
Housing and municipal economy, everyday services	2,010,000	53	109.0
Trade, public catering, materials and equipment, supply and sales	6,763,000	76	108.7
Arts	207,000	47	103.1
Public health, physical culture, social welfare	4,851,000	84	102.3
Culture	747,000	73	92.2

SOURCES: Calculated from figures given in Tsentral'noe statisticheskoe upravlenie, *Narodnoe khoziaistvo SSSR v 1975 g.* (Moscow, 1976), pp. 542–43; 546–47.

husband's job. Large numbers of women specialists reportedly work at jobs that could have been filled by less qualified persons. The underutilization of women is one more factor contributing to lower levels of remuneration even with comparable educational and professional attainments.

Soviet sources provide only fragmentary glimpses of male-female wage differentials, usually based on local surveys of particular groups of enterprises. One such study of factory workers in the mid-1960s found that the average wage of women workers was 69.3 percent that of males.[67] A second study, relying on a sample of 15,000 workers in Kievan light industrial enterprises, yielded a somewhat narrower differential: women's wages reportedly ranged from 83 to 90 percent of men's.[68] Finally, indirect evidence of a different kind is provided by a study of newlyweds in Kiev between 1971 and 1973. The average earnings of males in this sample were 116 rubles a month, compared to 84 rubles a month for their spouses; three-fourths of the men and one-third of the women were earning over 100 rubles a month.[69] These figures show a considerable resemblance to male-female income differences reported for several East European countries, where more complete data is available. A comprehensive study based on national income data for Czechoslovakia, for example, concluded that female earnings in 1973 were about 67 percent those of males, while in Poland they were 66.5 percent, and in Hungary, in the state sector only, they were 73 percent.[70]

The absence of national data makes it impossible to calculate with any precision the extent of the differential between average male and female earnings in the economy as a whole or to explore the relative weight of different factors in producing it. The high rates of full-time female labor-force participation in the USSR and the relative equality of women's educational attainments among the younger generation might be expected to reduce the influence of the two main factors that result in lower average wages for women in Western industrial societies. Nevertheless, a recent Western study which estimated that per capita female income in the USSR was roughly 87 percent that of males understates the likely differential.[71] The presence of considerable male-female wage disparities within individual enterprises as well as between male-dominated and female-dominated economic sectors suggests that female earnings are more heavily concentrated at the lower end of the wage scale. The published Soviet data themselves point to female earnings which fall between two-thirds

[67]A. L. Pimenova, "Sem'ia i perspektivy razvitiia obshchestvennogo truda zhenshchin pri sotsializme," *Nauchnye doklady vysshei shkoly: Filosofskie nauki*, No. 3, 1966, p. 40.

[68]N. A. Sakharova, *Optimal'nye vozmozhnosti ispol'zovaniia zhenskogo truda v sfere obshchestvennogo proizvodstva* (Kiev, 1973), pp. 28–31. The differentials in base pay were smaller than those found in supplementary wages.

[69]L. V. Chuiko, *Braki i razvody* (Moscow, 1975), p. 87.

[70]Benedikt Korda, "The Status of Women in a Socialist Country," *Osteuropa-Wirtschaft* 3 (1976): 205–14. Jan M. Michal, "An Alternate Approach to Measuring Income Inequality" (Paper presented at annual meeting of The American Association for the Advancement of Slavic Studies, Banff, 1974).

[71]William Moskoff, "An Estimate of the Soviet Male-Female Income Gap," *The ACES Bulletin* 16 (Fall 1974): 24. Moskoff's calculations were based on the first breakdown of wages by branch of the economy published in the USSR in three decades, *Trud v SSSR* (Moscow, 1968).

and three-fourths of male earnings. Moreover, the assumption that the second income in a family amounts to two-thirds the primary income is so widespread in Soviet economic writings as to be virtually axiomatic. Finally, recent studies of emigre families indicate female earnings which are 67 percent those of males.[72] In view of the tendency of Soviet authors to interpret similar wage differentials in capitalist countries as evidence of direct sex discrimination, a more comprehensive explanation of the presence of such differentials in the USSR and Eastern Europe would be instructive.

THE SOCIAL BASES OF OCCUPATIONAL SEGREGATION

The pattern of sexual stratification in the Soviet labor force that we have described is the result of several factors. The educational lag offers a partial but not sufficient explanation of the relative absence of women in important administrative and executive roles. In many areas the steady gains that one would anticipate by projecting earlier educational statistics onto the relevant professions have not occurred.

Differential aspirations appear to play a significant role. A lower proportion of Soviet women than men express an interest in a career rather than a job; only one-third of the women in a recent opinion survey expressed a desire to upgrade their skills, compared with over half of the male respondents.[73] But lower aspiration may reflect a realistic evaluation of the likely return on investments of additional time and energy; it may also reflect the greater claims on women's time made by household and childrearing tasks, which, as we shall see in Chapter VII, are still viewed as "women's work." The "double shift" of working wives means that they have demonstrably less leisure time for enhancing professional skills than their male counterparts.[74]

The differential valuation of occupations also continues to play an important role in shaping patterns of female labor-force participation. Recent Soviet sociological studies, as we have seen, trace the development of sex-based differences in the evaluation of different occupations back to early childhood. By the time students graduate from secondary school, these general orientations have influenced their evaluation of specific occupations.

We have discussed these differences in connection with educational orientations; it is useful to look at them once again in the light of our findings about occupational stratification. A study conducted in Lenin-

[72]Personal communication from Gur Ofer.
[73]G. V. Osipov and S. F. Frolov, "Vnerabochee vremia i ego ispol'zovanie," cited in David Lane, *Politics and Society in the USSR* (London, 1971), p. 355.
[74]*Ibid.* This survey of 2683 factory employees in Gorkii *oblast'* discovered that, while male respondents devoted 18.16 hours per week to improving professional qualifications, the corresponding figure for female respondents was 11.65 hours.

grad asked secondary school graduates to rank forty occupations in the order of their attractiveness.[75] The consistent tendency of girls to assign higher rankings to all teaching, medical, and cultural occupations and of boys to rank engineering and skilled technical positions more highly is extremely congruent with the distribution of men and women within the occupational structure. While men and women may seek somewhat different rewards from their jobs, the rating scale adopted by boys is far more congruent with the hierarchy of material rewards conferred by the economic system itself. Thus, differential preferences and valuations both reinforce and are in turn reinforced by the sexual segregation of the labor force.

More subtle prejudices, if not overt discrimination, also continue to play a role in shaping women's professional opportunities. Women are widely believed to have little initiative on the job, to be less creative, and to be less suited by nature for managerial positions, a number of Soviet studies found; although they deny that such views have any basis in fact.[76] Thus, deeply rooted attitudes about authority clearly affect the allocation of male and female roles. An intensive study of a team of scientific workers revealed that women as well as men expressed a preference for males in superordinate roles, with women preferred by both as subordinates.[77] The association of authority with males thus permeates Soviet writings. In the course of a far-reaching discussion of the recruitment and training of industrial executives, which extended over several issues of *Literaturnaia gazeta*, it took a letter from an irate female reader to point out that "for some reason it seems taken for granted that an executive is a man."[78]

But the character and values of the Soviet political system have also contributed to this pattern. The emphasis on participation in production as the guarantee of full equality, for example, neglected the political and cultural dimensions of sex roles, and these have proven more persistent and less responsive to economic arrangements than was anticipated. Only recently have Soviet scholars called for exploration of the psycho-historical roots of sex-based occupational preferences.

Moreover, the commitment to rapid industrialization, with the mobilization of manpower it entailed, created a climate hostile to changes in social relationships and values that might threaten the overriding objectives of productivity. Inadequate provision of child-care and household services was but one of a range of problems created by the pattern of

[75]V. V. Vodzinskaia, "Orientations Toward Occupations," in *Social Stratification and Mobility in the USSR*, ed. M. Yanowitch and W. Fisher (White Plains, N.Y. 1973).

[76]M. Pavlova, *Literaturnaia gazeta*, September 22, 1971, p. 13.

[77]V. N. Shubkin and G. M. Kochetov, "Rukovoditel', kollega, podchinennyi," *Sotsial'nye issledovaniia* 2 (1968): 143–55.

[78]*Literaturnaia gazeta*, September 15, 1976, p. 10.

economic choices. Differential patterns of schooling, which channel women
into the labor force at somewhat lower levels of skill, have reflected discriminatory admissions policies in higher education—policies that could
be readily altered if narrowly economic considerations were deemphasized
in favor of other priorities.

Several conclusions emerge from this brief survey of the participation
of women in the Soviet economy. First, the interaction of demographic
and economic pressures has played a critical role in bringing about high
rates of female employment. The deficit of males combined with the need
of an expanding economy for labor to provide the structural background
for the massive entry of women into the nonagricultural labor force. In
addition, economic organization has been a decisive factor in both encouraging and channeling the economic activities of Soviet women. The
command economy, with its system of central planning—which includes
educational and manpower planning—vastly enhances the capacity of the
political leadership to alter the economic roles of women. The centralization of political as well as economic authority has also facilitated the
development of programs to support new economic roles: maternal legislation, child-care facilities, educational opportunities. Finally, high rates
of participation were sustained by social and cultural norms that insisted
that women as well as men would find in paid employment the opportunity for personal satisfaction while contributing to the development of
the larger society.

Second, the organization of the Soviet economy made possible a very
high degree of control over the *terms* of women's entry into the labor force.
The maintenance of low wage levels has forced women into economic
roles even in the absence of extensive child-care facilities and other supporting institutions, leaving women without much freedom to choose not
to work or to reshape the terms of their employment to suit individual
needs. Under these conditions, women attempted to balance work and
family responsibilities by limiting their commitment to both.

The pattern of growth of the economy has also shaped women's roles.
In the economy of the 1920s, there was little change in women's roles.
They began to enter the labor force in large numbers, and in new areas,
only with the vast expansion inaugurated by the Five Year Plans, when
rapid industrialization created new opportunities for structural upward
mobility. Manpower needs have been more decisive than ideology in
shaping women's roles in the economic sector.

Thirdly, the distinctive character of Soviet economic development has
led to patterns of female labor-force participation that differ in some respects from those found in Western industrial societies. The emphasis on
heavy industry and the neglect, until recently, of agriculture, housing,
consumer goods, and the service sector have affected women's economic

roles in unique ways. The large proportion of women performing heavy, unskilled physical labor, in industry as well as in agriculture, and the high ratio of female engineers, technicians, and other specialists are just two examples of Soviet patterns that are distinctive among industrial societies.

Finally, the Soviet experience seems to suggest that, contrary to earlier expectations shaped by Marxist theory, economic participation does not, in and of itself, guarantee equality of status and authority for women, although it may be a necessary condition of equality. Even in this avowedly socialist society, the structure of authority remains hierarchical, and the proportion of women declines at successively higher levels of that hierarchy, even in the occupations in which they predominate.

SIX

Women and Power:
Changing Political Roles

It is good that the cook will be taught to govern
the state; but what will there be if a Commissar
is placed over the cook?   Nikolai Bukharin

IN studies of modernization, as in classical democratic theory, an expanding definition of citizenship has been viewed as either the
condition or the consequence of social progress.[1] Yet not until the twentieth century were political and civic rights extended to women on the
basis of equality with men.[2] Those who fought for female suffrage and
those who opposed it anticipated that it would have momentous implications for the development of modern political systems. But its consequences have been less dramatic than either friends or enemies envisioned.
Women have played a relatively limited role in public life, mobilized for
certain purposes at certain times, but without aspiring to leadership and
power.[3]

Even in the most highly developed and democratic societies, the political roles of women differ in important ways from those of men. Studies
of political behavior have documented the extent of these differences
across all areas of political life. For a wide range of activities, women's
participation is lower than that of men, whether one investigates voting,
political discussion, political letter-writing, party membership, or holding

[1]See, for example, Reinhard Bendix, *Nation-Building and Citizenship* (New York, 1964),
Ch. 3; Alice S. Rossi, ed., *John Stuart Mill and Harriet Taylor Mill: Essays on Sex Equality*
(Chicago, 1970), p. 73.

[2]For a study of the American feminist movement, see Eleanor Flexner, *Century of Struggle*
(Cambridge, Mass., 1966).

[3]Martin Gruberg, *Women in American Politics* (Oshkosh, Wisc., 1968); Kirsten Amundsen,
The Silenced Majority (Englewood Cliffs, N. J., 1971); Maurice Duverger, *The Political Role
of Women* (Paris, 1955); Jane Jacquette, ed., *Women and Politics* (New York, 1974).

party or public office.[4] The declining proportion of women at successively higher levels of political authority appears to be universal.[5]

Not only is the level of female participation lower, but the patterns of participation are different as well. Across a variety of dimensions the political attitudes and behavior of women are clearly distinguishable from those of men. Women voters, a number of studies conclude, tend to have a lower sense of political efficacy, to focus more heavily on local than on national issues, to be more conservative in their political values, more responsive to issues with moral overtones, more likely to personalize politics, and less comfortable with political conflict.[6] Even women who enter actively into political life, and who come to play leading roles within political parties or governmental institutions, differ substantially from their male counterparts in their career patterns and affiliations, despite important changes in recent years that are narrowing these differences.[7] But many writers have pointed to the low level of meaningful political participation by women as one of the key factors that inhibits their ability to defend their interests as a group.

Political scientists have offered a variety of explanations for the "apoliticism" of women.[8] For the most part, they do not distinguish women from other groups with low political involvement—the young, minorities, the socioeconomically deprived—and female apoliticism is attributed to the same motivational factors.[9] Other explanations attach greater weight to the sexual basis of political roles but differ over the relative importance of nature and culture.[10] A currently fashionable, if controversial, approach stresses the biological origins of political behavior and argues the existence of a fundamental connection between maleness, aggression, and

[4]A. Campbell, P. Converse, W. Miller, and D. Stokes, *The American Voter* (New York, 1960); Duverger, *Political Role of Women;* Amundsen, *Silenced Majority;* Gruberg, *Women in American Politics;* Robert Lane, *Political Life* (New York, 1959).

[5]Robert Putnam, *The Comparative Study of Political Elites* (New York, 1976). In this respect, the pattern of women's political roles resembles that of ethnic minorities.

[6]Campbell, Converse, Miller, and Stokes, *American Voter;* Gruberg, *Woman in American Politics.*

[7]Edmond Constantini and Kenneth Craik, "Women as Politicians: The Social Background, Personality, and Political Careers of Female Party Leaders," *Journal of Social Issues,* 28 (1972): 217–36; Jeane Kirkpatrick, *Political Women* (New York, 1974).

[8]See the discussion by Lynne Iglitzin, "Political Education and Sexual Liberation," *Politics and Society* 2 (Winter 1972): 241–54.

[9]*Ibid.,* p. 248; also Robert Dahl, *Modern Political Analysis* (Englewood Cliffs, N. J., 1970), pp. 77–84.

[10]For a review of the literature on the physiological bases of psychological differences between men and women, see Judith Bardwick, *The Psychology of Women: A Study of Bio-Cultural Conflicts* (New York, 1971). See also Eleanor E. Maccoby, ed., *The Development of Sex Differences* (Stanford, 1966), and Naomi Weisstein, "Psychology Constructs the Female" in *Women in Sexist Society,* ed. Vivian Gornick and Barbara K. Moran (New York, 1971).

politics.[11] Still other writers have given more emphasis to patterns of socialization that encourage boys to become independent, self-reliant, and achievement-oriented, while girls are rewarded for obedience, dependence, and nurturant behavior.[12] Yet even writers who emphasize the effects of cultural conditioning in definitions of masculinity and femininity tend to view such effects as the expression of biological or psychological forces. Thus, Fred Greenstein argues, politics "although not of deep interest to children of either sex, is more resonant with the 'natural' enthusiasms of boys."[13]

The assumptions and expectations that underlie these views have no official counterpart in the Soviet Union. There, the "apoliticism" of women is treated as an expression of their inequality in capitalist society, rather than of a universal, biologically determined fate. Within the Soviet Union, official sources insist, the revolution brought women full equality in economic, political, and social life. By destroying the elitist foundations of bourgeois democracy, socialism opened the way for the democratization of political life and the full participation of women. Soviet authors therefore point with pride to an impressive array of statistics demonstrating that Soviet women take an active part in political life to a degree unique among contemporary societies. In the 1975 elections alone, they note, over one million women were elected as deputies to local soviets, nearly half the total.[14]

Yet even the most cursory acquaintance with the facts of Soviet political life invites a certain scepticism. Despite considerable efforts to integrate women more fully into political life and some success in drawing women into political careers, in the Soviet Union, as elsewhere, women are largely absent from the upper reaches of power. In substantive rather than ceremonial roles, in the key hierarchies of political and coercive power, and at the apex of the system as a whole, politics remains a male affair.

Nevertheless, despite the apparent universality with which the political roles of women decrease at successively higher levels of the pyramid of political authority, important variations in the scope, levels, and patterning of female political participation in different political systems suggest a range of questions for comparative analysis. Preliminary efforts to define the nature and limits of these variations in relation to the pattern of male

[11]Konrad Lorenz, *On Aggression* (New York, 1963); Robert Ardrey, *Territorial Imperative* (New York, 1966); Lionel Tiger, *Men in Groups* (New York, 1969). Tiger, for example, argues that "The sexual division of political and aggressive behavior in all communities has direct biological roots," p. 89.

[12]For a review of the literature, see Naomi Weisstein, "Psychology Constructs the Female," in Gornick and Moran, *Women in Sexist Society*, and Kate Millet, *Sexual Politics* (Garden City, N. J., 1970) pp. 220–33.

[13]Fred Greenstein, *Children and Politics* (New Haven, 1965), p. 127.

[14]*Pravda*, June 21, 1975, p. 2.

political roles offers promising avenues for future research. Moreover, in the Soviet Union itself, such significant changes in the character and orientations of its political elite have occurred during the past six decades that different opportunities for the scope and nature of female political participation may well be associated with successive political regimes.

A detailed investigation of the role of women at different levels of the Soviet system, and of the patterning of female political careers within it, may yield still further insights. The impact of educational and professional attainments on the scope and nature of female political participation invites attention, as does the larger relationship between developmental patterns and political mobility. Finally, the differentiation of male and female roles and orientations, which we have traced through the educational system and into the occupational structure, might be expected to have some bearing on the patterning of political roles as well. The degree of "professional convergence," to use the formulation of Heinz Eulau and John Sprague, between occupational roles and the skills demanded of political leaders may vary among political systems in ways that affect the access of women to political power. Here too the Soviet Union presents an interesting case for further exploration.[15]

In focussing attention on the scope and patterns of female political participation, it is important to avoid equating participation with responsiveness to women's needs. A political regime responsive to the needs and interests of particular groups is not necessarily one in which such groups are represented in proportion to their size. Nor would proportional political participation necessarily imply responsiveness to group interests, although it might enhance the opportunity for interest articulation.[16] However, despite the formal denial until recent years of the existence of distinctive group interests in Soviet society and the assertion that Party and governmental institutions represent the national interests of an essentially solidary society, Soviet sources are almost obsessive in their concern with group representation in political bodies. Statistics on the membership of soviets and of Party organs at all levels include breakdowns by sex, nationality, occupation, and occasionally socioeconomic class, and there is reason to believe, as we shall see shortly, that norms for these categories are explicitly established by the leadership. Given the widespread use of these data by Soviet authors to demonstrate the representative character of Soviet political institutions and the implicit acceptance of a microcosmic definition of representation, it may not be altogether inappropriate for Western scholars to use these same criteria in analyzing

[15]Heinz Eulau and John D. Sprague, *Lawyers in Politics: A Study of Professional Convergence* (Indianapolis, 1961).
[16]For a thoughtful discussion of different views of representation and their implications, see Hannah Pitkin, *The Concept of Representation* (Berkeley and Los Angeles, 1967).

the composition of representative institutions without necessarily equating proportionality with responsiveness.

At the outset, however, it should be noted that the definition of political
participation employed here is a necessarily restricted one. The absence
of Soviet data that would permit an evaluation of the subjective dimensions of political behavior oblige us to limit our investigation to political
activity alone. Moreover, our own usage will not draw a sharp distinction
between private citizens as political participants and political professionals
but will include both categories. Since our purpose is not to examine the
nature and intensity of political participation in the USSR relative to other
political systems in absolute terms, but rather to examine the patterns of
political activity of women relative to those of men, it is best served by
an inclusive rather than an exclusive definition of participation.

Nor will our usage draw the rigid distinction between mobilized and
autonomous participation urged by some writers.[17] The boundaries between them are uniquely difficult to distinguish in the Soviet case, and
the consequences of a high level of mobilized political activity are, in any
case, similar for women and for men. To be sure, for purposes of comparison with Western patterns of participation, a somewhat different
framework would be called for. Because the role of citizen has not been
highly institutionalized in the Soviet system, the dichotomy between the
political-bureaucratic vanguard and the masses of the population is particularly sharp. The occupants of state and Party positions have, in some
respects, more in common with Western administrative and military elites
than they do with Western politicians. Nonetheless, since we are investigating neither the motivations nor the efficacy of Soviet political participation, but rather the extent to which women are drawn into political
roles relative to men and the difference in their patterns of participation,
the problem need not detain us here.

FEMALE PARTICIPATION IN THE SOVIETS AND LOCAL GOVERNMENT

The revolutionary leadership that came to power in Russia in 1917 was,
as we have seen, committed to the establishment of full political equality.
Sustained by the conviction that sexual inequality was rooted in social
arrangements, the revolutionary leadership anticipated that changes in
economic organization, accompanied by simultaneous efforts to alter expectations and behavior, would ultimately draw women out of the limited
confines of private households and into public life. Full political partici-

[17]For a discussion of differing definitions of political participation, see Samuel Huntington and Joan Nelson, *No Easy Choice: Political Participation in Developing Countries* (Cambridge,
Mass., 1976). For an argument for excluding mobilized actions from a definition of political
participation, see Myron Weiner, "Political Participation: Crisis of the Political Process,"
in Leonard Binder, et al., *Crises and Sequences in Political Development* (Princeton, 1971),
p. 164.

pation for women depended on the political democratization that would accompany the transformation of economic relationships.

This view received explicit statement in Lenin's writings. The nationalization of the means of production and the expropriation of the exploiting classes destroyed the elitist foundations of bourgeois democracy, in his view. Political and administrative leadership, he had argued in *State and Revolution*, just before the Bolshevik seizure of power, would no longer be the specialized function of a small elite but would become activities in which the entire working population could participate on an equal basis. Writing in *Pravda* in 1919, Lenin elaborated on his vision of a society in which "every cook could learn to administer the state":

> In order to be active in politics under the old, capitalist regime special training was required, so that women played an insignificant part in politics, even in the most advanced and free capitalist countries. Our task is to make politics available to every working woman. Ever since private property in land and factories has been abolished and the power of the landowners and capitalists overthrown, the tasks of politics have become simple, clear and comprehensible to the working people as a whole, and to working women as well. In capitalist society the women's position is marked by such inequality that her participation in politics is only an insignificant fraction of man's participation. The power of the working people is necessary for a change to be wrought in this situation, for then the main tasks of politics will consist of matters directly affecting the fate of the working people themselves. . . . Here Soviet power opens up a wide field of activity to working women.[18]

But the commitment to democratization coexisted uneasily with an authoritarian model of political organization. In the postrevolutionary period, the expanding authority of central Party organs and the increasing bureaucratization of the Party apparatus gradually undermined fragile experiments in participatory democracy. The growing extent of popular political participation coincided with a narrowing of the scope of its influence.

These tendencies did not go unrecognized within the Party itself. It was Bukharin who pointed to the fundamental incompatibility of the "commune state" envisioned by the Left Communists with the increasing bureaucratization of political authority. "It is good," he said, "that the cook will be taught to govern the state; but what will there be if a commissar is placed over the cook? Then he will never learn to govern the state."[19]

The evolution of the Soviet political system since 1917 has been marked

[18]V. I. Lenin, "O zadachakh zhenskogo rabochego dvizheniia v sovetskoi respublike," in *Polnoe sobranie sochinenii (PSS)*, 5th ed., 55 vols. (Moscow, 1958–1965), 39: 202–3.

[19]Cited in Stephen F. Cohen, *Bukharin and the Bolshevik Revolution* (New York, 1973), p. 75.

by the gradual inclusion of ever larger numbers of women in networks of political activity. The efforts of the Zhenotdel in the early years of the new regime, and of the Party leadership more generally, to develop new channels through which women could be reached for purposes of political agitation and political recruitment were rewarded by slowly rising rates of political participation. Up to 1929 these changes reflected direct efforts at political mobilization. Subsequently, however, they also reflected the increasing recruitment of women into the labor force and professions and the expansion of educational opportunities and attainments.

The very scanty and not completely reliable statistics available for the period from 1917 to 1934 indicate that these early efforts to draw women into political activity had rather important results. The proportion of women who performed the most basic civic duty, that of voting in elections, rose steadily in both urban and rural areas, from 42.9 percent in urban areas in 1926 to 89.7 percent in 1934 and in villages from 28 percent to 80.3 percent.[20]

Efforts to extend the level and scope of political involvement by drawing women into the work of local soviets also achieved substantial results. The proportion of women deputies in local soviets rose in rural areas from 1 percent in 1922 to 10 percent in 1926 and to 27 percent in 1934, and in urban areas it rose from 5.7 percent in 1920 to 18 percent in 1926 and to 32 percent in 1934. The next two decades brought a narrowing of the rural-urban gap, but little increase in the proportion of female deputies between 1932 and 1955, when it stood at 35.2 percent. Since 1955, however, the proportion of women has steadily risen with each election, reaching 40.7 percent of all deputies in 1961, 44.6 percent in 1969, and 48.1 percent in the elections of 1975.

Indices of female representation in the soviets at higher levels of the political system show similar tendencies. Starting from relatively low levels in the immediate postrevolutionary period, women registered significant gains through 1934. Their proportion then stabilized for several decades, rising somewhat during World War II, and again in the past two decades.

Even to the present day, the proportion of female delegates to the soviets remains greatest at the local level and decreases at successively higher levels of the hierarchy. As Table 21 indicates, women constitute 48.1 percent of deputies to local soviets, 44.9 percent at the *oblast* or regional level, 35.4 percent at the Union Republic level, and 31.4 percent of deputies to the Supreme Soviet.

While the statistics appear impressive, their meaning is more problematic, since members of the soviets are not elected through a competitive

[20]V. V. Sokolov, *The Rights of Women Under Soviet Law* (Moscow, 1928), pp. 9–14; G. N. Serebrennikov, *The Position of Women in the USSR* (London, 1937), pp. 140, 209–10.

TABLE 21

PERCENT OF WOMEN AMONG DEPUTIES TO SOVIETS, BY LEVEL

Levels of Government	Percent of women				
	1959	1967	1970	1973	1975
Supreme Soviet of USSR	27	28[b]	30.5	31.4[c]	31.4
Supreme Soviets of the Union Republics	32	34	34.8	—	35.4
Supreme Soviets of the Autonomous Republics	32	35	38.0	45.4	39.1
Oblast Soviets	40[a]	43	44.5	44.9	
Local Soviets	41[a]		45.8	47.4	48.1

SOURCES: For 1959 and 1961, *Women and Children in the USSR*, (Moscow, 1963), pp. 109–10; for 1967, *Zhenshchiny i deti v SSSR* (Moscow, 1969) p. 89; for 1970, *Pravda*, June 20, 1970, pp. 1–2, and July 15, pp. 2–3; for 1973, *Pravda*, June 23, 1973, pp. 1, 3, 4; for 1974, *Pravda*, June 26, p. 3; for 1975, *Pravda*, June 21, 1975, p. 2.
[a]1961.
[b]1966.
[c]1974.

process. The composition of the single electoral slate, and therefore of the soviets themselves, is the outcome of political decisions made at higher levels of the system in which neither the aspirations of potential candidates nor the preferences of the electorate are influential.[21]

Moreover, the composition of the soviets is intended to provide wide representation of diverse occupational and social groups, indeed to contain a cross-section of the Soviet population. The consistent proportions of female delegates at each level across republics that vary greatly in their economic and cultural development suggests that the selection of delegates is guided by norms for sexual composition (as well as for proportion of Party members) that are established at the all-Union level. The occupational background of the delegates shows far greater variation between republics, suggesting that these norms are probably established at the republic level to permit greater flexibility in reflecting differences in regional economic geography.[22] As Table 22 indicates, in the most recent

[21]For a discussion of local elections, see Everett Jacobs, "Soviet Local Elections: What They Are, and What They Are Not," *Soviet Studies* 22 (July 1970): 67. See also Max E. Mote, *Soviet Local and Republic Elections* (Stanford, 1965); Howard Swearer, "The Functions of Soviet Local Elections," *Midwest Journal of Political Science* 5 (May 1961): 129–49.
[22]Ronald J. Hill, "Continuity and Change in Supreme Soviet Elections," *British Journal of Political Science* 2 (January 1972): 51–52.

TABLE 22

COMPOSITION OF DEPUTIES ELECTED TO LOCAL SOVIETS, 1975,
BY REPUBLIC, SEX, PARTY AFFILIATION, AND OCCUPATION

Republic	Total number	Percent female	Percent party members and candidates	Percent workers	Percent collective farmers
USSR Total	2,210,824	48.1	43.8	40.5	27.2
RSFSR	1,109,283	49.4	42.5	45.5	20.4
Latvian SSR	23,567	48.9	46.4	36.3	29.7
Moldavian SSR	33,898	48.8	48.2	29.0	38.8
Estonian SSR	11,076	48.3	44.7	44.4	21.5
Georgian SSR	49,248	48.1	43.3	35.2	32.1
Lithuanian SSR	28,277	48.0	44.3	34.5	31.4
Kirghiz SSR	25,898	47.9	42.2	37.3	30.7
Uzbek SSR	88,950	47.5	45.1	32.4	35.7
Kazakh SSR	120,690	47.4	40.5	57.5	09.8
Armenian SSR	26,325	47.0	43.2	42.7	24.9
Belorussian SSR	79,447	46.7	43.5	34.0	30.7
Tadzhik SSR	23,366	46.7	45.2	29.7	39.0
Ukrainian SSR	521,395	46.2	46.6	31.8	40.5
Azerbaidzh SSR	48,286	45.7	44.8	34.0	31.9
Turkmen SSR	21,118	44.8	43.0	25.0	43.2

SOURCE: Compiled from figures given in *Pravda*, June 21, 1975, p. 2.

local elections, held in 1975, the proportion of women deputies elected to the local soviets of each republic varied within a very narrow range, from a low of 44.8 percent in Turkmenistan to a high of 49.4 percent in the Russian Republic, while the ratio of workers and collective farmers fluctuated more widely.

Moreover, the high proportion of women among the Soviet deputies is not a real measure of political influence. The Supreme Soviet, technically the highest organ of state authority, gathers only briefly twice each year and plays a limited, if growing, role in the policy process. It cannot appropriately be compared with the parliamentary bodies of Western Europe and the United States, in which women play a smaller, but potentially more powerful, role.[23]

[23]The highest proportions of women in Western legislative bodies are found in Scandinavia. In 1971–72 approximately 21 percent of Swedish deputies were female; 17 percent in Denmark and 16 percent in Norway were female. The figure for West Germany is 8 percent and for Great Britain, 4 percent.

Even within this body of admittedly limited power, the patterns of recruitment, career affiliations, and turnover rates of women deputies differ
in important ways from those of their male counterparts. First, the degree
of Party affiliation distinguishes male and female deputies. While 980
male deputies to the 1970 Supreme Soviet were Party members and 110
were not, 171 female deputies belonged to the Party and 252 did not.[24]
Further, male and female deputies had divergent occupational backgrounds. High Party and government officials dominated the membership
of the Supreme Soviet, and these were largely male. The female deputies
were predominantly collective farmers, doctors, and teachers. Finally, the
selection process resulted in much higher turnover rates for female deputies than for males. While the overall rate of re-election from 1966 to 1970
was 43.4 percent, more than half of the male deputies were re-elected, as
opposed to 15.3 percent of the females. Two of twenty-six teachers were
re-elected, and one of the eighteen medical workers. However small the
political impact of the deputies may be for institutional reasons, the lack
of continuity and experience reduces the potential effectiveness of the female deputies still further.

While there are no data available that would make possible a comparison of the political orientations of female and male deputies along the lines
that have been attempted for several Western political systems, fragmentary evidence suggests that the educational backgrounds and career affiliations of the female deputies direct their participation toward issue areas
involving health, cultural affairs, and public welfare. An analysis of the
participants in Supreme Soviet debates between 1966 and 1973 revealed
that the female deputies contributed to discussions of health policy, marriage and family law, labor legislation, and education in some proportion
to their numbers, but played a negligible role in discussions of planning,
budgetary matters, and foreign affairs.[25]

It is really at the local level, where these concerns are the dominant
ones, that women make their most substantial contribution to civic affairs.
Through the Standing Commissions of the local soviets, through the deputies' groups, and through their contacts with local social or public organizations, including the women's councils (*zhensovety*), the soviet deputies
supervise and coordinate a vast array of activities concerned with housing,
education, culture and health, local industry and trade, and social services.[26] Detailed evidence about the position of women in the executive

[24]Hill, "Continuity and Change," pp. 51–52.
[25]Based on a table of participants in Supreme Soviet debates prepared by Jerry Hough
for a new revised edition of Merle Fainsod's *How Russia is Ruled*, which was kindly shared
with the author.
[26]David Cattell, who observed these commissions in action, insists their independence
and extensive role are exaggerated in Western accounts; *Leningrad: A Case Study of Soviet
Urban Government* (New York, 1968), pp. 61–64. For a different perspective, and an illu-

committees of local soviets and not merely in their overall composition is not available, but if the distribution of positions in the executive committee of one Leningrad district soviet is typical, women form the bulk of the clerical and specialist staff, about half of the heads of divisions, and one-fourth of the deputies to the chairman (Table 23).

The role of women in other local government agencies awaits detailed investigation. In the city of Moscow, where one might expect to find a relatively high proportion of educated women with political and economic expertise, surprisingly few women hold responsible positions. They constituted between 5 and 10 percent of officeholders between 1950 and 1970, and only infrequently served as heads of governmental agencies, even those concerned with health and education.[27]

A more detailed account of the position of women in local government in Leningrad is possible. Between 1948 and 1965, 26 out of a total of 340 members of the City Executive Committee and department heads were women. Eight of these were members of the Executive Committee, heading no departments and serving one term only. Six women served as one of the four to seven Vice-Chairmen of the Committee during this time, and one served as Secretary. Finally, seven women served as heads of departments not carrying with them positions on the Executive Committee: departments for Social Security, Cultural Enlightenment, Film, Organization and Instruction, and General Housekeeping.[28]

WOMEN IN THE COMMUNIST PARTY

If we are concerned not merely with the extent and forms of political participation by women but also with the access of women to positions of political leadership, then we must turn our focus away from the soviets to examine more closely the role of women within the Soviet Communist Party. Because the Party is a selective political elite with a monopoly of power within the Soviet system, Party membership is the indispensable condition for a professional political career, as well as for high-level man-

minating portrait of the activities of a local soviet, see Theodore Friedgut, "Community Structure, Political Participation and Soviet Local Government: The Case of Kutaisi," in *Soviet Politics and Society in the 1970's,* ed. Henry Morton and Rudolf Tokes (New York, 1974). The *zhensovety* occupy themselves with local questions of particular relevance to women, such as child care, health, education, and consumer services, thereby enshrining "women's concerns" in Soviet political life as, in effect, a counterpart of "women's work" in the economy. For a more elaborate discussion of their activities, see N. Zaripova, "Zhenshchiny—Aktivnye stroiteli kommunizma," *Kommunist* 12 (1965): 29–32.

[27]Personal communication from James Oliver, Department of Government and Politics, University of Maryland, who kindly shared data collected for a study of the Moscow political elite.

[28]Personal communication from David Cattell, Department of Political Science, University of California at Los Angeles, who kindly shared data gathered for a study of the Leningrad political apparatus.

TABLE 23

PROPORTION OF WOMEN OCCUPYING POSITIONS IN THE EXECUTIVE
COMMITTEE OF A LENINGRAD DISTRICT SOVIET

Position	Women as percent of total
I Chairman, his deputies, and secretary of the executive committee	
1962	24.9
1964	24.9
1966	24.9
II Directors and deputy directors of divisions, directors of sectors	
1962	63.1
1964	59.1
1966	40.0
III Specialists (instructors, inspectors, and others)	
1962	87.2
1964	82.2
1966	92.9
IV Clerical personnel	
1962	100.0
1964	100.0
1966	100.0

SOURCE: V. G. Lebin and M. N. Perfilev, *Kadry apparata upravleniia v SSSR* (Leningrad, 1970), p. 176.

agerial positions in the economic and the state bureaucracies. Election to Party membership is both a reward for significant achievement and the condition for further opportunities for political and professional advancement. The role of women within the Party is therefore a sensitive indicator of their position in the larger society.

Table 24 reveals the changing patterns of female membership in the Communist Party from 1920 to 1976. There were relatively few women Communists at the time of the revolution and civil war: only 41,212 women, constituting less than 8 percent of the total membership, were recorded in the Party census of 1922. Their proportion reached 9.2 per-

TABLE 24
WOMEN MEMBERS OF THE COMMUNIST PARTY
1920–1977

Year	Total number of women	Women as percent of total
1920	45,297	7.4
1922	41,212	7.8
1924	46,728	9.9
1926	128,807	11.9
1930	219,338	13.1
1932	—	15.9
1934	—	16.5
1934[a]	395,763	14.7
1937	293,059	14.8
1939	333,821	14.5
1941	—	14.9
1946	1,033,115	18.7
1950	1,312,418	20.7
1952	1,276,560	19.0
1956	1,414,456	19.7
1961	1,809,688	19.5
1966	2,548,901	20.6
1967	2,647,074	20.9
1971	3,195,556	22.2
1973	3,412,029	23.0
1977	3,947,616	24.7

SOURCES: T. H. Rigby, *Communist Party Membership in the USSR, 1917–1967* (Princeton, 1968) p. 361; I. Kapitonov, *Kommunist*, No. 3, (February 1972): 35; *Partiinaia zhizn'*, no. 14, 1973; *Partiinaia zhizn'*, no. 21 (November 1977): 32.

[a]*Partiinaia zhizn'* gives the 1934 percentage as 14.7 without indicating the month for this data. Rigby's figure is the total recorded for January. Using the lower figure for 1934 would minimize the impact of the subsequent purges on female membership.

cent in urban areas and sank to 4.5 percent in the countryside.[29] By social origin and occupation, the women Communists differed from the male membership of the Party in these early years. A far higher proportion of the women than men were employees, while the peasantry was underrepresented among them. By 1926, for example, when 25.4 percent of the Party membership was of peasant origin, only 14.9 percent of the women fell into this category. Conversely, 27.3 percent of the women were employees, compared with only 17.4 percent for the Party as a whole.

[29]*Izvestiia*, January 23, 1923, pp. 46–47.

The nationality composition of the female party membership also diverged from the general pattern. In 1922, when women constituted 8 percent of the total membership, they represented 24.1 percent of the Jewish membership, 19.8 percent of the Finns, 18.7 percent of the Letts, 14.5 percent of the Estonians, and 7.2 percent of the Russians.[30] Among the non-Western nationalities of the Party, women were strongly underrepresented. Female Party membership was therefore highly correlated with education in the early years. By the 1930s, however, massive recruitment efforts in the countryside and the entry of women into the industrial labor force had reduced these divergences, and the occupational and nationality background of women Communists increasingly approximated the pattern within the Party as a whole.

The relatively low proportion of women in the Party in the early Soviet years began to rise in the middle and late 1920s, as a result of intensive recruitment efforts spurred by the activities of the Zhenotdel. By 1932 their proportion of Party membership had doubled to 15.9 percent, and it reached a high of 16.5 percent in 1934. In absolute numbers the growth was even more impressive, rising from 38,500 in 1924 to 500,000 in 1932. The mass purge (*chistka*) of 1933–1934, which was primarily directed at the inactive and least disciplined members of Party organizations, struck the female contingent with particular severity. Moreover, although the Five Year Plans were drawing women into the industrial labor force in massive numbers during these years, Party recruitment focused on the new and largely male managerial and technical elite. Only during World War II did the proportion of women begin to rise again, as the female membership trebled between 1939 and 1946.[31] The proportion stabilized in the postwar period, and did not begin to rise again until the mid-1960s. By 1970 the proportion of women exceeded 22 percent, by 1973 it had reached 23 percent, and in 1977 women constituted 24.7 percent of a total Party membership of 16.2 million (Table 24).

The rising proportion of women in the Party is the result of an intensive recruitment campaign that has been under way since the mid-1960s. Between 1956 and 1961, women constituted 18 percent of new candidate members, a proportion slightly below their share in the Party as a whole. Their share among new candidates increased to 21.7 percent between 1962 and 1965, 25.7 percent between 1966 and 1970, and 29.5 percent

[30]Merle Fainsod, *How Russia is Ruled*, 2nd ed. (Cambridge, Mass., 1963), pp. 254–55.

[31]Similar patterns of entry of women into political leadership roles occurred elsewhere during World War II. The proportion of women in the British House of Commons, the Japanese House of Representatives, the French Parliament, and the U.S. House of Representatives all reached a peak during and just after World War II. For a suggestive theoretical treatment of this phenomenon in a broader context, see Jean Lipman-Blumen, "Role de-Differentiation as a System Response to Crisis: Occupational and Political Roles of Woman," *Sociological Inquiry* 43 (April 1973): 105–30.

between 1971 and 1975.[32] In 1971 Party officials proudly announced that women constituted 29.2 percent of all candidate members, while in some regions they formed as much as 40 to 50 percent of new recruits.

In some of the less developed republics the political mobilization of women has taken a particularly intensive form. In the Moslem regions of the USSR, the recruitment of women into political life has joined the larger struggle against traditional values and institutions. Here, recruitment to Party membership started from extremely low levels. In 1927, when the proportion of women in the Party had reached 12 percent for the USSR as a whole, women comprised a mere 4.7 percent of the Tatars, 2.5 percent of the Bashkirs, 2.1 percent of the Kazakhs, and 0.7 percent of the Tadziks in the Party membership.[33] In order to raise the representation of women in Moslem areas to equal the proportion of women in the Party more generally, particularly strenuous recruitment efforts had to be made.

The membership figures for the Turkmen and Tadzhik Communist Parties demonstrate the pattern that prevailed more generally (Table 25). The lag in the proportion of women by comparison with the all-Union average was essentially overcome by the mid-1930s as a result of massive recruitment efforts. During World War II the numbers and proportion of women rose dramatically as women were recruited into the Party to replace men mobilized for military service. In 1944 female membership reached an all-time high of 29 percent in Turkmenistan and 30.3 percent in Tadzhikistan. In the immediate postwar period, however, the proportion of women declined sharply; demobilization of the more than half the Party membership serving in the armed forces caused the female percentage to plummet, although in absolute terms the number of women remained stable.[34]

The figures for female Party membership do not include a breakdown by ethnic background. If the ethnic composition of male and female cadres is assumed to be similar, then roughly 60 percent of the total female membership of the Party in Tadzhikistan is Tadzhik or Uzbek, and the remaining 40 percent are of Russian or another nationality. The proportion of native women is probably far lower, however, particularly in Turkmenistan. Only for the year 1966 are there figures for ethnic background,

[32]*Partiinaia zhizn'*, No. 4, July 1973, p. 14; and I. Kapitonov, *Kommunist*, No. 3, February 1972, p. 35; *Partiinaia zhizn'*, No. 10, May 1976, p. 14.
[33]T. H. Rigby, *The Communist Party Membership in the USSR* (Princeton, 1968), p. 362.
[34]A similar pattern prevailed in Uzbekistan and Kirgizia. The proportion of women in the Uzbek Communist Party stood at 31.5 percent in 1944 and declined to 19.5 percent in 1950 and 13.4 percent in 1962. In Kirgizia women comprised an extraordinary 38.5 percent of the Party membership in 1944, falling to 19.4 percent in 1950. Gerald Sperling and Elia Zurich, "The Social Composition of the Communist Parties of Central Asia," *Studies of the Soviet Union*, New Series, 8 (1968): p. 30.

TABLE 25

FEMALE PARTY MEMBERSHIP, TURKMENISTAN AND

TADZHIKISTAN, 1925–1974

	Turkmenistan			Tadzhikistan		
Year	Total party membership	Total women	Percent	Total party membership	Total women	Percent
1925	5,240	170	3.2	435	14	3.0
1932	15,883	1,715	10.8	12,671	1,016	8.0
1933	17,005	2,155	12.7	14,329	1,290	9.0
1936	6,475	776	12.0	5,153	—	—
1938	6,908	829	12.0	4,715	700	15.0
1941	19,084	2,595	13.6	14,500	2,270	15.0
1944	17,219	5,018	29.1	15,020	—	30.3
1945	19,284	5,384	27.9	16,890	4,783	28.0
1946	23,502	5,802	24.7	19,645	4,551	23.0
1950	33,463	6,272	18.7	31,234	5,970	18.0
1956	37,488	7,253	19.3	35,124	6,417	18.0
1960	45,152	8,437	18.7	47,920	9,024	19.0
1962	50,287	9,426	18.7	55,853	10,976	18.7
1967	62,679	11,379	18.2	76,001	13,686	18.0
1971	—	12,884	18.4	86,491	—	—
1974	—	—	—	92,062	17,420	18.9

SOURCES: Compiled from data in *Kommunisticheskaia Partiia Turkmenistana v tsifrakh: 1925–1966* (Ashkhabad, 1967), pp. 1–194; Teresa Rakowska-Harmstone, *Russia and Nationalism in Soviet Central Asia: The Case of Tadzhikistan*, (Baltimore, 1970), pp. 100–1; Gerald Sperling and Elia Zurich, "The Social Composition of the Communist Parties of Central Asia," *Studies on the Soviet Union*, New Series, 8 (1968): 30–45; *Kommunisticheskaia Partiia Tadzhikistana v tsifrakh* (Dushanbe, 1974), pp. 4, 12.

and they reveal that of the 11,084 female Party members, 3,826 were of Turkmen nationality.[35] The persistence of traditional values and behavior in Moslem regions, and the underrepresentation of local women in educational institutions and in the skilled labor force, continues to inhibit their full political participation. Recent complaints in the press suggest that the recruitment of women may have actually declined slightly in recent years. While the proportion of women within the Party actually exceeds all-Union levels in some republics, in Central Asia it remains lower than the national average and it includes large numbers of Russians and other non-native personnel.

If we look again at female Party membership, this time in the context of the overall demographic structure of the USSR, the recent increases

[35]*Kommunisticheskaia Partiia Turkmenistana v tsifrakh, 1925–1966* (Ashkabad, 1967), p. 190.

have been more impressive than they might otherwise appear. Although one out of every five Party members in the postwar period was a woman, the fact that adult females until recently outnumbered males by roughly 40 percent meant that the chances of being selected for Party membership in the mid-1950s were about one in eight for a man and one in forty for a woman. Since this demographic imbalance has been partly rectified in recent years as the ratio of young adult males to females becomes more even, a seemingly stationary percentage of women Party members actually conceals a slight improvement in the chances of women being selected for Party membership.

But despite the increased recruitment of women in recent years, they remain grossly underrepresented in proportion to their ratio in the population as a whole. As Table 26 demonstrates, the degree of Party saturation among men is presently four to five times greater than that for women, with only slight variations for each age cohort. Thus, 14.1 percent of all Soviet males over the age of eighteen and only 3.7 percent of all females are Party members. Since it has often been argued that the underrepresentation of women within the Party is a function of educational lag, what is striking is that the ratio of male to female saturation in fact remains constant even when level of education changes. At the lower range of educational achievement, roughly 7 to 8 percent of all men and 1.4 to 1.8 percent of all women over age thirty with primary or incomplete primary education are Party members. But the ratio is almost identical for men and women with complete higher education. Approximately 54 percent of all men over age thirty with higher education and only 13.6 percent of all such women are Party members.[36] Although one's chances of becoming a Party member increase dramatically with educational level, its effects are far greater for men. Educational attainment does not in fact equalize women's chances.

WOMEN IN THE POLITICAL ELITE

The underrepresentation of women that characterizes Party membership is even more striking in the realm of Party leadership, particularly at higher levels of the apparatus. In the Party organization itself, as in the government structure, the higher one moves in the hierarchy, the lower the proportion of women in positions of leadership. Women are found in greatest number as first secretaries in primary Party organizations, where they form roughly one-third of the total.[37] They also appear with some

[36]Jerry Hough, "Party 'Saturation' in the Soviet Union," in *The Dynamics of Soviet Politics*, eds. Paul Cocks, Robert V. Daniels, and Nancy Whittier Heer (Cambridge, Mass., 1976), pp. 125–26.

[37]They were 30.4 percent of primary party organization secretaries in 1960 and 33.4 percent in 1966; *Partiinaia zhizn'* 6 (March 1972): 26.

TABLE 26

PARTY SATURATION AMONG MEN AND WOMEN BY AGE GROUP, 1973

Age group	Men			Women		
	Total population in age group	Number of party members[a]	Degree of party saturation (percent)	Total population in age group	Number of party members[a]	Degree of party saturation (percent)
18–25	16,727,000	682,000	4.1	16,212,000	152,000	.9
26–30	6,834,000	893,000	13.0	6,985,000	209,000	3.0
31–40	17,985,000	3,692,000	20.5	18,751,000	889,000	4.7
41–50	14,909,000	3,358,000	22.5	18,497,000	974,000	5.3
51–60	7,821,000	1,792,000	22.9	11,904,000	636,000	5.3
61+	8,754,000	992,000	11.3	20,859,000	552,000	2.6
Total	73,080,000	11,409,000	14.1	93,208,000	3,412,000	3.7

SOURCE: Jerry Hough, "Party 'Saturation' in the Soviet Union," in Paul Cocks, Robert Daniels, and Nancy Whittier Heer, *The Dynamics of Soviet Politics*, (Cambridge, Mass., 1976), pp. 121–22.

[a]The figures for the number of Party members in each age group are approximations, based on the assumption that the age distribution of Party members for each sex reflects the age distribution of the total population group for each sex.

frequency as first or second secretary of *raion* (district) level Party committees, particularly in large urban areas. In Leningrad in 1964, according to David Cattell, 21 of 107 secretaries of *raion* and city organizations were women.[38] But the marginal role of women in positions of authority at the local level was pointedly described in an authoritative recent review of Party cadre policy by the Department of Party Construction in the Central Committee Academy of Social Sciences. Only 134 of all urban and district Party secretaries in the USSR as a whole in 1973 were women, under 4 percent of the total.[39]

Few women are known to have held the post of *oblast'* (regional) first secretary. The three detailed case studies of Party organization at the regional level, for Smolensk up to 1939, for Stalingrad from 1955 to 1966, and most recently for the Russian Republic and Ukraine, suggest that at this level Party leadership is largely a male affair.[40] An investigation by Joel Moses of the composition of all regional Party committees in the Russian and Ukrainian republics between 1955 and 1973 identified 26 women among the total of 810 *obkom* bureau members, or 3.2 percent of the total.[41] In nine of the twenty-five regions, no women served on the *obkom* bureau during this entire period of time, and in only five regions were two or more women elected simultaneously.

Given the low proportion of women within the regional Party leadership, it is not surprising that few have penetrated to the highest levels of the Party elite. Because of the centralization of authority within the Soviet system, a rough indication of the relative importance of members of the political elite and of their relative potential for influence in the decisionmaking process is given by their formal position within the Party hierarchy. At the top of this hierarchy stands the Party Politburo. Only one woman, Ekaterina Furtseva, has ever been a member of the Politburo, and she served for only three years.

Below the Politburo is the Central Committee, incorporating in its membership the political and administrative elite of the Soviet Union. The Central Committee elected at the 24th Congress of the Communist Party on April 8, 1971, had a total of 396 members, of whom 241 were full members and 155 alternates. Fifteen of the total were women, 6 full members, and 9 candidates. Not only is this low proportion—just 3.8 percent—striking in itself, but equally striking is the still lower propor-

[38]Personal communication from David Cattell.

[39]V. A. Kadeikan et al., eds. *Voprosy vnutripartiinoi zhizni i rukovodiashchei deiatel'nosti KPSS na sovremennom etape* (Moscow, 1974), pp. 192–93.

[40]Merle Fainsod, *Smolensk Under Soviet Rule* (Cambridge, Mass., 1958); Philip Stewart, *Political Power in the Soviet Union: A Study of Decision-Making in Stalingrad* (New York, 1965); Joel Moses, *Regional Party Leadership and Policy-Making in the USSR* (New York, 1974).

[41]Joel Moses, "Women in Political Roles," in *Women in Russia*, eds. Dorothy Atkinson, Alexander Dallin, and Gail Warshofsky Lapidus (Stanford, 1977).

tion of these who are professional political leaders. While the male membership of the Central Committee was dominated by members of the state and Party apparatus, only nine of the female members had made careers in Party or government. A tenth, Valentina Nikolaevna Tereshkova, was the well-known astronaut. The other five were honored workers rather than distinguished public figures, unidentifiable in any directories of prominent Soviet leaders. While this category accounted for only a small fraction of the male membership of the Central Committee and Central Auditing Commission, a third of the women fell into it. A similar pattern emerged from the 25th Party Congress held in March 1976. A total of fourteen women were elected to Central Committee membership, eight as full members and six as candidate members (Table 27). Since the size of the Central Committee had increased to 426 members, the proportion of women was now only 3.3 percent.

The role of women in the Central Committee bears no correlation to the proportion of women in the general Party membership. The election of Kollontai, Stasova, and Iakovleva to the Central Committee at the 6th Party Conference in August 1917, which then numbered thirty-one persons, meant that women formed over 9 percent of the Central Committee membership at a time when less than 8 percent of total Party membership was female. This figure was never again reached. Since 1918 the proportion of women in the Central Committee has fluctuated within a narrow range, never exceeding 4.2 percent of the total (Table 28). Thus, the gradual expansion of women in the general membership of the Party is not correlated with a growing role in positions of leadership.

Women are virtually absent from the upper levels of the Party apparatus itself. Furtseva was the only woman among the Secretaries of the Central Committee in the postwar period, and there have been few, if any, women among the heads or deputy heads of Central Committee departments or among the heads of its sections.[42]

A similar situation prevails at the top levels of the state apparatus. Only two women have held ministerial positions in the postwar period—Furtseva, who was serving as Minister of Culture at the time of her death in 1974, and Mariia S. Kovrigina, who was Minister of Health in the mid-1950s. Thus, the deliberations of both the Party Secretariat and the Council of Ministers have occurred largely without benefit of a female presence.

The marginal role of women in the Soviet political elite is most strikingly documented in the pages of comprehensive directories of the occupants of elite positions. One such directory, *Party and Government Officials of the Soviet Union, 1917–1967*, includes the members of all central

---

[42]Jerry F. Hough, "Women and the Women's Issue in Soviet Policy Debates," in Atkinson, Dallin, and Lapidus, *Women in Russia*.

TABLE 27
WOMEN ELECTED TO CENTRAL COMMITTEE OF THE CPSU
25TH PARTY CONGRESS, 1976

Full Members	Position
Biriukova, A. P. (1976; Candidate 1971)	Secretary, All-Union Central Council of Trade Unions
Dement'eva, R. F. (1976; Candidate 1971)	Secretary for Trade and Services, Moscow Gorkom
Ivannikova, M. S. (1971)	Weaver, cotton fabric factory
Karpova, E. F. (1976; Candidate 1966)	Deputy Chairman, RSFSR Council of Ministers
Kruglova, Z. M. (1976; Central Auditing Commission 1966)	Chairman of Presidium, Union of Soviet Societies for Friendship and Cultural Relations with Foreign Countries
Lykova, L. P. (1976; Candidate 1952)	Deputy Chairman, RSFSR Council of Ministers
Nikolaeva-Tereshkova, V. V. (1971)	Cosmonaut; Chairman, Committee of Soviet Women
Popova, M. G. (1971)	Crane operator, Nakhodka port
Candidate Members	
Fominykh, A. M. (1966)	Brigade leader of swine breeders, Belovskii kolkhoz
Kolchina, O. (1961)	Deputy Chairman, Presidium, RSFSR Supreme Soviet
Poberei, M. T. (1966)	First Secretary, Leninsk raikom, Volgograd oblast
Shevchenko, A. F. (1966)	Milkmaid; manager of a sovkhoz branch, Kiev oblast
Ulitina, L. V. (1976)	Coremaker, Machine-Building Plant, RSFSR
Eliseeva, N. G. (1976; Central Auditing Commission, 1971)	Deputy Chairman, Leningrad City Executive Committee

SOURCE: *Pravda*, March 6, 1976, p. 2.
NOTE: Date represents year first elected to Central Committee.

TABLE 28

FEMALE MEMBERSHIP IN CENTRAL COMMITTEE,
CPSU 1912–1976 (INCLUDING CANDIDATE MEMBERS)

Year	Total CC	Total women	Percent of women
1912	12	1	8.3
1917	31	3	9.7
1918	22	1	4.5
1919	27	1	3.7
1920	32	0	0.0
1921	40	0	0.0
1924	87	2	2.4
1927	121	5	4.0
1930	138	4	2.9
1934	139	3	2.2
1939	139	3	2.2
1952	236	7	3.1
1956	254	10	3.9
1961	330	11	3.3
1966	360	15	4.2
1971	397	15	3.8
1976	426	14	3.3

SOURCES: Calculated from data in Edward Crowley, et al., eds., *Party and Government in the Soviet Union 1917–1967* (Metuchen, N. J., 1969); *Pravda*, April 9, 1966, p. 2; *Pravda*, April 10, 1971, p. 2; Leo Gruliow, ed., *Current Soviet Policies: The Documentary Record of the 24th Congress of the Communist Party of the Soviet Union* (Columbus, 1973), pp. 186–95; *Pravda*, March 6, 1976, p. 2; Central Intelligence Agency Reference Aid, *The CPSU Central Committee and Central Auditing Commission—Members Elected at the 25th Party Congress* (Washington D.C., 1976).

government bodies from 1917 and of all major Party organs from the founding of the Social Democratic Party in 1898. Of the approximately 2,100 names listed in the directory, a total of 77, or 3.4 percent, were identifiable as women.[43] A second source is a directory compiled in 1973 of the occupants of all major state and Party positions at the republic level from 1955 to 1972. Of the roughly 2,500 names included in the index, a total of 109, or 4 percent, could be identified as women.[44]

[43]Edward Crowley, et al., eds., *Party and Government Officials of the Soviet Union,' 1917–1967* (Metuchen, N. J., 1969).
[44]Grey Hodnett and Val Ogareff, *Leaders of the Soviet Republics, 1955–1972* (Canberra, 1973).

THE PATTERN OF FEMALE POLITICAL ROLES

The roles of women in the Soviet political system differ from those of
men not only in their more limited scope but also in the ways in which
they are patterned. The broad outline of these patterns is a relatively familiar one. Few, if any, women are to be found in positions in the central
organs of coercion—the police and military—or within the diplomatic
corps. On the other hand, they are found in large numbers in such areas
as cultural affairs, health, social security, light industry, and consumer-
related services. As we have noted, the only two women to have held
ministerial positions at the national level in recent years were responsible
for Culture and Health.

A similar pattern recurs at the republic level. Some 109 women have
held responsible positions in the republic state and Party leadership
since 1955. As Table 29 indicates, over one-fourth of the total number
of these occupancies involved the supervision of cultural and educational
affairs: Minister of Culture or Minister of Education, for example, or
Head of the Party Central Committee's Department for Science and Culture or Schools. (The position of Minister of Foreign Affairs is included
in this category because it is a partially ceremonial one, concerned with
propaganda activities, and is usually held simultaneously with the position
of the Minister of Culture or Deputy Chairman of the Council of Ministers for Cultural Affairs.) If we add to this category a second related
group of functions involving ideological and propaganda activities, such
as Head of the Central Committee Department for Propaganda or Komsomol First Secretary, we have accounted for over 40 percent of all female
occupancies. A third area in which women tend to be found involves
welfare functions and includes positions in republican ministries and Central Committee Departments for Social Security and Health, as well as
the Chairmanship of the Trade Union Council. Finally, almost one-fifth
of female occupancies involve responsibility for light and food industry
and for the provision of local services.

The whole range of republic-level leadership positions, then, falls into
three categories. First, there are positions that are reserved for women or
frequently occupied by them, although not all occupants of these positions
have always been women. The Ministry of Social Security in the Russian
Republic, for example, has apparently been reserved as a women's position since Stalin's death. The head of the Party Central Committee
Women's Department, a position that was abolished in the late 1950s, was
another position reserved for women, and indeed accounted for one of the
four women to hold a leadership position in Estonia between 1956 and
1973 and one of the five in such positions in Lithuania.[45] With the increas-

---

[45] A Central Committee Department for Women's Affairs existed in Azerbaidzhan, Estonia, and Kazakhstan until 1957, in Kirgizia until 1956, in Lithuania until 1956, in Moldavia

ing attention given in recent years to the provision of everyday services, and the recent creation of ministries or Central Committee departments in some republics to supervise this function, these positions may come to be viewed as appropriate for female appointees. Second, there are positions to which women have had access, although women are not frequently found in them. Finally, there are positions—the vast majority— to which women have never been appointed.

It would appear that regional variations in female political mobility are the function of political choices rather than of cultural or developmental factors alone. The impact of different cultural traditions on the access of women to responsible positions and the way in which these traditions shape women's roles deserve separate study, but there is little apparent correlation between level of development more generally, or female educational attainments, and access to these particular elite positions.[46] Estonia and Lithuania, for example, have had only half as many women in positions of leadership at the republic level as Latvia, while the largest numbers of women are found in some of the Central Asian republics, where the promotion of women to high level positions within the Party and government has received great attention. Kirgizia, Turkmenistan, Tadzhikistan, and Azerbaidzhan account for almost half of the 109 women in republic-level leadership positions. The recruitment of local women in particular has been emphasized, though in some cases their influence may be more symbolic than real.[47] The Central Committee and Auditing Commission of the Tadzhik Communist Party, for example, included a substantial proportion of women of local nationality between 1948 and 1956—between 10 and 14 percent of the Central Committee total—while there was never more than one woman of Russian nationality on these bodies at any time.[48] Yet within the Central Committee apparatus the sit-

until 1956, and in Tadzhikistan until 1956. These departments were abolished in 1956 and 1957 in all republics.

[46]A regression analysis of the relationship between female educational attainments and the proportion of women in administrative categories covered by the 1970 census reports yielded no significant correlation. I am extremely grateful to Jerry Hough for his help in investigating this problem.

[47]The argument that Soviet nationality policy more generally has assigned to native elites ceremonial rather than substantive authority has been made by a number of authors. But the parallels between the role of female political elites and of native cadres are striking. As Massell has expressed it, "having been mobilized from a particular tradition and ethnic matrix, Central Asian specialist elites and political cadres, instead of being designated for full membership in the ruling stratum, were in effect relegated to precarious interstitiality in politics and culture. Instead of becoming full-fledged political actors in their own right, they were designated as political and cultural brokers . . . in their own societies—to act on behalf of forces beyond their control, and to be neither fully a part of their own native milieu nor a fully integrated part of the world of their Russian sponsors." Gregory Massell, "Modernization and Nationality Policy in Soviet Central Asia: Problems and Prospects," in Cocks, Daniels, and Heer, *The Dynamics of Soviet Politics*, p. 287.

[48]Teresa Rakowska-Harmstone, *Russia and Nationalism in Soviet Central Asia: The Case of Tadzhikistan* (Baltimore, 1970), p. 103.

TABLE 29
DISTRIBUTION OF WOMEN IN REPUBLIC LEADERSHIP BY
FUNCTIONAL GROUPS
(AS A PERCENT OF TOTAL NUMBER OF OCCUPANCIES)

Group 1	Education Science and Culture[a] Foreign Affairs	26.7
Group 2	Social Security Health[b] Trade Union	17.8
Group 3	Propaganda/Ideology Women's Affairs Komsomol Radio and Press	17.1
Group 4	Industry and Transport Light and Food Industry[c] Local Industry	11.6
Group 5	Economy Planning Statistics Trade and Finance	8.9
Group 6	Administrative Justice Control	6.2
Group 7	Everyday Servicing Communal Economy	6.2
Group 8	Construction Building Materials Industry	2.7
Group 9	Supreme Soviet	1.4
Group 10	Agriculture Forestry	1.4
		100

SOURCE: Based on data in Grey Hodnett and Val Ogareff, *Leaders of Soviet Republics, 1955–1972* (Canberra, 1973), and compiled by Val Ogareff.
[a]Mainly in culture.
[b]Predominantly in social security.
[c]Predominantly in light and food industry.

uation was reversed.[49] A large Russian majority, which included many women, dominated the apparatus, while it contained few female native cadres. Local cadres, and especially women, were most prominent in symbolic positions and in those areas that required direct contact with the local population and a knowledge of local languages—areas like agitprop, culture, and work among women—while Russians dominated those departments concerned with administration and with technical and economic affairs.

The reasons why women in positions of leadership at the republic and national levels tend to be concentrated in relatively few functional areas become clearer if we take a closer look at the career patterns and affiliations of female members of the regional elite. Of 116 women identified by Moses who served in some capacity at the regional level in 1970, almost half were responsible for ideological and cultural activities.[50] Only six of the total served as industrial secretaries or in industrial departments, and an additional ten had functional responsibilities for agriculture. In most cases, they were supervising activities in areas where women predominated, and their responsibilities tended to involve primarily rural regions and to be directed toward policy arenas of lower priority and status. Where major cultural institutions or research institutes fell within the province of a position, it tended to be occupied by a male.

The tendency of female professional and political leaders to be assigned to a limited range of functional responsibilities is equally pronounced in the careers of the twenty-six women members of *obkom* bureaus. Moreover, although the sample is too small to permit firm generalizations, the career patterns of the twenty-six women at the *obkom* level studied by Moses differed from those of their male counterparts in several other rather striking respects. While the typical male *obkom* member was recruited from a position outside the region and was then rotated between several positions and functional responsibilities to enable him to acquire a variety of skills and experiences, the typical female *obkom* member was a "local," recruited from a lower position within the region itself. She characteristically held only one position during her entire tenure on the bureau, either retaining it for a long period of time or serving only briefly before reassignment to a lower ranking position. Over a quarter of the women, and only 3 percent of the men, had held the same position for more than a decade. Only two of the twenty-six women were promoted to higher positions outside the region, in both cases becoming Minister of Social Security in the Russian Republic. As Moses suggests:

> If a highly mobile "generalist," tested frequently in several different leadership positions and locales, is preferred in assignments to the central organs, then

[49]*Ibid.*, p. 106.
[50]Moses, "Women in Political Roles," in Atkinson, Dallin, and Lapidus, *Women in Russia*.

even the female elite in these twenty-five regions would be seriously disqualified for further promotion considerations by the parochialism of their political associations and by the limited geographical context in which they have been able to prove their leadership capabilities.[51]

The different male and female career patterns within the Party leadership and within the political elite more generally may in turn be traced back to differences in educational background. As we have seen, Soviet studies of the occupational preferences and valuations of schoolchildren indicate the existence of substantial sex-linked differentiation, with boys attaching greater value to technical occupations and girls valuing teaching, medicine, and cultural work more highly. These preferences are in turn reflected in patterns of educational enrollment. Women are heavily concentrated in medical and pedagogical institutes and in the humanities faculties of higher educational institutions. Yet it is precisely those industrial, technical, and agricultural specializations, which men tend to enter in larger proportions, that have the greatest "professional convergence," to use the phrase of Eulau and Sprague, with the skills demanded of political leaders in the Soviet system. Just as law and politics have common role requirements in the American political system, so do these specializations contribute to the exercise of Party leadership in the Soviet context. Thus, the concentration of women in educational and cultural specializations at early stages of their professional careers shapes the positions they come to occupy within the Party elite as well.

Finally, these political roles may be more congruent with the family responsibilities of women political professionals. The lower pressure for geographical mobility, the less demanding training involved, and possibly even the less competitive environment of ideological and cultural work by comparison with industrial assignments, may also make these areas more attractive to women with family responsibilities. We might also speculate that the lower mobility of women is also related to interruptions in the development of their political careers. Women appointed to *obkom* bureaus were typically recruited at relatively late stages of their careers. All the female *obkom* bureau members in 1973, with the exception of the Komsomol First Secretary, were well past fifty years old, while the average age of all female officials studied by Moses was forty-five to fifty.[52] Without actual data on the marital status and family situation of these women, however, the relative weight of family responsibilities by comparison with other factors cannot properly be assessed.

[51]*Ibid.*
[52]*Ibid.*

THE POLITICAL MARGINALITY OF WOMEN: TWO EXPLANATIONS

The explanations that have been advanced to account for the marginal political role of women in all political systems fall into two broad categories. One group of explanations focuses on the problems of supply, taking the lower level of motivations and achievement of women themselves as the central factor. The other emphasizes the demand side, insisting that both overt and subtle patterns of discrimination operate to screen women out of political roles.

A number of factors are responsible for the inability or unwillingness of women to actively seek political careers, factors that are themselves shaped in part by the particular features of the Soviet system and the varied and complex demands it makes of its citizens. Party membership itself entails heavy responsibilities. To advance within the Party apparatus requires a high degree of mobility, as well as an enormous commitment of time and energy beyond the demands of a job or profession. As one member of a local Party bureau complained in a letter to *Pravda*:

> Each of us is obliged to attend in the course of one month: two sessions of the Party bureau, one meeting for all Party members in the garage, two sessions of the People's Control group and one general meeting each of the shop Party organization's Communists, the column trade union and the brigade.
> To this we must still add the quarterly meetings of the People's Control groups and of the Party organization *aktiv*, conferences, etc. Add participation in ad hoc commissions and People's Control inspections—sometimes lasting several days—and there goes your week! All our month's free days turn out to be taken up by volunteer work.
> Of course, each of us has a family, too, for which time must be allotted.[53]

Although the substantial educational attainments and professional accomplishments of Soviet women could conceivably enhance their level of political exposure, equip them with the requisite political skills, and motivate them to seek political careers, conflicting tendencies push in a different direction. The extensive involvement of Soviet women in full-time jobs or professional careers, added to the burden of family responsibilities that are not widely shared by men, may reduce the willingness of women to take on Party responsibilities as well. Those who do take an active role tend to do so at the local level, avoiding the mobility that would accompany a more ambitious political career.

The absence of sufficiently extensive data concerning the marital and family status of female Party members and leaders, their class background, occupations, or career patterns and affiliations, make it impossible to determine the extent to which these factors do in fact shape the

[53]"Party Life: How Can Time Be Found?" *Current Digest of the Soviet Press (CDSP)* 21 (1969): 21.

political roles that women might otherwise play. It is quite possible that, given the very high proportion of widowed or unmarried women in the older age cohort, family responsibilities alone would account for only a part of the problem.

It would also be useful to distinguish the effects of such objective constraints from those of more general role expectations that result from patterns of socialization—to inquire whether the socialization of women directs them away from the political arena and from leadership roles at a relatively early age, even before real marital or family obligations take on importance. The more substantial role of women in positions of leadership within the Komsomol deserves investigation, although it would appear that Komsomol work is a channel into precisely those ideological functions that women perform within the Party but not into the industrial positions that are an avenue to political mobility.[54]

A final explanation points to the paucity of women with the necessary skills and qualifications for positions of leadership. It focuses upon the relatively late entry of women into the educational system, the skilled labor force, and managerial level positions and suggests that the time lag explains the lack of women in the key positions and occupations from which Party leaders are recruited. Qualified women are simply not yet available in sufficiently large numbers.

While the consequences of the time lag are important and deserve attention, this argument is not without its problems. First, it assumes the existence of an evolutionary process with increasing entry of women into positions of leadership over time. Yet we have already seen that regional differences in female political roles bear little relationship to developmental level, and that while female Party membership declines with educational level, relative saturation rates are constant for men and women at each level. Moreover, even in the professions that women have dominated for several decades—medicine and education—their role declines as one moves higher in the hierarchy of status and authority. There appears to be no direct and simple correlation between educational attainment, occupational achievement, and recruitment to political roles. Party recruitment is the consequence of internal decisions reflecting organizational and political needs and is therefore shaped by a somewhat different constellation of factors than those which shape the recruitment of women into economic roles.

Additionally, to assume that Party recruitment occurs at relatively late stages of a career is to ignore the youthful complexion of a substantial

[54]Only a small proportion of Party secretaries whose career patterns were studied by Jerry Hough had Komsomol backgrounds; *The Soviet Prefects* (Cambridge, Mass., 1969) p. 73. Hough emphasizes the importance of technical expertise and managerial experience in appointments of Party secretaries at the local and regional level in recent years.

proportion of new Party recruits. Nearly three-fourths of the Party membership in 1967 had joined the Party after 1946, and over half were under age forty.[55] Indeed, the membership of the Party experienced its longest period of sustained growth between 1954 and 1964, increasing by more than 70 percent. It was therefore recruiting from among a pool of better educated young people in an age group in which the educational attainments of women were at least comparable to those of men.

Finally, to focus exclusively on the level of achievement of women as an explanation of their underrepresentation within the Party is to view the Party as a mere mirror of the distribution of status and power within Soviet society rather than as an institution that actively shapes it. The under-representation of women in the Party does not merely reflect lower levels of achievement. It enhances and perpetuates the problem. Precisely because Party membership constitutes a major channel of social mobility within the Soviet system and is a condition of access to elite status, the relatively low proportion of women in the Party membership and leadership limits their future occupational and professional options. Conversely, the active recruitment of women into the Party and their assignment to a variety of functional responsibilities and positions of leadership would enhance their skills and experience and alter the structure of other opportunities available to them.

Thus, we must direct our attention to the problem of demand as well as supply, and we must emphasize the importance of Party recruitment and assignment policies for the political role of women. As we have already noted, recruitment policies seem to account more directly for the noted variations in female membership than any other factor. The impact of recruitment policies was even more dramatic in those cases where, despite extremely low levels of education and skill among women, their percentage of membership rose quickly to match the nationwide norms. In recent years, the steady growth of the Party and its efforts to recruit more actively among under-represented groups have been conducive to the increased entry of women, as have efforts to strengthen the Party's representation in newly growing areas of the economy, the white-collar and service sectors, in which women play a predominant role.

But it is clear that within the Party itself there is considerable hesitation in promoting women to positions of real authority. Khrushchev considered this a serious problem, complaining to the 20th Party Congress in 1956 that "many Party and Soviet bodies exhibit timidity about putting women in executive posts. Very few women hold leading Party and Soviet positions, particularly as party committee secretaries."[56] The legacy

[55]Leonard Schapiro, "The 24th CPSU Congress: Keynote—Compromise," *Problems of Communism* 20 (July-August 1971): 4.
[56]*Pravda*, February 15, 1956.

of traditional role stereotypes is even more persistent in Soviet Central Asia, where the promotion of local women to key positions in the Party and state hierarchy is still considered to be a major problem, attributed to the "survival in the minds of many leaders of feudal bey attitudes." The Secretary of the Tadzhik Communist Party himself complained that even when women were placed in executive positions at the insistence of higher authorities, they were often quietly removed subsequently.[57]

The hesitation of Party officials to assign female Party activists to positions of authority finds fictional expressions as well. In one recent story, a Party official strikes the two female names from a list of candidates for appointment as Party representative to a research institution, reflecting to himself: "It was not that he had a low opinion of women [as Party leaders] in general. In textile mills, schools, hospitals, cafeterias, a woman, he granted, could do all right. But for a research institute or a plant—surely, there was no shortage of men in the Party?"[58] This form of role stereotyping, which involves a reluctance to place women in positions of authority over males, tends to perpetuate a pattern in which women rise to important positions only in institutions and economic areas of relatively low priority and status, traditionally defined as "women's fields," and to limit their entrance into fields that give more direct access to power. It is precisely at this juncture that the marginal political status of women joins the broader pattern of educational and occupational stratification we have already sketched. The educational and professional roles of women lack congruence with the skills and orientations demanded for political leadership, confining women to a narrow range of political roles with limited opportunities for upward mobility.

The hesitation in promoting women to responsible positions and the reluctance of women to accept them have been explicitly recognized as problems within the Party. At a plenary session of the Ivanovo Province Party Committee convened in July 1975 to discuss questions of women's economic and political participation, it was noted that a number of Party organizations had given insufficient attention to promoting female cadres. This failure was attributed to the presence of "a certain psychological barrier" that resulted in a situation where "on the one hand, a number of leaders fear to entrust women with responsible positions, and on the other, women themselves demonstrate timidity, doubting their strength and refusing, under various pretexts, a transfer to leading work."[59]

The political and developmental priorities of the system itself reinforce the political marginality of women. The Party's self-definition at different

[57]Rakowska-Harmstone, "Russia and Nationalism," p. 173.
[58]D. Pavlova, "Sovest'," cited in Xenia Gasiorowska, *Women in Soviet Fiction* (Madison, 1968), p. 210.
[59]*Partiinaia zhizn'*, no. 16, August 1975, p. 44.

stages of its evolution, as well as its recruitment policies, affects the availability of women for political roles. Explanations that emphasize the lack of motivation and ability on the part of women, or outright discrimination against them, ignore the extensive interaction between the structure of opportunity and the structure of individual choices.

This analysis of patterns of female political participation in the Soviet Union enables us to draw several broad conclusions about the forces that have shaped women's political roles. There has clearly been a long-term growth of involvement of women in public affairs, particularly at the local level and in the activities of the soviets. Economic development and rising educational attainments have been associated here, as elsewhere, with rising rates of female participation in political activities of various kinds. The tempo of this growth has been uneven, however, fluctuating in response to changing political requirements.

The most intensive efforts to bring women into new political roles have occurred in the context of broader redefinitions of political priorities. In the first fifteen years of Soviet rule, for example, a period in which the new leadership was committed to transforming traditional roles and relationships and sought to establish legitimacy by gaining support from new social groups, a variety of innovative policies was designed to bring women into political life. In the Central Asian regions of the USSR as well, political priorities encouraged the intensive recruitment of women to elite positions.

While the vast mobilizations of the Five Year Plan at first brought a new wave of female recruits into the ranks of the Party, the advance stopped in 1932. The shift in values and the bureaucratization of the political system that accompanied the consolidation of Stalin's rule demanded new political qualities. The purges, which decimated the prerevolutionary generation of politically aware and active women, and the rapid pursuit of industrialization facilitated the upward mobility of men into managerial and administrative positions in the state and Party hierarchy, to the virtual exclusion of women. The involvement of women at lower levels of the political system continued to increase slowly, but their role at higher levels remained stable until the exigencies of war created new but ultimately temporary opportunities. In recent years the increasing involvement of women at lower levels of the political system has been a function of efforts to widen the social bases of the political system and to extend the Party's influence in the newly expanding sectors of the economy.

Our survey further suggests a rather low correlation between increased mass involvement at lower levels of the political system and access of women to positions of political leadership. So few women have been members of the Central Committee during its entire history that efforts to discern long-term trends are distorted by the small size of the sample. Moreover, while the two or three female members of the Central Committee in earlier years were important political figures in their own right, in recent years many have been appointed for symbolic reasons, to give a more populist aura to the elite by recognizing the contributions of outstanding workers and peasants. Although increasing numbers of women serve as Party secretaries at lower levels of the system and women are found in substantial numbers within the apparatus itself, they have not been given recognition and promotion to leading positions in substantial numbers in recent years.

Nor is the role of women within the Party leadership highly correlated with the increasing participation of women in the labor force and in professions in roles requiring professional expertise and executive authority. In the entire period from 1939 to 1959, when the role of women in the labor force and in professional and managerial positions was increasing dramatically in many areas, the proportion of women among full-time secretaries of primary Party organizations increased by only 1 percent, while their proportion of general Party membership actually declined. The intensified recruitment of women to meet the wartime emergency was not sustained in the postwar period, when many women who had moved into important positions were replaced by men returning from the front. Thus, although there are periods in which political and economic needs coincide, there is little evidence of either a correlation between levels of political participation and political leadership or a close correlation between economic roles and political ones.

Finally, the Soviet sources show a rather limited insight into the whole range of problems surrounding the process of socialization into sex roles that has become such an important area of inquiry in Western sociology. Little attention has been devoted to the questions of role stereotyping and the influence of role models in political socialization. The emphasis in Marxist-Leninist theory on the economic sources of inequality obscures the ways in which the distribution of status and authority may be rooted in other mechanisms. The rather crude materialism of Soviet social analysis has resulted in a tendency to underestimate the psychological origins of attitudes toward authority and power.

Consequently, although the Soviet regime has brought about a dramatic alteration in the occupational aspirations and roles of Soviet women, the efforts to alter political roles have been less far-reaching in their consequences. Although the level of mass political participation has increased dramatically as a result of Soviet policy, no comparable successes have been achieved in drawing women into positions of political leadership.

Many of the generalizations about patterns of female political participation found in the behavioral literature seem to describe the Soviet scene
as well. Here, as elsewhere, the participation of women is greatest in areas
closest to traditional feminine concerns: public health, education, local
trade, and services. Women's political activity is greatest at the local level
and in contexts that are not stepping stones to national political careers,
while men remain dominant in the centers of national power: the army,
the bureaucracy, the police, and the Party.

SEVEN

Women and the Family: Changing Attitudes and Behavior

While growing prosperity since the end of World War II has strengthened the family, the positive influence is not as direct as had been expected. Life shows that improved conditions and equal rights for both sexes do not automatically strengthen the institution of marriage.

A. Kharchev

IN asserting, in 1919, that "the family is ceasing to be a necessity for its members as well as for the state,"[1] Aleksandra Kollontai was passing a judgment that even five decades later appears premature. The 1970 census recorded the existence of some 58.7 million families in the USSR, embracing 94 percent of the Soviet population.[2] This evident attachment to the institution of the family by its members is exceeded only by that of the state itself. When Khrushchev insisted, at the 22nd Party Congress in 1961, that "those who maintain that the family will become less important in the transition to communism and that with time it will disappear are entirely wrong,"[3] he was merely reiterating what has been the official Soviet position since the mid-1930s, a position that the present leadership has reaffirmed.

The survival of the family as an important social institution and the dramatic shift in official attitudes toward it had important consequences for the status and role of women. The patterns of political authority and economic development associated with Soviet modernization affected the structure and functions of the Soviet family. Its performance of critical

---

[1]Aleksandra Kollontai, *Sem'ia i kommunisticheskoe gosudarstvo* (Moscow, 1919), p. 6.
[2]T. N. Roganova, "Chislo i sostav semei v SSSR," in *Vsesoiuznaia perepis' naseleniia 1970 goda: Sbornik statei*, ed. G. M. Maksimova (Moscow, 1976), p. 269.
[3]*Pravda*, October 19, 1961, p. 8.

social functions rested on a sexual division of labor within the family that limited the expansion of female roles outside it. As a consequence, while a major thrust of Soviet efforts over several decades has been to enhance the participation of women in economic and political life, both the form of this participation and its limits are largely determined by women's continuing family responsibilities, imposing severe constraints on the equal participation of women in public domains, creating strains in values and behavior at all levels of the social system, and posing critical problems for public policy in the decades ahead.

From the earliest days of the Soviet regime, radical changes in the family were perceived to be essential to the achievement of sexual equality. The attitudes and behaviorial patterns that characterized the traditional patriarchal household would have to be ruptured in order to engage women more actively in public life. At the same time, it was expected that new forms of economic and political participation would have a reciprocal impact on domestic roles. Authority and independence acquired in public arenas would enhance women's status and power within the family. Early controversies raged over the degree to which family change was a cause or a consequence of broader socio-economic changes and over whether direct or indirect measures would prove more efficacious at inducing it. But the family was an explicit object of public policy from the start, and its transformation was viewed as a necessary condition of altering patterns of participation and authority in the wider society.

In their amalgam of apocalyptic vision and interventionist disposition, as in their recognition of the crucial interdependence of public and familial roles, Soviet perceptions and strategies stood in striking contrast to Western approaches. In the United States in particular, the family has been viewed as a quintessentially private and autonomous, if not sacred and inviolable, institution, rather than as a fit subject of governmental intervention. Its contribution to individual fulfillment has been emphasized more than its performance of vital social functions. The value attached to family privacy and autonomy has obscured the degree to which implicit assumptions about male-female relations, family patterns, and reproductive behavior are embedded in public policy in the United States. Marriage and divorce laws, tax measures, and social insurance and welfare programs, to cite just a few examples, embody specific assumptions and values with respect to sex roles and family behavior, whose provisions in turn shape the economic and social context in which private choices are made.[4]

[4]The often archaic assumptions underlying American statutory law and the struggle to alter the law to conform to contemporary social realities are examined in Leo Kanowitz, *Women and the Law: The Unfinished Revolution* (Albuquerque, 1969), and Lenore Weitzman, "Legal Regulation of Marriage: Tradition and Change," *California Law Review* (July–September 1974): 1169–1288. The anachronistic and discriminatory provisions of administrative

The Soviet leadership, by contrast, has shown greater awareness of the potential influence of social constraints and incentives in shaping individual behavior. By approaching the family as a social as well as a biological institution, Soviet leaders anticipated that its forms and functions would change in relation to the wider social environment. They treated the family as a malleable institution that was properly the object of public policy. The distinctive impact of Soviet policies and priorities, as well as the effects of such universal developmental processes as industrialization and urbanization, has shaped the features of the contemporary Soviet family in fundamental ways.

At the same time, the family is more than the passive object of broader economic and political pressures. As a fundamental agency of socialization, as a supplier of essential productive, reproductive, and emotional services, and as a basic unit of decision-making that mediates the relation of public and private domains, the family has been an active subject as well as an object in the drama of social change. However much its evolution has been shaped by the policies and priorities of the Soviet regime, it has itself exerted an influence on outcomes, facilitating certain types of changes while serving as a stubborn barrier to others and assimilating new pressures and opportunities into older attitudinal and behavioral patterns.

This pivotal role of the family as both subject and object of broader social changes has thrust it to the center of attention and concern in recent years, and not only in the USSR. The family stands at the vortex of a broad array of critical social issues in developing and industrial societies alike, raising profound and controversial problems for contemporary public policy. The terms of current controversies over the present condition and future evolution of the family in the USSR, however, bear the imprint of distinctive expectations and commitments. The comfortable assumption that the liberation of women and the reform of the family go hand in hand in a socialist society, and that they generate marital stability and high rates of reproduction, has been shattered by rising divorce rates and declining fertility. These trends evoke enormous anxiety, challenging as they do the complacent assertion that Soviet conditions make possible an optimal combination of female social participation with marriage and motherhood. By drawing attention to the acute strains resulting from conflicting pressures at all levels of the social system and the consequent serious implications for regime priorities, current patterns of family behavior have forced a fundamental reconsideration of a whole range of economic and social policies bearing on both the future of the family and the meaning of sexual equality.

---

regulations regarding unemployment insurance, social security benefits, federal survivor and disability insurance, and public assistance programs are discussed in Colquitt Walker, "Sex Discrimination in Government Benefit Programs," *Hastings Law Journal* (November 1971): 277–94.

We can attempt here only a brief and tentative analysis of the broad implications of Soviet development for the fate of the family and of the effects of changes in family structure and functions on female roles, identity, and status, teasing out of the fragmentary data some indications of current patterns and trends. The theoretical importance of the family as the link between macro-societal changes in the political-economic domain and the evolution of culture and personality is matched by its actual mystery,[5] and in this respect the Soviet family remains a particular enigma. Changes in family policies can be traced with relative ease, though without direct testimony of the concerns that prompted them or the decision-making process of which they were an outcome; evidence of their impact on family behavior eludes our grasp. The social history of the Soviet family in all its social and cultural diversity awaits systematic investigation by Soviet and Western scholars alike.

In this necessarily brief and preliminary overview, three issues will form the focus of our concern. The first is the evolution of official perspectives and policies. Here, we will be examining the family as an ideological construct—as an expression of official perceptions, attitudes, and priorities—at successive stages of Soviet development. The second of our concerns will be with basic patterns and trends in actual family behavior. Using a number of demographic indicators, we will analyze the impact of broader economic and social changes on family structure and behavior as manifested in patterns of marriage, divorce, and reproduction. Finally, we will investigate the role of women within the family itself, directing our attention to patterns of family authority and the sexual division of labor. This overview will permit us to draw some broader conclusions about the way in which the relationship of the family to the economic system has both accommodated and constrained an expansion of female occupational roles. As this analysis will reveal, those aspects of Soviet development that have tended to promote the equality of women have been substantially offset not merely by the persistence of traditional values but by economic and political priorities and by patterns of authority that have sustained and reinforced the differentiation of male and female roles.

FEMALE LIBERATION AND FAMILY COHESION: CONTRADICTORY IMPERATIVES IN SOVIET FAMILY POLICY

The evolution of Soviet family policy reflects an underlying tension between the conflicting requirements of female liberation and social cohesion. In classical Marxist theory, as in early Soviet policy, the transformation of the family was perceived to be essential to the liberation of

[5]Christopher Lasch, "The Family and History," *The New York Review of Books*, 20 (November 13, 1975): 33.

women. This transformation was envisioned as involving two distinct but related processes. First, it required a shift of functions from the family to the wider society. The nationalization of industry and the modernization of agriculture would deprive the household of the economic resources that sustain patriarchal authority, while the expansion of public education and child care and the social provision of household services would reduce the significance of the family in performing these functions as well. The burden of traditional responsibilities would thus be lifted from the shoulders of women, freeing them to participate in social production and in public life. Secondly, the transformation of the family required the establishment of equality in marriage. Equal rights in law, augmented by equal economic resources, would create a new symmetry in male-female relations and provide the foundations for sexual equality within the family itself.

Although official Soviet writings insist on the continuity of Soviet orientations toward the family and deny that revolutionary commitments were subsequently repudiated, the actual evolution of family policy has taken a more complex course.[6] As we have seen, the increasing reliance on the family for the performance of important social tasks combined with resource constraints generated by other economic priorities to inhibit the transfer of family functions to social institutions and to encourage a growing preoccupation with maintaining the family's stability and cohesion.

The evolution of Soviet family policy has therefore been marked by the tension between conflicting priorities. On the one hand, female independence and equality are enshrined in Soviet law, in clear recognition of the contribution of egalitarian and individualistic norms to the tasks of national development. At the same time, concurrent efforts to stabilize and strengthen the family as a fundamental social institution have come into conflict with these norms, forcing successive readjustments in the balance between the two goals in response to changing political priorities. The effort to balance these contradictory needs can be traced over a wide range of issue areas.

As we observed earlier, in the first years of the Soviet regime the conflict of contradictory imperatives was minimal. The weakening of the family served both the needs of insurgency and the goals of liberation and equality. Freedom of marriage and divorce was therefore emphasized, and

---

[6]If Western studies have on occasion exaggerated the hostility of the early Soviet regime to the family, current Soviet writings, by contrast, attach insufficient weight to this radical millenarian current. The shift in orientation that reached a climax in the mid-1930s is projected backward in time, creating an impression of continuity and consistency that is not altogether warranted; see, for example, the critique of Western treatments by A. G. Kharchev, "Sem'ia i sotsializm," *Kommunist* 37 (May 1960): 53–63. Although the view that the family would ultimately "wither away" as a social institution received serious expression within the revolutionary left, the mainstream of Party thinking sought the radical reform of the family rather than its total destruction.

state regulation was held to a minimum. Over time, however, the increasing reliance on the family for the performance of a broad array of socially important tasks strained against the initial treatment of the family as a relatively autonomous, spontaneous, and self-governing small group.

The critical stance toward the family embodied in Soviet legislation in the immediate postrevolutionary period reflected a conviction that the replacement of familial with individualistic values was essential to the social mobilization of women. Initial commitments to the transfer of family functions to the larger society, to equality in marriage, and to a redefinition of women's roles expressed a desire to destroy the foundations of traditional social hierarchies and to redirect energies away from private and family-centered concerns toward a productivity-oriented and competitive public arena.

Missing from initial Soviet perceptions was full awareness of the interdependence of male and female roles, identities, and statuses. The assumption that sexual liberation was largely analogous to class, generational, and ethnic liberation neglected the distinctive problems this interdependence raised for sexual equality. Only when the mobilization of women proved so threatening to males that it endangered other regime priorities did the explosive potential of sexual liberation become apparent.

Similarly, a full awareness of the social functions performed by the family was also largely missing from initial Soviet perceptions. Here, too, the complacent assumption that the transformation of the family was somehow congruent with all other desirable changes involved an underestimation of potentially conflicting goals. Consequently, when a shift of policy did eventually come, it was abrupt in form and dramatic in content.

This shift was motivated by the economic and political requirements of Stalinism and was made possible by the destruction of the socioeconomic framework in which the traditional family was embedded. As we have seen, from the mid-1930s on the family was assigned an increasingly critical role in sustaining new patterns of authority, maintaining a high birthrate, and maximizing the productivity of the labor force by accommodating itself to female employment outside the home while still providing a full range of domestic services. The intensification of state demands on the family was accompanied by an augmentation of state regulation. A social interest in the consequences of marriage now took precedence over the need for freedom and autonomy within it. The value attached to family stability was expressed by restricting the freedom to marry, divorce, or choose not to bear children.

But Stalinist policies did not effect men and women in identical ways. On the contrary, the new family legislation enshrined a double standard in Soviet law by compelling women alone to bear the consequences of extramarital sexual activity. Paternity was no longer treated as a biological

238   *Women in Soviet Society*

fact but as a legal obligation deriving only from registered marriage. Maternity, by contrast, was assigned social consequences whether or not it was associated with legal marriage, for it carried full responsibility for an illegitimate child. In this way the influence of female biology on destiny was enhanced by Soviet law.

The new family policies did, of course, offer additional protection and increased financial benefits to mothers. In this respect the state was, in effect, offering women compensation to offset the claims that could no longer be made against men. But insofar as family stability was perceived to conflict with the equal treatment of women, the former took clear precedence.

The subordination of sexual equality to political needs encountered sharp and widespread criticism in the years following Stalin's death in 1953. Advocates of a reform of family law based on a return to Leninist principles directed their criticisms to precisely those provisions which sacrificed the needs of the family as a voluntary association to the interests of the state. Thus, Anna Pergament, an expert on civil and family law and a leader of the reform movement, insisted in 1956 that the real reasons for the 1944 family edict be explicitly acknowledged: "It may be possible to show that the retreat from the principle [of equality of men and women] is dictated by *more important state interests*—which is incorrect in our opinion—but one must not deny that indubitable fact."[7] The reformers went on to point out that the effects of the Stalinist legislation directly subverted its original intent. Severe restrictions on legal divorce simply resulted in the de facto dissolution of marriage and the creation of new families outside the scope of state regulation altogether. The treatment of illegitimacy, far from buttressing the family, actually encouraged extramarital liaisons by freeing men from responsibility for their consequences. It was not support payments that threatened the stability of the family but extramarital relations themselves. The victims of Stalinist policy were ultimately the children; they suffered economic discrimination and social stigma through no fault of their own.[8] Thus, the proponents of reform —and women figured prominently among them—called for changes in family policy that would restore freedom of marriage and divorce, grant equal rights to all children regardless of the relationship of their biological parents, and assign equal responsibility to mothers and fathers alike.

The persistence of a double standard of sexual morality in Party and legal circles posed a serious obstacle to reform. In conversations with a number of conservative officials and jurists, Peter Juviler was informed

[7]Peter H. Juviler, "Family Reforms on the Road to Communism," in *Soviet Policy-Making*, eds. Peter H. Juviler and Henry W. Morton (New York, 1967), p. 35.
[8]*Ibid.*, p. 58. Several different estimates indicate a figure of approximately eight million illegitimate children for the 1950s. See also Juviler's "Soviet Families," p. 57.

that "a woman is a maid only once and must guard her female honor" and that "we must protect the family, the male [pause] . . . and the female."[9] Opponents of the proposed reforms united moralism with self-interest in their fear that the stability of legal families would be threatened by granting unwed mothers the right to open paternity suits. The possible injustice to males of unfounded suits and the disruptive effects such suits might have on other families were deemed greater dangers than the unfair treatment of several million unwed mothers.[10] Opponents of reform insisted, moreover, on the intimate connection between family stability and high fertility. Since Khrushchev himself took credit for having suggested the 1944 edict and stressed the national importance of high birthrates, a reform of Soviet family law awaited his departure from the political scene.

The new family codes, including a reform of divorce in December 1965 and the Basic Principles of Family Law of June 27, 1968, did not go quite so far as the reformers would have wished. Yet on the whole they struck a more reasonable balance between the interest of the state in family stability and the need for greater freedom and equality in personal relationships. Divorce procedures were simplified and fees reduced considerably.[11] Restrictions on medical abortions were also lifted, and reliance was now placed on moral suasion rather than legal prohibition for both divorce and abortion. The new legislation did not return to Leninist precedents; the refusal to recognize unregistered as well as registered marriages was unmistakable evidence that initial commitments to family revolution had been superseded. But the treatment of illegitimacy was modified to permit voluntary acknowledgement of paternity or firm evidence of its acknowledgement and to eliminate the stigma of the "blank space" on a child's birth certificate by allowing the entry of a name and patronymic.[12]

The evolution of Soviet family law has thus reflected shifting official appreciations of the family's role. A willingness to dispense with its functions in the interests of individual freedom and equality was succeeded by new legal arrangements that subordinated both individual freedom and

[9]Juviler, "Family Reforms," p. 47.

[10]*Ibid.*, p. 58.

[11]In cases where both parties seek divorce, and no children are involved, simple registration and a three-month wait are all that are necessary. Court proceedings are required in contested cases and in cases where there are minor children.

[12]Anna Pergament has continued to press for still further reforms in the treatment of children born out of wedlock. She argues that, since state allowances to single mothers are considerably lower than the contributions of a father to a child's support, it is not in the child's interest to restrict the definition of paternity. The narrow list of factors presently establishing paternity is biased against young female workers and office employees, in her view, because their difficult housing and economic circumstances make it impossible to claim joint residence with the child's father. She would therefore amend present laws to allow consideration of any circumstances that would reliably confirm the child's descent from the respondent ("Razvitie sovetskogo zakonodatel'stva o brake i sem'e," *Sovetskoe gosudarstvo i pravo* 9 [September 1975]: 47–51).

female equality to the support and protection of the family. While current Soviet policies reaffirm the desirability of family cohesion, they do so in the context of a more flexible response to individual needs.

A similar tension between the recognition of female equality and the support of family cohesion is manifested as well in the treatment of women in contemporary Soviet family law. A commitment to female independence and equality is balanced by the assignment of special rights and responsibilities to motherhood. The legal rights of women are largely unaffected by marriage itself, in contrast to both continental and common law legal practice. Marriage is not considered to be a device for the economic support of women; males are not assigned the responsibility of support nor are women assigned the reciprocal obligation of providing domestic services. The right to retain a maiden name in entering marriage, to enjoy equal personal and property rights, to control an equal share of community property, and to refuse to accompany a husband in a change of domicile are all enshrined in Soviet legislation. In contrast to American legal practice, not even the definition of rape is altered by the fact of marriage; in principle, nothing prevents the prosecution of a husband for the rape of his wife.[13]

The equal treatment of women gives way to special protection in connection with motherhood rather than marriage. In cases of divorce, no alimony is paid to wives, unless they are disabled, but child support is legally mandated. Neither a pregnant woman nor the mother of an infant under one year of age may be divorced by her husband without her consent. Moreover, pregnancy or motherhood is usually a mitigating factor in the sentencing of women for criminal offenses. In short, the social value attached to reproduction is reflected in the special rights as well as responsibilities of mothers.

The central place the family has come to occupy in official values is expressed even more dramatically in the current reassessment of collective as opposed to family-centered approaches to child-care and household services. Both the socialization of child care and the socialization of household work were intimately associated with the weakening of the family in early Soviet writings. Not surprisingly, a reappraisal of these earlier orientations is under way.

To be sure, a revival of enthusiasm for the collective upbringing of children was evident during Khruschchev's ascendancy. Renewed dis-

---

[13]Twenty-five American states do not permit the prosecution of a husband for rape (*San Francisco Chronicle*, January 25, 1977, p. 1). The legal codes of the various Soviet republics also differ somewhat in their provisions concerning women and the family. For an extensive treatment of Soviet legal practices see E. M. Vorozheikin, *Brak i sem'ia v SSSR* (Moscow, 1973), and Peter H. Juviler, "Women in Soviet Law: Rights, Penalties and Obligations," in *Women in Russia*, eds. Dorothy Atkinson, Alexander Dallin, and Gail Warshofsky Lapidus (Stanford, 1977).

cussion of the nature and requisites of the future Communist society evoked a mixture of populism and utopianism that permeated discussions of education as well as other policy issues. The collectivist vision, still defended by Strumilin, perceived the self-centeredness of the family to be a barrier to communal solidarity. In a critique of "momism" worthy of Philip Wylie, Strumilin warned of the harmful social consequences of maternal egoism:

> Such a mother regards her child, even if he is an ordinary dunce, as a miracle of nature and the apex of perfection. She protects him from his playmates, from the heat, cold and fresh and air, filling him with sweets and medicines, heaping toys and knick-knacks on him, protecting him from all extra mental strains. As a result, mother's little boy, unless subject to other influences, will grow up to be a self-adulating individual sneering at all that surrounds him, in short, a useless individual, a *stilyag*, a good-for-nothing who will never find his place in Soviet life.[14]

Collective upbringing, in the view of its advocates, combined the virtues of proper socialization with the benefits of efficiency. The education of children, they insisted, was far too important to the future Communist society to be left in the hands of untrained and overprotective mothers. The children's collective offered a superior form of upbringing, one that "can do more to inculcate the best social habits than the most sympathetic and loving mother. Prompt and effective reaction on the part of such a collective to all anti-social manifestations prompted by the egoistic disposition of the child are sure to nip them in the bud."[15]

Strumilin himself advocated a program of collective upbringing from infancy. "Emerging from a hospital every Soviet citizen would be assigned to a nursery, then to a kindergarten maintained day and night, then to a boarding school from which he would enter independent life—taking a job in production or continuing his studies in his chosen profession."[16] Khrushchev's own enthusiasm for an expansion of boarding schools was motivated by his desire to weaken what he considered to be the undesirable influence of elite families on the education and placement of children, an influence that impeded his efforts at status equalization. Views such as these, however, did not represent the mainstream of Party opinion, and their political influence proved short-lived. Khrushchev himself repudiated Strumilin's more radical views at the 22nd Party Congress in 1961, denying, in effect, any intention to attack the family as such. The

[14]S. G. Strumilin, "Communism and the Worker's Daily Life," *Novyi mir*, No. 7, 1960; translated in *The Soviet Review* 2 (1961): 10. See also Jerome Gilison, *The Soviet Image of Utopia* (Baltimore, 1975), pp. 102–9. Gilison's heavy reliance on sources of the Khrushchev period may account for the excessive emphasis he gives to the communalist orientation.
[15]Strumilin, "Communism."
[16]*Ibid.*

effort to create a mass network of boarding schools failed to survive his own political demise in 1964.[17]

In recent years a somewhat different emphasis has come to the fore. Current Soviet writings insist on the critical importance of the family in the socialization of young children and offer abundant evidence of what are seen to be the limitations of collective upbringing. Considerable public support for home care of infants amid increasing disenchantment with public day-care facilities has been expressed, particularly among intelligentsia families.[18] In passages reminiscent of American writings of the 1950s, Soviet pedagogues proclaim that the family alone can provide the individual attention that encourages the development of a particular child's unique potential.

The positive association between family upbringing and academic achievement is more a source of satisfaction than of alarm in recent Soviet work. But it is the family's socializing function that takes on special importance in current writings.[19] The ties of affection, respect, and trust that are found in families are now recognized to be essential to the proper moral upbringing of children. While educational institutions are well-suited to imparting knowledge, they are far less effective at inculcating

[17]Thus, the number of boarding schools increased dramatically from 1956, when Khrushchev first espoused them, until 1963–1964, at which point enrollments began to decline. Secondary boarding schools were abolished by decree, exceptions being made only for special elite schools for science, math, languages, and the arts (Juviler, "Soviet Families," p. 53). It should also be kept in mind that, contrary to much Western writing on the subject, the boarding schools were not elite institutions but contained a preponderance of children from broken or unstable families. They also served a rural clientele.

[18]The leveling effects of day-care facilities appear to be responsible for the lack of enthusiasm of many culturally advantaged families from a purely educational standpoint. Moreover, a number of studies have pointed to increased proneness to illness and retarded emotional development as possible negative effects of nursery schools. A recent documentary novella about the life history of a sixteen-year-old criminal, "Down the Staircase," by Valerii Agranovskii, provoked a stormy controversy by placing part of the blame for the boy's downfall on his unhappy kindergarten experience. Several respondents came to the defense of the kindergarten, insisting that assembly-line treatment was far from characteristic of Soviet schools and that the author posed a false conflict between impersonal collective upbringing and the spiritual comfort and affection offered by the family setting. Other respondents, however, refused to blame the family alone and insisted that the author had been, if anything, insufficiently critical of the defects of educational institutions; *Current Digest of the Soviet Press (CDSP)* 28, No. 49 (1976): 17–20.

[19]See, for example, V. Titarenko, "Vliianie semeinykh otnoshenii na uspevaemost' detei," in *Problemy byta, braka i sem'i*, ed. N. Solov'ev, Iu. Lazauskas, and Z. Iankova (Vilnius, 1970), pp. 172–76; R. Gurova, "Sem'ia i shkola," in Solov'ev, et al., *Problemy byta, braka i sem'i*, pp. 200–11. This trend bears a striking similarity to American child-rearing norms of the 1950s as depicted by Philip Slater. The concern with internalization of values rather than external conformity and the emphasis on the full development of the unique potential of each child placed a heavy responsibility on parents and particularly on mothers. In the American context it accompanied the new emphasis on feminine domesticity and gave support to the insistence that a career outside the home constituted a serious and potentially harmful distraction from the tasks of child socialization (*The Pursuit of Loneliness*, [New York, 1976], pp. 62–87).

appropriate values. As a recent pedagogical text explains: "A whole series of character traits are very important for the formation of communist awareness, feelings and characteristics, and only the family can impart them. The family is that social organization which is based upon love and which alone can foster this feeling."[20] Precisely because family upbringing joins authority with affection, it provides the essential condition for the internalization of adult values.

The new importance assigned to the socializing functions of the family is partly a function of new perceptions of the requirements of "developed socialism," to use the official formulation. A reduced reliance on external coercion as a mechanism of social control makes the internalization of norms of critical political importance. As problems of Communist up-bringing come to the center of official attention, a reconsideration of the potential contribution of the family to this process is called for. At the same time, the willingness of the present Soviet leadership to permit a certain crystallization of status hierarchies makes it unnecessary to challenge the potential influence of the family on educational and social placement, as Khruschev attempted to do. In the present political context, the family provides a valued supplement to the influence of educational institutions.

Current Soviet writings similarly attach new importance to the role of the family in providing household services. Where household work was once slated for extinction, to be gradually replaced by the social provision of everyday services, many aspects of household work are now seen by some commentators as constituting desirable contributions to family cohesion. Here, too, linger residues of earlier controversies. Some writers still envision the future Communist society as one in which communal social forms will replace individualistic and family-centered ones: "Under Communism the transition will be completed from the presently-existing separate household economies and individual services to a collective economy and social satisfaction of the daily needs of the people. Collective forms of social economy and communal services will predominate."[21] They predict that "communist society will have a well-arranged system of social feeding. Individual preparation of food in domestic conditions will disappear of itself, as domestic weaving, for example, did in the past."[22]

This vision has been questioned in recent years by a growing number

[20]Cited in Ludwig Leigle, *The Family's Role in Soviet Education* (New York, 1975), p. 26. A similar emphasis on the family's importance in character formation is found in A. G. Kharchev, *Brak i sem'ia v SSSR* (Moscow, 1964), pp. 267–72. Kharchev even mentions the positive contribution that religion can make to child socialization. The authority attributed to God, he suggests, offers an additional measure of social control, compensating in some degree for parental loss of authority (p. 278).
[21]*O kommunizme: kniga dlia chteniia* (Moscow, 1963), p. 380.
[22]*Ibid.*

of analysts who anticipate that the improvement of consumer and social services will assist rather than replace the family. Such analysts defend the retention of significant roles by the family in a future Communist society on the grounds that communal arrangements will not permit the satisfaction of increasingly diverse and individual needs, tastes, and life styles. A virtual apotheosis of the family dinner is offered by a leading family sociologist, A. G. Kharchev, who maintains that Communism "will not mean the compulsion in every instance to use social institutions for the satisfaction of the daily needs of society. Domestic dinners, lunches, domestic evenings and receptions undoubtedly will be preserved in that degree to which they will be necessary for the family in the satisfaction of its needs for 'domestic happiness' and socializing with friends in a home-like atmosphere."[23] Indeed, current writings go even further, not only extolling the virtues of "domestic happiness" but also suggesting that, even though a transfer of family functions to the larger society is for the first time within reach, it should be rejected in the interests of maintaining, even artificially, the function of the family as a social unit.

The potential implications of this reversal of official attitudes become clear in the recent insistence of two sociologists that excessive hopes have been attached to the possibility of shifting the burden of household work to external social institutions. Emphasizing diversity rather than homogeneity as the hallmark of Communist society, they argue that, "to the extent that every family is unique, its household is adjusted to the habits, tastes and temperaments of its members." In a dramatic inversion of revolutionary values, they conclude with the statement: "In the final analysis, the household serves to consolidate the family, and so, many or some aspects of housework cannot be wholly absorbed by the service sector even when the latter is able to [do so] . . . The normal functioning of the family—that primary cell of the socialist social organism—is incompatible with the absolute socialization of *byt* [everyday life]."[24]

Thus, whether in connection with the education and socialization of children or in relation to the provision of everyday services, Soviet sources now assign the family a central and enduring role. The continuing shift

[23]Kharchev, "Sem'ia i sotsializm"; see also his *Brak i sem'ia v SSSR*, p. 319–20.
[24]L. A. Gordon and E. V. Klopov, *Chelovek posle raboty: sotsial'nye problemy byta i vnerabochego vremeni* (Moscow, 1972), pp. 355, 105. The word *byt* has a rich and complex set of meanings that have no simple English equivalent. As an economic category, it includes all those activities and services performed within and outside the home that are essential to the reproduction of labor power, as in *bytovoe obsluzhivanie*, or everyday and consumer services. As a cultural category, it conveys the notion of a total way of life, or life style, including a culturally dictated selection from available alternatives. See the further discussion in A. Kharchev, "Byt i sem'ia kak kategorii istoricheskogo materializma," in Solov'ev, et al., *Problemy byta*, pp. 9–22, and in Stephen and Ethel Dunn, *The Study of the Soviet Family in the USSR and in the West* (American Association for the Advancement of Slavic Studies, forthcoming).

of some child-care and housekeeping functions to the larger society is officially supported and made possible by substantial new investments in public child care and in consumer services. But the total institutionalization of child care, as well as the complete socialization of household services, is officially rejected, not merely postponed to a more affluent future. The revolutionary antithesis of society and family has vanished; its place has been taken by a new image of partnership in fulfilling shared goals.

The full significance of this shift in orientations toward the family can only be appreciated in the larger context of Soviet political evolution in the post-Stalin period. Austerity was a hallmark of Stalinism. The diversion of resources from consumption to investment was sustained by a system of values that emphasized the virtues of asceticism and sacrifice, the postponement of immediate comforts on behalf of a long-term accretion of economic and military power. Conformity was secured through coercion; in both political and economic life, the repression of demand depended on an extensive apparatus of controls.

Even during Stalin's lifetime, the Soviet system relied on positive incentives as well as on coercion and terror. Particularly in the post-war period, as Vera Dunham has eloquently demonstrated,[25] a tacit rapprochement between the Soviet leadership and the resilient middle class was based on a shared interest in social mobility and material rewards. In the years since Stalin's death, the partial dismantling of controls has depended on a still greater responsiveness to popular needs. Increased reliance on incentives rather than coercion as a mechanism of political and economic control was perceived to be a condition of eliciting greater popular initiative. By devoting greater resources to the development of light industry and to consumer goods and services, the Soviet leadership proclaimed the satisfaction of consumer needs to be an important criterion of regime performance. In this respect, both the Khrushchev and the Brezhnev regimes exhibit a common commitment to affluence.

What distinguishes one regime from the other is not a reliance on material incentives as such, but rather the structure of the incentive system. An emphasis on collective as opposed to individual forms of consumption was characteristic of the Khrushchev era. While this emphasis can be traced through a whole range of investment decisions, it was most dramatically evident in the decision to restrict the production of automobiles for private use. The priority given to social rather than private consumption was expected to act as a constraint on family power, particularly within the elite, and as a device to channel family behavior in desired directions. Under Khrushchev, then, the allocation of resources served

[25] Vera S. Dunham, *In Stalin's Time: Middle Class Values in Soviet Fiction* (Cambridge, England 1976).

a transformationist impulse and was designed to create a more egalitarian socialist community by challenging the status and prerogatives of established elites. The shift to a more bureaucratized and hierarchical pattern of political control under Brezhnev is associated with a diminution of measures directed at the equalization of status and a reliance on a pattern of incentives more directly tailored to individual contribution. Reviewing the basic guidelines of the Tenth Five Year Plan at the 25th Party Congress in March 1976, Kosygin summarized the approach of the present leadership in these words:

> As before, the policy the Party pursues in the field of income and consumption proceeds from the premise that the principal means of increasing the population's income is pay raises, which account for three-fourths of the entire increment in income. The aim of this policy is not only to increase working people's consumption systematically, but also to intensify the incentive role of wages, salaries, and collective farmers' pay, making them more dependent on the end results of production and its increased efficiency.[26]

The effect of these policies is to channel a greater share of resources into private rather than socially organized forms of consumption and leisure, enhancing the sphere of activities in which the family occupies a central place and strengthening its economic and placement functions relative to the larger social community.[27] Public discussion of proposals to introduce installment credit to permit the mass purchase of automobiles, to encourage the construction and rental of *dachas* so that family vacations might supplement or replace those organized through enterprises or children's organizations, to expand the private supply of services to supplement the limited and inadequate state sector, and to extend the principles of cooperative housing to the creation of parent cooperative nursery schools are among the many manifestations of these new trends.

The increasing "privatization" of Soviet life and the reassertion of familial values likely to result from recent trends will not have precisely the same consequences for the stratification system that it might in Western societies. The potential threat of such privatization to collective solidarity is constrained by the absence of private ownership of the means of production; by a hierarchical and bureaucratized political system, which gives the Party elite ultimate control over mobility and rewards for

[26]Report by A. N. Kosygin, Chairman of the USSR Council of Ministers, to the 25th Congress of the Communist Party of the Soviet Union, March 1, 1976, reported in *Pravda*, March 2, 1976, p. 3.

[27]To cite just one example, a detailed sociological investigation of the effects of the shift from a six- to a five-day work week in the late 1960s found that the increase in leisure was largely devoted to family-centered social activities when it involved stable rather than shifting work schedules for husbands and wives; L. A. Gordon and N. M. Rimashevskaia, *Piatidnevnaia rabochaia nedelia i svobodnoe vremia trudiashchikhsia* (Moscow, 1972).

achievement; and by centralized control over the allocation of resources, which limits the play of market forces. Within these limits, the new importance assigned to the family and the increasing resources that it will have at its disposal are likely to have a considerable impact on patterns of sexual stratification. Welcome as these trends may be to a population that has had all too little occasion to enjoy the benefits of privacy, consumer goods, and leisure, their consequences for the position of women may be more problematic. To the extent that the Soviet definition of female equality depended on the devaluation of the family rather than on a transformation of sex roles as such, a strengthening of consumption-oriented and familial values will create new demands on women as well as offer them new benefits. It is therefore likely to heighten the already-considerable tension between women's family and work roles and, in the absence of countervailing pressures for an expansion of female status and opportunities outside the family, to sustain a sexual division of labor within it.

CURRENT TRENDS IN FAMILY BEHAVIOR:
MARRIAGE, DIVORCE, AND REPRODUCTION

The massive economic and social changes associated with the Soviet period have had far-reaching consequences for Soviet family life. The disruption of traditional family structures that accompanied industrialization and urbanization was intensified in Soviet conditions by the extraordinary scope and tempo of change.[28] Changes that occurred over an extended period in Western development were compressed into a relatively brief span of time in the Soviet Union, forcing a rapid transition from peasant to blue-collar culture that stamped the Soviet family with distinctive features. High rates of geographical and social mobility accelerated the disintegration of many of the social supports associated with traditional kinship and community structures. Politically directed change imposed additional elements of instability. To the disruptive effects of forced industrialization, collectivization, political terror, purges, and war were added the generational tensions induced by the massive indoctrination of children into radically new values and behavior. The cumulative impact of all these factors undermined the bases of family solidarity and encouraged the individuation and self-assertion of family members.

In many instances, to be sure, and particularly among the intelligentsia, these pressures served to enhance the cohesion of the family in response. As a locus of loyalty and intimacy the family provided a refuge, a temporary escape from the tensions and pressures of the larger political en-

[28]A classic treatment of the relationship of family structure to broader patterns of social change is William J. Goode, *World Revolution in Family Patterns* (New York, 1963). Edward Shorter's *The Making of the Modern Family* (New York, 1975) offers an extensive guide to current research.

vironment.[29] It thus preserved and transmitted important residues of earlier cultural orientations and life styles, even while assimilating and adapting to new attitudes and patterns of behavior. But the very resilience and persistence of the family as a central unit of Soviet social life was evidence of its inner transformation in adapting to a new environment.

The most far-reaching of the changes that the Soviet family has undergone involves its economic role. The shift from agricultural to industrial production and the collectivization of agriculture undermined the traditional peasant household as an institution in which ownership of land enhanced the power of the family as a social unit. The nationalization of industry had a parallel effect in the urban milieu, transferring authority from family to state and limiting the ability of the household head to utilize control over economic resources to assure authority within the family. The decline of the family as a productive unit and the separation of household from employment were not accompanied by the separation of large numbers of women from social production, as in the development of the European and American middle class. Instead, female employment occurred in conditions less favorable to family needs but more independent of family control. Finally, to the extent that access to education, occupational status, and income became relatively independent of the family unit, the bases of paternal authority were further weakened.

At the same time, the expansion of public education removed from the family another of its major functions, the preparation of offspring for adult occupational roles. As first primary and then secondary education became virtually universal, increasing numbers of children were removed from the family environment for substantial portions of the day. Even young children were cared for by an expanding network of preschool institutions in urban areas. Organized youth groups, sport and cultural activities in after-school hours, and summer vacation programs involved yet a further encroachment of external agencies on the family's traditional responsibility for education and socialization. The prevalence of a six-day work week until recently, the pattern of long working hours for women as well as men, and the relative rarity of work schedules that permitted families to vacation together, further reduced the place of family-centered activities in Soviet urban life to a degree that was probably unprecedented.[30]

[29]On the basis of refugee interviews, Kent Geiger concluded that the family was more united by the arrest of a member by the state than by the failure of a husband to earn an adequate income. See Kent Geiger, "Deprivation and Solidarity in the Soviet Urban Family," *American Sociological Review* 20 (1955): 57–68. The positive association of political pressure and family solidarity is also documented in Alex Inkeles and Raymond Bauer, *The Soviet Citizen: Daily Life in a Totalitarian Society* (Cambridge, Mass., 1961), chs. 8 and 9.

[30]The Israeli *kibbutz* would appear to be a partial exception, but insofar as it functions as a closely knit and relatively small community in which mothers staff the children's houses, it functions in important respects as an extended kinship group.

The reproductive functions of the family have also diminished in the more industrial regions of the USSR. The shift from agricultural to industrial production and the state's assumption of responsibility for welfare and social insurance reduced the economic value of children and transformed them from asset to burden. As the desire for children came to be weighed against competing social values—and competing demands on time, energy, and resources—urban families tended to have fewer children and to increase their investment in the psychological, emotional, and intellectual development of each child.[31]

The erosion of traditional patterns of family organization and behavior and the massive shift of resources and authority from family to external agencies limited the power of the family to compel, constrain, or influence individual behavior. This loss of authority, however, was accompanied, in the view of Soviet family sociologists, by the increasing importance of the family in providing psychological stability, emotional satisfaction, and sexual gratification to its members. Soviet treatments overstate the degree to which economic, religious, and familial considerations in marriage have been replaced by affection, but it appears that here, as in other modern societies, the emotional demands on marriage are increasing in intensity.[32] The combination of diminished authority and increased emotional importance—or what Soviet authors describe as the "purification" of family life —is also a major cause of the family's growing instability.

[31]For a discussion of the shift from "quantity" to "quality" in orientations toward child-rearing, see Judith Blake, "Are Babies Consumer Durables?" *Population Studies* 22 (March 1968): 5–25. A similar pattern is documented in a Soviet article comparing a 1929 survey of child-rearing practices with one conducted in 1969: N. Kharitonova, "K voprosu o sotsial'noi dinamike sem'i i semeinogo vospitaniia: Iz opyta sravnitel'nogo issledovaniia," in Sovetskaia Sotsiologicheskaia Assotsiatsiia (henceforth SSA) *Dinamika izmeneniia polozheniia zhenshchiny i sem'ia*, 3 vols. (Moscow, 1972), 1: 134–43.

[32]Although Soviet treatments of marriage patterns stress the replacement of economic and other considerations by ties of affection and romantic love, there is considerable evidence to suggest that material considerations continue to play a significant role in the selection of marriage partners. This is clearly the case with respect to the persistence of such traditional marriage practices as the payment of bride price and other customary arrangements in Soviet Central Asia. The influence of economic and status considerations are indicated in a recent letter from a young worker to the editors of *Literaturnaia gazeta* criticizing this pattern, recounting the disintegration of his own relationship with a woman friend when she became a student. Complaining of the condescension shown by students toward workers, he writes: "Many of them do not hide the fact that they entered higher school not out of any sense of vocation but rather for calculating reasons. They do not care what sort of specialists they become; they are concerned with their 'future position in society.' They are not attracted to people in workers' occupations. If one of them marries, the first thing he or she reports is not what sort of person his or her spouse is but rather who he or she is. If he is an engineer, that means the marriage is a successful one; if not, the person has made a stupid mistake." Translated in *CDSP* 28, No. 18 (1976): 11. Access to apartments and to residence permits in Moscow and Leningrad have also been mentioned in Soviet sources as among the more reprehensible motivations for marriage. At the same time, several writers have questioned whether "love matches" are necessarily more successful than those based on rational calculation. The latter may provide a firmer foundation for marital stability; Iuri Riurikov, *Literaturnaia gazeta* 29 (July 17, 1974): 13.

In the absence of more direct sources of information, a number of demographic indicators offer important clues to current patterns and trends in Soviet family behavior. As we have noted, the family remains a central fact in the lives of most Soviet citizens. Moreover, the nuclear family is overwhelmingly the norm. Almost two-thirds of the 58.8 million households recorded in the 1970 census consisted of a married couple with or without children, and another 11 percent were single-parent families without other relatives present.[33] The extended family was therefore relatively uncommon, accounting for under one-fourth of all Soviet families, and a high proportion of these were concentrated in the Central Asian and Transcaucasian republics. Slightly more than 14 million individuals in a total Soviet population of 241.7 million lived outside families, three-fourths of them women, and of these almost half were sixty years of age or older.[34]

The average Soviet family in 1970 was comparatively small, consisting of 3.7 persons. This national average, however, conceals important regional differences. For the USSR as a whole, four-fifths of urban families and two-thirds of rural families had two to four members. In the Central Asian republics, by contrast, at least 70 percent of all families had four or more members. Moreover, these regional differences actually increased in the eleven-year interval between the census of 1959 and that of 1970. The apparent stability of family size for the USSR as a whole is the product of two contradictory trends: stable or decreasing family size in the urbanized regions of the Slavic and Baltic republics and an increase, of considerable proportions in some cases, among the Moslem populations of Central Asia and in republics like Azerbaidzhan, Armenia, and Georgia, which are predominantly agricultural and where traditional family systems and cultural values have remained most stable.[35]

Marriage rates declined somewhat in the interval between censuses, although the ratio of families to population remained stable.[36] The decline was particularly sharp between 1960 and 1965, when it dropped from 12.1 to 8.7 per thousand. The period since 1967 has been marked by rising

[33]T. N. Roganova, "Chislo i sostav semei v. SSSR," in *Vsesoiuznaia perepis' naseleniia 1970 goda: sbornik statei*, ed. G. M. Maksimova (Moscow, 1976), p. 269.

[34]This figure represents an increase from the 9 million recorded in 1959, and amounts to 5.9 percent of the total population. It does not include members of families living separately from them. *Ibid.*, p. 262–63.

[35]The smallest family size—3.1—is found in Estonia, and the largest—5.4—is found in Tadzhikistan; *Ibid.*, p. 265. Average family size rose from 4.6 to 5.3 in Uzbekistan, 4.5 to 5.1 in Azerbaidzhan, 4.7 to 5.4 in Tadzhikistan, and 4.5 to 5.2 in Turkmenistan.

[36]The actual number of men and women married rose almost 25 percent; according to the 1970 census, 107,200,000 men and women were married, compared with 86,500,000 in 1959 (*Zhurnalist* 1 [January 1974]: 72–73; translated in *CDSP* 26, No. 18 [1974]: 6–7). It should be noted that the census records both registered and unregistered marriages, while the marriage rates are based on registered marriages only.

TABLE 30

REGISTERED MARRIAGES AND DIVORCES, USSR, 1940–1976

	Registered marriages[a]		Registered divorces			U.S.
Year	Number	Per 1,000 population	Number	Per 1,000 population	Per 1,000 marriages	Divorces per 1,000 population
1940	1,228,793	6.3	205,605	1.1	167	2.0
1950	2,080,817	11.6	67,353	0.4	32	2.6
1960	2,591,509	12.1	270,227	1.3	104	2.2
1965	2,008,673	8.7	360,424	1.6	179	2.5
1966	2,087,599	8.9	646,095	2.8	309	
1967	2,131,888	9.0	646,295	2.7	303	2.7
1970	2,365,259	9.7	636,232	2.6	269	2.9
1971	2,460,000	10.0	644,800	2.6	262	3.7[b]
1973	2,516,267	10.1	678,883	2.7	270	4.4
1974	2,606,700	10.3	743,400	2.9	285	4.5
1975	2,722,800	10.7	783,400	3.1	325	4.8
1976		10.1		3.4		

SOURCES: Tsentral'noe statisticheskoe upravlenie, *Narodnoe khoziaistvo SSSR za 60 let* (Moscow, 1977), p. 74; Tsentral'noe statisticheskoe upravlenie, *Naselenie SSSR 1973; statisticheskii sbornik* (Moscow, 1975), p. 150. See also: for 1940–1969, *Vestnik statistiki* 2 (1969): 92; for 1970–1974, *Zhenshchiny v SSSR* (Moscow, 1975), pp. 97, 100; for divorces in 1966, *Zhurnalist* 1 (January 1974): 72–73. The number of divorces per 1,000 marriages was reported to be as high as 408 in 11 major cities in 1973, reaching 425 in Leningrad and 436 in Moscow; Perevedentsev, *Literaturnaia gazeta* 18 (April 30, 1975); for the U.S., *San Francisco Chronicle*, February 9, 1977, p. 1. In the U.S. in 1974 there were a total of 2,233,000 marriages and 948,000 divorces, and a marriage rate of 10.5 per 1,000 population. Recent Soviet figures are found in *Vestnik statistiki* 12 (1975), pp. 89–90 and 11 (1976), pp. 88–89.

[a]Since these statistics do not distinguish first from subsequent marriages, the figures for marriage and divorce are not totally independent of each other. In 1973, 14.6 percent of males and 13 percent of females marrying had been married before; *Naselenie SSSR 1973*, p. 172.

[b]1972

marriage rates, and an average of 2.4 million new marriages has been recorded annually in the past few years (Table 30). Interestingly, more women than men reported themselves married. The census recorded an excess of 1,345,000 wives[37]—possibly a testimony to the comparatively greater value women attach to the marital state, an indication of differences in male and female definitions of unregistered cohabitation, or an effort to protect children born out of wedlock.

The census figures clearly indicate the favorable effect of an improved sex ratio on women's opportunity to marry. By 1970, the ratio of males to females in the USSR was normal for all ages under forty-three, although

[37]L. E. Darskii, *Formirovanie sem'i* (Moscow, 1972), p. 44.

TABLE 31
NUMBER OF MEN AND WOMEN MARRIED,
PER THOUSAND, BY AGE GROUP, USSR,
1959 AND 1970

	Men		Women	
Age Group	1959	1970	1959	1970
16–17	5	4	29	26
18–19	41	39	171	186
20–24	274	289	501	559
25–29	800	772	759	827
30–34	922	887	776	853
35–39	953	933	725	839
40–44	962	946	623	790
45–49	963	952	549	719
50–54	956	952	485	603
55–59	943	948	433	501
60–69	908	920	361	371
70 & over	739	778	169	196
Total population 16 and over	695	722	522	580

SOURCE: Tsentral'noe statisticheskoe upravlenie, *Itogi vse-soiuznoi perepisi naseleniia 1970 goda: Tom 2* (Moscow, 1972), p. 263. It should be noted that the census records reported marriages, not only registered ones.

there remained a surplus of 19 million females in the older age group.[38] Not surprisingly, then, the census figures reveal an increase in the proportion of women married in every age group with the exception of the youngest, where a rising age of marriage shows its influence.

For males, however, the opposite is the case (Table 31). One of the most dramatic trends revealed by the recent census is the decline in the proportion of married men between the ages of twenty-five and fifty-five. The 2.7 percent increase between 1950 and 1970 in the overall proportion of married males (compared with 5.8 percent for women) resulted from in-

[38]The ratio of men to women varied considerably among republics. Since those republics with smaller deficits of males also had higher ratios of married women, this variation may account for a part of the patterns described. In 1970 there were 855 men for every 1,000 women in the USSR as a whole, but the proportion ranged from a low of 825 in the Ukraine, 838 in the RSFSR and 842 in Latvia to highs of 968 in Tadzhikistan and 970 in Turkmenistan. Tsentral'noe statisticheskoe upravlenie, *Itogi vsesoiuznoi perepisi naseleniia 1970 goda. Tom 2: Pol, vozrast i sostoianie v brake naseleniia SSSR, soiuznykh i avtonomnykh respublik, kraev i oblastei* (Moscow, 1972), p. 9.

creases in the twenty to twenty-four and over–fifty-five age cohorts. For all other males the proportion married decreased. This trend is particularly striking in the twenty-five to twenty-nine age group, where over 25 percent of all men were unmarried in 1970, a sharp increase from the figure of 20 percent recorded in 1959. This trend is not uniform throughout the USSR. In Uzbekistan, for example, the proportion of married males declined for all age groups between 1959 and 1970. The figures for Lithuania, on the other hand, a republic that ranks relatively high in indices of modernization, show increases in the proportion of males married in all categories (Table 32). Estonia and Latvia show a decrease in the thirty to thirty-nine age cohort only. These figures may, therefore, reflect a narrowing over time of the wide differences in marital patterns between urban and rural areas and between the less and more developed republics, rather than merely a decline in the attractiveness of marriage to males in the most modern regions. Nevertheless, this trend has been a source of

TABLE 32

NUMBER OF MEN AND WOMEN MARRIED, PER THOUSAND,

UZBEKISTAN AND LITHUANIA, 1959 AND 1970

	Uzbekistan				*Lithuania*			
	1959		*1970*		*1959*		*1970*	
Age Group	*M*	*F*	*M*	*F*	*M*	*F*	*M*	*F*
16–17	17	40	8	47	3	10	3	8
18–19	88	406	50	343	20	93	29	106
20–24	354	729	314	715	194	384	245	480
25–29	821	882	805	905	627	668	682	767
30–34	937	867	914	909	825	750	846	821
35–39	956	839	945	907	880	755	898	823
40–44	958	747	950	851	897	713	918	790
45–49	959	681	950	799	900	685	921	748
50–54	954	591	943	686	901	631	914	677
55–59	949	539	935	593	886	558	900	609
60–69	922	346	909	406	852	421	873	481
70+	824	140	823	185	710	162	745	241
Total for all 16 and above	720	630	714	642	649	525	706	596

SOURCE: Tsentral'noe statisticheskoe upravlenie, *Itogi vsesoiuznoi perepisi naseleniia 1970 goda: Tom 2* (Moscow, 1972), pp. 264–65.

real anxiety among Soviet social scientists, who, at least until recently, insisted that Soviet policy had created optimal conditions for the flourishing of marriage and the full blossoming of family relationships, and who tended to view high rates of marriage and births as analogous to high rates of steel production—irrefutable evidence of the superiority of the socialist system.

A possible explanation of this trend suggests itself for consideration, although any firm conclusions must await the availability of more comprehensive data. If it is the case, as Gary Becker has attempted to demonstrate, that the economic benefits of marriage are optimized by a sharp division of labor within the family in which household services are exchanged for support, its attractiveness might be expected to diminish in conditions of high female labor-force participation.[39] The widening range of options available to women as a result of increased educational attainments and employment opportunities should create acceptable alternatives to marriage, as well as enhance female leverage within it, while reducing the potential value of marriage to men. Declining rates of marriage and rising rates of divorce might therefore be expected in circumstances where female education, employment, and status are most advanced.

The emergence of such a pattern in the USSR was forestalled by demographic trends that had a countervailing effect. Throughout Soviet history, but particularly in the postwar period, the severe shortage of males created an extremely asymmetrical marriage market. The effect of such a market was to make marriage an extremely attractive prospect to men by giving them an unusual degree of leverage both in the choice of marriage partners and in the terms of the marriage itself. Under these circumstances, the diminution of the sexual imbalance in recent years adversely affects the bargaining position of males while increasing its rewards to women. This might in turn account for the observed tendency for a lower proportion of males in the prime age groups to marry.

Yet a third trend in current family behavior, and one that is especially troubling to many Soviet commentators, is the rising rate of divorce. As Table 30 indicates, the simplification of procedures introduced in the mid-1960s was followed by a sharp increase in divorce rates, from 179 to 309 per thousand marriages. Here too, national averages conceal wide variations among regions. The number of divorces remains extremely low in

---

[39]This view is advanced most systematically by Gary Becker in "A Theory of Marriage," *Journal of Political Economy*, Pt. I, 81 (July–August 1973): 813–47; Pt. II, 82 (March–April 1974): pp. 511–22. While Becker's initial definition of "utility" is sufficiently broad as to encompass a wide range of values, his subsequent discussion tends to confine its meaning to economic variables. It should also be pointed out that Becker's model assumes a marriage market with a wide range of choices available. In a society like the USSR, where 85 percent of all able-bodied women are employed, the limited availability of nonworking wives restricts the range of male options in this respect.

the Central Asian republics, but reaches over 400 per thousand marriages in the major cities of the USSR.[40]

The Soviet data are not sufficiently comprehensive to permit a detailed analysis of the motives and patterns of marital breakdown,[41] but Soviet analysts cite alcoholism as the single most important cause of marital dissolution. Approximately half of all divorce actions are reportedly brought by women, and the overwhelming majority cited their husbands' drunkenness as the grounds for divorce.[42] Adultery was the second major reason reported. Incompatibility, infidelity, loss of affection, and parental interference were most often described by males as the causes of divorce; sexual incompatibility has not until recently been discussed as a separate factor. Following in the footsteps of Pirandello, several American family sociologists have asserted that every marriage is really two marriages: his and hers. Yet a third has been discovered in the USSR: the marriage perceived by the courts in determining the causes of divorce. A detailed examination of 637 divorce cases involving Belorussian collective farmers noted that the causes of divorce were perceived quite differently by each of the three parties. Charges of drunkenness were denied by husbands but upheld by courts, while husbands' claims that "parental interference" was a cause of divorce usually meant the wives' parents objected to the drinking bouts in question (Table 33).

[40] In the Russian and Ukrainian republics in 1973, for example, the number of registered divorces was 3.2 and 3.0 per thousand population, respectively. The highest figures were recorded for Moscow (5.1) and Leningrad (5.5). (The 8.6 per thousand recorded in Magadan *oblast* may reflect the unusually high concentration of population in prime age groups.) The figures for Uzbekistan, Tadzhikistan, Georgia, and Armenia were 1.1, 1.1, 1.1, and 0.9; Tsentral'noe statisticheskoe upravlenie, *Naselenie SSSR 1973: Statisticheskii sbornik* (Moscow, 1975), pp. 150–65. For an analysis of divorce patterns based on data for the 1960s, see Denis Peter Mazur, "Correlates of Divorce in the USSR," *Demography* 6 (August 1969): 279–86.

[41] No comprehensive collections of data on divorce in the Soviet Union are presently available, nor are there as yet any detailed analyses of its causes, patterns, and consequences. A number of useful contributions based on relatively limited data include Kharchev, *Brak i sem'ia v SSSR*, Ch. 5; N. Solov'ev, "Razvod, ego faktory, prichiny, povody," in Solov'ev, et al., *Problemy byta*, pp. 111–27; N. G. Iurkevich, *Sovetskaia sem'ia: funktsii i usloviia stabil'nosti* (Minsk, 1970); B. Urlanis, *Literaturnaia gazeta*, February 7, 1970, p. 12; L. Chuiko, *Braki i razvody* (Moscow, 1975); R. Achylova, "Izmenenie polozheniia zhenshchin pri sotsializme kak faktor formirovaniia novykh vzaimootnoshenii mezhdu suprugami v kirgizskikh sem'iakh," in SSA, *Dinamika izmeneniia*, 1: 17–19; V. T. Kolokol'nikov, "Brachno-semeinye otnosheniia v sfere kolkhoznogo krest'ianstva," *Sotsiologicheskie issledovaniia*, No. 3 (July-August-September 1976), 78–87; N. G. Iurkevich, "Motivy zakliucheniia i stabil'nost' braka," in Solov'ev, et al., *Problemy byta*, pp. 99–110.

[42] A. G. Kharchev, writing in 1964, reports a figure of 40 percent; *Brak i sem'ia v SSSR*, p. 212. Kolokol'nikov's more recent study of a rural sample reported 50 percent; *Sotsiologicheskie issledovaniia*, p. 78. Kolokol'nikov's study also revealed that almost 25 percent of the husbands had a second family by the time their first marriage was officially dissolved and over 12 percent had permanent ties with another woman. The comparable figures for wives were 11 percent and 6 percent. The author of the study concluded that divorced women had fewer chances of remarriage than their former husbands and that "many divorced collective farm women face a very real prospect of spending the rest of their lives alone—'neither bride nor widow,' as the folk saying has it."

TABLE 33

THE CAUSES OF DIVORCE AMONG BELORUSSIAN COLLECTIVE FARM FAMILIES, 1970–1973, IN THE OPINION OF WIVES, HUSBANDS, AND THE COURTS

	In the opinion of		
Causes of divorce	*Wives*	*Husbands*	*The courts*
Alcoholism	44.3	10.6	38.7
Incompatibility	6.7	22.2	15.1
Infidelity	12.6	15.3	9.4
Frivolous grounds for marriage	2.0	4.5	8.5
Prolonged separation (for objective reasons)	3.8	3.1	5.4
Loss of affection for unspecified reasons	8.6	12.3	5.3
Cruelty	5.6	0.6	3.6
Sentencing to deprivation of freedom (3 years or more)	2.6	2.1	3.3
Physical or mental illness	1.7	2.6	2.1
Interference by parents or other relatives	4.4	11.3	1.5
Sterility	0.7	1.0	0.8
Physiological incompatibility	0.3	0.5	0.3
Other reasons	6.7	6.0	6.0

SOURCE: V. T. Kolokol'nikov, "Brachno-semeinye otnosheniia v sfere kolkhoznogo krest'-ianstva," *Sotsiologicheskie issledovaniia 3* (July-August-September 1976): 82.

Tensions induced by intense workday pressures on both males and females and extremely crowded living conditions, which provide little privacy, may also be assumed to play a heavy role. Finally, light-hearted and frivolous marriages based on only brief acquaintance have come in for a heavy share of criticism. A high proportion of marriages lasting one year or less involves spouses between twenty and twenty-four years of age, although such marriages account for a relatively small proportion of total divorces. The figures for 1973 indicate that 38 percent of all divorces involved marriages of ten or more years' duration, 41 percent involved marriages of three to nine years' duration, and 20 percent involved marriages of two years or less.[43]

[43]Calculated from figures given in Tsentral'noe statisticheskoe upravlenie, *Naselenie SSSR 1973*, p. 176. A comparison of these percentages with those given by Kharchev in 1964 (*Brak i sem'ia*, p. 212) shows a considerably lower percentage of brief marriages and a higher proportion of marriages of long duration. Marriages of one year or less, for example, account for 18 percent of divorces in Kharchev's figures but only 4 percent in the national figures for 1973, while marriages of ten to twenty years duration accounted for 14 percent of divorces in Kharchev's figures and 28 percent in those for 1973. Marriages of twenty years or more formed 4 percent of Kharchev's total and 10 percent in 1973. The two sets of statistics are not strictly comparable, however, as Kharchev's are based on court records of

Some writers view these rising divorce rates without excessive alarm, even interpreting them as evidence of female liberation and genuine sexual equality. As one prominent economist and demographer, A. Vishnevskii, affirmed in a recent discussion, "I believe that up to a certain point the increase in the number of divorces is evidence not of the destruction of the institution of the family but of its strengthening, of its adaptation to new conditions."[44] High rates of remarriage are cited as evidence that divorce reflects a desire to change partners rather than a rejection of marriage as such.[45] Others, however, like Perevedentsev, view the prevalence of divorce as a serious social problem and see in it a manifestation of a dissatisfaction with the institution of marriage itself.[46] A study by Solov'ev that found that 71 percent of divorced men and only 50 percent of divorced women wished to marry again is cited as evidence of a troubling disenchantment.[47] Moreover, the fact that only half of divorced men and an even lower proportion of divorced women actually remarry is offered as further confirmation of this view.[48]

As a result of these trends, the marriage prospects of older women are especially bleak. The tendency for older men to marry considerably younger women is accentuated by the particularly large size of the younger age cohort born in the postwar period. Moreover, higher rates of remarriage among divorced males and the excess of widows over widowers are reflected in the fact that the proportion of women married begins to decline with the thirty-five to thirty-nine age cohort. Ninety-four percent of males aged forty to forty-four are married, compared to 79

the city of Leningrad in the absence of national statistics for the earlier period. Iurkevich's study of marital instability based on Belorussian data of the mid-1960s also pointed toward high divorce rates in the early years of marriage. Two-thirds of all divorces occurred in the first five years of marriage, one-third in the first year and 16 percent in the first three months; "Motivy zakliucheniia i stabil'nost' braka," in Solov'ev, et al. *Problemy byta*, pp. 99 –100. The Ukranian figures reported by Chuiko are similar to the national averages; *Braki i razvody*, p. 136.

[44]*Komsomol'skaia pravda*, May 14, 1975, p. 4.

[45]A. Gorbovskii, "Odin iz aspektov vozdeistviia intellektualizatsii na dlitel'nost' brachnykh otnoshenii," in SSA, *Dinamika izmeneniia*, 3: 60–71.

[46]*Komsomol'skaia pravda*, May 14, 1975, p. 4. See also N. Iurkevich and S. Burova, *Literaturnaia gazeta* 40 (October 1, 1975), p. 13; and N. Solov'ev, "Razvod, ego faktory, prichiny, povody" in Solov'ev, et al., *Problemy byta*, pp. 111–12. Solov'ev describes two opposing points of view toward divorce that, in his opinion, prevent a proper scientific understanding of the problem. One supports total freedom of divorce, ignoring the moral essence of marriage, while the other declares freedom of divorce to be an amoral phenomenon, views divorce itself as a misfortune or a tragedy, and sees rising divorce rates as evidence of the general destruction of the family.

[47]Larisa Kuznetsova, *Literaturnaia gazeta*, January 1, 1975, p. 12.

[48]B. Urlanis, *Literaturnaia gazeta*, February 7, 1970, p. 12. Urlanis gives a figure of 354,000 males and 313,000 females entering second marriages in 1967. For 1973, the figures for remarriages in general are 369,643 males and 333,309 females; Tsentral'noe statisticheskoe upravlenie, *Naselenie SSSR 1973*, p. 172. Only in the cohorts under age twenty-four do female remarriage rates exceed those of males.

percent of women, and in the forty-five to forty-nine age group, 95 percent of males compared to only 71 percent of women are married (Table 31). Only one woman in nine in the thirty to thirty-five age group got married in 1970, and the number of women who marry after age thirty-five is infinitesimal.

Limited opportunities for older women to marry, combined with the strong desire to bear a child, may in turn account for the paradoxical fact that, despite an overall increase in the proportions of women entering marriage, rates of illegitimacy are comparatively high and may actually be increasing among older age cohorts of women. (Table 34). Illegitimate children account for one out of every ten live births.[49] In the city of Perm in 1966, one-fourth of all births to women aged thirty-five to thirty-nine and almost one-third of those aged forty to forty-four were extramarital. The high illegitimacy rates among older age groups suggest the presence of deliberate intent, particularly in light of the extensive use of abortion as a method of birth control in the Soviet Union. The figures therefore indicate that a high value is attached to children even in the absence of marriage, and perhaps especially in its absence. As Kingsley Davis has suggested, the more disappointing life is in other ways, the more rewarding children may be.[50] The very possibility of raising children even outside marriage may offer many women a positive alternative to settling for a marriage that has serious limitations. Unlike a younger group of unwed mothers, for whom the birth of a child is a great misfortune, these are women who, in the words of one writer, are "independent, self-confident and capable of heading a family."[51] The Soviet press has carried a number of letters from such proud and outspoken unwed mothers calling for greater public recognition and approval and demanding that the very definition of the family be altered to encompass a mother and child.

Changing public attitudes toward sexual morality are an additional factor in the declining attractiveness of marriage to males insofar as such attitudes encourage the satisfaction of sexual desires outside it. Although materials on sexual behavior are relatively sparse, several recent studies

[49]B. Urlanis, *Literaturnaia gazeta*, February 7, 1970, p. 12. Detailed figures for Saratov province in 1969 indicated that 8.7 percent of all births were out of wedlock, with half of these registered in the mother's name alone; Larisa Kuznetsova, *Literaturnaia gazeta*, April 4, 1973, p. 12. M. Tol'ts gives figures of 22.8 per hundred in 1950 and 11.7 per hundred in 1964 for Novosibirsk, and figures of 15 per hundred in 1959 and 12.1 per hundred in 1968 for Perm; "Kharakteristika nekotorykh komponentov rozhdaemosti v bol'shom gorode," in *Demograficheskii analiz rozhdaemosti*, eds. D. I. Valentei et al. (Moscow, 1974), pp. 45–56. Although high rates of illegitimacy were also characteristic of the postwar period, the deficit of males at that time was largely responsible.

[50]Kingsley Davis, "Population Policy and the Theory of Reproductive Motivation," *Economic Development and Cultural Change* 25 (Special supplement 1977): 176.

[51]L. Kuznetsova, *Literaturnaia gazeta*, April 4, 1973, p. 12. See also George St. George, *Our Soviet Sister* (Washington, D.C., 1973), pp. 73–78.

TABLE 34
ILLEGITIMATE BIRTHS PER THOUSAND UNMARRIED WOMEN, BELORUSSIA, 1959 AND 1970

Age group	1959	1970
15–19	2.7	7.1
20–24	16.3	73.9
25–29	36.8	98.1
30–34	39.1	87.2
35–39	27.1	47.2

SOURCE: Larisa Kuznetsova, "Obeshchal zhenitsa," *Literaturnaia gazeta*, April 14, 1973, p. 12.

point to increasing acceptance of both premarital and extramarital sexual relations, particularly among males, and higher acceptance among Leningrad University professionals than among students.[52] A survey of Leningrad students indicates that over 50 percent of the men and 14 percent of the women had their first sexual experience by the age of eighteen, with an additional third of the men and half of the women reporting such experiences between the ages of nineteen and twenty-one. The persistence of a double standard of sexual morality is indicated by another survey of Leningrad students and research personnel. In this study, women as well as men considered premarital sexual relationships to be more permissible for men than for women, and women made a much sharper distinction between sexual relationships with a loved one and those with an acquaintance.

The availability of sex outside marriage, the declining proportion of married males in the twenty-five to fifty-five age bracket, the high proportion of unmarried older women, and the possibility that continuing urbanization and economic development will result in further declines in the rate of marriage have all generated serious concern in official circles. Social scientists and journalists vie in inventing measures to encourage marriage, particularly among bachelors, and to provide greater opportunities for singles to become acquainted. The breakdown of traditional social networks, as well as the enthusiasm for technological solutions, is evident in the search for new institutional arrangements to promote ac-

[52] A. G. Kharchev and S. I. Golod, "Molodezh' i brak," in Leningradskii gosudarstvennyi universitet, *Chelovek i obshchestvo* (Leningrad, 1969), p. 137; S. I. Golod, "Sociological Problems of Sexual Morality," translated in *Soviet Sociology* 8 (Summer 1969): 3–23.

quaintanceship. Leningrad has its Over-30 Evenings, while thriving
Friendship Clubs in Riga and Novosibirsk have pressed for official sponsorship and support. Proposals for a "public compatibility service" that
would apply "the findings of science" to everyday life have also found
their advocates. The age of computer dating in the USSR may be at hand.[53]

For women who do marry, status and opportunities vary with the cultural traditions and levels of development of different regions. The combination of early marriage and a large male-female age gap at the time of
marriage is a common pattern in traditional societies and is an indication
of women's limited status and opportunities outside the family by comparison with the value attached to female reproductive potential within
it. Early marriage is, therefore, usually associated with limited education
and employment and early childbearing. This pattern is not characteristic
of the Soviet Union as a whole; in 1973 the average age of men at marriage
was twenty-four years and five months and the average age for women
was twenty-two years and seven months. But here, too, the variations
among republics are extremely great.

In Lithuania, for example, eight of every thousand sixteen- and
seventeen-year-old women were married in 1970, compared with forty-
seven in Uzbekistan and seventy-two in Armenia.[54] For 18- and 19-year-
olds the corresponding figures are 106 for Lithuania, 343 for Uzbekistan
and 268 for Armenia. In the single year 1973, four percent of all men who
married were under 20, by comparison with 27 percent of all women.[55]
The lowest proportion of youthful marriages among women and the narrowest age difference between males and females at the time of marriage
was recorded for Estonia. In a republic like Uzbekistan, by contrast, a far
higher proportion of women married at an early age—37 percent of the
1973 total were under age twenty—and the male-female difference is
much larger, with only 3.7 percent of the total of men marrying under
age twenty.

These variations in marriage patterns coincide with variations in reproductive behavior. While the single-child family is now the norm in the
urban regions of the Slavic and Baltic republics, large families are widespread among the non-Slavic populations. As Table 35 indicates, only 1
percent of all worker and white-collar families in the urban areas of the
Russian Republic have four or more children, compared with 25 percent

[53]See, for example, proposals to establish a computer dating service and the enthusiastic
reponse of readers reported in *Nedelia*, No. 36 (September 6–12, 1976): 6–7; and Iuri Riurikov, *Literaturnaia gazeta*, July 17, 1974, p. 13. *Literaturnaia gazeta* published two personal
advertisements from readers seeking partners as an experiment in its November 17, 1976
issue (p. 13), and reported a flood of letters in response (December 22, 1976, p. 13). Over
80 percent of the total came from women, most of whom were over age thirty-five.
[54]Tsentral'noe statisticheskoe upravlenie, *Itogi vsesoiuznoi perepisi* 2, pp. 263–66.
[55]Tsentral'noe statisticheskoe upravlenie, *Naselenie SSSR 1973*, p. 172.

TABLE 35

BREAKDOWN OF WORKER AND WHITE-COLLAR FAMILIES BY NUMBER OF CHILDREN, BY REPUBLIC, 1972

Number of children:	Urban Areas					Rural Areas[a]				
	1	2	3	4	5 or more	1	2	3	4	5 or more
USSR	57.6	33.6	5.7	1.7	1.4	38.1	32.9	14.8	6.8	7.4
Russian SSR	61.6	32.9	4.4	0.8	0.3	42.6	35.6	13.7	4.6	3.5
Ukrainian SSR	61.4	34.7	3.4	0.4	0.1	47.6	39.0	10.5	2.1	0.8
Belorussian SSR	54.6	39.0	5.6	0.7	0.1	38.0	35.0	18.6	5.7	2.7
Uzbek SSR	37.8	28.6	14.1	8.8	10.7	20.6	18.4	18.3	16.8	25.9
Kazakh SSR	46.1	37.4	10.0	3.4	3.1	28.3	27.4	20.2	10.9	13.2
Georgian SSR	42.0	41.7	13.2	2.5	0.6	34.1	38.1	16.2	7.8	3.8
Azerbaidzhan SSR	36.1	33.2	15.0	9.0	6.7	13.4	16.8	15.8	17.8	36.2
Lithuanian SSR	57.9	34.4	6.1	1.1	0.5	37.7	37.8	16.4	6.5	1.6
Moldavian SSR	59.6	33.8	5.1	1.1	0.4	43.0	30.8	13.7	7.5	5.0
Latvian SSR	66.4	29.8	3.2	0.3	0.3	51.8	36.1	8.9	1.6	1.6
Kirgiz SSR	43.0	34.0	11.0	5.5	6.5	25.7	25.8	15.8	13.2	19.5
Tadzhik SSR	33.9	30.9	12.7	9.1	13.4	17.3	22.0	13.5	15.2	32.0
Armenian SSR	32.3	35.4	20.7	9.5	2.1	20.7	21.2	25.5	19.7	12.9
Turkmen SSR	34.7	27.5	13.3	9.0	15.5	18.8	18.3	17.4	16.7	28.8
Estonian SSR	60.3	35.2	3.4	0.9	0.2	46.5	35.1	14.4	3.7	0.3

SOURCE: Tsentral'noe statisticheskoe upravlenie, *Zhenshchiny i deti v SSSR* (Moscow, 1975), pp. 92–96.

[a] Collective farm families are not included. In all republics their proportion of one-child families is significantly lower and of four-or-more-child families significantly higher than these figures.

of all such urban families in Turkmenistan. The proportion of large families is greater still in rural areas, constituting almost half of the total in Uzbekistan, Tadzhikistan and Turkmenistan, and more than half the total in Azerbaidzhan. Nevertheless, because the regions of high birthrates comprise a relatively small proportion of the total Soviet population, the trend toward smaller family size in the more developed regions has resulted in a considerable decline in the Soviet birthrate as a whole.[56]

This brief overview of Soviet demographic indicators has pointed to the emergence of two distinct patterns of family behavior in the USSR today. Among the Moslem populations of Soviet Central Asia, and to a lesser extent in republics such as Azerbaidzhan, Armenia, and Georgia, the tenacity of traditional patterns of family life is evident. The limited impact of industrialization and urbanization on the local nationality and the persistence of traditional cultural norms are revealed in lower levels of female education, limited female labor-force participation outside agriculture, and the predominance of early marriages and large families. Here, customary norms and behavior enjoy wide scope and are manifested in a high degree of family stability, limited geographical mobility, and high birthrates. Family practices have proven far more resistant to change than legal norms and educational patterns.

A very different pattern of family behavior characterizes the urban and industrial regions of the USSR, particularly the Baltic and Slavic populations. High levels of female education and labor-force participation are accompanied by lower rates of marriage, later marriage age, high rates of divorce, and declining family size. These trends have been the focus of anxious discussion in recent years, challenging as they do the expectation that sexual equality and rising living standards in a socialist society would automatically promote a high degree of marital satisfaction and stability. As the dean of Soviet family sociologists noted ruefully: "While growing prosperity since the end of World War II has strengthened the family, the positive influence is not as direct as had been expected. Life shows that improved conditions and equal rights for both sexes do not automatically strengthen the institution of marriage."[57]

A number of Soviet analysts have explicitly recognized that family instability and declining birthrates in the more industrial regions of the USSR are a manifestation of serious strains within the family itself. While the internal dynamics of Soviet family life is only now emerging as a subject of scholarly investigations, it is likely that the changes in women's

[56]From a figure of 45.5 births per thousand in 1913, it had fallen to 31.2 per thousand by 1940, 26.7 per thousand in 1950, and a low of 17 per thousand in 1969. It has risen slightly since then, reaching 18.0 in 1974; Tsentral'noe statisticheskoe upravlenie, *Narodnoe khoziaistvo SSSR v 1974 gody* (Moscow, 1975), p. 44. A more comprehensive discussion will follow in Chapter VIII.
[57]A. G. Kharchev, *Zhurnalist* 11 (November 1972): 58–61.

roles outside the family that we have been exploring thus far, as well as changes in the role of the family itself, have affected attitudes and behavior within the family in ways that offer some clue to current trends. Accordingly, we will turn our attention to the pattern of authority and roles and the sexual division of labor within the family itself.

FAMILY POWER STRUCTURE AND THE SEXUAL DIVISION OF LABOR

The expectation that the increased participation of women in the economic and political life of the community would have a direct and favorable effect on the role and status of women within the family was, as we have seen, a central feature of Soviet approaches to sexual equality. This expectation was embodied in three interconnected assumptions: that industrialization and the growing social provision of household and child-care services would gradually reduce the burden of domestic chores; that women would be the principal beneficiaries of this trend, gaining thereby the time needed to improve professional qualifications and to participate more fully in public affairs; and that rising female educational and occupational attainments would reduce disparities of status and power within the family itself, resulting in greater equality and a more democratic structure of authority.

The Soviet association of female economic and political participation with family equality has its counterpart in Western sociological and feminist theory.[58] Focusing on the resources that men and women bring to marriage as the key to family power structure, this literature attributes male dominance in family relationships to differences in the comparative participation of males and females in the broader social system. As a prominent family sociologist puts it, "insofar as marital power is measured in terms of decisions governing transactions between the family and the external system, the comparative participation of the husband and wife in the external system will determine the balance of power."[59]

If it is indeed the case that education, age, occupational status, income, and social participation constitute critical resources bearing on family authority, reducing the disparity in the distribution of such resources be-

---

[58]The classic statement of the resource theory of family power is Robert O. Blood, Jr., and Donald M. Wolfe, *Husbands and Wives: The Dynamics of Married Living* (Glencoe, 1960), Ch. 2 and 3.

[59]Robert O. Blood, Jr., "The Measurement and Bases of Family Power: A Rejoinder," *Marriage and Family Living* 25 (November 1963): 475–76. This approach suffers from an excessive emphasis on the external basis of personal resources and a tendency to restrict the scope of resource theory to economic resources. Similar criticisms are raised in David Heer, "The Measurement and Bases of Family Power: An Overview," *Marriage and Family Living* 25 (May 1963): 133–39. A thoughtful critique of the general literature on family power structure is presented in Constantina Safilios-Rothschild, "The Study of Family Power Structure: A Review 1960–1969," *Journal of Marriage and the Family* 32 (November 1970): 539–52.

tween men and women in the larger society should create greater sharing
of authority within the family and a more egalitarian pattern of decision-
making.

The Soviet experience deserves the attention of sociologists and feminists alike, for it provides a unique setting in which to test this expectation. Since the broad economic and political changes that we have traced
so far involve a substantial alteration in the relative resources of men and
women in the larger society, they might reasonably be expected to have
a major impact on female power, status, and roles within the family.
While the available evidence is still too meager to offer convincing confirmation of this expectation, a substantial body of Soviet research is devoted to exploring the impact of macro-societal changes on internal family
relationships.

Unquestionably, the Soviet period has brought fundamental changes
in the comparative resources of males and females. The gradual equalization of male and female attainments is reflected in the fact that 90 percent of all marriages involve partners of similar educational levels.[60] Indeed, it is frequently the case that the educational level of women not
only equals but even exceeds that of their husbands, particularly in the
early years of marriage.

Employment is another potential source of enhanced female power.
Women's involvement in work outside the home, removed from direct
control by husbands, creates new structural possibilities for personal autonomy while simultaneously giving women an independent role as breadwinners. The tendency for women to be concentrated in economic sectors
where prevailing wage levels are low means that women remain, for the
most part, the secondary wage earners, but this is not always the case.
Several recent studies of small samples of urban families found that
women's earnings equalled or exceeded those of their husbands in roughly
one-third to one-half the households.[61] Even in families where women's

[60]Kharchev, *Brak i sem'ia*, p. 196; A. Daniliauskas, "O sotsiologicheskikh aspektakh èt-
nograficheskogo izucheniia byta rabochikh i kolkhoznikov Litovskoi SSSR," in Solov'ev, et
al., *Problemy byta*, p. 75.

[61]At least four different studies of the relative income of wives and husbands indicated
that the wife's income equaled or exceeded the husband's in a substantial number of cases.
The wife's income exceeded the husband's in 18 percent of the families in Study 1; 20.5
percent in Study 2; 8 to 18 percent in Study 3; and 7 percent in Study 4. The wife's income
equaled the husband's in 33 percent of the families in Study 1; 22.6 percent in Study 2; 8
to 21 percent in Study 3, and 19 percent in Study 4. The wife's income was less than the
husband's in 49 percent of the families in Study 1; 56.9 percent in Study 2; 71 to 79 percent
in Study 3; and 74 percent in Study 4. Study 1: A. G. Kharchev, *Brak i sem'ia*, p. 223 (300
families in sample); Study 2: A. E. Kotliar and S. Ia. Turchaninova, *Zaniatost' zhenshchin v
proizvodstve* (Moscow, 1975), p. 139; Study 3: N. A. Sakharova, *Optimal'nye vozmozhnosti
ispol'zovaniia zhenskogo truda v sfere obshchestvennogo proizvodstva* (Kiev, 1973), p. 31 (650 families in sample); Study 4: A. L. Pimenova, "Sem'ia i perspektivy razvitiia obshchestvennogo
truda zhenshchin pri sotsializme," *Nauchnye doklady vysshei shkoly: Filosofskie nauki*, No. 3
(1966): 40 (550 families in sample).

earnings are lower, the relative narrowness of the margin is itself an indication of the vital contribution of female income to the family budget and its potential implications for family power.

To note that Soviet women enter marriage with greater educational and occupational status and with independent incomes is not, however, to demonstrate that these presumed resources have actually had the expected effect on the position of women within the family or to define its scope and nature. Moreover, even if Soviet families are indeed undergoing a dramatic evolution from a traditional, patriarchal form of organization characterized by the subordination of women to a modern and egalitarian structure in which authority and power are more equally shared, only comparative investigations will make it possible to distinguish the effect of changes in female resources from the effect of other macro-social forces.

Clearly, Soviet ideology has altered the fundamental bases of female status through its devaluation of domestic roles and its emphasis on education and employment as the source of social prestige. It is also likely that female access to education, employment, and independent income enhance women's freedom of choice in entering and leaving marriage by reducing the value of the resources gained through marriage relative to those obtainable outside it. These are by no means minor matters, and they have enormous significance in and of themselves for female status and opportunities for self-realization. But the effect of these changes on the intrafamily distribution of power is far more elusive. Indeed, Soviet social scientists have devoted considerable effort to attempting to operationalize indices of female status within the family without thus far achieving very great success.

Using traditional structural-functional theoretical paradigms, Soviet treatments of family behavior have focused on two issues: family power structure and the division of domestic labor. The studies of family power structure have themselves taken several forms. A first approach treats male participation in household chores as an index of female power. A positive relationship between female employment outside the home and male help within the household is cited as evidence that employment enhances women's power within the family. Thus, one such study found that, in families where women held no paid outside jobs, men's expenditures on housework were 8.3 percent that of women's, but in families where women held such jobs this proportion climbed to 24 percent.[62]

[62]L. V. Ostapenko, "Vliianie novoi proizvodstvennoi roli zhenshchiny na ee polozhenie v sem'e (po materialam obsledovaniia v vyshnevolotskom raione kalininskoi oblasti)," *Sovetskaia ètnografiia*, No. 5, (1971): 95–102; translated in *Soviet Sociology* 12 (Spring 1974): 85–99. See also Kharchev, *Brak i sem'ia*, p. 260. These findings are consistent with those reported in an American study by Robert O. Blood, Jr., and Robert L. Hamblin, "The Effects of the Wife's Employment on the Family Power Structure," in *A Modern Introduction to the Family*, eds. Norman W. Bell and Ezra F. Vogel (Glencoe, 1960), pp. 137–42, and

Whether male sharing in domestic chores is an appropriate measure of female power is problematic, given the possible effect of other variables. Indeed, some of the more sophisticated Western studies suggest that the greater participation of husbands in household chores in families with working wives should be seen not so much as a durable change in the distribution of power but as a temporary accommodation to specific situational pressures.[63] Indeed, the difficulties involved in demonstrating a causal relationship between female authority and male participation in domestic chores has led several scholars to question whether this entire approach is a fruitful one.

A second group of investigations has focused on patterns of decision-making within the family as an index of female power. Still relatively unsophisticated in their research design, these studies take as evidence of women's authority in family affairs the fact that in a high proportion of families women control the family purse, influence major economic decisions, and have a decisive voice in child-rearing.[64] Here, too, the Soviet

---

with the results of cross-national studies surveyed by Stephen J. Bahr, "Effects on Power and Division of Labor in the Family," in *Working Mothers: An Evaluative Review of the Consequences for Wife, Husband and Wife*, eds. Lois W. Hoffmann and F. Ivan Nye (San Francisco, 1974), pp. 167–85. The most recent and sophisticated Western studies, however, point to an opposite conclusion, finding no significant variation in the average amount of time husbands spend in family roles associated with wives' employment when age, class, number of children and other variables were controlled; K. Walker, "Time Spent by Husbands in Household Work," *Family Economics Review* (June 1970): 8–11, and Martin Meissner, 'Sur la division de travail et l'inégalité des sexes," *Sociologie du Travail* 17 (1975): 329–50, and "Women and Inequality," *Our Generation* 11 (Winter 1976): 59–71.

[63]Blood and Hamblin, "The Effects of the Wife's Employment," p. 141. See also Constantina Safilios-Rothschild, "The Study of Family Power Structure: A Review 1960–1969," *Journal of Marriage and the Family* 32 (November 1970): 539–52; Stephen J. Bahr, "Comment on 'The Study of Family Power Structure: A Review 1960–1969,'" *Journal of Marriage and the Family* 34 (May 1972): 239–44; and Bahr's "Effects on Power," pp. 181–85. Blood and Hamblin did not themselves interpret an alteration of roles as a more egalitarian pattern of family power and insisted that theories of family power structure relying on economic determinism were of limited utility in describing the relationships that obtain in primary groups. The Soviet studies assume the correlation of male participation in household chores with greater family egalitarianism without providing the evidence necessary to connect the two or controlling for the range of possible variables. See Z. M. Iuk, *Trud zhenshchiny i sem'ia* (Minsk, 1975), pp. 92–93, for a review of such studies, and Kharchev, *Zhurnalist* 11 (November 1972): 58–61, as an example of the genre. Neither the Western nor the Soviet studies have tested for the effects of relative male-female income.

[64]A. L. Pimenova, "Novyi byt i stanovlenie vnutrisemeinogo ravenstva," *Sotsial'nye issledovaniia* 7 (1971): 34–45. In a study of 595 Leningrad worker families, for example, Pimenova found that wives handled 61 percent of small purchases alone and were involved in 84 percent of large purchases. Decisions about leisure tended to involve equal participation by both spouses. See also V. Ivanov, "Dal'neishee izmenenie polozheniia zhenshchiny v rabochei sem'e (na materiale BSSR)," in SSA, *Dinamika izmeneniia*, 1: 42; E. Musaev, "Rol' professional'noi i sotsial'noi aktivnosti zhenshchin Turkmenistana v razvitii sovremennoi Turkmenskoi sem'i," in SSA, *Dinamika izmeneniia*, 1: 81–83; and M. Pankratova, "Izmeneniia v semeinykh otnosheniiakh sel'skikh zhitelei SSSR," in SSA, *Dinamika izmeneniia*, 1: 90–92. When husbands' and wives' responses were compared, it was found that males considered a higher proportion of actions to have been taken jointly and fewer by wives alone.

research does not adequately address the whole range of issues involved in family decision-making. Comprehensive analyses should distinguish routine from critical decisions, evaluate the relative ranking of preferences across a broad spectrum of issue areas, and concern themselves with the definition of the decisional agenda itself. Moreover, it is sometimes difficult to distinguish women's power from women's burdens. In many instances, the dominant role of women in Soviet families is the result of male default rather than sharing, is especially characteristic of unstable or unhappy marriages, and is often associated with male alcoholism.[65] Finally, the relegation of decision-making over certain areas to a particular spouse usually entails the relegation of certain tasks as well and may express the power of the "relegating spouse" over the "implementing" one rather than a genuine sharing of authority.

A third group of Soviet studies is distinguished by a focus on authority patterns rather than decision-making as a criteria of female status within the family. The view that changes in the economic and social roles of women have enhanced their authority within the family is supported by evidence that the traditional designation "head of the household" is undergoing fundamental change. The Soviet studies are not consistent about the precise nature of this change: some conclude that the whole concept "head of the household" is becoming, if not archaic, then purely formal as traditional male domination loses its substance, while others argue that the traditional concept is gaining new meaning by virtue of the fact that women are increasingly identified as the "head of the household."[66]

A fourth and more promising approach to the study of family power structure, pioneered by Zoia Iankova, a prominent family sociologist, involves an effort to construct a typology of family patterns based on a more complex and multidimensional set of criteria.[67] By ranking families in terms of their resemblance to one of several "ideal types," ranging along a continuum from the most autocratic (defined as "traditional") to the most democratic (defined as "modern"), such an approach opens the possibility

---

[65] Iurkevich, for example, reports that shared decision-making tends to predominate in happy marriages, while female dominance is characteristic of unsuccessful ones; *Sovetskaia sem'ia*, pp. 188–89.

[66] A. L. Pimenova, "Novyi byt," pp. 41, 43. The fact that 57 percent of spouses interviewed denied the very existence of "headship" in their families is used to support the first view, although a somewhat different position is implicit in data showing that women were identified as "head of the household" in 3 percent of rural families studied and 30 percent of urban ones. In all of these studies, however, the absence of a single and clear definition of "headship" makes the findings difficult to interpret. Respondents' views may reflect the influence of traditional cultural norms or the assignment of legal responsibility as much as an assessment of the real distribution of power. In some cases female headship simply reflects male absence.

[67] Zoia A. Iankova, "Struktura gorodskoi sem'i v sotsialisticheskom obshchestve," *Sotsiologicheskie issledovaniia* 1 (July–September 1974): 100–109; V. Golofast, "Poriadok raspredeleniia funktsii i napriazhennost' v sem'e," in SSA, *Dinamika izmeneniia*, 3: 47–59.

of longitudinal comparisons over time. Further investigations may be able to identify the proportion of families at any given moment that correspond to one of the ideal types and to trace the scope and direction of change.

All of these approaches, however, with the possible exception of the last, suffer at present from serious problems of conceptualization, methodology, and evidence—problems that limit their usefulness in addressing the critical issues they raise. For example, the absence of any benchmarks or of a comparative frame of reference makes it impossible to assess the extent and direction of change over time. Furthermore, the Soviet investigations have not explored systematically the full range of variables that might affect the observed outcomes nor attempted to distinguish the relative weight of each. The "legacy of the past" is assigned responsibility for the persistence of inegalitarian patterns of power and authority with little discussion of the ways in which specifically Soviet patterns of economic development and political authority may have reinforced traditional patterns. In this respect, the Soviet studies represent less an effort to explore the complex relationship of different dimensions of social change than a tendency to assemble evidence to support already-established conclusions.

Even with greater methodological sophistication, the study of family power poses inherent problems. As in community power studies, the tendency to treat power as quantitative rather than relational and as additive rather than situational simplifies the research design at the cost of distorting reality. Moreover, the treatment of resources in terms of objective socioeconomic attributes neglects the role of psychological, sexual, and emotional factors in marital interactions and the complex pattern of exchanges that underlie them. Finally, the utility of formal organizational models for the study of marital relationships is itself open to question. As one Soviet scholar has pointed out, the transfer of terms like "division of labor," "democratization," or "decision-making process" from the study of formal organizations to the study of the family rests on an analogy that may be inappropriate to the study of spontaneous, self-organizing, small groups.[68] All these difficulties make it questionable whether studies of marital power will offer a fruitful avenue for exploring the effects of broader social changes on the family position of women.

If the focus on family power as a criteria of female equality poses virtually insurmountable obstacles to sociological investigation, a focus on the intrafamilial allocation of time may offer more promising results. At a minimum, a comparison of male and female patterns of time expenditure could yield some insights into the sexual division of labor within the family and permit a more reliable analysis of the relationship between do-

[68]A. I. Prigozhin, "Sem'ia kak organizatsionnyi fenomen," in SSA, *Dinamika izmeneniia*, 1: 97–102. A similar skepticism is expressed by Blood and Hamblin, "The Effects of the Wife's Employment," pp. 141–42.

mestic and extrafamilial roles. Insofar as these patterns either constrain or enhance the ability of spouses to augment economic or political resources outside the family, they impinge directly on the allocation of societal opportunities, statuses, and roles. Moreover, to the extent that the division of labor within the family reflects differences of status and power as well as differences of aptitude and preference, such a study of time allocation may offer indirect evidence about the sources of marital conflict.

The distribution of free time within the family, for example, might well serve as one criterion of egalitarianism in family relationships. To the extent that genuine equality entails equal opportunities for personal development and self-fulfillment, a division of labor that yields equal amounts of leisure for husband and wife might be taken as evidence of equality in the allocation of responsibilities and rewards. Given the high proportion of Soviet households in which women as well as men work full time outside the home, the pressures for equal sharing of domestic chores and leisure there should be particularly strong.

Time-allocation analyses also offer several methodological advantages. Increasing Soviet interest in the problems of social planning and in the rational use of time has made the study of time budgets a major area of sociological research. The large number of time-budget studies conducted in the Soviet Union makes it possible to place far greater confidence in the patterns they reveal than is possible in areas where research is more fragmentary. Between 1959 and 1965, for example, over 100,000 man-days of human activity were recorded for analysis, providing an unusually large data base on which to draw. In addition, the availability of time-budget studies conducted in the USSR in the 1920s and 1930s, as well as a twelve-nation study including the USSR conducted in the 1960s, provides both temporal and cross-national benchmarks for the evaluation of the contemporary Soviet data.[69]

---

[69]These advantages, it should be added, are partially offset by a number of limitations, some intrinsic to the methodology of time-budget studies in general and others specific to the Soviet studies. There are great difficulties attached to the treatment of simultaneous or interpenetrating activities, for example, which affect the standardization of data. The recording of activities of short duration also is subject to variation because of its high sensitivity to differences in interviewing technique and data collection.

The Soviet investigations in particular suffer from some additional shortcomings. The samples were composed almost exclusively of workers in large urban centers. The virtual absence of data from small settlements or from rural areas makes it impossible to draw broader conclusions or to compare the effect of different cultural patterns, levels of industrialization, and urbanization on family time use. Moreover, in most cases the studies did not control for other critical variables, such as age, family structure, income, or socioeconomic status.

The term "free time" is itself a source of ambiguity. To some extent, it is a residual category, accounting for the time available after work, physiological needs, and housekeeping have been attended to. Yet while "work" and "physiological needs" are sharply defined and relatively constrained activities, "housework" and "free time" are both highly elastic and

The major findings of the Soviet time-budget studies are summarized in Table 36. As this composite portrait indicates, the amount of time both sexes spend at work is roughly equal, as is the amount of time devoted to physiological needs. In both cases, the figure for women is slightly lower than that for men; one study found, for example, that women sleep one hour less than men each night. The major differences between male and female time budgets are found in the two remaining categories, "housework" and "free time." Women spend between two and two-and-one-half times as much time on housework as men, while men have over one-and-a-half times as much free time as women. Thus, women spend twenty-eight hours per week on the average on housework, compared to about twelve hours per week by men, while the figures for "free time" are roughly the reverse.

Within the housework category itself, a sharp division of labor on the basis of sex is evident. Certain activities, such as gardening and household repairs, are predominantly male activities and account for over half of all housework performed by men. A second group of activities are predominantly female but are shared to some degree by males. Shopping and cleaning house fall into this group; women spend some six hours per week shopping, compared to three hours for men. Other types of housework, including cooking and laundry, fall into a third category, for they are largely the domain of women. Laundry, for example, consumes six hours a week for women and fifteen to twenty minutes for men. Cooking is another task which is almost exclusively performed by women, requiring ten to twelve hours a week from women and one and a half hours from men. [70]

---

to some extent mutually interdependent. The allocation of time between these two categories tends to be inversely related and involves elements of choice as well as necessity.

Moreover, the reporting of data in terms of these broad categories obscures important male-female differences in the pattern of time expenditure within categories, which would stand out sharply if more refined categories were employed. Finally, the time spent with children is not treated consistently. Some of the earlier studies failed altogether to distinguish "care of children" from "upbringing of children," while later studies included the first under "housework" and the second under "free time." For a more elaborate treatment of the methodology and findings of Soviet time-budget studies, see Michael Paul Sacks, *Women's Work in Soviet Russia* (New York, 1976), Chs. 5 and 6.

[70]A similar pattern emerged in a study of Lithuanian families that focused specifically on the division of household activities. The three chores that women alone performed in the largest percentage of cases were preparing dinner (69 percent), washing and ironing (67 percent), and shopping (64 percent), while the only two activities engaged in by men alone to any considerable degree were minor repairs (68.1 percent) and paying bills (29.9 percent). The highest percentage of jointly performed activities were cleaning and dishwashing, which were shared in about one-third of the families. This study also indicated that certain types of child care are largely performed by women. In 81.2 percent of the families women alone bathed, fed, and dressed children and, in 78.2 percent of the families, also took them to and from the nursery or kindergarten. Males helped with children's schoolwork in 14 percent of the cases. Ia. Andriushkiavichene, "Zhenskii trud i problema svobodnogo vremeni," in Solov'ev, et al., *Problemy byta* pp. 82–83.

TABLE 36

A COMPARISON OF TIME BUDGETS OF MALE
AND FEMALE WORKERS

Time-budget categories	Percent of week devoted to given activity		Ratio of time spent by females in given category to that of males
	Males	Females	
Working time			
Low	28	27	
High	32	31	
Average	30	29	.96
Physiological needs			
Low	38	37	
High	42	40	
Average	41	39	.95
Housework			
Low	5	11	
High	10	22	
Average	8	19	2.37
Free time			
Low	16	9	
High	25	17	
Average	21	13	.62

SOURCES: L. A. Gordon and E. V. Klopov, *Chelovek posle raboty* (Moscow, 1972); V. D. Patrushev, *Vremia kak ekonomicheskaia kategoriia* (Moscow, 1966); G. S. Petrosian, *Vnerabochee vremia trudiashchikhsia v SSSR* (Moscow, 1965); G. A. Prudenskii, *Vnerabochee vremia trudiashchikhsia* (Novosibirsk, 1961); V. A. Artemov, V. I. Bolgov, and O. V. Volskaia, *Statistika biudzhetov vremeni trudiashchikhsia* (Moscow, 1967); G. V. Osipov and S. F. Frolov, "Vnerabochee vremya i ego ispol'zovanie," in G. V. Osipov, ed. *Sotsiologiia v SSSR*, Vol. 2 (Moscow, 1965).

NOTE: The table was compiled by transforming the data presented in the above studies into percentages of time in a seven-day week in the interest of standardization. In the Soviet usage, "working time" includes both actual work and time connected with work, as in travel; "physiological needs" include eating, sleeping, and self-care; "housework" includes shopping, food preparation, care of the household and possessions, and direct physical care of young children; "free time" includes hobbies, public activities, activities with children, study, and various forms of amusement and rest.

As two specialists on time budgets noted, "there is at present no real tendency to redistribute labor in the kitchen. . . . The basic hope for liberating working women from excessive work in feeding the family is therefore connected not with a redistribution of this work by drawing men into the kitchen, but with factors that further reduce time spent on preparing food and on related activities."[71] The time-budget data are therefore quite consistent with the findings of other sociological studies based on interviews, which concluded that nearly 75 percent of all domestic duties fall exclusively to women, while the remainder are shared with husbands and other family members.[72]

While the Soviet time-budget studies do not, for the most part, explore systematically the effect of different variables on patterns of time usage, several hypotheses can be offered on the basis of the available data. First, important male-female differences in the treatment of housework reveal the independent effects of different socialization and values. For example, in a situation where men and women confront identical physical environments—among single students living in dormitories—male students spend five to six hours per week on household chores, while female students spend eighteen hours per week, or three times as much time, on these activities.[73]

Second, this male-female differential increases with marriage. While the total amount of free time available to married males and females alike is lower than that for singles, the twelve-hour gap recorded for unmarried youth rises to eighteen to twenty hours in young families.[74] It may therefore be the case that, as a consequence of marriage, men gain more in services than they contribute, while the opposite is true for women. Thus, a

[71]L. A. Gordon and E. V. Klopov, *Chelovek posle raboty* pp. 117–18.

[72]Z. Iankova, "O bytovykh roliakh rabotaiushchei zhenshchiny," in Solov'ev, et al., *Problemy byta*, p. 43. See also G. A. Slesarev and Z. A. Iankova, "Zhenshchiny na promyshlennom predpriiatii i v sem'e," in *Sotsial'nye problemy truda i proizvodstva*, ed. G. V. Osipov and Ia. Shchepanskii (Moscow, 1969), pp. 430–31, for the authors' conclusion that, in 70 to 75 percent of worker families, women carry virtually the entire burden of domestic labor. The proportion is even higher among the Leningrad and Kostroma families studied by Kharchev and Golod: in 81.5 percent of Leningrad families and 97 percent of those in Kostroma, the working wife alone carries the burden of domestic chores, with the bulk of assistance coming from mothers and mothers-in-law rather than husbands; A. G. Kharchev and J. I. Golod, *Profesional'naia rabota zhenshchin i sem'ia* (Leningrad, 1971), pp. 70–75. A similar situation prevails among rural families, although the data are less detailed and comprehensive. V. T. Kolokol'nikov ("Brachno-semeinye otnosheniia," p. 84, a study of Belorussian collective farm families) concluded that, although women's participation in agricultural labor was comparable to that of men, only 58.6 percent of male respondents participated to any degree in housework.

[73]L. A. Gordon and E. V. Klopov, *Chelovek posle raboty: Sotsial'nye problemy byta i vnerabochego vremeni: Prilozhenie* (Moscow, 1972), p. 14. Female students, for example, tend to cook their own meals rather than eat out, thus devoting additional expenditures of time to shopping for food. They also spend more time caring for rooms, clothing, and possessions than do male students.

[74]*Ibid.*, p. 98.

comparison of broken with intact households indicates that working mothers with one child and no husband present spend from three to eight hours less time per week on housework than working mothers with husbands present.[75] These figures suggest that the share of housework contributed by men does not balance the additional time expended in caring for them. An irate letter to *Literaturnaia gazeta* added graphic detail to bare statistical fact:

> Although women are now legally equal to men, male psychology has not changed. For many women, marriage means a working day equal to a man's, plus another working day at home. Men seldom view marriage as a joint venture. A man I know is a good example. When he married, he couldn't boil water and he felt imposed upon if his wife asked him to go to the bakery. After his divorce, he lived alone and became a wonderful cook and housekeeper. But when he remarried he reverted completely to type.[76]

Third, the male-female differential appears to increase with age, although it is difficult to distinguish age from stages in the life cycle that bring additional responsibilities. Indeed, family structure is the major determinant of how much free time is available to adults. The birth of a first child has the most dramatic impact, bringing about a sharp increase in domestic chores and a decrease in the time devoted by women to study. The presence of relatives reduces the expenditure of time on household chores, but only marginally.

Fourth, educational level appears to have an important effect on the allocation of time to domestic chores, but not necessarily on the participation of males in them. A higher level of education is almost always accompanied by a decline in the time devoted to housework. Moreover, this correlation is even stronger for women than it is for men. Education may therefore be associated with a greater tendency to devalue housework, with a greater ability to organize it efficiently, and, perhaps most important, with both the incentive and the ability to devote resources to acquiring household appliances and services. Still, the five most prevalent daily activities of women with specialized education differed little from those of women with four grades of schooling or less, but differed considerably from those of comparable males.

Finally, although the effects of socioeconomic or occupational status are even more difficult to tease out of the individual data, the evidence indicates that the male-female division of labor does not necessarily become more equal at higher levels of the social hierarchy. Contrary to the views of a number of Soviet social scientists, the reduction of time devoted by

---

[75]G. S. Petrosian, *Vnerabochee vremia trudiashchikhsia v SSSR* (Moscow, 1965), p. 106. See also Michael Paul Sacks, *Women's Work*, p. 124.

[76]L. Yanina, "Only Romeos!" *Literaturnaia gazeta*, May 12, 1971, p. 12; translated in *CDSP* 23, No. 24 (1971): 28.

women to housework appears to occur not so much as a result of greater male participation but through the acquisition of household appliances and services made possible by higher levels of income. Indeed, it appears that blue-collar males devote more time to housework and spend less time on study and on public affairs than their white-collar counterparts. The latter—particularly those males engaged in demanding careers—devote more time to work, to study, and to social participation, and less time to household chores, than any other category.[77] Thus, the male-female division of labor is not necessarily more equal among the technical and professional intelligentsia; indeed the reverse appears to be the case.

Unfortunately, no data are available that would enable us to analyze the effects of relative male and female income on the sexual division of labor. A number of Western studies have suggested that the members of families allocate time according to their comparative advantage in the production of market and domestic goods and services, and that comparative advantage is in turn determined by a combination of relative wage rates and efficiency in home production.[78] If this hypothesis is correct, we might expect to find that, in families where the income of the wife is substantially higher than that of the husband, he would play a comparatively greater role in domestic production than in families where the wife's income is lower. Unfortunately, the effects of relative income on the family division of labor has not been systematically studied by Soviet sociologists—nor, for that matter, by Western ones—but if such a trend was indeed emerging in the USSR, it is likely that it would receive prominent mention in Soviet writings.

It would appear, then, that the division of labor within the Soviet family is shaped by ecological factors that limit the effects of increased female resources or egalitarian values. The correlation between egalitarian values and actual behavior is in any case rather weak; in a group of families studied by A. Pimenova, an equal division of household labor was favored by

[77]B. Grushin, *Svobodnoe vremia: aktual'nye problemy* (Moscow, 1967), pp. 52–56. Similar findings were reported in a recent study of 6,000 rural regions: M. Pankratova, "Izmeneniia v semeinykh otnosheniiakh sel'skikh zhitelei SSSR," in SSA, *Dinamika izmeneniia*, I: 92. See also *Sotsial'naia struktura sel'skogo naseleniia SSSR* (Moscow, 1971). A similar pattern appears to prevail among the better-educated strata of the working class. Both male and female workers with higher or secondary specialized education devote less time to housework and more time to educational and cultural pursuits than workers with lower levels of education, but the male-female differential is actually wider in these groups. E. B. Gruzdeva, "Osobennosti obraza zhizni 'intelligentnykh rabochikh'," *Rabochii klass i sovremennyi mir* 2 (March–April 1975): 96.

[78]Gary S. Becker, "A Theory of the Allocation of Time," *Economic Journal* 75 (September 1965): 493–517; Jacob Mincer, "Market Price, Opportunity Costs and Income Effects" in *Measurement in Economics: Studies in Mathematical Economics and Econometrics*, ed. Carl F. Christ (Palo Alto, 1963); Reuben Gronau, "The Intrafamily Allocation of Time: The Value of the Housewives' Time," *American Economic Review* 63 (September 1973): 634–51; George Farkas, "Education, Wage Rates, and the Division of Labor Between Husband and Wife," *Journal of Marriage and the Family* 38 (August 1976): 473–83.

63 percent of women and 55 percent of men but was practiced in only 12 percent of the families.[79] Thus, the participation of males in household chores may be better interpreted as a necessary response to the situational pressures confronted by the family as a result of the combined burden of work and domestic responsibilities on women. To the extent that alternative assistance is available—either in the form of help from other relatives or in the form of household appliances and services that the family can afford to purchase—the male contribution is reduced. Similarly, the competition of other legitimate and valued activities—further education, a demanding career, political responsibilities—also justify a reduction of the male contribution to domestic chores. The relative absence of both these alternatives in blue-collar families may therefore explain the tendency for the domestic division of labor to be more equal.

In the light of these patterns, it may be unrealistic to assume that further economic development will bring with it a dramatic decline in women's household responsibilities and a sharp increase in the time available for recreation and leisure, for improving professional qualifications, and for participating more actively in public affairs. As we have already noted, a comparison of family time budgets in the 1960s with those recorded four decades earlier reveal only a modest decline in the time devoted to household chores. Moreover, several Soviet analysts point out that women's domestic responsibilities have actually increased in the interim because there are now fewer adults in the household available to share them and because new demands frequently supplement, rather than replace, the old.[80] In this respect, the Soviet data appear to support an American study that concluded that gains produced by labor-saving technology in the last few decades have not been translated into substantial increments of leisure. The effect of industrialization and of increased so-

[79] A. Pimenova, "Sluzhbi v sem'e," in Solov'ev, et al., *Problemy byta* pp. 150–53. These findings are congruent with those of Western studies, which indicate that although egalitarian values are professed more frequently in middle-class than in blue-collar families, and greater deference to males is found among the latter, actual behavior does not always correspond. The basis of deference shifts, with highly educated males defending their low participation in household work on the grounds of their professional responsibilities rather than their sex. Mirra Komarovsky, *Blue-Collar Marriage* (New York, 1962), pp. 220–35; William J. Goode, *World Revolution and Family Patterns*, pp. 21–22.

[80] As Zoia A. Iankova has persuasively argued, women have not simply lost their former duties; they have also acquired new ones. As the requirements of the household have changed, higher standards of household maintenance and new demands in the realm of child upbringing have created new female responsibilities; "O semeino-bytovykh roliakh rabotaiushchei zhenshchiny," *Sotsial'nye issledovaniia* 4 (Moscow, 1970), p. 77. At the same time, the breakup of extended families means that tasks once shared between two generations of women now fall exclusively on the wife. These two trends, Iankova argues, have actually resulted in increased burdens for women, which have not been compensated for by the development of everyday services; "O bytovykh roliakh rabotaiushchei zhenshchiny," in Solov'ev, et al., *Problemy byta*, pp. 43–44. See also Iuri Riurikov, *Literaturnaia gazeta*, November 17, 1976, p. 13.

cietal complexity has not been so much to reduce the time devoted to household chores as to alter their nature and to reduce their physical burden.[81]

These trends may be further strengthened if the present emphasis on familial values grows. Improvements in housing and consumption are not likely to have a one-dimensional effect; they may lighten the physical burden of domestic chores while raising standards and expectations so that the overall time devoted to family activities is maintained or increased. A Soviet woman voiced the frustration of countless American counterparts in writing:

> Yes, a washing machine frees me from heavy physical work . . . .but now if there is the slightest spot on the linen I toss it into the washing machine. But after all, the washing machine doesn't iron. The time that I formerly spent washing clothes I now spend ironing. If there had not been a washing machine in the house I would not so quickly toss the linen into the wash-basin. Everyday appliances free the housewife from heavy physical strains—shaking out rugs, washing clothing, heating and carrying water, but the time it takes to carry out all the household tasks has remained the same as it used to be.[82]

The mechanization of a number of household tasks and the further development of consumer services may have a more immediate impact on the chores performed by males and redound more directly to their benefit. It is unlikely that such measures will justify the excessive hopes placed in them as the ultimate solution to the burdens women presently confront.

The elasticity of domestic responsibilities highlighted in these studies suggests, therefore, that future reductions in female working time will not necessarily result in the greatly increased leisure that many Soviet writers anticipate. The additional time is more likely to be devoted to child care and domestic responsibilities than to study, social participation, or leisure pursuits. The shift from a six-day to a five-day work week in 1967 had just this effect, the authors of a study based on the industrial city of Taganrog conclude. The increase in free time it yielded was comparatively greater for men than for women, because the relative share of time that males devoted to domestic chores actually declined as a result of the shift.[83] With a six-day work week, the time expenditure of males on household chores was half that for women: 16.1 hours per week compared with 32.9. With the shift to a five-day work week, the male share dropped to 40 percent: 12.8 hours per week compared with 30.5 for women.[84]

[81]Joann Vanek, "Time Spent in Housework," *Scientific American* 231 (November 1974): 116–20.

[82]E. Marok, *Literaturnaia gazeta*, December 19, 1973, p. 13.

[83]Gordon and Rimashevskaia, *Piatidnevnaia rabochaia nedelia*, pp. 62–69.

[84]*Ibid.*, p. 24. Gordon and Rimashevskaia further point out that, while 87 percent of the women surveyed had hoped to be able to enjoy one day free of household chores, a far lower proportion were actually able to do so; p. 88.

A similar pattern emerged in a recent experiment with shortening the workday of women factory workers. Although the shorter day had the desired effect of providing more time for the supervision and upbringing of children, it had as well the unanticipated effect of increasing the time women devoted to household chores.[85] In fact, a high proportion of the women who participated in the experiment reported that their husbands took advantage of the opportunity to shift additional household duties to their wives. More extensive measures to shorten women's workday to free more time for the supervision of children and the performance of household tasks may therefore reinforce a sexual division of labor by weakening the rationale for a more equal sharing of domestic responsibilities.

The sexual division of labor within the family has important consequences for the Soviet family itself and for the larger social system. The "double burden" placed on women by the combination of full-time employment and heavy family responsibilities serves to free men to pursue educational and occupational advancement while restricting the mobility of women. Thus, the unequal division of household chores is responsible for the limited amount of free time available to women for raising technical and professional qualifications. Women's educational efforts virtually cease with the birth of the first child,[86] while men's ability to continue with their studies is not adversely affected by family responsibilities. As two Soviet authors explicitly recognize, men combine employment with study by limiting the time they devote to family chores, at the expense of other members of the household, who in effect subsidize these educational pursuits.

> From everything that we know about the structure of urban life, we can assert that it [free time] is obtained by increasing the housework of working and non-working women—mothers, wives, and other relatives. This is the "contribution" that they make to their children's and husbands' further education. And much evidence . . . shows that this is no "loan" repaid with interest, but a "free

[85]E. V. Porokhniuk and M. S. Shepeleva, "O sovmeshchenii proizvodstvennykh i semeinykh funktsii zhenshchin-rabotnits," *Sotsiologicheskie issledovaniia* 4 (October-November-December 1975): 102–108. An earlier experiment in Kostroma found that a one-hour reduction of working time yielded half an hour of free time, with the other half-hour devoted to household chores; V. N. Pimenova, *Svobodnoe vremia v sotsialisticheskom obshchestve* (Moscow, 1974), p. 131.

[86]Ostapenko reports that only 2 percent of the rural women in his sample continued their education after marriage; "Vliianie novoi proizvodstvennoi roli," p. 92. In a sample of urban factory workers, according to Kotliar and Turchaninova (*Zaniatost' zhenshchin v proizvodstve* [Moscow, 1975], pp. 125–26.), 17.9 percent of unmarried women workers were continuing their studies, compared to 3.8 percent of those married. Among women workers without children, 11 percent were involved in efforts to improve educational and technical qualifications. The proportion dropped to 4.5 percent among those with one child, to 3.0 percent among those with two, and to zero for those with three or more children. (It is not clear whether or not the correlation of study with number of children is a subset of the first set of data.)

grant." Consequently, a cause that is on the whole progressive is "paid for" not just by society and not just by those of its members who obtain the fruits of a higher education. Combination of work and study has become so widespread in the USSR partly because it has been supported by the other part of society —people who often do not participate in study at all and even suffer a certain loss on education's account.[87]

Thus, high rates of female labor-force participation in the USSR do not preclude the participation of women in what Arlie Hochschild has described as the "two-person career."[88] By freeing males from the performance of routine household maintenance and child care, which would otherwise divert time and energy from educational and professional activities, Soviet women in effect advance the professional mobility of males at the sacrifice of their own.

THE ARTICULATION OF WORK AND FAMILY ROLES:
A STRUCTURAL ANALYSIS

On the basis of our analysis of female occupational and family roles, it is now possible to view the sexual division of labor within the Soviet family in the context of the broader pattern of roles that integrate the family and the larger economic system. The partial segregation of male and female roles within this system can be seen as a mechanism that served to cushion the impact of women's entry into new occupational roles on social structure, family organization, and authority patterns.[89]

We may begin by distinguishing work and family as two arenas in which Soviet males and females both participate, yielding four analytically distinct roles that are structurally integrated with each other: female work roles, female family roles, male work roles, and male family roles. For men and women alike, work and family roles are to some degree inversely related and compete with each other for time and energy. The articulation of these two roles, however, differs for men and women in critical respects.

As we have seen, in the case of women it is family roles that are assigned primacy and that are permitted to define the nature and rhythms of female employment. As one Soviet analyst frankly acknowledged: "Women do indeed choose easier jobs, with convenient hours, close to home and with pleasant co-workers and managers, but not because they lack initiative. They choose these jobs because their combination of social roles is dif-

[87]Gordon and Klopov, *Chelovek posle raboty*, pp. 200–201.

[88]Arlie Russell Hochschild, "Inside the Clockwork of Male Careers," in *Women and the Power to Change*, ed. Florence Howe (New York, 1975), pp. 47–80.

[89]This analysis owes much to a suggestive paper by Joseph H. Pleck, "Work and Family Roles: From Sex-Patterned Segregation to Integration" (Paper presented at the annual meeting of the American Sociological Association, San Francisco, August, 1975).

ficult."[90] Women's family responsibilities are permitted to intrude into work roles; indeed, the conditions of female employment in the USSR are specifically designed to accommodate family responsibilities to a degree that is virtually unprecedented in industrial societies. Provisions for pregnancy leaves, arrangements for nursing infants during work hours, and exemptions of pregnant women and mothers from heavy work, overtime, or travel away from home are predicated on the view that these are exclusively female responsibilities and that they take a certain priority that work arrangements must accommodate. The illness of family members is responsible for high rates of female, not male, absenteeism. Thus, women tend to view work from the perspective of their roles as wives and mothers; work satisfaction depends less on the content of the work itself than on its convenience in relation to family responsibilities.

This limited insulation of female work roles from family roles results in characteristic patterns of female behavior. As two Soviet specialists in female employment concluded from their interviews with working women, "many female workers stated that when at work they cannot put the house and children out of their mind. The women value jobs requiring simple automatic responses that can be performed adequately despite these mental distractions."[91] Under these circumstances, it is understandable that married women are seriously underrepresented in enterprise activities requiring additional commitments of time and energy, as well as in volunteer movements and in public affairs more generally. Even married women and mothers who might assign a lower priority to family roles in their personal scale of values and orientations confront pressure to accommodate the heavy burden of domestic responsibilities—pressure that adversely affects their full participation in the labor force and compels them, in varying ways and degrees, to limit their commitment to work.

Precisely the opposite is the case for males. For men, it is work roles that take precedence and that are permitted to impinge on family roles when the need arises. Thus, male work roles are structured on the assumption that men may literally "take work home" with them. An extensive network of evening and correspondence courses attended overwhelmingly by males, the numerous assignments requiring travel away from home, and the proliferation of Party meetings and responsibilities in which males play a predominant role are all predicated on the view that these constitute legitimate claims on male time and energy even if

[90]M. Pavlova, *Literaturnaia gazeta*, September 22, 1971; see also A. G. Kharchev, and S. I. Golod, "Proizvodstvennaia rabota zhenshchin i sem'ia," in *Sotsial'nye problemy truda i proizvodstva*, ed. G. V. Osipov and Ia. Shchepan'skii (Moscow, 1969), p. 442; Ia. Andriush-kiavichene, "Zhenskii trud i problema svobodnogo vremeni," in Solov'ev et al., *Problemy byta*, p. 86.
[91]A. G. Kharchev and S. I. Golod, *Professional'naia rabota zhenshchin i sem'ia* (Leningrad, 1971), pp. 63–64.

they are carried out at the expense of family responsibilities. Under these circumstances, the limited contribution of males to household chores, like the limited commitment of women to occupational roles, is a manifestation not of individual shortcomings but of socially patterned roles. The fact, as Kharchev put it, that "while men often think about production work at home, women frequently think about domestic concerns at work"[92] reflects a fundamental difference in the structure of male and female work and family roles. The boundaries between work and family are permeable, but in opposite directions for men and women.

Just as work and family roles are interdependent and mutually reinforcing for each sex separately, so too are male and female roles interdependent in both the economy and the family. As we have seen, women are integrated into the labor force in segregated and subordinate roles. Horizontal occupational differentiation and vertical stratification by sex effectively shield male roles from competition by women and limit the situations in which females exercise authority over males. Specifically, norms that classify whole occupations as especially suitable for female labor or that assign women authority primarily when it is exercised over other women create a dual labor market that partially insulates male work roles from the effects of increased female employment and that sustains the predominance of males in positions of leadership and responsibility.

A parallel pattern of roles is found within the family itself. Norms that sustain a sexual division of labor within the family by defining housework and child care as preeminently "women's work" also serve to insulate the male role from pressures for increased participation in domestic work as women take on paid employment. The effect is to create a domestic counterpart to the dual labor market in which, as Pleck suggests, one part of the labor supply does not take on certain types of work even when there is a surplus of it, while the other part is overworked and leaves needed work undone.[93] At best, men "help" with housework and child care; no redefinition of male roles is involved.

The residual elements of ascription that characterize the sexual division of labor within both the occupational system and the family, combined with the differential permeability of the work-family boundary for males and females, acted as buffers that reduced and cushioned the strains created by changing female roles. By limiting the impact of macro-societal changes associated with female employment outside the home on the sphere of family relationships, it facilitated the adjustment of males to changes in female roles. In Parsonian terms, the dual linkages that female employment created between the occupational and family systems were

---

[92]Kharchev, *Zhurnalist* 11 (November 1972): 60–61.
[93]Pleck, "Work and Family Roles," p. 12.

partly deprived of their potential for conflict by maintaining residual elements of a sexual division of labor in both spheres.

Nevertheless, the effects of the structure of work and family roles that we have been describing were not altogether benign. By creating a certain asymmetry between the transformation of female work roles and the relative stability of male family roles, such a structure created two specific sources of strain. The first is the potential for conflict between males and females over the division of domestic responsibilities; the second is the tension between female work and family roles.

The unequal division of domestic labor between husbands and wives in conditions of full-time female labor-force participation has been identified by a number of Soviet analysts as a major locus of female dissatisfaction and resentment, an important contributing factor in marital instability, and a potential source of increasing disenchantment with the institution of the family itself. The tensions it creates receive direct expression in contemporary Soviet fiction. Natalia Baranskaia's evocation of a "week like any other" in the harried life of a young Soviet wife and mother captures the findings of innumerable time-budget studies in one dramatic image of the family evening: the husband, poring over newspapers and professional journals; the wife, herself employed at a scientific research institute, swallowed up in laundry, mending, child care, and the next evening's dinner.[94]

Resentment is even more openly expressed in another literary episode:

> She rebels primarily against the de facto inequality of husband and wife in *byt*: "Only to the uninformed person does it appear that man and wife are always together. In fact, here's how it looks: in the evening he shuts himself up with a book and she cooks, washes, mends . . . Her sex puts an obligation on her, you understand! That mangy skirt! It obliges her to serve! You are called to the table to finish an interesting piece of work, an article. You've begun a dissertation. Or you want to go out all summer with a prospecting group. Who has time for that? You have to sacrifice. And to boot what you like best and find most interesting . . . I know intelligent, talented women whom the family has turned into day laborers. It ate their talent . . . With borshch and cutlets . . . And here's the way it turns out: people get married in order not to eat in restaurants and carry clothes to the laundry, in order to have a cook and a laundress at home. But I don't want it!" And she adds: "All the same, the family is a survival. All the same, women will one day tear it up from the inside."[95]

The family division of labor, connected as it is with not only family power structure but also with the organization of Soviet life more broadly, is ultimately a profoundly political issue. While male-female conflicts are

[94]Natalia Baranskaia, "Nedelia kak nedelia," *Novyi mir*, No. 11 (November 1969): 23–55.
[95]V. Pertsovskii, "Ispytanie bytom," *Novyi mir*, No. 11 (1974): 250.

indirectly alluded to in a number of Soviet writings, one sociologist has
come very close to conceptualizing it as a structural problem involving
fundamental conflict between groups.

> The overall shortage of free time gives rise to a very curious phenomenon—
> a kind of struggle among different groups for free time. It is conducted in two
> forms. In the first place, certain groups, in order to provide themselves with
> comparatively more leisure time, resort to the shortening of certain necessary
> obligations. For example, the technical intelligentsia as a whole, and especially
> the men among them, spend significantly less time than others with their chil-
> dren; of course, they gain some time in this way, but the cause of childrearing
> hardly gains by it. In the second place, there is a direct struggle for free time
> among various groups. In the latter case it can be observed that certain groups
> not only refuse to fulfill certain necessary obligations, but shift them to the
> shoulders of other groups. This is precisely the way in which men act in re-
> lation to women, making use of the long-standing traditions of *byt*.[96]

In this remarkable statement is a recognition that the allocation of free
time, and implicitly the sexual division of labor itself, has an important
political dimension. To the extent that unconstrained time is a valued
resource—and indeed there are proposals by Soviet economists to assign
it an economic value to facilitate macro-economic and social planning[97]
—it is the focus of increasing competition and conflict.

This competition has the potential to become especially acute in Soviet
conditions precisely because of the degree to which the traditional rationale for a sexual division of labor has been eroded. In nonindustrial or
peasant communities, the allocation of time within the family is not as
central or potentially explosive an issue because of the role of the household unit in production and the absence of a sharp distinction between
work and leisure. It is only in the context of industrial organization, where
work and family are separated and where the "workday" has become a
sharply delimited time span in the public sector, that the fundamental
asymmetry in the relationship of economy and family raises the problem
of asymmetry between male and female roles. Even so, in a context where
marriage can be viewed as the exchange of economic support for domestic
services, the sexual division of labor has important elements of reciprocity
in which both partners may reap considerable, if not precisely equivalent,
benefits.

In the Soviet context, however, the extensive full-time employment of
women as well as men creates a strong presumption in favor of an equal
sharing of domestic responsibilities by challenging the premises on which
the traditional division of labor once rested. The persistence of an unequal

---

[96]B. Grushin, *Svobodnoe vremia: aktual'nye problemy* (Moscow, 1967), pp. 57–58.
[97]V. Shapiro, "Iskusstvennoe regulirovanie pola potomstva—novyi faktor v planirovanii
sem'i," in SSA, *Dinamika izmeneniia*, 3: 178–89.

division of labor under new conditions is therefore a potential source of tension and conflict.

While most Soviet writings assign the blame for this continuing inequality to the persistence of traditional values and expectations, which lag behind changes in real conditions, a few have gone so far as to suggest that it has structural causes and implications relating to the pattern of social domination itself. In a brief but suggestive passage, one Soviet sociologist links sexual differentiation to the effort of males to use social distance to maintain masculine authority. Female subordination, he concludes, is the result of a system of social stratification by sex, and male "parasitism" in family life is one of its major manifestations.[98]

Although Soviet social scientists have not been tempted to pursue further the structural underpinnings and theoretical implications of the sexual division of labor, they have been sufficiently alarmed by its potential for marital conflict and family instability to define it as one of the two most critical and urgent problems stemming from the present structure of family and work roles. Indeed, the work of Iurkevich in particular has emphasized the critical importance of the family division of labor to marital stability, and has attempted to demonstrate that marital satisfaction is greatest where domestic responsibilities are most evenly shared (Table 37).

TABLE 37
MARITAL SATISFACTION AND THE DESIRED AND ACTUAL DIVISION OF DOMESTIC RESPONSIBILITIES

Division of domestic responsibilities between spouses	In happy marriages		In unhappy marriages	
	Ought to be (percent)	Is (percent)	Ought to be (percent)	Is (percent)
Entirely or almost entirely carried out by the wife	—	14.00	—	58.56
Husband helps wife	39.76	48.40	41.74	28.83
Both carry out each chore	58.23	30.40	52.17	6.31
Other answer or no answer	2.01	7.20	6.09	6.30
Total	100.00	100.00	100.00	100.00

SOURCE: N. G. Iurkevich, *Sovetskaia sem'ia: Funktsii i usloviia stabil'nosti* (Minsk, 1970), p. 190.

[98]See, for example, N. Kostiashkin, *Molodoi kommunist*, No. 8 (August 1976): 79–84.

The second problem is the extreme tension between female work and family roles as they are presently defined. International studies of family time budgets have demonstrated that working women everywhere devote less time to domestic labor than do housewives, and in this respect Soviet women are no exception. Indeed, the very volume of male complaints testifies to its impact on family life. As one aggrieved husband complained to *Literaturnaia gazeta:*

> A woman earns almost as much as a man. She considers herself independent and equal. The man's prestige in the family has been thoroughly shaken and is determined only by his prestige on the job. The woman has already stopped thinking of how to surprise her husband with a tasty dinner, and more often she surprises him by cooking nothing at all.[99]

But women's effort to limit family commitments has far more ominous implications for larger Soviet priorities and objectives. It entails as well a direct and explicit effort to limit family size. Low birthrates in the regions of high female labor-force participation and the predominance of one-child families in urban milieus are the most dramatic and, from the point of view of the Soviet leadership, the most extreme, undesirable, and indeed threatening manifestations of women's resistance to the combined pressures of work and family roles. By impinging on the entire range of economic, political, and military preoccupations and priorities of the current Soviet leadership, such manifestations have compelled a fundamental reconsideration of a whole spectrum of policies involving the scope and definition of female roles. It is to an analysis of these perceptions, reassessments, and recommendations, and their implications for public policy, that we now turn.

[99]L. Kuznetsova, *Literaturnaia gazeta*, July 12, 1967, p.12.

EIGHT

Sex Roles and Public Policy:
The Spectrum of Reassessments
and Proposals

> Equal rights presuppose essentially unequal rights
> for various social groups in the society. In order
> to eliminate the disproportion in the development
> of the personality of men and women, women
> must enjoy additional opportunities relative to
> men. . . . This signifies the creation of "privi-
> leges" for women.
> A. G. Zdravomyslov, V. P. Rozhin, V. A. Iadov

IN the late 1960s, over a century after discussions of the "woman question" first agitated intellectual circles in London, Paris, and St. Petersburg, sexual equality had emerged once again as a subject of political controversy. In the context of profound anxiety over the nature and direction of social change, the sharpening perception of the social consequences of modernization—and of the dilemmas inherent in dealing with these consequences—provoked once again a fundamental reconsideration of the position of women.

A number of problems common to both Soviet and Western society contributed to the revival of discussion of women's roles. The persistence of sexual inequality in the family, in the labor force, and in political life evoked increasing frustration, resentment, and criticism, in circumstances that encouraged growing assertiveness on the part of women themselves. But the reassessment of women's roles in the USSR in recent years has also been provoked and facilitated by two distinctive sets of concerns stemming directly from current economic and political priorities, the first deriving from the urgent need for a more effective use of scarce labor resources and the second from an equally urgent need to halt a decline in the birthrate.

Among the serious problems that have compelled a fundamental re-consideration of previous assumptions and institutional arrangements, the declining birthrate is unquestionably of prime importance. Its ominous implications for political and military power, for the supply of labor re-sources, and for ethnic integration have brought demographic problems to the forefront of political concern. At the same time, the virtual exhaustion of Soviet labor reserves makes future economic growth dependent on in-creased labor productivity and on the optimal utilization of all available labor resources. Given the irreplaceable contribution of women to both produc-tion and reproduction, the conflicting requirements of these two overarch-ing priorities create profound dilemmas for current Soviet policy.

These dilemmas are made all the more acute by a growing recognition that present arrangements fail to provide optimal conditions for the har-monious combination of women's dual roles. As Brezhnev himself ex-plicitly acknowledged in an address to the Trade Union Congress in March 1977, "we men . . . have thus far done far from all we could to ease the dual burden that [women] bear both at home and in production."[1] The rapid growth of female labor-force participation in the past fifteen years has not been matched by a corresponding expansion of everyday services. This failure, in the view of many critics, places such enormous burdens on women as to compromise their ability to function adequately in both work and family roles. Mounting evidence of its adverse effects has made the Soviet family itself, as well as the role of women within it, the focus of anxious scrutiny. Rising divorce rates, signs that marriage itself is declining in attractiveness, increasingly serious problems of ju-venile delinquency, widespread alcoholism, and many additional signs of general family instability have offered tempting themes to a burgeoning number of sociologists, journalists, legal specialists, and social critics, call-ing into question the compatibility of women's employment with family responsibilities as these are presently defined. In scholarly publications and symposia, in the mass media, and increasingly in key political journals as well, the causes and consequences of current problems, and possible measures to influence them, have been the subject of an intense debate in which questions of sex roles occupy a central place.[2]

[1]*Pravda*, March 22, 1977, p. 1.

[2]For several examples among many, see the round-table discussion of demographic prob-lems and policies, "Sotsial'no-filosofskie problemy demografii," published in three issues of *Voprosy filosofii* 9 (September 1974): 84–97; 11 (November 1974): 82–96; and 1 (January 1975): 57–78; L. A. Gordon, E. V. Klopov, and L. Onikov, "Sotsial'nye problemy byta," in the authoritative Party journal *Kommunist* 17 (November 1974): 49–60; "Sem'ia," the lead editorial in the organ of the Party Central Committee, *Sovetskaia kul'tura*, February 4, 1974, p. 1; and the report of a meeting of the Ivanovo region Party committee specifically convened to discuss the role of women that appears in *Partiinaia zhizn'*, no. 16 (August 1975): 44–45. The observance of International Women's Year in 1975 gave additional impetus to discus-sions of women's roles; the large number of conferences and meetings devoted to this theme

There is strong, if often circumstantial, evidence that the Soviet leadership has not only tolerated the growing heat and scope of this debate but has actively encouraged it. In fact, it may be said that it is precisely the regime's growing sensitivity to the unexpectedly complex interaction of social and economic issues that has been, in good part, responsible for the officially sponsored proliferation of social science research in the last decade and for the enhanced prestige and greater investigative freedom accorded to social analysts in specified issue areas. Current Soviet discussions are therefore exceptionally important from a theoretical as well as a policy-oriented perspective, for they point to the fundamental interdependence of economic and family institutions.

THE RECOGNITION OF CONTRADICTIONS IN WOMEN'S DUAL ROLES

The starting point of current Soviet discussions is a recognition that the dual roles of women create contradictions from which even socialism cannot entirely spare the family. The very admission that Soviet society has not yet solved this problem is both a refreshing departure from traditional assertions and an essential condition for a reassessment of past policies and current priorities. In analyzing the causes and implications of current problems and in developing recommendations for their resolution, social scientists have played a major role.

The basic contradiction is defined differently by different writers. For Zoia Iankova, it is fundamentally a contradiction between women's old and new roles; according to Kharchev and Golod, it is a "contradiction between woman's activity in her occupation and her social role as wife and mother";[3] while for a third sociologist, N. V. Panova, it is a conflict whose origin lies less in women's dual roles than in the excessive burdens attached to one of them: "It is impossible not to see that the many-sided and active participation of women in the life of the society poses its problems, and gives rise to its contradictions, above all to contradictions connected with the overburdening of working women with the fulfillment of family duties."[4]

These contradictions, in the view of a number of social analysts, produce a series of undesirable outcomes for women themselves, for the family, and for the larger society, and result, in the words of Kharchev and

provided a forum for airing a variety of problems connected with the utilization of women in the labor force, their limited participation in political life, and the burdens imposed by the slow development of everyday services.

[3]Z. Iankova, "O bytovykh roliakh rabotaiushchei zhenshchiny," in *Problemy byta, braka i sem'i*, ed. N. Solov'ev, Iu. Lazauskas, and Z. Iankova (Vilnius, 1970), p. 44; A. G. Kharchev and S. I. Golod, *Professional'naia rabota zhenshchin i sem'ia* (Leningrad, 1971), p. 162; see also A. G. Kharchev, "Byt i sem'ia kak kategorii istoricheskogo materializma," in Solov'ev, et al., *Problemy byta*, pp. 18–19.

[4]N. V. Panova, "Voprosy truda i byta zhenshchin," in Solov'ev, et al., *Problemy byta*, p. 92.

Golod, "in serious losses to our entire society in the ethical, social, demographic and economic spheres."[5] Such contradictions engender, first of all, an extreme degree of nervous strain and fatigue, whose effects are documented at length in studies by sociologists and medical researchers. Secondly, the cumulative pressures of work and family responsibilities adversely affect not only women's health but also their opportunities for professional and personal development. As a consequence, "even in conditions of socialism there are preserved elements of real inequality between women and men."[6] Finally, society as a whole pays a high price for the overburdening of women. "The contradictions between the professional and family roles of women," Kharchev points out, "engender tensions and conflicts in internal family relations, lead to a weakening of control over the conduct of children and a deterioration of their upbringing, and, finally, is one of the basic causes of the declining birthrate."[7]

Paradoxically, some of these new problems are perceived to stem from the very success of the Soviet regime in achieving high levels of female labor-force participation at relatively low cost. The greater the reliance on female labor resources, and the more limited the investment in services to sustain it—as is apparent, for example, in the industrial regions of European Russia—the higher now appear to be the costs both to women and to the regime. Conversely, the lower the level of female education and labor-force participation, and the greater the resistance of traditional norms and patterns of behavior to penetration by new Soviet values and modes of action—as, for example, among the peoples of the Caucasus and Central Asia—the greater the degree of family stability and the higher the levels of fertility.

There can be little doubt that the impact of these contradictory trends has come to be felt all the more strongly in that it has helped to bring to the fore the explosive implications of one of the major unresolved tensions in Soviet political life: interethnic tension. Any resolution of current dilemmas may very well require the development of a regionally differentiated set of policies as well as an intricately interwoven pattern of resource allocation in the context of a uniform and national program that will not arouse local sensitivities. The effort to develop a comprehensive population policy is therefore fraught with especially great dangers and risks.

Furthermore, a number of possible approaches to current dilemmas risk exacerbating male-female tensions as well as divisions based on ethnicity. The greater the investment in educational and professional attainment on the part of women, the more acutely they appear to resent the absence

[5]Kharchev and Golod, *Professional'naia rabota zhenshchin*, p. 163.
[6]Kharchev, "Byt i sem'ia," in Solov'ev, et al., *Problemy byta*, p. 19.
[7]*Ibid.*, pp. 19–20.

of commensurate roles and opportunities for self-assertion, and the greater the potential for conflict with males, both in the workplace and within the family.

Finally, many of the new initiatives for which a wide range of analysts now actively press would require a major commitment of resources and an unprecedented level of intervention in wholly new areas of social and personal life—intervention, at that, in conditions of high uncertainty where outcomes are quintessentially unpredictable.

As a number of recent writings indicate, the customary parsimony of the Soviet leadership in funding new social programs has been encountering sharp challenges. As we shall see, the mounting pressure by specialized elites and the indications of their frustration have found expression in a growing number of explicit pronouncements. A warning by Iurkevich—that the enormity of the emerging problems precludes an easy, and inexpensive, solution—is but one typical indication of the resistance of at least some social scientists to the demand for quick (and no doubt cheap) ways out. As Iurkevich puts it:

> in the majority of cases, the measures capable of yielding a favorable effect demand from society considerable outlays and efforts. Everyone knows that in technology the introduction of any innovations is impossible without corresponding expenditures. But in the area of social relations, the kinds of recommendations that are frequently expected of scholars are those capable of resolving serious social problems without "capital investments." This is unrealistic. Policies in the field of family relations corresponding to the current needs and possibilities of our society are completely unthinkable without additional expenditures.[8]

These expenditures, he is quick to add, will be more than compensated by their results.

For new proposals to be compelling, they had to point to the dire consequences of further inaction by the Soviet leadership. For the demographers, the task was relatively easy; just such a rationale was available in the prediction that the failure to develop a comprehensive demographic policy would raise what would ultimately be the gravest danger of all: the danger of depopulation. The sociologists focused their attention on the family itself, warning that its growing instability augured ill both for the birthrate and for the proper socialization of the younger generation. To economists, it was the exhaustion of labor resources that posed critical problems and urgently required vast new investments to improve the quality of productive inputs. Thus, not unexpectedly, the representatives of different academic disciplines selected from the available social reality

[8]N. G. Iurkevich, *Sovetskaia sem'ia: funktsii i usloviia stabil'nosti*, (Minsk, 1970), pp. 203–4.

Women in Soviet Society

those dimensions of the problem most directly relevant to their particular scholarly concerns.

The presence of widespread alarm among social analysts and their general agreement that radical new departures were vital did not mean that they shared any single definition of precisely what was problematic, or of the solutions any particular problem demanded. Indeed, three distinct orientations can be distinguished in current Soviet writings, differing in their focus of concern, in their perception of its causes, and in the recommendations that flow from their diagnoses.[9] Furthermore, the three different action schemes presented for the consideration of policy elites embody fundamentally different conceptions of women's potential contribution to "developed socialism." These differing factual and evaluative assessments of present problems stem in part from divergent assumptions about male and female roles. They begin with different characterizations of how men and women differ and what consequences these differences ought to have for social organization and behavior, and end with policy recommendations that have distinctly different implications for the allocation not only of resources but of social roles.[10]

The first policy orientation tries, in effect, to straddle the issue. It attempts to reconcile the need for high levels of female labor-force participation with the desire for higher birthrates by proposing a series of measures to reduce the burdens of women's dual roles. Relatively orthodox in its assumptions and moderately reformist in orientation, it views the present balance of work and family roles as optimal and focuses on short-

---

[9]This discussion shares with Franklyn Griffiths the view that a focus on the process of interest articulation is likely to prove more fruitful in the study of the Soviet policy process, and less burdened by methodological difficulties, than a focus on interest groups; Franklyn Griffiths, "A Tendency Analysis of Soviet Policy-making," in *Interest Groups in Soviet Politics*, eds. H. Gordon Skilling and Franklyn Griffiths (Princeton, 1971), pp. 335–78. It therefore directs attention to the substantive issues raised in current public debates, focusing on the process of interest articulation rather than on the major institutional actors. A more comprehensive analysis of the formation of current Soviet social policy and its implications for the study of the Soviet policy process will be developed in a separate monograph by the author now in preparation, "Toward Social Planning: Social Science and Public Policy in the USSR, 1965–1977."

[10]As theorists of social stratification have frequently pointed out, the distribution of social roles involves the evaluation as well as the differentiation of functions and persons. Insofar as sex is one basis for the assignment of social roles, sex differentiation has an important normative as well as behavioral component. The existence of biological and psychological differences between men and women is beyond question; the social consequences attached to them are problematic and vary among different social systems. Questions of what differences are viewed as socially relevant ones, what they are relevant to and under what conditions, are central to the investigation of distributive systems. Precisely because sex-role norms are entwined with the allocation of social functions, their investigation needs to be integrated into the general study of social systems. For a more comprehensive discussion, see Harriet Holter, *Sex Roles and Social Structure* (Oslo, 1970), and her "Sex Roles and Social Change," *Acta Sociologica* 14 (1971): 2–12.

comings in the service sector and in specific conditions of female employment as the sources of unnecessary strain.

A second orientation reflects a far greater sense of doubt about present arrangements and views current demographic trends with serious alarm. Critical of policies that subordinate women's primary biological and social functions as wives and mothers to short-term economic needs, it proposes to redress the imbalance by elevating the social status and material rewards associated with reproduction.

A third orientation stands in dramatic opposition to any pressure to diminish women's role in production and advocates instead its intensification. Adamantly opposed to proposals that would, in effect, encourage women to revert to traditional roles as wives, mothers, and homemakers to even a limited degree, this orientation emphasizes the critical importance of high rates of female labor-force participation to the national economy, while also stressing the equally critical importance of female economic participation for women's social status and personal development and satisfaction. Accordingly, it advocates a further extension of women's roles in economic and political life on terms of greater equality with men and a reduction in the family burdens that inhibit it. The solution, in this view, lies not only, or even primarily, in the extension of everyday services but in the fundamental redefinition of male-female relationships. The goal, in this case, is quite clear: the increasingly equal sharing, by men and women, of functions, responsibilities, and rewards.

Although these three broad approaches have been sharply delineated for analytical purposes, in reality the boundaries between them are far from rigid. Many specific recommendations—for example, those calling for improvements in consumer services—cannot be exclusively indentified with a single orientation. Moreover, within each of these categories, the measures proposed are motivated by a broad range of considerations, ranging from the most instrumental and calculating manipulation of female roles in the service of state interests to the superficial invocation of official priorities on behalf of simple humanitarian goals. No measures are introduced without some reference to the larger social interest that they would serve, as well as to their potential benefits to women. Thus, while the relative weight of different considerations in any particular instance cannot be easily established, and the overlapping of such considerations is in many instances quite extensive, the three approaches deduced here do represent three identifiable tendencies in Soviet official and semiofficial writings.

These orientations represent, in effect, alternative strategies for dealing with a number of critical domestic issues. Therefore, before turning to a more systematic analysis of these three basic orientations and their implications for the future development of women's roles, it will be helpful first to examine the two overarching imperatives that provide the framework of current debates, the first stemming from the demographic trends that give heightened importance to women's reproductive potential, and the second deriving from the scarcity of labor resources that make women's future role in production of vital national concern. In short, we shall examine current Soviet perceptions of women as both a reproductive and productive resource.

DEMOGRAPHIC PROBLEMS AND PUBLIC POLICY: WOMEN AS A REPRODUCTIVE RESOURCE

In current Soviet reassessments of women's roles, advocates of measures to enhance the status and rewards associated with maternity occupy a central place. Viewing the declining birthrate with profound alarm and identifying as its basic cause an excessive emphasis on female labor-force participation at the sacrifice of women's reproductive potential, a number of prominent Soviet demographers (of whom the most outspoken have been Boris Urlanis of the Institute of Economics of the USSR Academy of Sciences and Viktor Perevedentsev of the Academy's Institute of the World Labor Movement) have advocated a comprehensive and far-reaching population policy designed to bring about a reversal of current demographic trends.

The declining birthrate requires dramatic new departures in Soviet economic and social policy, in their view, because of its ominous implications for Soviet economic growth, political and military power, and ethnic balance in the years ahead. Throughout the Soviet period, and until the 1960s, the tendency for successive cohorts of women to bear fewer and fewer children was partially offset by declining mortality. More recently, however, the combination of declining birthrates (Table 38) and level or rising mortality rates has resulted in a sharp drop in net population increase, from 18 per thousand in 1960 to 8.9 per thousand in 1976, a projected 7.5 per thousand in 1990, and possibly 5.8 per thousand in the year 2000. Despite a temporary reversal in this trend in the past few years as the result of the entry of a large age cohort into the prime childbearing age, the problem is likely to become progressively more acute later in the century.[11] The disparity between what a number of Soviet

[11]From a rate of 45.5 births per thousand in 1913 the figure fell to 31.2 per thousand in 1940, 26.7 per thousand in 1950, and a low of 17 per thousand in 1969. It has risen slightly since then, reaching 18.0 in 1974; Tsentral'noe statisticheskoe upravlenie, *Narodnoe khoziaistvo SSSR v 1974 gody* (Moscow, 1975), p. 44. At the same time mortality rates, which reached a low of 7.1 per thousand in 1960, rose to 9.5 per thousand in 1976 and are likely to continue to rise in the next few decades. As a result of both these trends, by the year 2000 the size of the Soviet population will have increased to just under 310 million, rather than the 340-350 million projected by earlier Soviet analyses. Unpublished estimate, Foreign Demographic Analysis Division, U. S. Department of Commerce. For an excellent review

demographers consider an optimal rate of reproduction and the actual rate, which in some regions falls below the replacement rate, is, in their view, sufficiently alarming to require that highest priority be given to eliminating the possibility of a future decline in population, "regardless of any considerations that may be advanced from an economic, ecological, sociological or any other point of view."[12]

Why declining fertility rates should be a source of anxiety among Soviet analysts in a world where zero population growth is seen by many as the only solution to resource constraints becomes apparent in the light of their concern with several distinctive aspects of Soviet economic and political development.[13] First and foremost is the potential effect of a stable or shrinking population on future economic growth. In the face of a mounting labor shortage and of male and female participation rates that already approach the demographic maximum, expanding population is considered vital to continued economic growth. Although efforts are underway to shift from an extensive to an intensive pattern of economic development and to compensate for labor shortages by encouraging technological innovation and increased labor productivity, in the past few years it has nonetheless proven necessary to rely on imports of foreign labor (that is, from Eastern Europe) to overcome specific shortages. Labor constraints in the prime industrial regions of the USSR—especially Russia and Siberia—are likely to become even more acute in coming decades because a growing proportion of new labor supply will be located in regions—such as Central Asia—where relatively low levels of industrialization and low rates of out-migration have already produced a labor surplus.[14] The complex problems involved either in shifting Central Asian labor resources to regions of labor scarcity or in accelerating industrial development in Central Asia itself preclude an easy or rapid resolution of current dilemmas.

---

of Soviet fertility trends, see Murray Feshbach and Stephen Rapawy, "Soviet Population and Manpower Trends and Policies," in U.S. Congress Joint Economic Committee, *Soviet Economy in a New Perspective* (Washington, D.C., 1976), pp. 113–54; Frederick E. Leedy, "Demographic Trends in the USSR," in U.S. Congress Joint Economic Committee, *Soviet Economic Prospects for the Seventies* (Washington, D.C., 1973), pp. 428–84; Warren Eason, "Demographic Problems: Fertility," in U.S. Congress *Soviet Economy in a New Perspective*, pp. 155–61. Recent Soviet treatments include B. Ts. Urlanis, *Problemy dinamiki naseleniia SSSR* (Moscow, 1974), and A. Ia. Kvasha, *Problemy ekonomiko-demograficheskogo razvitiia SSSR* (Moscow, 1974).

[12]Urlanis, *Problemy dinamiki naseleniia SSSR*, p. 283.

[13]These concerns are spelled out in a number of books and articles, but most directly in Urlanis, *Problemy dinamiki naseleniia SSSR*, and in Perevedentsev's contribution to the *Voprosy filosofii* round-table discussion, "Neobkhodimo stimulirovat' rost naseleniia v nashei strane," 11 (1974): 88–92. See also Helen Desfosses Cohn, "Population Policy in the USSR," *Problems of Communism* 22 (July–August 1973): 41–55.

[14]For an illuminating discussion, see Murray Feshbach, "Prospects for Massive Out-migration from Central Asia During the Next Decade," mimeographed (Washington, D.C., Foreign Demographic Analysis Division, U.S. Department of Commerce, 1977).

TABLE 38

NUMBER OF BIRTHS PER THOUSAND FEMALES BY AGE OF MOTHER, 1926/27–1973/74 AND
TWO-YEAR MOVING AVERAGE OF THE CRUDE BIRTHRATE 1960/61–1973/74

Age of mother	1926/27	1938/39	1954/55	1960/61	1963/64	1968/69	1971/72	1973/74
Total births 15–49	159.1	139.5	86.2	90.6	78.4	65.3	67.2	66.8
15–19	38.2	32.8	15.6	35.2	22.7	28.9	32.4	33.3
20–24	259.4	214.4	146.9	164.8	162.6	157.0	173.9	173.4
25–29	269.0	230.6	172.9	160.7	145.6	128.8	137.1	134.8
30–34	224.5	183.5	127.6	110.1	97.6	92.0	84.3	79.3
35–39	171.6	131.7	74.4	60.7	52.0	47.4	49.4	45.5
40–44	90.8	68.1	35.4	23.5	21.4	16.2	14.6	14.4
45–49	23.0	19.0	7.1	4.8	3.9	3.4	2.0	1.7
First births 15–49				34.5	28.0	25.0	29.2	29.8
Second births 15–49				24.7	21.8	17.6	18.1	18.6
Third births 15–49				12.9	11.2	7.6	6.9	6.7
Fourth births 15–49				7.5	6.6	4.7	3.7	3.4
Fifth and higher order births, 15–49				10.9	10.8	10.4	9.3	8.4
2-year moving average of the crude birth rate				24.2	20.4	17.1	17.8	17.7

SOURCE: Compiled from Warren Eason, "Demographic Problems: Fertility," in *Soviet Economy in a New Perspective*, U. S. Congress Joint Economic Committee (Washington, 1976), pp. 158–59.

In addition to its contribution to future labor resources, expanding population is also thought to be necessary to maintain an optimal balance between the productive and the dependent segments of the population. The growing weight of pensioners in the total Soviet population is placing increasing strains on the system of social services. The proportion of adults eligible for pensions, for example, rose from 10 percent in 1950 to 15 percent in 1970 and is likely to reach 20 percent by the year 2000.[15] The combination of an aging population and more liberal pension benefits will constitute an increasing drain on resources in coming decades.

Less openly discussed, but clearly a further source of concern, is the effect of current demographic trends on military and political power. Perevedentsev's view that "a country's position in the world, all other things being equal, is determined by the size of the population,"[16] is unlikely to be confined to demographers. Frequent comparisons of Soviet population trends with those of the United States, Japan, and China indicate a serious preoccupation with the strategic implications of population dynamics and prompted one recent suggestion that the Soviet leadership adopt as its goal the maintenance of a constant ratio between the size of the world population and that of the USSR.[17]

Beyond the declining birthrate itself, moreover, its implications for the ethnic composition of the Soviet population is a cause of particular alarm. While the single-child family is now the norm in the Slavic and Baltic republics, large families are widespread among the non-Slavic populations. As we noted in Chapter VII, only 1 percent of all families in the urban areas of the Russian Republic have four or more children, compared with 25 percent of all urban families in Turkmenistan. The proportion of large families is greater still in rural areas, constituting almost half of the total in Uzbekistan, Tadzhikistan, and Turkmenistan, and even more in Azerbaidzhan.

Demographic disparities resulting from economic and cultural patterns that affect desired family size will be further compounded in coming decades by regional variations in marriage and divorce rates and in the age structure of the population. As Table 39 reveals, the rate of births per thousand population in the Central Asian republics is roughly two-and-a-half times greater than in the Baltic and Slavic republics. Moreover, since the age structure of the latter republics is also associated with higher mortality rates, the net differences in population growth are even greater than differences in the birthrate alone. Net increases in population range

[15] Feshbach and Rapawy, "Soviet Population and Manpower Trends," in U.S. Congress, *Soviet Economy in a New Perspective*, p. 115.

[16] *Literaturnaia gazeta*, March 20, 1968, p. 11.

[17] E. D. Grazhdannikov, *Prognosticheskie modeli sotsial'no-demograficheskikh protsessov* (Novosibirsk, 1974); V. Perevedentsev, *Voprosy ekonomiki*, no. 6 (June 1976): 127–33; for a similar concern see Perevedentsev, *Literaturnaia gazeta*, March 20, 1968, p. 11.

TABLE 39

POPULATION GROWTH IN THE USSR, BY REPUBLIC,
1976 (PER 1,000 POPULATION)

Republic	Births	Deaths	Net increase
USSR total	18.4	9.5	8.9
RSFSR	15.9	10.0	5.9
Ukraine	15.2	10.2	5.0
Belorussia	15.7	8.8	6.9
Uzbekistan	35.3	7.1	28.2
Kazakhstan	24.3	7.2	17.1
Georgia	18.2	7.8	10.4
Azerbaidzhan	25.7	6.6	19.1
Lithuania	15.7	9.6	6.1
Moldavia	20.6	9.0	11.6
Latvia	13.8	12.1	1.7
Kirgizia	31.3	8.2	23.1
Tadzhikistan	38.2	8.5	29.7
Armenia	22.7	5.5	17.2
Turkmenistan	34.7	7.7	27.0
Estonia	15.1	12.0	3.1

SOURCE: Tsentral'noe statisticheskoe upravlenie, *Narodnoe khoziaistvo SSSR za 60 let* (Moscow, 1977), pp. 72–73.

from 1.7 per thousand for Latvia to 29.7 per thousand for Tadzhikistan.

As a consequence of these variations, an increasing share of future net population growth will be provided by the Moslem populations of the Central Asian and Transcaucasian republics. In 1959 these republics accounted for just over 12 percent of all births in the USSR; by 1970 their share had risen to 20 percent. The disparity is even more dramatic with respect to the natural increase in population overall. In 1959 these republics accounted for 15 percent of the total, and 11 years later for 30 percent.[18] The profound implications of these trends for the supply and quality of military manpower, as well as for the nature and availability of future labor resources, have not escaped the attention of Soviet analysts and policy makers. Thus, while the high fertility rates in these regions are in some respects a welcome compensation for the low rates prevailing elsewhere, they create additional and delicate problems of their own.

Finally, current demographic trends pose particular difficulties for a political system committed to controlling the direction of social change

[18]Tsentral'noe statisticheskoe upravlenie, *Naselenie SSSR 1973: Statisticheskii sbornik* (Moscow, 1975), pp. 69–83.

because they raise what Gregory Massell has aptly called "the specter of a chartless voyage."[19] The educational attainments and economic independence of women that are a source of such pride are also associated with high divorce rates and declining fertility, while high fertility rates are found precisely among the least "liberated" Soviet women, whose levels of education and labor-force participation are lowest. Not only do these trends challenge the heretofore unquestioned assumption that socialist societies are characterized by a steady increase in population, they also raise the prospect that desired goals may be fundamentally incompatible. The difficulty of evaluating these trends and the extreme ambivalence of official reactions to them are not surprising, for they compel attention to the unintended consequences of Soviet policies and priorities. Increasing official encouragement of social research, including demography, in recent years—albeit within sharply delimited parameters—and the concomitant revival of interest in social planning offer compelling evidence of both a new recognition of societal complexity and a continuing commitment to directed social change.

In attempting to define an optimal pattern of population growth and in proposing a series of measures with this objective in mind, the advocates of a comprehensive demographic policy proceed on the assumption that family preferences must be reconciled with societal needs. The right of the state to influence family behavior is largely unquestioned; acquiescence in unregulated family behavior is rejected as "demographic nihilism." In the words of one prominent Soviet demographer, A. Ia. Boiarskii: "Soviet science has a peculiarly active relationship to reality; it is obliged not only to explain it but to alter it. In the light of this one can no longer preserve the approach to demographic processes . . . as something purely exogenous in relation to the national economic plan and the policies of the state."[20]

Similarly rejected is the view that global resource constraints require limits on population growth, a view that is stigmatized as "Malthusianism." This does not, however, preclude efforts to reduce fertility in the Moslem regions of the USSR. While the subject is too sensitive to permit extensive public discussion, there are a number of indications that birthrates in these regions are considered to be excessive. At a meeting sponsored by the Academy of Sciences in 1975, a participant from Turkmenistan noted that "from the standpoint of economic and social interests,

[19]Gregory Massell, *The Surrogate Proletariat: Moslem Women and Revolutionary Strategies in Soviet Central Asia, 1919–1929* (Princeton, 1974), pp. 41–43. Massell is here referring, of course, to the problem of adapting revolutionary theory and practice to the unique and unanticipated set of conditions presented by the Central Asian milieu. Certain parallels with the contemporary situation nevertheless suggest themselves.
[20]Cited in David M. Heer, "Recent Developments in Soviet Population Policy," *Studies in Family Planning* 3 (November 1972): 259.

this highly expanded type of population reproduction in Turkmenia and other republics with similar birthrate indices is less than optimal. The present high birthrate makes it virtually impossible for mothers to work."[21] Another distinguished contributor urged that every effort be made to encourage vocational education for women in Central Asia and to involve them in social production, and further recommended that public health agencies increase the effectiveness of different contraceptive methods and publicize methods of birthrate regulation more widely.[22] The need for a regionally differentiated demographic policy is thus explicitly, if delicately, acknowledged. In a discretely worded passage, a leading Soviet demographer, A. Ia. Kvasha, suggested its contours:

> For the U.S.S.R., where there exist large regional differences in the processes of reproduction of the population—from approximately stationary to greatly expanding, and where, moreover, these differences are largely determined by different levels of fertility, it is an important question whether demographic policy should vary by region of the country. If one proceeds from the view that demographic policy should primarily be directed at the creation of a single optimum type of population reproduction in the nation, then there should exist a single general direction of demographic policy for the entire country. For example, if we consider optimal a type of reproduction of population which is characterized by a net coefficient of 1.0–1.2 . . . with such parameters . . . it is necessary to stimulate by various measures the birth of first, second and third children in the family . . . but beginning with the fourth child all measures of an encouraging nature should cease, or at a minimum significantly weaken. Such a system might stimulate fertility in areas where it is low and at the same time further the lowering of fertility in areas where it is very high.[23]

Insofar as the reduction of fertility in these regions is to a considerable degree a function of female education and employment, its form and pace will depend on the outcome of larger political conflicts surrounding the allocation of resources to the industrialization of Soviet Central Asia.

With respect to the non-Moslem regions of the USSR, it is the problem of declining birthrates that dominates discussions of population policy. A partially successful effort to free demography from rigid ideological constraints has made it possible to acknowledge that changes in reproductive behavior are the result of objective social processes that are universal in their impact.[24] Urbanization, rising levels of education, improvements in the status of women, and growing material and cultural demands all tend to be inversely correlated with fertility in industrializing societies; in this respect the Soviet Union is no exception. But the thrust of the

[21]R. Galetskaia, "Sferi demograficheskoi politiki," *Voprosy ekonomiki* 8 (August 1975): 152.
[22]*Ibid.*, p. 149.
[23]A. Ia. Kvasha, *Problemy ekonomiko-demograficheskogo razvitiia*, pp. 139–40.
[24]For a treatment of the ideological and institutional constraints that continue to inhibit the development of the discipline, see Helen Desfosses [Cohn], "Demography, Ideology and Politics in the USSR," *Soviet Studies* 28 (April 1976): 244–56.

pronatalist orientation is to identify specific features of Soviet development that have reinforced these broader trends and to propose a broad spectrum of measures designed to mitigate their effects, if not to reverse them altogether.

One might have expected the advocates of a comprehensive population policy to recommend the use of legal and administrative constraints to alter reproductive behavior. The restriction of abortions is the most obvious measure of this kind, and one that would be likely to have a wide impact, given the fact that abortion continues to be the major method of birth control in the Soviet Union today. It is estimated that some eight million abortions are performed annually, amounting to more than double the number of live births in some areas.[25] If recent experience in Rumania offers any guidance, such a measure might have a positive if small effect on present birthrates. However, such a course of action has not been adopted in the USSR thus far nor is it supported by the most prominent advocates of a comprehensive population policy, despite ample Soviet and East European precedent. Insisting that abortion, like contraception, is merely an instrument for limiting family size rather than a cause of the trend to do so, opponents of such restrictions have warned that they consider them to be inadmissible in principle, ineffective in practice, and potentially harmful in their effects.[26] The advocates of more energetic governmental initiatives have therefore directed their attention to measures that would alter the social and economic context of reproductive behavior rather than attempt to coerce behavior itself.

The first group of such recommendations may be broadly classified as measures designed to enhance fertility potential. Insofar as low marriage rates, late marriage age, and a high degree of marital instability have an adverse, albeit indirect, effect on fertility, the aim of this first set of proposals is to expand the pool of married females in the prime reproductive age cohort.[27] A rise in the marriage rate could be achieved, in the view

[25]Jerzy Berent, "Causes of Fertility Decline in Eastern Europe and the Soviet Union," Part I, *Population Studies* 24 (July 1970): 281. Soviet sources indicate that roughly 25 percent of birth control is carried out through contraception, and 75 percent through abortion; A. Verbenko, "Tol'ko zhelannye deti," *Literaturnaia gazeta*, July 31, 1968, p. 12. Moreover, the incidence of abortion has risen substantially since its legalization in 1955. According to one Soviet specialist, between 1955 and 1965 the total of legal and illegal abortions increased by a factor of four. E. A. Sadvokasova, *Sotsial'no-gigienicheskie aspekty regulirovaniia razmerov sem'i* (Moscow, 1969), p. 117.

[26]Sadvokasova, *Sotsial'no-gigienicheskie aspekty;* Verbenko, "Tol'ko zhelannye deti," p.12. The very persistence of such warnings, however, is an indication that the issue remains controversial. Indeed, in a recent round-table discussion of demographic problems sponsored by *Voprosy filosofii*, at least one of the participants, V. P. Bochkov, commented on the harmfulness of abortions and explicitly stated that the number of pregnancies ought to correspond to the number of actual births; "Sotsial'no-filosofskie problemy demografii," Part II, *Voprosy filosofii* 11 (November 1974): 83.

[27]For a useful treatment of the range of factors that affect fertility, see Kingsley Davis and Judith Blake, "Social Structure and Fertility: An Analytic Framework," in *The Family: Its Structure and Functions*, ed. Rose Laub Coser (New York, 1964), pp. 629–64.

of a number of writers, by official sponsorship of new institutional arrangements to facilitate acquaintanceship—clubs, social activities, and
even computer dating services. Furthermore, the state might provide additional incentives to marriage in the form of financial aid to newlyweds
and priority in the assignment of apartments.[28] Finally, more serious attention to the social consequences of economic decisions is called for. For
example, the failure of planning agencies to take social and demographic
factors into consideration in the siting of new enterprises has resulted in
the creation of cities with an overwhelming preponderance of a single sex.
In these "cities of bridegrooms" and "cities of brides" the opportunities
for marriage are severely limited.[29] Consequently, joining social to economic planning would help to create more favorable conditions for acquaintanceship and marriage and would presumably have a beneficial effect on fertility rates as well.

A reduction in the proportion of late marriages would be a further contribution to reproductive potential, although by no means do all demographers share Perevedentsev's enthusiasm for a campaign to encourage
early marriages. A few have expressed concern that the social maturity
essential to marital stability is not often found among eighteen- and nine-
teen-year-olds, and that "love at first sight" does not necessarily provide
a solid foundation for future family life. Moreover, insofar as early marriage and childbearing limit the further education of young women, particularly given the reluctance of educational bureaucracies to accommodate the needs of student-parents, the potential costs of early marriages
may outweigh their benefits.[30] Further research has therefore been recommended by a number of social analysts who fear that hasty campaigns
may prove more harmful than the problem they attempt to resolve.

Finally, marital instability itself is seen as contributing to lower fertility. The two are mutually reinforcing, as family sociologists have pointed
out, in that the very fragility of marriage accentuates the tendency of
women to have only one child, while the presence of few or no children
simplifies the dissolution of marriage. Furthermore, low rates of remarriage and low birthrates in second and subsequent marriages further de-
press population size.[31] In an effort to stem the rising rate of divorce, a

[28]Perevedentsev, *Literaturnaia gazeta*, August 30, 1972, p. 12.

[29]*Ibid.* See also A. E. Kotliar and I. Kirpa, "Demograficheskie aspekty zaniatosti v gorodakh raznymi promyshlennymi strukturami," *Vestnik statistiki* 7 (1972): 12–18.

[30]See, for example, the debate between Perevedentsev and A. Vishnevskii in *Komsomol'-
skaia pravda*, May 14, 1975, p. 4. The Ministry of Higher and Specialized Secondary Education was urged to develop a clear-cut policy for dealing with married students. Inadequate dormitory facilities and other regulations that force women to choose between study
and motherhood were the subject of criticism by Vishnevskii; *Literaturnaia gazeta*, January
12, 1977, p. 13.

[31]A recent study, for example, found that 35 percent of all divorces involved couples
without children, and that female fertility rates in second marriages were only 30 to 40
percent those in first marriages; L. P. Chuiko, *Braki i razvody* (Moscow, 1973), pp. 173ff.

number of analysts have proposed that the waiting period prior to marriage be lengthened, that marriage counseling be introduced on a wide scale, that sex education be included in secondary school programs, and that other financial measures be undertaken to alleviate the economic stresses that young families often confront.[32] The failure to synchronize work schedules, which compels husbands and wives to vacation separately, comes in for particular criticism. A number of analysts have suggested that marital stability would be enhanced by arranging vacation schedules to permit families to spend this time together, and such analysts have urged the construction and rental of private *dachas* for family vacations.[33]

Proposals such as these would extend the scope of public policy into relatively uncharted terrain. They would also, as a matter of course, vastly enhance the importance of social scientists in analyzing, predicting, and directing the process of social change. In assuming a degree of public responsibility for the encouragement and support of personal relationships, in pressing for a consideration of social priorities in economic decisions, and in advocating the allocation of considerable resources for new social needs, these proposals envision a serious commitment of public resources to activities that were hitherto considered to be largely outside the public domain.

In addition to proposing measures that would enhance fertility potential, a number of social scientists have also pressed for a second group of policies designed to alter social values in favor of large families. Placing the blame for low birthrates on social trends that have altered the costs and benefits of children, and devalued reproduction by comparison with other social and personal goals—such as improvements in living standards, female education, labor-force participation, and cultural and leisure pursuits—they advocate a national effort to stimulate the desire for children. In order to achieve an optimal figure of 2.65 children per family, a veritable campaign has been launched to persuade young couples that having at least two and preferably three children is a patriotic duty as well as a guarantee of family happiness. Recent Western studies that point to the advantages enjoyed by only children do not receive wide circulation; Soviet writers deplore the "hothouse" atmosphere of small families and insist that only in larger families are the dangers of egoistic individualism averted and a proper socialist upbringing assured. Some even go so far as to assert that the antisocial tendencies of only children are man-

---

[32]See, for example, Perevedentsev, *Literaturnaia gazeta*, August 30, 1972, p. 12. A recent study of divorce by L. Chuiko pointed to the difficult housing conditions of young newlyweds as a particular source of strain. On the basis of data from the Ukraine, she reported that only 5 to 7 percent had an apartment of their own, and that 20 percent had their own room in the apartment of one set of parents.

[33]Z. M. Iuk, *Trud zhenshchiny i sem'ia* (Minsk, 1975), pp. 201–2.

ifested in the especially high proportion of juvenile delinquents among them.[34]

As one demographer was sufficiently candid to admit, however, nearly everyone who opposes the single-child family in theory has only one child in fact. The growing emphasis on quality rather than quantity in reproduction (based as it might be on the ancient Leninist dictum "better fewer, but better"), has led a number of demographers to warn that depriving children of siblings is an excessive price to pay for "quality." As G. Kiseleva graphically put it:

> While the absolute majority of families want a first child, the thought of a second puts them off: Why deny themselves something else they want? And it might crimp the style of the first child.
>
> Parents often misjudge the needs—and the capabilities—of their first child, burdening him with a heavier load of music lessons, foreign language classes and athletics than they themselves could handle between the two of them. Five or eight years later they realize that in fact he is not another Mozart. But then his childhood is gone—if he ever had one. Wouldn't it be better to take the money, time and energy that such parents put into turning their child into a Leonardo da Vinci and "give" him not a drawing teacher who bores him, or another expensive and hateful box of paints, but a little sister or brother instead?[35]

It is clear, however, that any serious effort to bring about a reversal of current trends will require more than just public campaigns. Recognizing that a major shift of attitudes and motivations is involved, demographers and sociologists have recently directed their attention to the social-psychological bases of reproductive behavior in a number of promising investigations to identify relevant values and dispositions.

Yet a third group of recommendations is premised on the view that living conditions rather than reproductive motivation are the major obstacle to increased family size. These recommendations, therefore, are intended to reduce the material burden of childrearing by offsetting more of its costs. (Although the distinction between measures that reduce the costs of bearing and raising children and those that act as a direct incentive to fertility is not a sharp one, we shall treat incentives to fertility as a fourth category to be explored shortly.)

These proposals are based on the findings of extensive demographic surveys which indicate that an overwhelming majority of Soviet families have fewer children than they actually desire. While almost four out of

[34]M. Alemaskin, *Literaturnaia gazeta*, February 14, 1973, p. 11. The author cites two 1970 studies of juvenile delinquents that concluded that large families have a smaller proportion of problem children than smaller ones, but the evidence cited does not, on the face of it, actually sustain this conclusion, nor is any causal relationship demonstrated.

[35]G. Kiseleva, *Literaturnaia gazeta*, July 4, 1973, p. 13. See also B. Urlanis, *Literaturnaia gazeta*, September 27, 1972, p. 13.

five women surveyed considered two or three children to be optimal, four out of five Soviet families in fact have only one or two children.[36] A number of problems surround the interpretation of "desired number of children." Nonetheless, many Soviet demographers have drawn from these studies the conclusion that specific material difficulties—most notably limited financial resources, poor housing conditions, and the lack of space in preschool institutions—are responsible for the apparent gap between ideal and actual family size. This conclusion is reinforced by other studies based on interviews with women themselves: in Chuiko's investigation of newlyweds in Kiev, for example, 40 percent of the brides insisted that improved housing was the essential precondition of their willingness to bear as many children as they considered ideal. In view of the fact that from a societal perspective children constitute a resource, while from the point of view of an individual family they represent a cost, the harmonization of family preferences with societal needs, it is argued, depends on an increased level of financial support.

To be sure, these arguments are seriously challenged by a number of Soviet analysts. Investigations of the relationship between family income and fertility, they point out, have yielded contradictory results, demonstrating that subjective evaluations of family needs play a crucial mediating role between income and fertility.[37] If this is indeed the case, then material incentives are unlikely to have a positive impact on reproductive behavior. The presumed association between the availability of preschool facilities and birthrates meets with equal scepticism. In the view of a number of demographers, the availability of institutional child care is a condition of female employment rather than a contribution to fertility, especially in light of the fact that the birthrate is lowest in precisely those urban regions where the child-care network is most extensive.

Finally, the very desirability of relying on material incentives has been questioned by still others who fear that a program of direct grants will

[36]V. A. Belova and L. E. Darskii, *Statistika mnenii v izuchenii rozhdaemosti* (Moscow, 1972).

[37]A summary of the contradictory findings of several studies of the relationship of income and fertility is presented in Heer, "Recent Developments in Soviet Population Policy," p. 262. The report of an all-Union symposium on demographic and family problems held in October 1975 came to a similarly ambivalent conclusion. Some participants noted that small families were more common among high-income groups than among those with low incomes. The number of children per family in the highest income group was 2.57 (ideal) and 1.87 (expected), while the corresponding figures for the lowest income groups were 4.10 and 4.23. At the same time, it was argued, there is an emerging tendency for high-income families to have a higher birthrate than those with smaller incomes. A survey showed that in republics with a low birthrate, families with a monthly income of 151 to 210 rubles averaged 1.94 children, those with an income of 451 to 600 rubles averaged 2.05 children, and families whose income reached 901 or more rubles had 2.49 children. No connection was found between income and number of children, however, in families where the wife had a higher education (V. P. Tomin, "Vsesoiuznyi simpozium po demograficheskim problemam sem'i," *Sotsiologicheskie issledovaniia* 2 [April-May-June 1976]: 189).
    See also V. A. Belova et al., *Skol'ko detei budet v sovetskoi sem'e* (Moscow, 1977).

minimize the degree of social control over family expenditures, and that it would be preferable to allocate resources to collectively organized forms of consumption. Advocating just such a course Piskunov and Steshenko argue,

> collectively organized forms of consumption permit a social collective not only to implement its control over correct and purposeful utilization of the means of existence and the very process of their consumption but consciously to influence the shaping of new needs. . . . The development of free and subsidized goods and services makes it possible to solve the problems of demographic policy within the overall set of strategic tasks of social policy as a whole.[38]

These criticisms notwithstanding, the interest in and pressures for measures to offset some of the costs of raising children remains considerable. Indeed, their advocates have made a concerted and partially successful effort to persuade the Soviet leadership to undertake a number of new initiatives along these lines. The extension of maternity leave benefits to *kolkhoz* women and the liberalization of sick leave benefits for parents of young children represented official implementation of the recommendations of a scholarly symposium on women's employment and the family held in Minsk in 1969.[39] Additionally, a new program of partially paid maternity leave for up to a year to supplement existing provisions for 112 days of paid maternity leave was promised at the 25th Party Congress in 1976.[40] But the most significant of these new initiatives—for it represented a new departure in Soviet population policy—was the enactment of a new family allowance program on September 12, 1974.

By the late 1960s, it was widely acknowledged that the family allowance program first introduced under Stalin acted more to redistribute income to large families than to encourage fertility. The fact that the Soviet program provided such allowances only for fourth and higher-order births, that the benefits extended only four years, that the actual amounts involved were extremely small, and that the share of child benefits in the total social assistance program was declining was the subject of unflattering comparisons with foreign, and particularly East European, models. The views of Iurkevich, writing in the late 1960s, reflected a broader con-

---

[38]V. P. Piskunov and V. S. Steshenko, "O demografLcheskoL politike sotsialisticheskogo obshchestva," in *Demograficheskaia politika*, eds. V. P. Piskunov and V. S. Steshenko (Moscow, 1974), pp. 21–22.

[39]The original recommendations were published as an Appendix in A. G. Kharchev and S. I. Golod, *Professional'naia rabota zhenshchin*, pp. 161–70. Maternity leave payments were raised to 100 percent of salary without distinction by category of employment in 1973.

[40]Kosygin announced at the Congress that "provisions have been made for putting into effect a number of new social measures using these [public consumption] funds, among them giving women partially paid leave to care for infants until they reach the age of 1"; *Pravda*, March 2, 1976, p. 3. This intention was reaffirmed in Baibakov's report to the Central Committee plenary session in 1976; *Izvestiia*, October 28, 1976, pp. 2–4. No precise terms were mentioned.

sensus among the emerging community of demographers and sociologists
that new initiatives were overdue:

> As a whole, the Soviet state and society spends comparatively more than any
> other state in the world on the protection of maternity and childhood (the
> maintenance of children's preschool institutions, pioneer and other children's
> camps, etc.). But it is appropriate to pose the question of restoring the leading
> position in the area of direct material assistance to the family for the mainte-
> nance of children as well. This is not merely a question of the prestige of the
> world's first socialist state but also a question of simple necessity, and at the
> same time, of justice. . . . It goes without saying, that the increase in expen-
> ditures on public forms of family services (nurseries and kindergartens, ex-
> tended-day groups in the schools, etc.) is a necessary thing. But if we wish to
> stimulate fertility and consider that social upbringing must be combined with
> that of the family, the expenditures of society must increase in both directions,
> harmoniously supplementing each other.[41]

The Soviet leadership was apparently persuaded of the desirability of
such reforms. At the 24th Party Congress in 1971, Kosygin announced
the Party's intention of introducing a program of child allowances, and
three years later it was finally enacted. The new program provided for
monthly payments of twelve rubles for each child under eight to families
whose total per capita income did not exceed fifty rubles per month.
Moreover, its actual effects suggest that careful attention was given to
designing a plan that, while national in scope and uniform in application,
would nevertheless produce differentiated outcomes, maximizing the benefits to smaller urban families and forestalling a massive flow of new resources to regions of high fertility.[42]

The introduction of this new program constituted a significant new
departure in Soviet social policy and a substantial new commitment of
resources. It virtually doubled the number of children covered—the proportion rising to 37 percent of all children under age eight—and involved
a fivefold increase in total expenditures, from 395 million rubles for the
old program in 1974 to a combined total of 2.195 billion rubles for both
programs together.[43] While it thus met the minimum demands of the advocates of new initiatives, it was nonetheless relatively modest in comparative terms. It represented an expenditure of 0.6 percent of national
income in 1974, compared with a figure of 3.2 percent for similar social
programs in France in 1972.[44] Moreover, twelve rubles per month per

[41]N. G. Iurkevich, *Sovetskaia sem'ia: Funktsii i usloviia stabil'nosti* (Minsk, 1970), pp. 40–
41. Heer has argued that Soviet programs and priorities were in fact antinatalist in their
effects; "Recent Developments in Soviet Population Policy," p. 258.

[42]This view is supported by David Heer's analysis of the impact of the two programs on
different types of families; "The New Direction of Soviet Population Policy," mimeographed (Center for Population Research, Los Angeles, 1976), Table 2.

[43]*Ibid.*, pp. 9–10.

[44]*Ibid.*

child was a relatively modest figure compared with the government's subsidy of preschool institutions, which amounted to twenty-seven to thirty-three rubles per month per child. While the new allowances helped to offset some of the costs associated with bearing and raising children and possibly underscored the notion that the production and care of children is not merely a private concern of parents but a socially valued activity, they could hardly, of themselves, constitute a powerful incentive to reproduction.

In welcoming the new family allowance program as a promising beginning, Urlanis and Perevedentsev made it clear that still further measures would be required to achieve a real resolution of the demographic problem. As Urlanis insisted: "It is appropriate to consider the decisions of the 24th Congress of the Communist Party of the Soviet Union as a definite step in the direction of perfecting a demographic policy. They ought to be followed by new decisions which will safeguard an important and priceless element of the future productive forces of our country—its population."[45]

The further measures Urlanis alluded to represent the central thrust of the entire pronatalist position, as well as its most controversial dimension. Differing from the preceding measures in its purpose, the magnitude of expenditures involved, and the method of calculation, this fourth and final component of a comprehensive demographic policy involves, in the words of one Soviet author, "transforming maternity, in one degree or another, into professional, paid social labor."[46] At the core of this proposal is a willingness to forgo the short-term advantages of high rates of female labor-force participation in the interest of a long-term population increase. This objective would be accomplished by compensating women workers for remaining home to bear and raise children. Direct financial subsidies, tailored not to the direct cost of children but to the opportunity cost of female labor, and on a scale sufficient to motivate women to withdraw from the labor force, are intended as an inducement to increasing family size.

Furthermore, because extended maternal leave would adversely affect the level of benefits women might claim at retirement, the advocates of such programs also support a modification of the entire pension system to reflect the social value of maternity. Pension benefits in this scheme would reward child-rearing as well as production and would depend on the number of children raised as well as on labor-force participation.[47]

Advocates of such an approach draw heavily on East European expe-

[45]Urlanis, *Problemy dinamiki naseleniia SSSR*, p. 306.
[46]Cohn, "Population Policy in the USSR," p. 55.
[47]V. Perevedentsev, *Zhurnalist*, no. 9 (1974): 50; see also Iurkevich, *Sovetskaia sem'ia*, p. 41.

rience in arguing that such programs are demonstrably effective in raising birthrates. In Hungary, for example, where the most far-reaching of such maternal leave programs has been in effect since 1959, women workers receive a paid leave amounting to the equivalent of one-half the average wage for a period of up to three years after the birth of a child.[48] An eight percent rise in the Hungarian birthrate between 1959 and 1969 is, in the view of Urlanis, compelling evidence of the potential benefits of such an approach.

The major defect of the Hungarian model, as Urlanis sees it, is its failure to scale payments to actual wages. By tying family allowances to the number of children and fixing maternal leave payments at a uniform level, the Hungarian program maximized the fertility incentive to low-income families while minimizing its effect on families with higher levels of education and professional attainment. Its social impact was therefore problematic, in the view of Urlanis:

> In these circumstances, when a woman receives a wage above the average level, her material interest in enlarging her family diminishes. As a result, there arises the well-known inequality in the possibility of using the allowances. Thus, 73 percent of the women with a primary education took advantage of the allowance, 61 percent of those with a secondary education, and only 30 percent of those with higher education.[49]

A sliding scale of benefits tied to wage levels is therefore advocated by Urlanis as the condition of a more equal distribution of fertility outcomes among social strata.

The high costs of such a program, in the view of its supporters, will be more than offset by its future benefits. Over the long run the increased wealth that a larger labor force will generate will compensate for the short-term budgetary outlays that programs such as these would require. How-

---

[48]The extended leave follows the normal five months of maternity leave at full salary and involves monthly payments of 600 forints, or 36 percent of the average annual wage in 1972. This payment is supplemented by a family allowance for second and higher-order births that rises abruptly and cumulatively with each ensuing birth. The two together amount to 71 percent of the average wage with the third child and rise to 95 percent with the birth of the fifth (Robert J. McIntyre, "Pronatalist Programs in Eastern Europe," *Soviet Studies* 27 [July 1975]: 369–70). A favorable review of East European programs by a Soviet author that appears to be directed at current discussions is R. Galetskaia, "The Demographic Situation in Comecon Member Nations," translated from *Voprosy èkonomiki* 4 (1974), in *The Soviet Review* 16 (Spring 1975): 34–55.

[49]Urlanis, *Problemy dinamiki naseleniia SSSR*, p. 298. A similar reservation is expressed by Piskunov and Steshenko. If fixed grants are set at a high level, in their view, they would undermine the entire system of economic incentives in the production sphere, while setting them at a low level deprives them of any potential for stimulating fertility and transforms them into a family assistance program for low-income households. However, they are also opposed to proposals that tie support to income levels because such schemes increase the dependence of children's opportunities on the socioeconomic level of their parents; "O demograficheskoi politike," in Piskunov and Steshenko, *Demograficheskaia politika*, pp. 18–24.

ever, immediate and tangible benefits are expected as well, for the proponents of direct incentives share the conviction that the extensive employment of mothers of young children is not the asset it is usually assumed to be, but an arrangement for which Soviet society pays a high economic and social price.[50]

Among the economic costs of maternal employment the most significant are undoubtedly the major expenditures associated with the construction and staffing of preschool institutions. Some four to five hundred rubles annually are required to maintain a single child, and of this total the government subsidizes roughly four-fifths. Rising standards of care in recent years, combined with rising costs of construction and maintenance, have made the institutional care of young children an increasing drain on public funds. These costs rose 34 percent between 1965 and 1970 alone; the average cost of constructing a single place in a nursery was reported to be 980 rubles.[51] A cutback in the network of nurseries would generate substantial savings, which might be earmarked for maternal leaves instead. Additionally, a large number of personnel would be released for employment elsewhere and could be transferred to the kindergartens or to other areas of the economy where labor is in short supply.

A social as well as an economic loss results from the institutional care of young children, in this view. On the one hand, Soviet pronatalists emphasize strongly the positive contribution of maternal affection to the emotional development of young children, even drawing on the authority of Dr. Spock to make their point. On the other hand, the pronatalists point up the negative aspects of present arrangements, including the greater vulnerability to illness of children in institutional settings. Nurseries are thus seen to be as problematic from the standpoint of health as they are with respect to psychological development. Moreover—as the argument goes—the frequent illness of children is partly responsible for high rates of absenteeism among working mothers, creating an additional drain on wage and benefit funds that is not offset by any corresponding gains in productivity. Thus, according to the calculations of one recent analysis, the cost of working mothers is 1.8 to 3.4 times as high as that

---

[50]This argument is developed at greater length, with supporting computations, by K. Vermishev, "Stimulirovanie rosta naseleniia," *Planovoe khoziaistvo* 12 (December 1972): 102–7. See also his "Chto obshchestvo vygodnee," *Literaturnaia gazeta*, January 22, 1969, p. 12. Similar concerns expressed in more ambiguous form appear to underlie a study which concluded that the proportion of women employed in the socialized sector of the economy exceeded an optimal level, and that societal interests would be served by a better balance between work in the public sector and in the household; A. E. Kotliar and S. Ia. Turchaninova, *Zaniatost' zhenshchin v proizvodstve* (Moscow, 1975), especially p. 16.

[51]Kvasha, *Problemy ekonomiko-demograficheskogo razvitiia*, p. 138. Overall expenditures on preschool and other child-care facilities increased 2.5 times between 1960 and 1970, rising from 1.725 million to 4.298 million rubles; *Vestnik statistiki* 1 (January 1976): 96.

of nonworking mothers, even in the absence of labor contributions by the latter group.[52]

Thus, the desirability of family care for young children, the feasibility of providing it by shifting resources toward a program of maternal leaves, and the potentially beneficial effect of such measures on future fertility are mutually reinforcing features of the pronatalist position. For all of these reasons, Perevedentsev argues,

> I am in agreement with the opinion of the demographers who consider that there are no gounds for increasing the number of nurseries. It is more fitting to allocate the corresponding funds for the development of kindergartens. If, during the 1920s when the nurseries first developed on a mass scale, children from the worst family conditions found themselves in a better situation, now, not infrequently, everything is the opposite. Nursery children are more often sick and lag in physical, emotional and intellectual development behind children raised at home. From the demographic viewpoint it is preferable if the small child stays with his mother.[53]

Concurring in this view, Urlanis concludes that "to the extent there has been an improvement in the living conditions of the Soviet family, it is necessary to direct our efforts to the curtailment of nurseries and the expansion of the network of kindergartens."[54]

Although these arguments have not gone unchallenged, across a broad range of policy issues, a Soviet pronatalist orientation has come to be asserted with growing vigor and self-confidence. A central thesis is stressed without hesitation: while a number of socioeconomic factors need to be taken into account, pronatalist policies must command high priority and must be pursued by the state with determination, as well as with suitable material and administrative and ideological support. By the same token, issues of sexual equality and of women's opportunity for social participation and personal development are generally side-stepped, implicitly devalued or redefined, or altogether ignored.

LABOR UTILIZATION AND PUBLIC POLICY:
WOMEN AS A PRODUCTIVE RESOURCE

The exhaustion of the vast labor reserves that for several decades fed the expanding Soviet economy stands at the center of a second constellation of problems presently confronting Soviet policy makers. Where

[52]Vermishev, "Stimulirovanie rosta naseleniia," p. 106.
[53]V. Perevedentsev, "Sem'ia: vchera, segodnia, zavtra," *Nash sovremennik* 6 (1975): 131. The view that it is economically more efficient and socially more desirable to pay mothers to remain at home to care for their own children, rather than to subsidize public day care to facilitate female labor-force participation, has influential supporters in current American discussions as well; see Mary Jo Bane, *Here to Stay: American Families in the 20th Century* (New York, 1976).
[54]Urlanis, *Problemy dinamiki naseleniia SSSR*, p. 300.

economic growth once depended on the ability to draw hitherto untapped segments of the population into the industrial labor force, it is now critically dependent on the ability to increase labor productivity. The resulting shift from an extensive to an intensive strategy of economic development makes the optimal utilization of scarce labor resources of paramount economic and political importance.

In the light of these larger concerns, proposals such as those of Perevedentsev and Urlanis—which would substantially reduce the level of female labor-force participation—are unlikely to be implemented in the absence of conclusive demonstration of their necessity. The lack of a consensus even among demographers themselves about the importance of high birthrates and the outright opposition of specialists in related areas make the case in favor of them even less persuasive.

Opposition to such policies stems first and foremost from a refusal to treat the stimulation of fertility as an overriding economic and political priority. A number of prominent demographers, including A. Ia. Kvasha of the Center for the Study of Population Problems at Moscow University, economists specializing in problems of labor resources, including V. B. Mikhailiuk and N. A. Sakharova, and sociologists of family and *byt* such as Kharchev, Slesarev and Iankova, direct their criticism at what they view as the narrow focus of such proposals. Insisting, in effect, that human beings are more than merely reproductive machines and that broader economic priorities as well as the needs and preferences of women themselves deserve consideration, these critics argue that population policy must conform to the larger requirements of the economy and society as a whole. As Piskunov and Steshenko put it: "The demographic problem in socialist society does not have so simple a solution as some demographers think. It is a complex social problem that must not be replaced by the narrower problem of activating the generative function of the population. Demographic policy must be seen as an organic component of the total socioeconomic policy of a socialist society."[55] Noting, moreover, that demographic measures compete with other claims on the national budget, Kvasha pointedly reminded his colleagues: "The resources of a nation, even the richest, are not unlimited. The general dimensions of demographic investments, their share of the national income, are largely determined by the form of social structure and also by the specific conditions of the nation. Moreover, besides the demographic investments, there are other important articles of expense for the government."[56]

Sceptical of the urgency of increased fertility, opponents of the proposed demographic policies have directly challenged the association of

[55]Piskunov and Steshenko, "O demograficheskoi politike," in Piskunov and Steshenko, *Demograficheskaia politika*, pp. 15–27.
[56]Cited by Heer, "Recent Developments in Soviet Population Policy," p. 264.

population size with national power. They insist, rather, that technological and qualitative indices are more significant measures than purely quantitative ones: "Ideas are often expressed that a contracting population reproduction might negatively influence the international prestige of the state. But at present this authority is based above all on economic and technical progress and not by the total number of 'souls' in the nation."[57]

Similar considerations are voiced with respect to economic growth. As V. A. Boldyrev affirmed at a *Voprosy filosofii* round table in 1974, economic development depends on the quality of the labor force and on its ability to exploit the possibilities of modern technology, not merely on its size.[58] The major source of economic growth in a developed socialist society, in this view, is not through an expanding labor force but through more intensive methods of production and increasing labor effectiveness. From this perspective, a stable level of population is sufficient, obviating the need for additional demographic investments and permitting a concentration of resources and efforts on increasing productivity. Indeed, to the extent that the trend toward one- or two-child families reflects an intensification of parental investments in the education and development of the individual child, its emphasis on quality rather than quantity is seen as altogether congruent with broader social needs.

This position receives further support from those who attach social as well as economic importance to the role of women in the labor force and who seek to improve its terms. Proposals to encourage the withdrawal of mothers from the socialized sector are depicted as a "step backward,"[59] an effort to recreate a division of labor on the basis of sex. Unsparing in their criticisms, opponents of such measures argue that by withdrawing from activities most highly valued in the society at large, by accepting an oppressive financial dependence, and by sacrificing skills and opportunities for professional development during a critical period in their careers, women would suffer a loss of status and authority within their families as well as in society as a whole. Rejecting the argument that paid maternal leave is more economically advantageous than the construction of preschool institutions, Piskunov and Steshenko affirm:

> The [social] cost involved in obtaining the necessary demographic effect is not at all a matter of indifference to society. . . . If women today were offered the opportunity simply to raise children and keep house, a majority of women would hardly accept it. At the present time, the interests of socialist society in the "woman question," which consists of creating conditions for the all-round and harmonious development of women, and the interests of women

[57]*Ibid.*, pp. 263–64.
[58]V. A. Boldyrev, "Tendentsii razvitiia sotsialisticheskoi ėkonomiki i demograficheskaia politika," *Voprosy filosofii* 11 (1974): 84–88.
[59]N. Sonin, "Mesto prekrasnoi poloviny," *Literaturnaia gazeta*, April 16, 1969, p. 11.

themselves, whose participation in work outside the home has become an inseparable part of their lives, coincide in full. Therefore it is hardly desirable to undertake measures that can result in a violation of this correspondence. The question must be aimed at creating conditions under which participation in work outside the home will not have a negative effect on the generative function of women, and such that women will face no obstacles in working outside the home to the extent required by their own development as members of society building communism and to the extent that it does not conflict with the interests of family and children.[60]

Possibly the most compelling obstacle, given the scarcity of labor resources, is the negative effect of long interruptions in employment on skills and future productivity. A loss of the considerable social investment in the education of women, potentially greater resistance on the part of employers to hiring and training them, and the difficult problems of reentry have all been cited as arguments against such proposals.

Critics insist, therefore, that the growing role of women in social production is not only a desirable phenomenon but an objective and irreversible fact. Rejecting the argument that declining fertility is a product of high rates of female labor-force participation, Piskunov and Steshenko speak on behalf of a number of demographers and economists in asserting that "although voices have recently been heard contending that women's allegedly excessive activity in the economy is a factor in the decline of the birthrate to a most inauspicious level, the way to improve the present demographic situation lies not in reducing women's economic activity but in raising it further."[61] For proponents of this view, the more intensive utilization of female labor and its increased effectiveness form the starting point of current discussions.

Needless to say, the fact that women constitute over half the Soviet labor force would in and of itself invite attention to problems of female employment. Moreover, the few remaining reserves of labor outside Central Asia are largely made up of women who, because of family responsibilities as well as the absence of suitable employment, have not entered the labor market. Additionally, the disproportionate concentration of women in low-skilled and unmechanized work (especially in agriculture, in economic sectors of low productivity, and in conditions that generate high rates of turnover and absenteeism) only serves to emphasize the fact

---

[60]Piskunov and Steshenko, "O demograficheskoi politike," pp. 25–26. When questioned whether they would prefer to work at home for the same pay, 85 percent of the women surveyed responded negatively; G. A Slesarev and Z. A. Iankova, "Zhenshchiny na promyshlennom predpriiatii i v sem'e," in *Sotsial'nye problemy truda i proizvodstva*, eds. G. V. Osipov and Ia. Shchepan'skii (Moscow, 1969), p. 422.

[61]Piskunov and Steshenko, "O demograficheskoi politike," p. 23.

that prevailing patterns of female labor-force participation are a serious drag on the economy as a whole.[62]

It is these distinctive and problematic features of female employment that have drawn the particular attention of a number of labor resource specialists.[63] For them the issue is clear: since female labor (especially maternal employment) is dependent on the presence of a whole range of facilitating conditions in the larger environment, efforts to increase the effectiveness of such labor compel consideration of the interdependence of economic and social planning. The creation, in August 1976, of a new union-republic level State Committee on Labor and Social Problems to replace the State Committee on Labor and Wage Problems as well as the Republic level committees on Labor Resource Utilization offers some evidence of growing official awareness of this interdependence.

Current policy discussions and the recommendations flowing from them address five somewhat distinct sets of issues, which we shall consider in turn: (1) the optimal level of female labor-force participation; (2) the optimal distribution of female labor among different sectors of the economy; (3) the improvement of skill levels of the female labor force; (4) the adaptation of working conditions to the special needs of women workers; and (5) the creation of supporting institutions and arrangements in the larger society to maximize female labor productivity as well as ensure the compatibility of women's dual roles. Directed as they are to questions of paramount economic and political importance, these broader discussions have provided the framework for some extremely critical assessments of current employment patterns, as well as for the elaboration of a number of far-reaching proposals for reform.

Soviet discussions of the optimal level of female labor activity remain rather oblique. Published sources indicate the presence of three points of view, one advocating the diminution of female labor-force participation, a second calling for its further expansion, and a third committed to maintaining its continuity but reducing its intensity and channeling it "within reasonable limits."[64] We shall return to this question shortly; it is sufficient to note here that in all of these discussions, there is no attempt to specify in precise numerical terms what level of participation is considered "optimal." There appears to be widespread agreement that present levels

---

[62]See, for example, G. Sergeeva, "O professional'noi strukture rabotaiushchikh zhenshchin," *Planovoe khoziaistvo* 11 (November 1976): 37–46.

[63]For several examples of a larger genre, see N. A. Sakharova, *Optimal'nye vozmozhnosti ispol'zovaniia zhenskogo truda v sfere obshchestvennogo proizvodstva* (Kiev, 1973); A. E. Kotliar and S. Ia. Turchaninova, *Zaniatost' zhenshchin v proizvodstve* (Moscow, 1975); V. G. Mikhailiuk, *Ispol'zovanie zhenskogo truda v narodnom khoziaistve* (Moscow, 1970); Z. M. Iuk, *Trud zhenshchiny i sem'ia* (Minsk, 1975).

[64]Sakharova, *Optimal'nye vozmozhnosti*, p. 74.

of female employment exceed what would be desirable, given the underdevelopment of the service sector and the heavy burden of women's domestic responsibilities. Indeed, this view receives explicit endorsement in
Article 35 of the new Soviet constitution, which promises the gradual
reduction of working time for women with small children.

Soviet analysts express a similar uncertainty in their projections of future trends. On the one hand, the recognition that female employment
represents a response to economic pressures points toward a reduction of
participation rates as living standards improve. As two labor economists
noted: "The supply of female labor is more elastic [than that of males].
It depends to a greater degree on the extent to which a family's requirements are satisfied by the earnings of the head of the family (the male)
and by income from public consumption funds. The lower the level at
which these requirements are being satisfied, the more the family needs
earnings from its women."[65] On the other hand, these same authors note
that, while a certain number of women of working age do not work
because of their high family income, and that the impact of this factor is
likely to intensify in the context of future development, there is also a
countervailing tendency at work: high education and professionalism may
serve as strong incentives to uninterrupted employment. How these two
contradictory trends will work themselves out in practice remains a subject of some uncertainty in Soviet analyses. While the weight of economic
pressures tends to be emphasized by some writers, the dominant view
among sociologists (based, in part, on interviews with women workers)
is that, for the vast majority of women, employment yields satisfactions
that extend beyond its direct economic benefit.[66] Sociologists therefore
anticipate a continuing high female commitment to work as a valued social
activity rather than a decline in participation rates as a result of higher
living standards.

The pressures for more effective use of labor resources are also responsible for a new interest in the expansion of part-time employment. Until
relatively recently, the concentration of women in part-time jobs in Western capitalist societies was cited as evidence of their economic exploitation
and inequality. In the past few years, however, the Soviet search for
greater flexibility in the organization of production has transformed the

[65]V. Guseinov and V. Korchagin, "Voprosy trudovykh resursov," *Voprosy ekonomiki* 2
(February 1971): 45–51.
[66]A number of studies that attempted to ascertain whether women would continue to
work even if their income were no longer needed reported that between 70 and 85 percent
of respondents replied affirmatively; Mikhailiuk, *Ispol'zovanie zhenskogo truda*, p. 24. See also
Slesarev and Iankova, "Zhenshchiny na promyshlennom predpriiatii," p. 423; Z. Ia. Iankova, "Razvitie lichnosti zhenshchiny v sovetskom obshchestve," *Sotsiologicheskie issledovaniia*
4 (October-November-December 1975): 43; A. L. Pimenova, "Sem'ia i perspektivy razvitiia
obshchestvennogo truda zhenshchin pri sotsializme," *Nauchnye doklady vysshei shkoly: filosofskie
nauki* 3 (1966): 36–39.

Western experience with part-time work into a model worthy of socialist emulation. Advocates of expansion of part-time employment insist that because female equality in a socialist system is guaranteed by law, affirmed by ideology, and supported by a wide range of policies, and because part-time workers enjoy the same benefits as workers employed full time, the disadvantages inherent in part-time female employment in the West are obviated in the USSR.[67]

In the context of current economic priorities, the flexibility of part-time employment is clearly its major attraction. The creation of part-time jobs would expand the supply of labor by drawing into productive employment those segments of the population—primarily women—who are not now in a position to accept full-time work for reasons of health, age, family responsibilities, or the wish to continue their studies. Women who are full-time housewives or exclusively engaged in caring for children appear to be the major target of these proposals, but pensioners and students are also mentioned as additional reserves of untapped labor. Furthermore, it is argued, part-time jobs would offer added flexibility in those branches of industry which experience fluctuations in the need for labor and above all in the service sector, where "peak" periods of demand could be met in this way. The apparently higher productivity of part-time workers is also cited in its favor; one experiment using two part-time workers in place of one full-time worker yielded a 20 percent increase in output.[68] Lower labor turnover and a reduction in the time and money lost through absenteeism are among the additional anticipated benefits of this innovation.

Its potential advantages to individual workers, and particularly to women, are also emphasized by advocates. Part-time work would provide women with an opportunity to maintain the continuity of their employment even while children are young, to make an independent contribution to family income, and to enjoy the satisfaction of membership in a collective without the double burden that full-time work would entail. It is therefore advocated by many as an alternative to the extended maternity leaves favored by Urlanis and Perevedentsev, enabling women to maintain their involvement in social production without paying an excessively high cost.

Despite its proclaimed virtues, the actual opportunities for part-time

---

[67]Discussions of part-time employment include A. Novitskii and M. Babkina, "Nepolnoe rabochee vremia i zaniatost' naseleniia," *Voprosy ekonomiki* 7 (July 1973): 133–140; N. Shishkan, "Nepolnyi rabochii den' dlia zhenshchin v usloviiakh sotsializma," *Ekonomicheskie nauki* 8 (1971): 42–47; Kotliar and Turchaninova, *Zaniatost' zhenshchin v proizvodstve*, pp. 98–104; E. R. Martirosian, "Pravovoe regulirovanie nepolnogo rabochego vremeni," *Sovetskoe gosudarstvo i pravo* 10 (October, 1976): 54–61; B. Sukharevskii, "Nepolnyi rabochii den'; ego granitsy i effektivnost'," *Literaturnaia gazeta*, March 15, 1972, p. 10; Guseinov and Korchagin, "Voprosy trudovykh resursov," pp. 45–51.

[68]Kotliar and Turchaninova, *Zaniatost' zhenshchin v proizvodstve*, p. 101.

employment remain limited. Although these opportunities have expanded somewhat in the past few years, they constituted only 2.5 percent of total employment in 1974.[69] The intention of the present Soviet leadership to expand this form of economic participation has been clearly indicated in recent pronouncements, most notably in connection with the 25th Party Congress of 1976.[70] However, the prospect raises a number of issues that have not yet been resolved.

One group of obstacles to the expansion of part-time employment appears to come from enterprise management itself. The obvious difficulties in introducing flexible work shifts into standardized production schedules make it likely that any expansion of part-time work will occur either in industries with high proportions of female workers or through the creation of special sectors, assembly lines, or other arrangements where part-time workers will be partially segregated from the full-time labor force. The full implications of such arrangements for the position of women in the labor force have not been directly confronted.

An additional problem not yet resolved involves the terms on which part-time work will be remunerated. In principle, part-time workers are entitled to full benefits; in practice, however, the difficulties are numerous. As a specialist in labor law acknowledged, although the law states that part-time workers should not be granted less annual leave, accumulate less seniority, or be deprived of other rights as workers, "there are still many unanswered questions in this area."[71]

Even more significant is the evident disagreement over the payment norms for part-time work. The official view, reiterated in virtually all authoritative discussions, is that wages be in proportion either to time worked or to output.[72] A very different position, however, is taken by a number of sociologists and economists concerned with the special problems of female labor. In their view, at least one group of potential part-time workers—the mothers of small children—should be entitled to a shortened workday without any loss of pay.[73] Although the distinction between "part-time employment" and "incomplete workday" is not explicitly made in Soviet sources, these writers appear to have in mind a temporary shortening of the normal working day to four hours for the

[69]*Ibid.*, p. 102.

[70]A series of proposals for the establishment at enterprises of a "special allocation of work stations with shorter workdays and wages paid for the time actually worked" for women with two or more children was submitted to the Council of Ministers in the summer of 1976; V. Kurasov, *Izvestiia*, July 23, 1976, p. 2.

[71]E. R. Martirosian, "Pravovoe regulirovanie nepolnogo rabochego vremeni," *Sovetskoe gosudarstvo i pravo*, 10 (October 1976): 54–61.

[72]*Ibid.*

[73]Sakharova, *Optimal'nye vozmozhnosti*, pp. 47–49; Iuk, *Trud zhenshchiny i sem'ia*, p. 122; Iankova, "Razvitie lichnosti," pp. 44–46.

mothers of infants and five or six hours for mothers of very young children. The rationale behind these proposals rests on the argument that the definition of women's working time ought to include not only work in the socialized sector but work in the domestic economy as well. Moreover, some writers go so far as to insist that women have a right to an adjustment of their work norms because the expansion of everyday services has failed to keep pace with the expansion of female employment. In fact— as Sakharova sees it—the amount of time expended on everyday services in different regions as a result of differential development should be scientifically determined and work norms adjusted to compensate for regional variations.

The advocates of a shortened workday with no loss of pay appeal to more traditional forms of legitimation as well. The principle that working conditions should be adapted to the special physiological and psychological needs of women has a long history in Soviet theory, if not always in practice, although this particular use of tradition is quite unique. Lenin himself is drawn into the debate in defense of the principle that, while female participation in social production is a condition of equality, the intensity of female employment need not be identical to that of men. Finally, the recommendations of the Second International Trade Union Conference in Bucharest in 1964, as well as those of the Minsk symposium of 1969, serve as additional ammunition in the campaign.

Whether or not this panoply of arguments will succeed, such arguments are inherently suggestive and important in the Soviet context. At one level, they illuminate the way in which conventional formulas can be used on behalf of new and often socially progressive purposes. By refusing to exclude women's domestic chores from the definition of "work," and by arguing that working mothers have a "right" to be compensated for the "double shift" they perform because of the state's failure to provide appropriate conditions for their employment, the advocates of such measures are not only insisting that socially valued work be properly compensated; they are holding policy makers accountable for the shortcomings of current programs.

The distribution of women among different economic sectors and occupations is a second focus of current analyses. Extreme disproportions of men and women in different types of economic activity are the object of sharp criticism, although it is the extensive role of women in heavy and unskilled labor rather than their overrepresentation in more desirable occupations that is singled out for attack. The fact that two-fifths of working women in major occupations perform the simplest labor—as unspecialized agricultural workers, maids, porters, guards, practical nurses, unskilled workers, and warehouse employees—is a repeated theme, and the need to shift women from farm to nonfarm jobs and from unskilled to skilled occupations is seen as an important economic and social priority.[74]

Such a change in the structure of female employment is seen as depending in turn on more energetic efforts to improve the skill levels of female workers. In view of the limited enrollment of women in technical-vocational programs, dramatic new initiatives will be needed in order to raise the proportion of women among skilled workers in industry. Tolkunova for example, recommends reestablishing quotas for women in technical-vocational schools as the most effective way to accomplish this task.[75]

The special obstacles that family responsibilities place in the way of raising qualifications have suggested to other authors the need for more complex innovative approaches. After an extensive account of the low level of qualifications of female workers and their limited opportunities for professional advancement, one study concluded:

> The possibility of improving qualifications at work, in the schools, and in refresher courses is limited by the fact that between the ages 25–35 family responsibilities and childbearing still do not permit the majority of working women to study while continuing to work. The present system of raising qualifications in production is not adapted to working women with families, and the question of creating such a system in our country is not, for the present, resolved.[76]

The authors of this study point to a number of programs in other socialist countries, particularly the German Democratic Republic, as models of what might be done. The creation of special courses for such women, during working time. and without loss of pay, is but one of the many measures that, in their view, deserve consideration in the USSR, and they deplore the absence of any concern with these issues in the current social plans of enterprises.[77]

Given the considerable obstacles to a dramatic rise in the skill level of female industrial workers, however, the most significant changes in patterns of female employment in the years ahead are likely to involve a shift of women out of industry and into white collar work, as well as a further expansion of the largely female service sector. The proportion of women in the upper reaches of the professions is also likely to stabilize, if not actually contract, in the absence of new initiatives. The declining propor-

---

[74]G. Sergeeva, "O professional'noi strukture," pp. 37–46; M. Fedorova, *Voprosy èkonomiki* 12 (December 1975): 55–64, translated in *CDSP* 28 (June 2, 1976): 14–15. Sergeeva proposes that unskilled jobs be restructured on an hourly basis and used as a form of supplementary income, presumably for part-time workers and pensioners.

[75]V. N. Tolkunova, "K voprosu o ravenstve zhenshchin v trude i bytu pri sotsializme," *Sovetskoe gosudarstvo i pravo* 10 (1969): 129.

[76]Kotliar and Turchaninova, *Zaniatost' zhenshchin v proizvodstve*, p. 78.

[77]*Ibid.*, pp. 78–80.

tion of women in medicine offers evidence of the potentially adverse impact that demands for ever higher levels of training and expertise are likely to have on women's access to highly-skilled and responsible positions. However, there is no indication that these issues are as yet receiving the attention they deserve.

A fourth body of recommendations is addressed to the improvement of working conditions themselves. Persistent complaints that large numbers of women work at heavy physical labor, in unhealthy environments, or on irregular and night shifts indicate that existing protective labor legislation is not adequately enforced. One account, for example, reported that it was common for women to be obliged to work overtime and on rest days and that illegal dismissals were a frequent occurrence, and it criticized local trade unions and executive committees for their failure to correct such violations.[78]

The authors of several studies call not only for the observance of existing protective measures but also for their further extension. New technologies, they suggest, should be adapted to the physiological and psychological needs of women workers. A recent decree of the Council of Ministers directed at drawing women into more skilled and mechanized agricultural work is mentioned by many commentators as a possible model for new initiatives. The decree joined the customary exhortations with innovative new provisions: the construction of agricultural machinery especially adapted for women, a 10 percent reduction of production norms for them, and preferential pension arrangements.[79]

This precedent, in the view of a number of sociologists and labor economists, should provide the model for further measures. In the words of Slesarev, "The time has come to investigate the possibility of granting a preferential work regime to women."[80] A reduction in the working day of mothers should receive high priority; one group of authors proposes that free time be treated like wages, with disproportionately large increases granted to the most deprived categories as a priority. Furthermore, it is suggested, differentiated work norms for women ought to be developed on a broad scale. Citing Marx himself as authority, the authors of *Man and His Work* argue that "equalization in the social conditions for the development of the personality of male and female workers . . . [requires] the creation of 'privileges' for women."[81]

A fifth and final group of recommendations is addressed to improving the larger social environment that sustains female employment and above

[78]*Kazakhstanskaia pravda*, October 23, 1973, p. 3.

[79]Iankova, "Razvitie lichnosti," pp. 44–46.

[80]G. A. Slesarev, *Metodologiia sotsiologicheskogo issledovaniia problem narodonaseleniia SSSR* (Moscow, 1965), p. 136.

[81]Zdravomyslov, A. G., Rozhin, V. P. and V. A. Iadov, *Chelovek i ego rabota* (Moscow, 1967), p. 267. See also pp. 309–12.

all to improving the network of consumer and everyday services. The starting point of such efforts in recent years is the treatment of time as a valuable economic resource. This view, of course, is implicit in most Soviet investigations of time budgets, and it is frequently used to justify the allocation of increased resources to consumer services. As one economist put it:

> The economic evaluation of free time is necessary if there is to be a valid redistribution of social resources in favor of the service branches. The consideration of this factor radically alters our ideas concerning the relative economic effectiveness of various branches of the economy and demonstrates the superiority of a comprehensive socioeconomic approach over a narrowly commercial approach that ignores numerous factors contributing to social wealth.[82]

Assigning an economic value to free time creates a powerful economic justification for investments in consumer services. Public laundries, refrigerators, and rapid urban transit can all be demonstrated to generate substantial savings in time that more than compensate for the cost of the initial investment.

The importance of a more intensive utilization of scarce labor resources is repeatedly cited in support of efforts to expand and improve consumer services. Conventional complaints about the insufficient development of child-care institutions take on added urgency in view of current labor shortages. Characteristic of a large volume of such complaints was an outspoken letter to *Izvestiia* from Orenburg women, who blamed the shortage of kindergarten space for high labor turnover, and added that "if the women not now working—because [of the absence of] kindergarten and nursery accommodations—had worked, the [Orenburg Gas Industry] Association would have produced at least 30,000,000 rubles' worth of additional gas. That is what the shortage of preschool institutions costs!"[83] The editors of *Izvestiia* took up the complaint, commenting that "the problem raised is one of great state importance and great social significance," announcing that *Izvestiia* would henceforth monitor the construction and operation of preschool institutions, and concluding with the statement that it expected the appropriate ministries, departments, and local Soviets to reply to the questions raised.[84]

Similarly, the economic and social costs of inadequate consumer services have received much attention in recent years. In a passage reminis-

[82]N. Kostiashkin, "What is an Hour of Leisure Worth?" translated in *CDSP* 28 (December 29, 1976): 6.

[83]*Izvestiia*, April 11, 1976, p. 1.

[84]*Izvestiia*, April 11, 1976, p. 1, and April 17, 1976, p. 2. The campaign continued with the announcement on May 4 that the Presidium of the Russian Republic Council of Ministers had taken up the complaints raised by Orenburg workers, acknowledged that they merited serious attention and support, and instructed local executive committees to submit proposals for dealing with the problem.

Beginning in 1976, funds obtained from the nationwide *subbotnik* (voluntary Saturday work) were to be used to construct additional kindergartens, but one year later half the available total remained unspent.

cent of Strumilin's writings a half century earlier, Iankova points out that some 180 billion person-hours are devoted to housework each year, only 18 percent less than the total time spent on jobs.[85]

It would seem, on the basis of this spectrum of perceived problems and priorities, that future developments are likely to take two forms. The first involves the further mechanization of household work and the partial socialization of *byt*. The increasing production of labor-saving appliances such as refrigerators and washing machines, or, to use the Soviet term, the industrialization of everyday life, will help to lighten the burden of household chores while the expansion of child-care institutions and the development of public dining facilities will remove some chores from the household altogether. Indeed, some authors, such as Grushin, have argued for a more extensive investment in consumer services in preference to a shorter workday for women, on the grounds that the allocation of resources to these activities will yield a far greater saving of time and effort in the long run, while a shorter workday will sacrifice output without appreciably enhancing leisure.

Despite the sense of urgency evident in current writings, the highly centralized and bureaucratic pattern of economic planning and management characteristic of the Soviet Union and the traditional weight of the heavy industrial sectors are likely to be continuing impediments to the development of consumer services. The intrinsic difficulty of assigning quantitative goals to economic activities whose real objective is consumer satisfaction, where flexibility and individuation are preeminently valuable, underlies the continuing barrage of familiar grievances and new proposals. Moreover, the modest targets of the current Five Year Plan do not hold out the prospect of a rapid expansion and improvement in consumer services in the immediate future. Indeed, in this respect the 25th Party Congress marked a partial reversal of earlier trends, with renewed priority assigned to heavy industrial growth.

An increasing reliance on both private and cooperative arrangements is likely to be the other main outcome of current trends. A number of proposals along these lines have appeared in recent writings, suggesting the creation of parent cooperative nurseries and kindergartens in housing developments (possibly drawing on pensioners and adolescents for assistance), economic unions of families to share the burdens of shopping and child care, and even the reliance on "nannies" and governesses to supervise children. A group of Moscow sociologists headed by Iankova reported recently that one-third to one-half of all young parents surveyed favored such cooperative arrangements because of the inability of publicly organized consumer services and child care to meet current needs.[86] Similarly,

---

[85]Iankova, "Razvitie lichnosti," p. 46.
[86]Iu. Riurikov, *Literaturnaia gazeta*, November 17, 1976, p. 13. See also Iankova, "Razvitie lichnosti," p. 46.

if the apparent willingness to tolerate and even encourage private entre-
preneurial activities as a supplement to the public sector continues over
the long run, they will unquestionably play a rapidly growing role in the
social infrastructure.

In sum, the broad effects of current economic and political priorities
point to accelerating trends in the direction of the privatization and individuation of activities and life styles. To be sure, the shortage of labor
resources militates against any substantial reduction in the level of female
labor-force participation in the foreseeable future. But obvious demographic problems as well as new social concerns definitely point to a reduction in the intensity of such participation and to more flexible patterns
of employment, especially for mothers of young children. Further moves
in this direction, however, are likely to be accompanied by increasing
sexual segregation within the labor force, if, as seems likely, these initiatives attempt to provide the kinds of occupations and work settings that
will be suitable for such purposes. In these circumstances, a concerted
effort to improve the skill levels and professional development of women
workers and to provide opportunities commensurate with their skills will
be required to offset some of the adverse consequences of current demographic and economic priorities for the economic and social position of
women.

MASCULINE/FEMININE: A TENDENCY ANALYSIS
OF CONFLICTING SEX-ROLE NORMS

The policy debates provoked by the conflicting requirements of current
economic and political problems and priorities have brought conflicting
sex-role norms within the larger society into sharp focus. It is therefore
appropriate to conclude our discussion with a more detailed examination
of the three major orientations toward the allocation of roles outlined at
the start of this chapter and with a consideration of their implications for
the future position of women.

All three approaches share certain assumptions about sex roles that give
some indication of both the scope and the limits of contemporary Soviet
discussions. Soviet treatments of sex roles begin, virtually without exception, by emphasizing their biological basis. Indeed, the assumption that
biology determines destiny is expressed far more confidently in Soviet
writings than might be expected in a political culture that emphasizes a
materialist interpretation of social reality. Equality, Soviet writers insist,
is not to be confused with identity, an error widely attributed to American
feminism. Women are different.[87]

---

[87]As Zoia Iankova, a leading sociologist of female work and family, put it: "Many modern
feminist movements such as Women's Liberation in America interpret 'equality' as 'identity,'
but communist society does not consider the present development of the male population

References to nature, biology, and anatomy are used to explain differences in male and female social roles. The fact that women alone bear and nurse children is presented as conclusive demonstration that women have a primary and exclusive responsibility for household and childbearing. In contrast to their Western counterparts, Soviet analyses show no sensitivity to the distinction between reproduction—a biological fact—and childrearing or housekeeping—socially learned roles whose relationship to biology is not a given but requires explanation.[88] The equation of femininity, maternity, and domesticity is virtually universal, and the recognition that roles might be socially assigned rather than endowed by nature is largely absent.

Political and economic participation, by contrast, are defined as universal human roles rather than sex-specific ones. Biological differences are not viewed as a basis for excluding females from the occupational system nor for curtailing their participation in civic, economic, and educational arenas. Female employment has been fully incorporated into the definition of femininity itself. Yet a crucial assumption remains in force: Soviet women are defined as having dual roles; men are not.[89]

If we were to arrange sex-role norms along a continuum—at one end of which male and female roles are viewed in dichotomous and sterotypical terms and social roles are typed on the basis of sex, while at the other

---

to be a standard for the development of women, who should develop their own potentials regardless of any preconceived criterion;" "Razvitie lichnosti," p. 42.

[88]A thoughtful critique of the confusion between biologically based and socially engendered behavior in American social science with direct relevance for Soviet writings is Margaret Polatnick, "Why Men Don't Rear Children: A Power Analysis," mimeographed (Department of Sociology. University of California at Berkeley, 1973). One illustration of precisely the confusion she describes is a published interview with a member of the Presidium of the Committee of Soviet Women, who argued: "woman by her biological essence is a mother—a teacher-trainer (*vospitatel'nitsa*)" who has "an inborn ability to deal with small children, an instinctive pedagogical approach." She went on to defend the refusal to admit girls to 135 of 1,110 professions taught in technicums because of the need to consider girls' "motherly mission." Quoted in Jerry Hough, "Women's Issues in Soviet Policy Debates," in *Women in Russia*, eds. Dorothy Atkinson, Alexander Dallin, and Gail Warshofsky Lapidus (Stanford, 1977).

[89]Thus, two Soviet sociologists write of the tension between a woman's rights as a citizen and her "obligations connected with being a woman, such as family responsibilities," Slesarev and Iankova, "Zhenshchiny na promyshlennom," in Osipov and Shchepan'skii, *Sotsial'nye problemy truda i proizvodstva* p. 416. The absence of serious emphasis on family roles in male upbringing stands in striking contrast. As one writer put it: "Since childhood [men] are taught to believe that they must be good breadwinners, but little is said to them about the need to be a good family man. . . . The whole system of upbringing and the actual relationships of men teach them to be shy about discussing family affairs, to be embarrassed by their love for their wife and children. Even in the first days after marriage the young husband . . . demonstrates to his friends that he is not hurrying to be home, that there is nothing he is missing and that his having a family is not something so serious that it requires that he change his habits"; Viktor Isimbaliuk, "Étot zagadochnyi muzhchina," *Literaturnaia gazeta*, June 5, 1974, pp. 9–10.

end sex is transcended as the basis for allocating social roles—it would be apparent that Soviet sex-role norms do not range along its entire length and are generally not found at the extremes, but are concentrated within somewhat narrower parameters.[90] On the one hand, few Soviet writings altogether deny the relevance of sex for the assignment of at least some social roles. On the other hand, sex is not the basis for a rigid stereotyping of male and female roles that would exclude women from public arenas. What distinguishes various Soviet positions within these parameters is the degree of emphasis given to sexual differences, the consequences drawn from them, and their implications for the definition of female roles.

The first approach, which might be characterized as *assimilationist*, would be located near the center of this continuum. In a relatively traditional and orthodox fashion, given the Soviet context, it combines a positive attitude toward the assimilation of women into previously male roles in economic and political life with an emphatic recognition of distinctively female qualities, needs, and responsibilities. This assimilationist orientation—reflected in the writings of a number of Moscow sociologists of family and *byt*, including Kharchev, Iankova, Slesarev, Gordon, and Klopov, as well as in authoritative official pronouncements—takes for granted the fact of women's dual roles and indeed defends its desirability.[91] The problem lies not in the present balance between the two but in the absence of conditions that make possible their optimal combination. The essence of this position is conveyed in the following statement by Slesarev:

> despite the combining of two major functions [by women] it is impossible not to see that these functions stand in significant contradiction to each other: the participation of women in social production, as we demonstrated earlier, to a certain degree limits maternity, and maternity [in turn limits] the involvement of women in production. Of course, it should not be concluded from this fact that in order to obtain a higher level of reproduction of the population it is necessary to tie women once again to the hearth. The problem is confined to the need for society to provide women with a still greater possibility of combining joyous maternity with creative participation in social labor.[92]

Sociological studies based on interviews with women workers are drawn

[90]The conceptual rationale for such an approach is developed more fully in Marie Withers Osmond and Patricia Yancey Martin, "Sex and Sexism: A Comparison of Male and Female Sex-Role Attitudes," *Journal of Marriage and the Family* 37 (November 1975): 744–58. The absence of systematic Soviet attitudinal studies makes it impossible to analyze the degree of support attached to different positions or the direction of change. Consquently, comparisons with American survey data are unfortunately precluded.

[91]Examples of this approach include Iankova, "Razvitie lichnosti"; Kharchev and Golod, *Professional'naia rabota zhenshchin i sem'ia;* and the selections in N. Solov'ev, Iu. Lazauskas, and Z. Iankova, eds., *Problemy byta, braka i sem'i* (Vilnius, 1970).

[92]G. A. Slesarev, *Metodologiia sotsiologicheskogo issledovaniia*, pp. 127–28.

on as evidence that women themselves attach equal value to work and family roles and view them as mutually reinforcing rather than contradictory.

Female employment, in this approach, is one of the fundamental achievements of socialist society and the guarantee of sexual equality. At the same time, the need for further improvements in working conditions and the further extension of protective benefits to offset the heavy burdens of domestic responsibilities borne by women workers is explicitly acknowledged. Indeed, women's significant contribution to society is itself the justification for measures to ameliorate their difficult situation.

In the treatment of family roles the emphasis is also on ameliorative measures. The increasing production of consumer goods, especially of domestic labor-saving appliances, and the further development of the network of everyday services will relieve the household of its excessive burdens, obviating the need for any far-reaching changes in the structure of the family or work. Technological progress and social reforms introduced by a benevolent Party leadership are treated as the wellsprings of future improvements.

Sharply distinguished from this relatively moderate, reformist position is a second policy-orientation, which is far more critical of present social arrangements, which is based on very different assumptions about female capacities and needs, and which has radically different implications for social organization as well as for the allocation of economic resources. At its heart is an emphasis on *sexual differentiation* rather than assimilation and a belief that greater recognition of fundamental male-female differences is long overdue. Demographers such as Viktor Perevedentsev are the major proponents of this approach, supported by sociologists and social psychologists among others, who, in the manner of American functionalists, insist on the desirability of a sex-based division of functions cued to the distinction between instrumental and expressive roles. Declining birthrates, increasing marital instability, and juvenile delinquency are cited as evidence that the blurring of sexual differences has gone too far and that its undesirable social consequences are now manifest.

Masculinity and femininity, in this orientation, are viewed in dichotomous and stereotypical terms. In language reminiscent of American functionalist sociology of the 1950s, Igor Kon, a prominent social psychologist, offers a vivid survey of the biological and physiological differences between the sexes:

> Men significantly surpass women in speed and coordination of simple body movement, are better oriented in space, more easily assimilate mechanical habits and knowledge of any kind. On the other hand, women on the average surpass men in such operations which demand precise, quick, filigree move-

ments of the hands, out-do men in quickness and preciseness of perception, mechanical memory, in fluency of speech. Men and women are still more strongly differentiated by the tendency of their interests. These distinctions are manifested literally from the age of infancy. Boys are drawn to more active games of strength, connected with competition, risk; girls are oriented toward quieter activities, are more easily subjected to the influence of the surroundings. For them the psychological atmosphere of social intercourse has greater significance than its subjective content. . . . Men of all ages are more persistent and obstinate than women; they are more consistent emotionally. Women more often suffer from being neurotic, their emotional world is more fragile; therefore they especially value consistency in their social milieu and human intercourse.[93]

A stereotypical view of female skills, preferences, and temperaments permeates Kon's imagery. Furthermore, sexual assymmetry here is not presented merely as an objective fact; it is laden with evaluative overtones suggesting that women are not merely different but inferior.

A negative appraisal of femininity is far from universal within this second orientation; it has its counterpart in the equally stereotypical devaluation of males and the insistence by a number of analysts—usually, though not exclusively, women—that many valuable qualities and capabilities are uniquely female. However, despite their conflicting appreciations of males and females, in both cases the emphasis on distinctive male and female characteristics accompanies proposals designed to reinforce them. The "masculinization of women" and the "feminization of men" are fundamental sources of concern,[94] the roots of these social trends are anxiously analyzed, and a series of proposals is designed to inhibit further evolution in this direction.

This orientation has a number of implications for current policy. In defining an optimal balance between women's dual roles, it is maternity rather than labor-force participation that is emphasized. Motherhood and family responsibilities associated with it are treated as the most important

[93]I. Kon, "Muzhestvennye zhenshchiny? Zhenstvennye muzhchiny?" *Literaturnaia gazeta*, January 1, 1970, p. 12.

[94]See, for example, the round-table discussion of the feminization of boys recorded in *Literaturnaia gazeta*, October 15, 1969, "Vremia byt' muzhchinoi," which blames the problem on the feminization of the teaching profession and on the absence of strong male role-models within the family. See also *Literaturnaia gazeta*, October 8, 1969, p. 13, and January 1, 1970, p. 12. A more recent complaint about the "asexual" upbringing of Soviet children warned that "the tenderness and sensitivity prized in a woman can become weaknesses in a man"; *Izvestiia*, October 14, 1976, p. 5. The feminization of the secondary school system and its harmful effect on boys have been a particular focus of anxiety in recent Soviet writings; the issue was even aired at a session of the Supreme Soviet in July 1973. In a conversation reported by Jerry Hough, a member of the Presidium of the Committee of Soviet Women defended the preference now given to boys in admission to pedagogical institutes on the grounds that men teachers were needed in the upper grades so boys could benefit from "uncompromising male conversation"; "Women and the Women's Issue in Soviet Policy Debates," in Atkinson, Dallin, and Lapidus, *Women in Russia*.

function of women. Female employment is a subordinate priority; women's involvement in social production should not be permitted to detract from their central and basic social role as wives and mothers.

While not directly challenging the desirability of maternal employment in principle, there is, in this orientation, some tendency to view it as excessive or abnormal. High rates of female labor-force participation are portrayed as the consequence of particular historical pressures rather than a desirable and irreversible trend. These writers anticipate a "normalization" that will permit the temporary withdrawal of mothers from the labor force while children are young. As one demographer put it, the time has now arrived when the Soviet Union can afford the luxury of permitting a child to be raised by its own mother.[95] Within the labor force itself, normalization will mean an end to heavy labor for women, greater opportunities in light industry and the service sector, the extension of part-time work opportunities and more attention to employment patterns consistent with women's distinctive biological and psychological capacities.

Finally, this orientation emphasizes the unique and irreplaceable contribution of women within the family and seeks to assign it rewards and status commensurate with its social value. Social critics marshal a vast array of evidence to demonstrate that larger social trends have eroded the incentives to domesticity. As one mother of four reported, honorary titles and family allowances for mothers of large families notwithstanding, she has often been praised for her twenty-five years of uninterrupted employment but never for the fact that she is raising four children.[96] Another writer complained, "photographs of mothers of many children are nowhere to be seen. Maternity medals and orders are often presented without the proper publicity. Schoolchildren . . . are never introduced to Mother-Heroines, to women who have received the Order of Maternal Glory. But after all, this is very important—we should constantly instill respect for motherhood and special respect for mothers with large families."[97] Even Western proposals for pay for housewives[98] have been reported in the Soviet press, although the main focus of discussion is on family allowance schemes that would offer financial encouragement to women to withdraw from the labor force in order to bear and raise more children.

The insistence that domestic labor deserves greater prestige and rewards is not associated with any eagerness to encourage men to share it.

[95] B. Urlanis, *Literaturnaia gazeta,* March 3, 1971, p. 11.

[96] G. Kiseleva, *Literaturnaia gazeta,* July 4, 1973, p. 13.

[97] D. Novoplianskii, *Pravda,* November 29, 1972, p. 3.

[98] Z. Marok, *Literaturnaia gazeta,* December 19, 1973. This article, entitled "How Much is a Housewife Worth?" is a translation from the Yugoslav press; it concludes that the housewife performs so wide a range of specialized activities as to be deserving of pay equal to that of the director of a large corporation.

Indeed, an implicit assumption that such work is beneath male dignity can often be detected in the defense of a sharp division of labor within the household.[99] It follows, therefore, that nurturance and accommodation are highly valued feminine qualities. While these are usually associated with the performance of maternal functions, their emphasis is not altogether devoid of benefits to men as well, as these passages from letters received by *Literaturnaia gazeta* indicate:

> "Everybody agrees that it is necessary to liberate women from hard physical labor," Comrade Nebitov from Gatchina wrote, "but why separate a woman from the kitchen? Why deprive her of additional opportunities to manifest love and consideration for her husband? If only you could see with what tender attention my wife follows the trajectory of my first probing spoon from a plate of soup!". . . Here is the view of Comrade Vanyushin from Kaluga province: "Free a woman from the kitchen and you give her the freedom to be a silly hen. Who needs such a woman? Woman is supposed to adorn the family hearth, just as flowers adorn the meadows."[100]

The reassertion of more traditional ideals of femininity is accompanied by laments over the loss of traditional virtues. A letter to *Literaturnaia gazeta* from a seventeen-year-old young woman vividly conveys a nostalgic idealization of a society where male and female were more sharply distinguished:

> there is one aspect of the equality of the sexes that alarms me: women are becoming less feminine. There is more and more vulgar laughter, cigarette smoking and suggestive behavior. Girls even seem ashamed of tenderness, shyness or weakness. Sometimes I find myself thinking about finishing schools, where "noble young ladies" used to learn how to behave in public, walk nicely and dance gracefully. Of course, the spirit of these institutions is unacceptable to us, but it would be good to learn these things even now.[101]

Her proposal to recreate separate and sexually differentiated programs of upbringing for schoolchildren was greeted by an enthusiastic flood of letters, according to the editors of *Literaturnaia gazeta*. (This reaction confirms Philip Slater's hypothesis that an emphasis on the sexual differentiation of conjugal roles will usually be accompanied by pressures to increase sexual differentiation in the education of males and females.) Typical of the response was a letter from a Leningrad teacher, who wrote:

---

[99] As T. E. Chumakova put it, "There remains a very significant number of men who are able to help their wives in fulfilling household functions but who nevertheless avoid or simply refuse any form of household work, considering it unworthy of male dignity"; *Sem'ia, moral', pravo* (Minsk, 1974), p. 14.

[100] L. Kuznetsova, *Literaturnia gazeta*, July 12, 1967, p. 12.

[101] Irina Larina, "O mode i staromodnosti," *Literaturnaia gazeta*, September 8, 1976, p. 11.

Some negative aspects of women's independent status are all too evident these days—smoking, drinking, foul language, striving to engage in "free" love. The consequence of such behavior on the part of young women and girls is the severe harm they will do to the atmosphere of their own homes, for woman is "protector of the hearth" and plays a key role in raising her children.[102]

A second writer added:

In World War II our girls never lost their femininity, even at the front, yet nowadays you can hardly distinguish many girls from fellows. The other day, for instance, I saw a couple embracing, both of them shaggy, in trousers and heavy shoes, and I couldn't tell which was the fellow and which the girl. Finishing schools are alien to us from a social and political standpoint, it is true, but what about from a moral standpoint? In my opinion, girls ought to strive for nobility. I think that at a certain stage girls and boys should receive separate training in questions of morality and family upbringing.[103]

The excessive assertiveness of liberated Soviet women produces a lack of femininity that is responsible, according to still another male respondent, for the entire catalog of social problems that Soviet society presently confronts:

Most men are sick of coarse, ultramodern women who behave like cowboys. I can't prove it statistically but can suggest that one reason there are so many divorces is women's loss of femininity. Many men do not enjoy playing the role of orderly to their wives, after all. Every man, so far as I know, dreams of a tender, affectionate, modest woman, and there are fewer and fewer such. The consequences are terrible: thousands of men avoid marriage, thousands of children are raised as orphans even though their fathers are alive, and the women themselves react indignantly and deluge the newspapers with letters about incompatibility, matchmaking services and the like. No matter how far emancipation develops, women are primarily mothers, giving life to mankind. Bearing and raising children has always been and should continue to be the most important thing in a woman's life.[104]

The emphasis given to women's maternal roles in this perspective is attacked by advocates of a third and contrasting approach, equally critical of present arrangements but for an opposite reason. Feminist publicists like Larisa Kuznetsova and S. Berezovskaia, specialists in family law and sociology like Chumakova and Iurkevich (many of them working in the Belorussian and Baltic republics), and at least one influential political figure, L. Iu. Dirzhinskaite, Deputy Chairman of the Lithuanian Council

[102]I. Zimin, "Zerkalo otnoshenii," *Literaturnaia gazeta*, November 24, 1976, p. 11.
[103]A. Arkilovich, "Somnitel'nye ukrasheniia," *Literaturnaia gazeta*, November 24, 1976, p. 11.
[104]Grigorii Molodsov, "Devushka ili kovboi?" *Literaturnaia gazeta*, November 24, 1976, p. 11.

of Ministers, blame a number of social problems on the persistence of a
sexual division of labor rather than its diminution. The solution, in their
view, lies not in the intensification but in the *transcendence of sex* as the
basis for allocating social roles.[105]

The starting point of this approach is neither a defense of nor a direct
attack on sexual differentiation but a challenge to stereotypes that distort
female capabilities and needs. Far too much has been made of biological
differences, it is argued, particularly in view of the tendency of modern
technology to mitigate their social consequences. Women are far better
suited to the performance of traditionally male roles than is often believed,
while many of the traits usually associated with femininity are equally
desirable in men.[106] Without attempting to explore the structural roots
of sexual inequality, there is the suggestion that the persistence of traditional assumptions about female inferiority are to the benefit of men, defending "acquired positions" against new challenges.

In defining an optimal balance between women's dual roles, the advocates of sex-role transcendence emphasize the potential contribution of
work to women's sense of autonomy, identity, and fulfillment. Larisa
Kuznetsova, for example, deplores the excessive dependence of women
on family and personal ties. Noting that the breakdown of personal relationships leaves women especially vulnerable, adrift, and even prone to
engage in crime, she insists that work is a potential anchor that offers
security and stability in times of trouble. Kuznetsova therefore warns
young women: "When you hear that girls don't have to tear the stars out
of the sky, go through the university, and the rest of it, you should pay
attention, but only in order to do the opposite. The modern woman needs
a well-arranged career just as much as a well-arranged private life."[107]
The special importance of work in women's self-actualization, particularly
where professional careers are involved, receives particular emphasis in
this orientation. One outspoken Soviet writer, Maia Ganina, articulated
this view with eloquent clarity in a debate with Perevedentsev about female literary heroines.[108] Sharply criticizing the traditional Soviet feminine ideal of the "well-rounded woman" who joins love, work, and children in complete harmony, Ganina pointed out that it was humanly
impossible for a single personality to encompass all virtues. The involvement in careers, which Perevedentsev saw as a form of compensation for
missing, unsatisfying, or disappointing personal relationships with men
was for Ganina an expression of a genuine sense of vocation. Defending

[105]Two of the most comprehensive statements of this problem are Iurkevich, *Sovetskaia
sem'ia*, and Chumakova, *Sem'ia, moral', pravo*.

[106]L. Kuznetsova, *Literaturnaia gazeta*, June 25, 1975; July 16, 1975, p. 13.

[107]L. Kuznetsova, *Literaturnaia gazeta*, May 29, 1974, p. 12.

[108]"Neizbezhnost' garmonii," *Literaturnaia gazeta*, March 5, 1975, p. 14.

the virtue of assertiveness rather than accommodation, Ganina insisted that women with talent and commitment should be permitted the same passionate absorption in work that is considered genius in men but labeled neurotic sublimation in women.

The pattern of occupational roles is the subject of far-reaching criticism from commentators sharing this perspective. Not "protection" but assignment to positions of responsibility and leadership is called for: "Women have no need of 'light work,' but of qualified work, commensurate with their professional preparation and training, their education, and their talents,"[109] insisted one commentator. Authority, not merely work, should be as accessible to women as to men. If family obligations stand in the way of professional achievement, the emphasis should be placed on lightening them rather than on compelling the sacrifice of promising careers.

Finally, this approach calls for the replacement of a sexual division of labor within the family by a sharing of domestic roles. Sceptical of the potential contribution of technology to women's liberation from household chores, it emphasizes the need to redistribute burdens within the family itself. The persistent notion that household chores and child-rearing are "women's work" is sharply attacked. Insisting that these be treated as joint responsibilities, Lidia Litvinenko, herself a scientist, deplores the fact that official actions and pronouncements themselves sustain traditional definitions of female roles:

> When, say, a new meat grinder is invented, the article is headed "A Gift to Women," or when a new grocery store is opened, you read "Housewife Will Be Pleased." That's an outdated philosophy and should be criticized in the press. Such confusion of relations and condescension do a lot of harm; they prevent both men and women from learning the meaning of genuine equality. . . . The accent should not be on women's but on family housework. The husband should do as much as his wife.[110]

A more equitable sharing of responsibilities also demands, in this view, greater male participation in child-rearing. A redefinition of male roles within the family is perceived to be the condition of greater female opportunities outside it, as this passage makes clear:

> Of course, no one but a woman is able to give birth and to nurse a babe in arms. However, upbringing without the very active participation of the man of the house, the father, and from the very start, can bring nothing but harm, not only to the child but later on to all of society. Therefore, the traditional arguments in favor of the existing disproportion [between the wide participation of women in economic life and their limited access to positions of

[109]Berezovskaia, *Literaturnaia gazeta*, June 28, 1975, p. 12; for a similar view see also M. Sonin, *Literaturnaia gazeta*, April 16, 1969, p. 11.
[110]*Soviet Life*, no. 186 (March 1972): 52–53.

responsibility] cannot be accepted. Women can and must hold a far more significant place in managerial work than they do now.[111]

The increased participation of men in household responsibilities is treated as the necessary counterpart to the expansion of female public roles, restoring a symmetry in the articulation of work and family roles disrupted by Soviet industrialization. As Iurkevich succinctly puts it:

> The entry of women into the sphere of social production presupposes the return of men to the family (a partial return, of course, as partial as the departure of women from the family). If women had remained within the family, in order to produce the same quantity of material wealth it would have been necessary for men to work almost twice as much. From this point of view it is possible to say that women liberated men from half of their heavy work. Why, then, should some men not wish, in their turn, to take upon themselves half of "light" women's work?[112]

A similar view is expressed by the authors of a major study entitled *Man and His Work*. Pointing out that historically the burden of housework fell to women because men were the family breadwinners, they argue that a new situation has been created by the entry of women into the labor force. Under these circumstances, in their view, the moral justification for an unequal division of labor has been undermined.[113]

Emphasizing that new attitudes are a precondition for new patterns of behavior, a number of writers call for more systematic intervention by state, Party, and public organizations to publicize and inculcate egalitarian norms. The present system of training and indoctrination is, in their view, "one-sided," and fails to consider the specific demands of women. In a number of instances the activities of the Zhenotdel are not only explicitly recalled but are held up as a model of what might be done to inculcate in women a sense of dignity and a consciousness of their equal rights with men. As Zdravomyslov, Rozhin, and Iadov insist, "the urgency of these problems of training is not yet exhausted."[114]

Beginning from childhood, a number of analysts recommend, both in the family and in schools, efforts should be made to avoid a rigid stereotyping of male and female roles. Emphasizing the importance of concrete educational work in eliminating traditional stereotypes, they rec-

---

[111]M. Sonin, *Literaturnaia gazeta* April 16, 1969, p. 11.

[112]Iurkevich, *Sovetskaia sem'ia*, p. 192. The importance of greater male participation in household chores and child-rearing is also emphasized by L. Dirzhinskaite in "Sovetskaia zhenshchina—aktivnyi stroitel' kommunizma," *Partiinaia zhizn'* 20 (October 1975): 23–28, and even more strongly in two interviews in *Sovetskaia Litva*, April 27, 1975, p. 2, and December 29, 1975, p. 2. I am grateful to Joel Moses for drawing my attention to these interviews.

[113]Zdravomyslov, Rozhin and Iadov, *Chelovek i ego rabota*, pp. 310–11.

[114]*Ibid.*, p. 311.

ommend that it be bolstered by new legal codes that emphasize the joint and equal responsibility of both spouses for the maintenance of the household and the raising of children.

The view that men as well as women have dual roles distinguishes this orientation from those emphasizing either differentiation or partial assimilation of female to male roles. The very notion of sex roles is virtually transcended here in what amounts to an androgynous conception of human roles that are fundamentally alike for both men and women. Still, even those who adhere to this relatively sophisticated and novel view shy away from any suggestion that, if men are to share more fully in household responsibilities, more flexible work schedules are desirable for them as well. The overriding concern with productivity—and, most likely, with the perceived limits imposed by the political system on the dialogue as a whole—inhibits a full redefinition of male work roles, even among those analysts who go furthest in repudiating a sexual division of labor within the family.

However limited by comparison with Western treatments, the emphasis on role-sharing as the key to sexual equality has profound implications in the Soviet context. Rather than looking to technological progress and consumer affluence as the solvents of social inequality, such an approach focuses on the structure of authority itself, both within the family and outside it. Reforms in the allocation of resources that would lighten the burdens carried by the family are welcomed, but insofar as such changes would not decisively alter the definition of male and female roles themselves, they are seen as offering no final solution to the problem of equality.

It is thus the focus on role-sharing that distinguishes the orientation toward sex-role transcendence from that of the assimilationists, even those most committed to far-reaching reform. For the claims of the assimilationists are directed at the allocation of resources rather than the distribution of power. Potentially radical in the Soviet context and with far-reaching significance in their call for a reordering of priorities to serve human needs, they are more concerned with lifting the burdens that weigh on men and women alike than with the sexual division of labor. How the lines are drawn between the two approaches is perhaps best apparent in this comment by Zoia Iankova, probably the most eloquent advocate of the assimilationist position:

> it would be wrong to think that the division of chores evenly between husband and wife will revolutionize daily life. Sharing chores may improve the woman's position and establish a new type of relations within the family, but this is only a temporary measure that merely compensates for shortcomings in the services sector. Household chores impinge upon the social activity of men and women alike and cut into their free time. Thus, the main task is not to redis-

tribute tasks that hinder personal development but to eliminate them by introducing fundamentally new ways to carry them out.[115]

Minimizing the implications of a "new type of relations within the family," Iankova insists that improved conditions of everyday life are the key to women's position. All-purpose service enterprises, self-service shopping centers, cooperative household and child-care arrangements, mail order facilities, and the enlistment of volunteer workers in the supervision of children—measures such as these, in her view, will truly "revolutionize everyday life."

Desirable as such reforms may be, an exclusive emphasis on improving the material conditions of everyday life effectively diverts attention from the structure of authority itself. As we noted earlier, Soviet discussions of family power contain a veiled critique of authoritarian relationships in Soviet society more broadly, with the family as an implicit metaphor for the political order itself. The persistence of patterns of domination and subordination, and their legitimation through appeals to custom, biology, or social function, clearly extends beyond the confines of the family itself. In focusing on the fundamental bases of the allocation of social roles and rewards, the advocates of sexual equality based on the transcendence of sex raise fundamental questions about the distribution of power itself.

These conflicting approaches to the definition of femininity indicate the scope and limits of discussions of sex roles in contemporary Soviet society. As this analysis shows, the range of debate is itself significantly narrower than that found outside Soviet borders. The principle of equal rights is unchallenged, as is the view that women have dual roles. Even those who assign the family particularly great value do not argue that it should become a universal and exclusive preoccupation for women. At the same time, the family as a social institution is largely beyond criticism. Even if domestic chores are devalued, children clearly are not. From a comparative perspective, Soviet writings are conspicuously devoid of overt hostility to men, even though male behavior is a frequent target of criticism. Finally, and importantly, Soviet writings offer no structural interpretation of inequality nor any analysis of how patterns of social and sexual stratification may be rooted in the fundamental economic and political organization of the Soviet system itself.

[115]Iankova, "Razvitie lichnosti," p. 44.

NINE

Sexual Equality
and Soviet Policy:
Toward a Comparative Perspective

A policy which attempts to give women an equal
place with men in economic life while at the same
time confirming woman's traditional responsibility
for care of the home and children has no prospect
of fulfilling these aims. The division of functions
between the sexes must be changed in such a way
that both the man and the woman in a family are
afforded the same practical opportunities of participating in both active parenthood and gainful
employment.

The Status of Women in Sweden:
Official Report to the United Nations

THIS study has attempted to examine the way in which the
pursuit of modernization under Communist auspices shapes the scope and
limits of social equality in Communist systems. Drawing on the Soviet
experience, and focusing on the problem of sexual equality in particular,
it has argued that the transformation of social structure in Communist
systems was not merely an outcome but a deliberate instrument of a larger
strategy of development in which role change was perceived to be an important economic and political resource.

The preceding chapters have demonstrated that, despite a deliberate
expansion of female economic and political participation, the terms on
which it occurred both sustained and reinforced a pervasive asymmetry
of male and female roles. This asymmetry was not merely a consequence
of cultural lag but reflected, rather, a coherent, mutually reinforcing and
systematic pattern of official perceptions, priorities, and institutional arrangements that impinged on every dimension of social structure. Our
analysis of the implications of this pattern for the role of women in Soviet

335

society now makes it possible to draw a number of conclusions about the pattern of Soviet development and to locate it in a broader analytical and comparative framework.

In a recent influential study of social stratification in capitalist and Communist societies,[1] Frank Parkin concluded that, although structured inequalities were generated in both types of social systems, Communist systems evidenced both a greater disposition and a greater capacity to hold such inequalities in check. Societies in which egalitarian values occupied an important place and were joined to a command economy and a centralized, one-party political system generated, in his view, a greater degree of social equality than did societies in which the combination of a market economy and pluralist political system made it possible for privileged groups to maintain their economic and political dominance.

In the light of the issues raised in this study, Parkin's conclusion is open to serious qualification. While his analysis correctly points to the presence of specific attributes of Communist systems that both compel and facilitate an assault on certain dimensions of social inequality, it fails to address adequately either the conditions under which such an assault has been and can be pursued or the developmental priorities and structural characteristics that act as built-in constraints. As this study has suggested, the ideological underpinnings, economic organization, and patterns of political authority characteristic of Communist systems establish sharp limits to the achievement of equality even as they encourage a considerable degree of social leveling.

These constraints become especially apparent if the Soviet experience is approached from a broader comparative perspective. In the West, the emergence of sexual equality as an intellectual and political concern was, as we have seen, the expression of specific tensions in the modernization of Western society. The differentiation of economic and family institutions in the course of industrialization—predicated on the differentiation of male and female roles—was an expression of the distinctly different consequences that modernization entailed for men and women. By increasing the economic dependence of women, intensifying their isolation from newly developing public arenas, and assigning them a largely derivative status based on marriage and reproduction, the process of modernization initially tended to insulate the role of women from the implications of new norms.

Nonetheless, dependence, isolation, and derived status were themselves being called into question in Western society. The claim for recognition and participation in a new national community on the basis of an individualistic and universal conception of citizenship could not easily be con-

[1] Frank Parkin, *Class Inequality and Political Order: Social Stratification in Capitalist and Communist Societies* (London, 1971).

fined to men. Moreover, a number of technological and demographic trends which diminished the salience of biological differences called into question the legitimacy and the utility of sexual differentiation for a wide range of social roles, adding further to the pressures for a redefinition of women's position.

While these pressures pointed in a number of different directions, they tended, in the first phase of feminist activity, to coalesce around the demand for access to economic and political domains on equal terms with men. In nineteenth-century Russia, however, in the context of an enduring autocratic system based on traditional principles of legitimacy, obstacles to the development of a new civic community meant that the quest for sexual equality was ultimately assimilated into a general radical movement and subordinated to the achievement of larger social goals.

As we know, the commitment of the new Soviet regime to a radical transformation of political, economic, and social structures was accompanied by an effort to harness all available human energies—male and female alike—on behalf of national development. The utilization of women as a major economic and political resource, however, could not help but transform the very meaning of equality, ultimately draining it of libertarian and humanitarian underpinnings and infusing it with instrumental and utilitarian concerns. The emphasis in Western liberal thought on the elimination of obstacles to full participation was replaced in Russia by an emphasis on the obligation to contribute; sexual equality ultimately came to mean an equal liability to mobilization.

Undeniably, the concentration of economic and political power gave the Soviet leadership unprecedented leverage in assaulting the obstacles to new female roles. This power was far from unlimited, given the resistance of informal and intimate relationships to direct political manipulation, and its use on behalf of female emancipation threatened to compromise the achievement of other major goals. Nonetheless, the reliance on authority rather than consensus, on mobilization rather than reconciliation, on systemic change rather than piecemeal reform, and on the calculation of public rather than private benefits made it possible to manipulate the network of social pressures, incentives, and costs in ways that furthered a transformation of female roles.[2]

Additionally, the very atmosphere of crisis that surrounded the evolution of the Soviet system was itself an enabling condition of this transformation. The combined effects of rapid industrialization, agricultural

---

[2]For the distinction between ideological and pragmatic political systems, see Joseph La Palombara and Myron Weiner, *Political Parties and Political Development* (Princeton, 1966). The mobilization-reconciliation dichotomy is developed in David Apter, *The Politics of Modernization* (Chicago, 1965) and elaborated in Kenneth Jowitt, *Revolutionary Breakthroughs and National Development* (Berkeley and Los Angeles, 1971).

collectivization, political repression and war—and of the severe deficit of males that resulted—aided the breakdown of traditional social norms and institutions.[3] The cumulative effect of these circumstances was to draw women into new economic and political roles while at the same time weakening their leverage in male-female relationships.

Thus, as Soviet experience suggested from the very beginning, there was a critical distinction between mobilization and liberation. The fact that women were perceived as a major economic and political resource was compatible with an extreme degree of exploitation. The terms of female mobilization were therefore crucial. It may be said that in the Soviet context these terms tended to be extremely unfavorable to women. To be sure, the precise manner in which female resources would be utilized, and on what terms, was redefined at successive stages of Soviet development and depended on larger economic and political conditions. Without minimizing the implications of changing official perceptions, capabilities, and priorities for the opportunities and pressures that women confronted, it is nonetheless possible to point to a number of underlying—indeed built-in—constraints that, though differing in form and intensity at different points in Soviet evolution, consistently impinged on the transformation of women's roles.

The first of these constraints was the ambiguous ideological legacy of Marxism-Leninism itself. Despite the egalitarian impulse on which it rested, the treatment of sexual equality in the Marxist tradition was, as we have seen, both limited and contradictory. Indeed, the sexual division of labor was conspicuously absent from the enumeration of social contradictions that would vanish in a future Communist society. The emphasis on class rather than sex as the crucial social division; on the shift of family functions to the larger society rather than on a redefinition of male as well as female roles; and on women's distinctive biological characteristics and needs suggest a disposition to view the sexual division of labor as natural as well as an unwillingness to confront a set of issues that was potentially disruptive to class solidarity.

These limitations became even more pronounced with the adaptation of classical Marxism to the Russian environment. Drawing on the Russian radical tradition of the "common cause" rather than on Western forms of individual self-assertion, Soviet ideology demonstrated a particular propensity to subordinate libertarian to utilitarian concerns. In its treatment of equality writ large, as well as of sexual equality in particular, it served

---

[3]For a suggestive theoretical treatment see Jean Lipman-Bluman, "Role de-Differentiation as a System Response to Crisis: Occupational and Political Roles of Woman," *Sociological Inquiry* 43 (April 1973): 105–30, and "A Crisis Framework Applied to Macrosociological Family Changes: Marriage, Divorce, and Occupational Trends Associated with World War II," *Journal of Marriage and the Family* 37 (November 1975): 889–902.

to sustain, in effect, a "false consciousness" that directed attention away from the real structure of domination. The very recognition of structured inequalities came to be inhibited by an emphasis on formal equality of rights and opportunities. Moreover, the invocation of prerevolutionary conditions as the standard of reference emphasized the accomplishments of Soviet power; to the extent that sexual inequality was recognized to persist, it was treated as a "legacy of the past," in effect as a cultural rather than a political problem. Comparisons of relative male and female status were blunted by an inordinate emphasis on the biological determinants of female capabilities, while the unequal distribution of status, wealth, and power more generally was increasingly legitimized in functionalist terms. Thus, Soviet ideology functioned to obscure the presence of structured inequalities and to divert attention from the social allocation of roles.[4]

Soviet patterns of economic development constituted a second constraint on the achievement of sexual equality. While an expanding industrial economy and a severe deficit of males facilitated the absorption of women into the modern labor force, they did so in ways that preserved important features of a dual labor market and that insulated new female work roles from impinging on other aspects of social and family structure. An overriding concern with productivity stood in the way of more flexible work arrangements until very recently and resulted in the particularly intensive exploitation of female labor with only minimal accommodation of family and personal needs. Additionally, economic priorities that sacrificed the development of everyday services to the pursuit of economic and military power compelled the household to absorb the additional burdens of female employment; in effect, the intensification of women's unpaid labor within the family became the corollary of expanding female roles outside it.

Finally, Soviet patterns of political authority have precluded the emergence of a genuine civic culture that would permit the political participation of men and women alike as citizens rather than subjects. The Party's preemption of significant political roles, its control over recruitment to positions of political authority, and the close association of political authority with bureaucratic position are features of an authoritarian pattern of political rule in which women occupy a high proportion of symbolic and ceremonial positions and a low proportion of substantive and authoritative ones. The very recognition accorded women as a collectivity is itself a reflection of a subject political culture in which no autonomous group activity is permitted. Because Soviet political institutions are designed to inhibit the aggregation and representation of group interests,

---

[4]Certain parallels are suggested with the Soviet treatment of deviance as examined by Walter D. Connor, *Deviance in Soviet Society—Crime, Delinquency, and Alcoholism* (New York, 1972).

the responsiveness of the Soviet leadership to the special needs of women has not been the result of organized action by women on their own behalf but an expression of a paternalistic, if now more benevolent, pattern of political rule.

To locate the Soviet experience in a broader comparative perspective, it is helpful to first specify the range of possible ways in which sex roles may be patterned in modern industrial societies.[5] Implicitly or explicitly, and with varying degrees of conscious recognition in different societies, sex-role norms are reflected across the broad spectrum of public policy, creating a pattern of pressures, sanctions, incentives, and opportunities that defines the arena of private choices. Extending the analysis developed in Chapter VIII, we can conceive of societies organized on the basis of (1) a sharp differentiation of male and female roles; (2) the partial assimilation of female to male roles; or (3) the transcendence of sex as the basis for the allocation of social roles. Needless to say, these are analytical constructions or ideal types rather than specific social systems, but they are extrapolated from the underlying premises of public policy in a wide range of contemporary societies. While they may also be conceived as three stages in a developmental sequence, the boundaries between them are by no means sharp; indeed, the third model represents the logical outcome of a number of trends that are immanent in contemporary Western societies but not actually manifested in comprehensive and coherent form in any particular one.

The first pattern of social organization is characterized by a high degree of differentiation of male and female roles. This differentiation rests in turn on a sharp distinction of public and private arenas; while male activities are directed to public domains, women's activities center on the family and household. In some societies public activities are actually formally proscribed for women; the practice of seclusion in traditional Islamic and Hindu communities is an example of a particularly sharp segregation of male and female roles.[6]

The sharp distinction of male and female domains is sustained by prescriptive norms that characteristically derive social roles directly from biological differences. The emphasis on sexual complementarity, if not female subordination, is associated with an image of the social order as hierarchical and differentiated, in which men and women occupy a distinct and complementary place.

[5]For another effort to construct such a typology, based on structural arrangements that sustain different life options for women rather than implicit sex-role norms, see Constantina Safilios-Rothschild, "A Cross-Cultural Examination of Women's Marital, Educational, and Occupational Options," *Acta Sociologica* 14 (1971): 96–113.

[6]For an illuminating treatment of the social and symbolic implications of this pattern, see Hanna Papanek, "Purdah: Separate Worlds and Symbolic Shelter," *Comparative Studies in Society and History* 15 (June 1973): 289–325.

Public policy is typically directed toward the reinforcement of these roles. The legal and civic disabilities of women go hand in hand with high social esteem, and maternal and reproductive functions receive social support, often in the form of family allowance programs. Among modern industrial societies, those in which Roman Catholicism exercises social and political influence probably represent the closest approximation to this model; its assumptions are particularly deeply embedded in certain aspects of Christian doctrine. As is manifest in traditional theology, although all souls are viewed as equally precious to God, they are conceived as fulfilling very different earthly roles. Indeed, as a number of papal pronouncements have warned, to strive for a "false and unnatural equality with the male effects the ruin of the woman."[7] Work outside the home is not considered suitable for women, who are made by nature "for domestic labors, which greatly protect the chastity of the weak sex and correspond naturally to the well-being of children and the household."[8] Because maternity is the natural destiny of women, "the end to which the Creator has ordained her whole being," women's place is clearly within the home. The contribution of domestic and childbearing activities to the welfare of the community, as well as to the well-being of the family, deserves to be encouraged and rewarded; the Irish Constitution thus defines women's domestic activities as a service to the state itself and guarantees that no economic necessity will oblige women to undertake work outside the home to the neglect of household duties.

The underlying assumptions that characterize this model retain a certain potency in contemporary social values, but it is fair to say that the growing scope and intensity of female economic and political participation have eroded their structural basis.

A second model for the allocation of social roles is characterized by the partial assimilation of women into male roles in economic and political domains but also by the retention of traditional female responsibility for the family. Its fundamental premise is that women, but not men, have dual roles. The dominant system of values is formally egalitarian and universalistic: women are guaranteed equal legal and political rights and equal educational opportunities. At the same time, women are also assigned the primary responsibility for homemaking and child care. The expansion of female occupational roles can be sustained by a variety of child-care arrangements, including a reliance on other family members, on private domestic help, on publicly organized child-care facilities, or on some com-

[7]Pope Pius XI, "Casti connubi" *Encyclical*, 1930; see the discussion by Mary Cornelia Porter and Corey Venning, "Catholicism and Women's Role in Italy and Ireland," in *Women in the World: A Comparative Study*, eds. Lynne B. Iglitzin and Ruth Ross (Santa Barbara, 1976).

[8]Porter and Venning, "Catholicism and Women's Role," in Iglitzin and Ross, *Women in the World*.

bination of the three, but the locus of ultimate responsibility is still considered to rest with the woman.

This assimilationist model produces characteristic patterns of female economic and political participation. As is the case in the United States, as well as in a number of West European societies, a high proportion of women are engaged in nonfarm employment, with increasing numbers of married women and mothers entering the labor force.[9] Female employees are formally guaranteed equality of rights; Article 119 of the Treaty of Rome, for example, requires equal pay for equal work in all Common Market countries. Nevertheless, equality in practice is vitiated by the segmentation of the labor market, by level, by sector, and by skill categories. Female labor is treated as residual and supplementary, while opportunities for upward mobility are limited by lower educational attainments, lower continuity of employment, and indirect, if not outright discrimination. In political life, men and women are educated equally for citizenship and afforded equal rights of participation, but no special effort is made to encourage the exercise of such rights. Although patterns of female political participation vary with socioeconomic position, education, cultural patterns, and political institutions, levels of female participation are generally somewhat lower than those of males, and relatively few women play an active political role at the national level. The explicit recognition of women's dual roles is thus associated with significant constraints on equal participation in economic and political arenas.

A third and final model is one that attempts to transcend sex as a basis for the allocation of social roles. Starting with the premise that biological differences have only limited relevance for the allocation of social roles, it rests on the assumption that in modern society there are neither male nor female roles but only human ones. In the context of such roles, family and work have an important place in the lives of men and women alike. This model envisages the opportunity for men and women to participate fully in the whole range of public and private activities and the opportunity for both to move freely between instrumental and expressive behavior. In this sense, it is a model that entails the simultaneous and reciprocal redefinition of male and female roles in ways that expand the possibilities of each.[10]

[9] These trends are reviewed at greater length in Judith Blake, "The Changing Status of Women in Developed Countries," *Scientific American* 231 (September 1974): 137–47.

[10] The behavioral foundations for such an approach are provided by psychological experiments that demonstrate that traditional sex-role stereotypes restrict behavior in undesirable ways and that the integration of instrumental and expressive capacities is essential to effective human functioning; S. Bem and E. Lenney, "Sex-Typing and the Avoidance of Cross-Sex Behavior," *Journal of Personality and Social Psychology* 33 (1976): 46–54. Its social rationale and implications are spelled out in Alice Rossi, "Equality Between the Sexes: An Immodest Proposal," *Daedalus* 93 (Spring 1964): 607–52; and Eugene Litwak, "Technological Innovation and Ideal Forms of Family Structure in an Industrial Democratic Society," in *Families in East and West*, eds. Reuben Hill and Rene Konig (The Hague, 1970), pp 348–96.

An official report of the Swedish government to the United Nations in 1968 spelled out some of the conditions and possible implications of such an approach for public policy. In arguing that any lasting change in the economic and social position of women required the rejection of marriage as a device for their economic support, it challenged a basic premise of assimilationist strategies. Public policies that supported an exclusively familial role for women were criticized as a direct obstacle to the economic independence of women and to their ability to compete on equal terms in the labor market. As the report argued:

> A decisive and ultimately durable improvement in the status of women cannot be attained by special measures aimed at women alone; it is equally necessary to abolish the conditions which tend to assign certain privileges, obligations or rights to men. No decisive change in the distribution of functions and status between the sexes can be achieved if the duties of the male in the society are assumed *a priori* to be unaltered. The aim of reform work in this area must be to change the traditional division of labor which tends to deprive women of the possibility of exercising their legal rights on equal terms. The division of functions between the sexes must be changed in such a way that both the man and the woman in a family are afforded the same practical opportunities of participation in both active parenthood and gainful employment.[11]

Public policy in this model therefore assumes the obligation of both men and women to support themselves, as well as to jointly share in the responsibilities of parenthood. It repudiates the view that women alone have "two roles" by denying a biological connection between childbearing and child-rearing; the care and upbringing of children is viewed as a human role, not a female one. In economic life, it entails a commitment to full employment and to the elimination of a dual labor market, not merely through the entry of women into formerly male fields, but also through the entry of men into fields and professions previously dominated by women. The encouragement of part-time work and flexible work schedules for men and women alike is the condition of a more viable integration of family and employment. Educational policy is expected to support this goal by providing an equal and identical upbringing for boys and girls: both shop and domestic sciences are compulsory for all schoolchildren. Legislation affecting taxation, insurance, and family allowances is being rewritten to substitute parental benefits for those that accrue to one partner only, while in political life there has been an agressive recruitment of women aimed at achieving more equal levels and patterns of participation.

Variants of this approach have, of course, found some expression in modern Russian history as well. In the prerevolutionary writings of Mikhailov, in the novels of Kollontai, in individual letters to Soviet journals,

---

[11]The Swedish Institute, *The Status of Women in Sweden: Report to the United Nations, 1968* (Stockholm, 1968), p. 4.

Women in Soviet Society

and in the quest by some contemporary Soviet writers for a society based neither on patriarchy nor on matriarchy—in all these contexts there is an explicit recognition that the mere assimilation of women into male roles without a corresponding redefinition of both will continue to stand in the way of genuine liberation. But if we were to characterize the Soviet approach to sexual equality in the light of the broad typology just outlined, this much seems clear: while Soviet policy has been premised on the repudiation of extensive sex-role differentiation, its goal may be said to have been assimilation rather than sex-role transcendence. The central thrust of Soviet policy has been to superimpose new obligations of work and citizenship on more traditional definitions of femininity and to reshape to some extent the boundaries between public and family responsibilities —in short, to facilitate women's performance of both their roles—rather than to radically redefine both male and female roles.[12]

To be sure, the Soviet economy—like the economies of other East European systems—is distinguished by an unusual degree of reliance on female labor. High rates of female participation in the nonagricultural sector of the labor-force are supported in part by the extensive provision and partial public subsidization of child-care facilities. Additionally, official values emphasize the importance of women's economic independence and reject, in principle, the treatment of marriage as an arrangement in which economic support is exchanged for domestic and child-rearing services.

Nonetheless, because women's entry into new economic and political roles occurred in a context in which the primacy of women's family roles was explicitly affirmed and sustained by a wide range of facilitating measures, women's occupational mobility was also limited. To the extent that female responsibility for the internal management of the household was the condition of male achievement outside it, women entered the competitive arenas of economic and political life on fundamentally unequal terms with men. The more onerous the burden of domestic responsibilities, and the less able a given household to provide substitutes for female domestic labor, the greater the handicaps with which women confronted new opportunities. These handicaps were partly offset, as we have seen,

---

[12]A basically similar approach to female mobilization warrants the inclusion of China in this category, although the commitment to agricultural development and the effort to limit population growth have distinctive implications for the role of women. The focus of this study does not permit an extended treatment of the Chinese case, but several relevant studies include Gregory Massell, "Family Law and Social Mobilization in Soviet Central Asia: Some Comparisons with Communist China," *Canadian-American Slavic Studies* (Summer 1975): 374 –402; Shelah Leader, "The Emancipation of Chinese Women," *World Politics* 26 (October 1973); Marion Levy, *The Family Revolution in Modern China* (Cambridge, Mass., 1965); Ch'ing-k'un Yang, *Chinese Communist Society: The Family and the Village* (New York, 1968); Delia Davin, *Woman Work: Women and the Party in Revolutionary China* (Oxford, 1976); Marilyn Young, ed., *Women in China: Studies in Social Change and Feminism* (Ann Arbor, 1973).

by Soviet "affirmative action" programs, including investments in education, child care, and special conditions of employment. At the same time, however, the Soviet pattern of economic development, by limiting investment in urban infrastructure and in services, maintained pressure on the household to provide these services itself. As a consequence, Soviet patterns of modernization encouraged the integration of women into public arenas, but on terms that inhibited their full assimilation and that perpetuated and in some respects even reinforced the distinction between "men's work" and "women's work" in economic life, in politics, and in the family.

It is far from clear that the cumulative effects of current economic and social trends will result in the erosion of these patterns in the near—indeed foreseeable—future. Undeniably, increased investments in consumer goods and services will lighten the burdens of daily life under which Soviet women have long labored. However, there are a number of reasons why we might anticipate a growing differentiation of male and female roles in the years ahead. First, to the extent that a severe deficit of males, coinciding with a fundamental transformation of economic and social structure, created unprecedented pressures as well as opportunities for female mobility, the return to demographic "normalcy" for younger age cohorts, in the context of a relative saturation of elite positions, is likely to slow both the impetus and the real possibilities for the advancement of women in the educational and occupational structure.

Second, the evolution of the economy itself may serve to further reinforce the sexual segregation of the labor force. Increasing technical complexity and sophistication will be required of the industrial labor force in the years ahead, and women are likely to be forced out of skilled positions in the absence of fundamental reforms in the system of vocational education and on-the-job training. Similar trends are likely to develop in some of the professions, as the declining proportion of women physicians in recent years suggests. At the same time, the rapidly-growing service sector, with its relatively greater flexibility in accommodating part-time and irregular work, is likely to absorb increasing proportions of women who lack the specialized skills required in the industrial sector.

Finally, to the extent that the Soviet leadership actively attempts to increase the birthrate by raising the status and rewards associated with maternity and by reaffirming its present emphasis on the family's crucial role in the socialization of young children, the pressures and incentives which sustain high rates and intensities of female labor-force participation are likely to diminish correspondingly. The attractions of family-centered activities will be further enhanced if growing affluence is associated with more comfortable living conditions and the ability to afford increased female leisure.

Official encouragement of such implicitly "conservative" trends, and of the greater differentiation of male and female roles that would result from them, might well be welcomed by a considerable number of Soviet women themselves. For that matter, at this particular juncture of Russia's historical development, they might view it as a distinctly "progressive" solution. Coming as it does after decades of severe emotional and material deprivation and hardship, the promise of some respite and relaxation in an increasingly attractive privatized sphere is likely to hold, at least for a time, a considerable attraction. In the Soviet context, such trends indeed constitute a significant broadening of the range of options open to women. To be sure, they may not necessarily respond, as many demographers clearly hope they will, with a "baby boom" reminiscent of that in the United States during the 1950s. They may make altogether different use of new resources and leisure, utilizing new-found, more flexible options for cushioning their lives with unaccustomed comforts, and for enjoying all the appurtenances of romantic femininity. But to the extent that these new options effectively forestall a simultaneous redefinition of male roles in both economic and family life, they may intensify rather than diminish the differentiation of male and female roles.

Consequently, any genuinely radical departures in female roles and status and in male-female relationships and authority patterns more broadly in the years ahead are far more likely to take place in some Western societies—including the United States—than in the USSR. Despite the continuing obstacles, it is here that the most dramatic advances in women's educational and occupational attainments and in women's access to positions of political responsibility have been occurring in recent years. It is also safe to assume that it is in such democratic milieus as Sweden and the United States, which offer wide scope to the efforts of organized feminist movements, that the advances in sexual equality are likely to continue in the foreseeable future. And it is the Western feminist movement that is likely to provide the inspiration and the theoretical rationale for a truly fundamental reassessment of women's roles in modern society, including the USSR itself.

Selected Bibliography

Abramova, A. *Okhrana truda zhenshchin*. Moscow, 1972.

Abray, Jane. "Feminism in the French Revolution." *American Historical Review* 80 (February 1975): 43–62.

Acker, Joan. "Women and Social Stratification: A Case of Intellectual Sexism." *American Journal of Sociology* 8 (January 1973): 936–45.

Aminova, R. Kh. *Oktiabr' i reshenie zhenskogo voprosa v Uzbekistane*. Tashkent, 1975.

——. "Zhenshchiny Uzbekistana v avangarde stroitelei kommunizma." *Obshchestvennye nauki v Uzbekistane* 3 (March 1974): 3–39.

Amundsen, Kirsten. *The Silenced Majority*. Englewood Cliffs, N.J., 1971.

Aries, Philippe. *Centuries of Childhood: A Social History of Family Life*. Translated by Robert Baldick. New York, 1962.

Arutiunian, Iu. V. *Sotsial'naia struktura sel'skogo naseleniia SSSR*. Moscow, 1971.

Atkinson, Dorothy; Dallin, Alexander; and Lapidus, Gail Warshofsky, eds. *Women in Russia*. Stanford, 1977.

Babkina, M. "Nepolnoe rabochee vremia i zaniatost' naseleniia." *Voprosy ekonomiki* 7 (July 1973): 133–40.

Bahr, Stephen J. "Effects on Power and Division of Labor in the Family." In *Working Mothers: An Evaluative Review of the Consequences for Wife, Husband and Child*, edited by Lois W. Hoffman and F. Ivan Nye. San Francisco, 1974.

Bane, Mary Jo. *Here to Stay: American Families in the 20th Century*. New York, 1976.

Baranskaia, Natalia. "Nedelia kak nedelia." *Novyi mir* 11 (November 1969): 23–55.

Barker, G. R. "La Femme en Union Soviétique." *Sociologie et Sociétés* 4 (November 1972): 159–91.

Bebel, August. *Woman Under Socialism*. New York, 1971. (Originally published 1883).

Becker, Gary. "A Theory of Marriage." *Journal of Political Economy*, Part I, 81 (July–August 1973): 813–47; Part II, 82 (March–April 1974): 511–22.

Bell, Norman W., and Vogel, Ezra F., eds. *A Modern Introduction to the Family*. Glencoe, 1960.

Belova, V. A., and Darskii, L. E. *Statistika mnenii v izuchenii rozhdaemosti*. Moscow, 1972.

——; Bondarskaia, G. A.; Vishnevskii, A. G.; Darskii, L. E.; and Sifman, R. I. *Skol'ko detei budet v sovetskoi sem'e*. Moscow, 1977.

Bendix, Reinhard. *Nation-Building and Citizenship*. New York, 1964.

——. "Tradition and Modernity Reconsidered." *Comparative Studies in Society and History* 4 (April 1967): 266–73.

Benet, Sula, ed. and trans. *The Village of Viriatino*. New York, 1970.

Benston, Margaret. "The Political Economy of Women's Liberation." *Monthly Review* 21 (September 1969): 13–24.

347

Selected Bibliography

Berent, Jerzy. "Causes of Fertility Decline in Eastern Europe and the Soviet Union." *Population Studies*, Part I, 24 (March 1970): 35–58; Part II, 25 (July 1970): 247–92.

Bergmann, Barbara R., and Adelman, Irma. "The 1973 Report of the President's Council of Economic Advisors: The Economic Role of Women." *The American Economic Review* 63 (September 1973): 509–14.

Bilshai, Vera. *Reshenie zhenskogo voprosa v SSSR*. Moscow, 1956.

———. *The Status of Women in the Soviet Union*. Moscow, 1957.

Blake, Judith. "The Changing Status of Women in Developed Countries." *Scientific American* 231 (September 1974): 137–47.

Blaxall, Martha, and Reagan, Barbara. *Women and the Workplace: The Implications of Occupational Segregation*. Chicago, 1976.

Bliakhman, L. S., and Shkaratan, O. I. *NTR, rabochii klass, intelligentsiia*. Moscow, 1973.

Blood, Robert O., Jr. "The Measurement and Bases of Family Power: A Rejoinder." *Marriage and Family Living* 25 (November 1963): 475–77.

———, and Wolfe, Donald M. *Husbands and Wives: The Dynamics of Married Living*. Glencoe, 1960.

Bobroff, Anne. "The Bolsheviks and Working Women, 1905–20." *Soviet Studies* 26 (October 1974): 540–67.

Bochkareva, E., and Liubimova, S. *Svetlyi put': Kommunisticheskaia Partiia Sovetskogo Soiuza—borets za svobodu, ravnopravie i schast'e zhenshchiny*. Moscow, 1967.

Borisov, V. A. *Perspektivy rozhdaemosti*. Moscow, 1976.

Boserup, Esther. *Woman's Role in Economic Development*. London, 1970.

Bronfenbrenner, Uri. *Two Worlds of Childhood: US and USSR*. New York, 1968.

Brown, Donald, ed. *The Role and Status of Women in the Soviet Union*. New York, 1968.

Bryant, Louise. *Six Months in Red Russia*. New York, 1918.

Bystrianskii, Vadim A. *Kommunizm, brak i sem'ia*. Petrograd, 1921.

Campbell, A.; Converse, P.; Miller, W.; and Stokes, D. *The American Voter*. New York, 1960.

Cattell, David. *Leningrad: A Case Study of Soviet Urban Government*. New York, 1968.

Chafe, William H. *The American Woman: Her Changing Social, Economic, and Political Role, 1920–1970*. New York, 1972.

Chapman, Janet. *Real Wages in Soviet Russia*. Cambridge, Mass., 1963.

Chuiko, L. P. *Braki i razvody*. Moscow, 1975.

Chumakova, T. E. *Sem'ia, moral', pravo*. Minsk, 1974.

Churchward, L. G. "Soviet Local Government Today." *Soviet Studies* 17 (April 1966): 431–52.

Clements, Barbara. "Emancipation through Communism: The Ideology of A. M. Kollontai." *Slavic Review* 32 (June 1973): 323–38.

Cocks, Paul; Daniels, Robert V.; and Heer, Nancy Whittier. *The Dynamics of Soviet Politics*. Cambridge, Mass., 1976.

Cohen, Stephen. *Bukharin and the Bolshevik Revolution*. New York, 1973.

[Cohn], Helen Desfosses. "Population Policy in the USSR." *Problems of Communism* 22 (July–August 1973): 41–45.

———. "Demography, Ideology, and Politics in the USSR." *Soviet Studies* 28 (April 1976): 244–56.

Collins, Randall. "A Conflict Theory of Sexual Stratification." *Social Problems* 19 (Summer 1971): 3–12.

Collver, Andrew, and Langlois, Eleanor. "The Female Labor Force in Metropolitan Areas: An International Comparison." *Economic Development and Cultural Change* 10 (July 1962): 367–85.

Cook, Alice. *The Working Mother: A Survey of Problems and Programs in Nine Countries.* Ithaca, 1975.

———. "Equal Pay: Where Is It?" *Industrial Relations* 14 (May 1975):158–77.

Cooney, Rosemary Santana. "Female Professional Work Opportunities: A Cross-National Study." *Demography* 12 (February 1965): 107–20.

Coser, Lewis. "The Case of the Soviet Family." In *The Family: Its Structure and Functions*, edited by Rose Laub and Ruth Coser. New York, 1964.

Costantini, Edmond, and Craik, Kenneth. "Women as Politicians: The Social Background, Personality, and Political Careers of Female Party Leaders." *Journal of Social Issues* 28 (1972): 217–36.

Crowley, E., et al., eds. *Party and Government Officials of the Soviet Union, 1917–1967.* Metuchen, N. J., 1969.

Cuisinier, Jean, and Raquin, Catherine. "De quelques transformations dans le système familial russe." *Revue Française de Sociologie* 7 (October–December 1967): 521–57.

Current Digest of the Soviet Press. June 1968 through January 1977.

Dahrendorf, Ralf. *Essays on the Theory of Society.* Stanford, 1968.

Danilova, E. Z. *Sotsial'nye problemy truda zhenshchiny-rabotnitsy.* Moscow, 1968.

Darskii, L. E. *Formirovanie sem'i.* Moscow, 1972.

———, ed. *Rozhdaemost'.* Moscow, 1976.

Davin, Delia. "The Implications of Some Aspects of CCP Policy Toward Urban Women in the 1950's." *Modern China* 1 (October 1975): 363–78.

———. *Woman-Work: Women and the Party in Revolutionary China.* Oxford, 1976.

Davis, Kingsley. "Population Policy and the Theory of Reproductive Motivation." *Economic Development and Cultural Change* 25 (Special Supplement 1977): 159–79.

Deputaty verkhovnogo soveta SSSR. Vos'moi sozyv. Moscow, 1970.

———. *Deviatyi sozyv.* Moscow, 1974.

Dewar, Margaret. *Labor Policy in the USSR, 1917–1928.* London and New York, 1956.

De Witt, Nicholas. *Education and Professional Employment in the USSR.* Washington, D. C., 1961.

Documentazione sui paesi dell'est 11 (January 1975): *La condizione della donna nei paesi dell'est.*

Dodge, Norton T. *Women in the Soviet Economy.* Baltimore, 1966.

———. "Recruitment and the Quality of the Soviet Agricultural Labor Force." In *The Soviet Rural Community*, edited by James Millar. Urbana, Ill., 1971.

———, and Feshbach, Murray. "The Role of Women in Soviet Agriculture." In *Soviet and East European Agriculture*, edited by Jerzy F. Karcz. Berkeley and Los Angeles, 1967.

Dunham, Vera. "The Strong Woman Motif in Russian Fiction." In *The Transformation of Russian Society*, edited by C. E. Black. Cambridge, Mass., 1960.

———. *In Stalin's Time: Middle Class Values in Soviet Fiction*. New York, 1976.

Dunn, Stephen P. "Structure and Functions of the Soviet Rural Family." In *The Soviet Rural Community*, edited by James Millar. Urbana, Ill., 1971.

———, and Dunn, Ethel. *The Peasants of Central Russia*. New York, 1967.

———, and ———. "The Soviet Regime and Native Culture in Central Asia." *Cultural Anthropology* 8 (June 1967): 147–84.

———, and ———. *The Study of the Soviet Family in the USSR and in the West*. Columbus, 1977.

Duverger, Maurice. *The Political Role of Women*. Paris, 1955.

Dzhunusov, M. S. "O nekotorykh natsional'nykh osobennostiakh obraza zhizni v usloviiakh sotsializma." *Sotsiologicheskie issledovaniia* 2 (April–June 1975): 62–73.

Economic Report of the President. Washington, D. C., 1973.

Engels, F. *The Origin of the Family, Private Property, and the State*. New York, 1942. (Originally published 1884).

Fainsod, Merle. *Smolensk Under Soviet Rule*. Cambridge, Mass., 1958.

———. *How Russia Is Ruled*. 2nd ed. Cambridge, Mass., 1963.

Fallers, Lloyd. *Inequality*. Chicago, 1973.

Farnsworth, Beatrice. "Alexandra Kollontai: Bolshevism and the Woman Question." Paper delivered at the annual meeting of the American Historical Association, San Francisco, December 1973.

Feeley, Dianne. "Women and the Russian Revolution." *The Militant*, March 1971.

Feshbach, Murray. "Manpower Trends in the USSR: 1950–1980." U.S. Department of Commerce, Bureau of the Census, Foreign Demographic Analysis Division, May 1971. Mimeographed.

Field, Mark. *Soviet Socialized Medicine*. New York, 1967.

———, and Anderson, David. "The Family and Social Problems." In *Prospects for Soviet Society*, edited by A. Kassof. New York, 1968.

Fisher, Ralph. *Pattern for Soviet Youth: A Study of the Congresses of the Komsomol, 1918–1954*. New York, 1959.

Fitzpatrick, Sheila, ed. *Cultural Revolution in Russia, 1928–1933*. Bloomington, 1977.

Flexner, Eleanor. *Century of Struggle*. Cambridge, Mass., 1966.

Fogarty, Michael; Rapoport, Rhona; and Rapoport, Robert. *Sex, Career and Family*. Beverly Hills, 1971.

Galenson, Marjorie. *Women and Work*. Ithaca, N. Y. 1973.

Galetskaia, R. "Demograficheskaia politika: ee napravleniia." *Voprosy ekonomiki* 8 (August 1975): 149–52.

Gans, Herbert. *More Equality*. New York, 1973.

Gasiorowska, Xenia. *Women in Soviet Fiction*. Madison, 1968.

Geiger, Kent. *The Family in Soviet Russia*. Cambridge, Mass., 1968.

Gilison, Jerome. *The Soviet Image of Utopia*. Baltimore, 1975.

Gitelman, Zvi. *Jewish Nationality and Soviet Politics: The Jewish Sections of the CPSU, 1917–1930*. Princeton, 1972.

Glazer, Nathan. *Affirmative Discrimination: Ethnic Inequality and Public Policy*. New York, 1975.

Golod, S. I. "Sociological Problems of Sexual Morality." *Soviet Sociology* 8 (Summer 1969): 3–23.

Goode, William J. *World Revolution and Family Patterns.* New York, 1963.

Gordon, L. A., and Klopov, E. V. *Chelovek posle raboty: sotsial'nye problemy byta i vnerabochego vremeni.* Moscow, 1972.

———, and ———. *Chelovek posle raboty: sotsial'nye problemy byta i vnerabochego vremeni: Prilozhenie.* Moscow, 1972.

———, and Rimashevskaia, N. M. *Piatidnevnaia rabochaia nedelia i svobodnoe vremia trudiashchikhsia.* Moscow, 1972.

———; Klopov, E. V.; and Onikov, L. "Sotsial'nye problemy byta." *Kommunist* 17 (November 1974): 49–60.

———; ———; and Petrov, T. A. "K izucheniiu sotsialisticheskogo obraza zhizni: razvitie byta sovetskikh rabochikh v retrospektive i perspektive." *Rabochii klass i sovremennyi mir* 32 (1976): 33–20.

———; Neigol'dberg, V. Ia.; and Petrov, T. B. "Razvitoi sotsializm: blagosostoianie rabochikh." *Rabochii klass i sovremennyi mir* 20 (1973): 53–72 and 21 (1974): 15–33.

Greenstein, Fred. *Children and Politics.* New Haven, 1965.

———. "Sex-Related Political Differences in Childhood." *Journal of Politics* 2 (1961): 353–71.

Gronau, Reuben. "The Intrafamily Allocation of Time: The Value of the Housewives' Time." *American Economic Review* 63 (September 1973): 634–51.

Gross, Edward. "Plus ça change? Sexual Structure of Occupations Over Time." *Social Problems* 16 (Fall 1968): 198–208.

Gruber, Martin. *Women in American Politics.* Oshkosh, Wisc., 1968.

Grushin, B. A. *Svobodnoe vremia: aktual'nye problemy.* Moscow, 1967

Guseinov, V., and Korchagin, V. "Voprosy trudovykh resursov." *Voprosy ekonemiki* 2 (February 1972): 45–51.

Haavio-Mannila, Elina. "Convergences between East and West: Tradition and Modernity in Sex Roles in Sweden, Finalnd and the Soviet Union." *Acta Sociologica* 14 (1971): 114–25.

Halle, Fannina. *Women in Soviet Russia.* London, 1934.

———. *Women in the Soviet East.* New York, 1938

Hammer, Darrell. "The Dilemma of Party Growth." *Problems of Communism* 20 (July–August 1971) 17.

Harper, Samuel. *Civic Training in Soviet Russia.* Chicago, 1929.

Heer, David M. "The Measurement and Bases of Family Power: An Overview." *Marriage and Family Living* 25 (May 1963): 133–93.

———. "Abortion, Contraception and Population Policy in the Soviet Union." *Soviet Studies* 17 (July 1965): 76–83.

———. "The Demographic Transition in the Russian Empire and the Soviet Union." *Journal of Social History* 1 (Spring 1968): 193–240.

———. "Female Labor Force Participation Rates and Fertility in the USSR: Statics and Dynamics of the Relationship." Population Research Laboratory, University of Southern California, 1976. Mimeographed.

———. "The New Direction of Soviet Population Policy." Population Research Laboratory, University of Southern California, n.d. Mimeographed.

————— and Youssef, Nadia. "Female Status among the Central Asian Nationalities: The Melding of Islam and Marxism and its Implications for Population Increase." Population Research Laboratory, University of Southern California, n.d. Mimeographed.

Heidenheimer, Arnold, "The Politics of Public Education, Health, and Welfare in the USA and Western Europe: How Growth and Reform Potentials Have Differed." *British Journal of Political Science* 3 (July 1973): 315–40.

Hill, Ronald J. "Continuity and Change in Supreme Soviet Elections." *British Journal of Political Science* 2 (January 1972): 47–67.

Hochschild, Arlie, "A Review of Sex Role Research." *American Journal of Sociology* 78 (January 1973): 249–67.

Hodnett, Grey, and Ogareff, Val. "Leaders of the Soviet Republics 1955–1972." Canberra, 1973. Mimeographed.

Hoffberg, George. "Wages in the USSR, 1950–1966." U.S. Department of Commerce, Bureau of the Census, April 1968. Mimeographed.

Hollander, Paul. *Soviet and American Society: A Comparison*. New York, 1973.

Holter, Harriet. *Sex Roles and Social Structure*. Oslo, 1970.

—————. "Sex Roles and Social Change." *Acta Sociologica* 14 (1971): 2–12.

Hough, Jerry. "Party Saturation." In *The Dynamics of Soviet Politics*, edited by Paul Cocks, Robert V. Daniels, and Nancy Whittier Heer. Cambridge, Mass. 1976.

Huber, Joan, ed. *Changing Women in a Changing Society*. Chicago, 1973.

Huntington, Samuel, and Nelson, Joan. *No Easy Choice: Political Participation in Developing Countries*. Cambridge, Mass., 1976.

Iankova, Zoia A. "O semeino-bytovykh roliakh rabotaiushchei zhenshchiny." *Sotsial'nye issledovaniia* 4 (1970): 76–87.

—————. "Struktura gorodskoi sem'i v sotsialisticheskom obshchestve." *Sotsiologicheskie issledovaniia* 1 (1974): 100–110.

—————. "Razvitie lichnosti zhenshchiny v sovetskom obshchestve." *Sotsiologicheskie issledovaniia* 4 (1975): 42–51.

Iglitzin, Lynne, and Ross, Ruth. *Women in the World: A Comparative Study*. Santa Barbara, 1976.

Inkeles, Alex. *Social Change in Soviet Russia*. Cambridge, Mass., 1968.

—————, and Bauer, Raymond. *The Soviet Citizen: Daily Life in a Totalitarian Society*. Cambridge, Mass., 1961.

Institut Istorii Partii pri TsK Kommunisticheskoi Partii Kazakhstana. *Kompartiia Kazakhstana za 50 let (1921–71)*. Alma Ata, 1972.

Institut Istorii Partii pri TsK Kommunisticheskoi Partii Turkmenistana. *Kommunisticheskaia Partiia Turkmenistana v tsifrakh, 1925–1966*. Ashkhabad, 1967.

Institut Konkretnykh Sotsial'nykh Issledovanii AN SSR. *Sotsial'nye issledovaniia: Problemy braka, sem'i i demografii* 4 (Moscow, 1970).

—————. *Sotsial'nye issledovaniia: Metodologicheskie problemy issledovaniia byta* 7 (Moscow, 1971).

Institut Marksizma-Leninizma pri TsK KPSS. *KPSS v rezoliutsiiakh i resheniiakh*. 4 vols. Moscow, 1954–1960.

International Labour Office. *Yearbook of Labour Statistics, 1971*. Geneva, 1971.

Iuk, Z. M. *Trud zhenshchiny i sem'ia.* Minsk, 1975.

Iurkevich, N. G. *Sovetskaia sem'ia: Funktsii i usloviia stabil'nosti.* Minsk, 1970.

Ivanov. V. A. "Vazhnaia teoreticheskaia i ideologicheskaia problema." *Sotsiologicheskie issledovaniia* 1 (1975): 190–94.

Jacobs, Everett. "Soviet Local Elections: What They Are, and What They Are Not." *Soviet Studies* 22 (July 1970): 61–76.

Jancar, Barbara. "Women and Soviet Politics." In *Soviet Politics and Society in the 1970's,* edited by H. Morton and R. Tokes. New York, 1974.

Janos, Andrew. "The One-Party State and Social Mobilization: East Europe Between the Wars." In *Authoritarian Politics in Modern Society,* edited by Samuel Huntington and Clement Moore. New York and London, 1970.

Jaquette, Jane, ed. *Women and Politics.* New York, 1974.

Jowitt, Kenneth. *Revolutionary Breakthroughs and National Development: The Case of Romania 1944–1960.* Berkeley and Los Angeles, 1971.

———. "Inclusion and Mobilization in European Leninist Regimes." *World Politics* 28 (October 1975): 69–96.

———. "An Organizational Approach to the Study of Political Culture in Marxist-Leninist Systems." *The American Political Science Review* 68 (September 1974): 1171–91.

Juviler, Peter H. "Family Reform on the Road to Communism." In *Soviet Policy-Making,* edited by Peter H. Juviler and Henry W. Morton. New York, 1967.

Kadeikan, V. A. et al., eds. *Voprosy vnutripartiinoi zhizni i rukovodiaschei deiatel'nosti KPSS na sovremennom etape.* Moscow, 1974.

Kanowitz, Leo. *Women and the Law: The Unfinished Revolution.* Albuquerque, 1969.

Kassof, Allen, ed. *Prospects for Soviet Society.* New York, 1968.

Katz, Zev. "Hereditary Elements in Education and Social Structure in the USSR." University of Glasgow, Institute of Soviet and East European Studies, n.d. Mimeographed.

———. "Sociology in the Soviet Union." *Problems of Communism* 20 (May–June 1971): 22–40.

———. "Patterns of Social Stratification in the USSR." MIT Center for International Studies, Cambridge, Mass., April, 1972.

Kharchev, A. G. "Sem'ia i sotsializm." *Kommunist* 37 (May 1960): 53–63.

———. *Brak i sem'ia v SSSR.* Moscow, 1964.

———, ed. *Sem'ia kak ob"ekt filosofskogo i sotsiologicheskogo issledovaniia.* Leningrad, 1974.

———, and Golod, S. I. "Molodezh' i brak." In Leningradskii gosudarstvennyi universitet, Nauchno-issledovatel'skii institut kompleksnykh sotsial'nykh issledovanii (Uchenye zapiski, vypusk VI), *Chelovek i obshchestvo.* 1969.

———, and ———. *Professional'naia rabota zhenshchin i sem'ia.* Leningrad, 1971.

Kingsbury, Susan, and Fairchild, Mildred. *Factory, Family, and Women in the Soviet Union.* New York, 1935.

Kirkpatrick, Jeane J. *Political Woman.* New York, 1974.

Knight, Amy. "The Fritschi: Female Radicals in the Russian Populist Movement." *Canadian-American Slavic Studies,* (Spring 1975):1–17.

Kollontai, Aleksandra. *Sotsial'nye osnovy zhenskogo voprosa.* St. Petersburg, 1909.

———. *Red Love.* New York, 1927.

————. *A Great Love*. New York, 1929.

————. *Free Love*. London, 1932.

————. *The Autobiography of a Sexually Emancipated Communist Woman*, edited by Irving Fetscher. Translated by Salvator Attanasio. New York, 1971. (Originally published 1926)

————. *Izbrannye stat'i i rechi*. Moscow, 1972.

————. *Sexual Relations and the Class Struggle: Love and the New Morality*. Translated by Alix Holt. Bristol, England, 1972.

Kolokol'nikov, V. T. "Brachno-semeinye otnosheniia v sfere kolkhoznogo krest'ianstva." *Sotsiologicheskie issledovaniia* 3 (1976): 78–87.

Kolpakov, B. T., and Patrushev, V. D. *Biudzhet vremeni gorodskogo naseleniia*. Moscow, 1971.

Komarovsky, Mirra. *Blue Collar Marriage*. New York, 1962.

Kommunist. Selected issues, 1969–1974.

Kommunisticheskaia Partiia Sovetskogo Soiuza (KPSS). *Shestoi S"ezd RSDRP (Bol'shevikov). Protokoly*. (KPSS, 6th S"ezd). Moscow, 1958.

————. *Sed'moi Ekstremnyi S"ezd RKP (b). Stenograficheskii Otchet*. (KPSS, 7th S"ezd). Moscow, 1962.

Kommunistka. Selected issues, 1920–1928.

Kotliar, A. E., and Kirpa, I. "Demograficheskie aspekty zaniatosti v gorodakh s razlichnoi promyshlennoi strukturoi." *Vestnik statistiki* 7 (1972): 12–18.

————, and Turchaninova, S. Ia. *Zaniatost' zhenshchin v proizvodstve*. Moscow, 1975.

Krupskaia, Nadezhda. *O rabote sredi zhenshchin*. Moscow, 1926.

Kurtsikidze, E. G., et al., eds. *Kommunisticheskaia Partiia Gruzii v tsifrakh, 1921–1977 gg*. Tbilisi, 1971.

Kvasha, A. Ia. *Problemy ekonomiko-demograficheskogo razvitiia SSSR*. Moscow, 1974.

Lane, David D. *The Roots of Russian Communism*. Assen, Netherlands, 1969.

————. *Politics and Society in the USSR*. London, 1971.

Lane, Robert. *Political Life*. Glencoe, 1959.

Lapidus, Gail W. "Modernization Theory and Sex Roles in Critical Perspective." In *Women in Politics*, edited by J. Jaquette. New York, 1974.

————. "Political Mobilization, Participation and Leadership: Women in Soviet Politics." *Comparative Politics* 8 (October 1975): 90–118.

————. "USSR Women at Work: Changing Patterns." *Industrial Relations* 14 (May 1975):178–195.

Laslett, Peter. *The World We Have Lost*. New York, 1965.

Lenin, V. I. *Polnoe sobranie sochinenii*. 55 vols. 5th ed. Moscow, 1958–1965.

Lennon, Lotte. "Women in the USSR." *Problems of Communism* 20 (July–August 1971): 45–58.

Levkovich, M. O., et al., eds. *Bez nikh my ne pobedili by*. Moscow, 1975.

Levy, Marion. *The Family Revolution in Modern China*. New York, 1949.

Liegle, Ludwig. *The Family's Role in Soviet Education*. Translated by Susan Hecker. New York, 1975.

Lipman-Blumen, Jean. "Role de-Differentiation as a System Response to Crisis: Occupational and Political Roles of Woman." *Sociological Inquiry* 43 (April 1973): 105–30.

————. "A Crisis Framework Applied to Macrosociological Family Changes: Marriage, Divorce, and Occupational Trends Associated with World War II." *Journal of Marriage and the Family* 37 (November 1975): 889–902.

Lipset, Seymour Martin, and Bendix, Reinhard. *Social Mobility in Industrial Society.* Berkeley, 1959.

————, and Dobson, Richard. "Social Stratification and Sociology in the Soviet Union." In *Social Stratification and Mobility in the USSR*, edited by Murray Yanowitch and Wesley Fisher. White Plains, N. Y., 1973.

Literaturnaia gazeta. Selected issues, June 1968–May 1976.

Litviakov, P., ed. *Demograficheskie problemy zaniatosti.* Moscow, 1969.

Lloyd, Cynthia B., ed. *Sex Discrimination and the Division of Labor.* New York, 1975.

Luke, Louise E. "Marxian Women: Soviet Variants." In *Through the Looking Glass of Soviet Literature*, edited by Ernest Simmons. New York, 1953.

Lund, Caroline. "The Communist Party and Sexual Politics." *International Socialist Review*, March 1971.

Lunin, B., ed. *Goroda sotsializma i sotsialisticheskaia rekonstruktsiia byta.* Moscow, 1930.

Mace, David, and Mace, Vera. *The Soviet Family.* Garden City, N. Y., 1964.

Madison, Bernice. *Social Welfare in the USSR.* Stanford, 1968.

————. "Social Services for Families and Children in the Soviet Union Since 1967." *Slavic Review* 31 (December 1972): 831–52.

————. "Soviet Income Maintenance Policy for the 1970's." *Journal of Social Policy* Part 2, 2, (April 1973): 97–117.

Makarenko, Anton S. *The Collective Family: A Handbook for Russian Parents.* Translated by Robert Daglish. New York, 1967.

Maksimova, G. M. *Vsesoiuznaia perepis' naseleniia 1970 goda: sbornik statei.* Moscow, 1976.

Male, D. J. *Russian Peasant Organization Before Collectivization.* Cambridge, England, 1971.

Malia, Martin. *Alexander Herzen and the Birth of Russian Socialism: 1812–1855.* Cambridge, Mass., 1961.

Mandel, William. "Soviet Women and their Self-Image." *Science and Society* 35 (Fall 1971): 286–310.

————. "Soviet Women in the Work Force and Professions." *American Behavioral Scientist* 15 (November–December, 1971): 255–80.

————. *Soviet Women.* New York, 1975.

Marshall, T. H. *Class, Citizenship and Social Development.* Garden City, N. Y., 1964.

Martirosian, E. R. "Pravovoe regulirovanie nepolnogo rabochego vremeni." *Sovetskoe gosudarstvo i pravo* 10 (October 1976): 54–61.

Mason, Karen Oppenheim; Czajka, John L.; and Arber, Sara. "Change in U. S. Women's Sex-Role Attitudes, 1964–1974." *American Sociological Review* 41 (August 1976): 573–96.

Massell, Gregory. "Law as an Instrument of Revolutionary Change in a Traditional Milieu." *Law and Society Review* 2 (February 1968): 179–228.

————. *The Surrogate Proletariat: Moslem Women and Revolutionary Strategies in So-*

viet Central Asia, 1919–1929. Princeton, 1974.

———. "Family Law and Social Mobilization in Soviet Central Asia: Some Comparisons with Communist China." *Canadian-American Slavic Studies*, (Summer 1975):374–402.

Matskovskii, M. S., and Ermakova, O. V. "Tendentsii izmeneniia tematiki issledovanii po sotsiologii sem'i." *Sotsiologicheskie issledovaniia* 4 (1976): 88–97.

Matthews, Mervyn. *Class and Society in Soviet Russia*. New York, 1972.

Mazur, Denis Peter. "Reconstruction of Fertility Trends for the Female Population of the USSR." *Population Studies* 21 (July 1967): 33–52.

———. "Correlates of Divorce in the USSR." *Demography* 6 (1969): 279–86.

———. "Fertility and Economic Dependency of Soviet Women." *Demography* 10 (February 1973): 37–52.

———. "Relation of Marriage and Education to Fertility in the USSR." *Population Studies* 27 (March 1973): 105–16.

McIntyre, Robert J. "Pronatalist Programs in Eastern Europe." *Soviet Studies* 27 (July 1975): 366–80.

McNeal, Robert H. "Women in the Russian Radical Movement." *Journal of Social History* 5 (Winter 1971–1972): 143–63.

Michal, Jan. "An Alternate Approach to Measuring Income Inequality." Paper presented at the Conference of the International Slavic Association, Banff, August 1974.

Mikhailiuk, V. B. *Ispol'zovanie zhenskogo truda v narodnom khoziaistve*. Moscow, 1970.

Millar, James R., ed. *The Soviet Rural Community*. Urbana, 1971.

Millett, Kate. *Sexual Politics*. Garden City, N. Y., 1970.

Monich, Zinaida I. "The Professional and Paraprofessional Component in the Structure of the Rural Population." *Soviet Sociology* 12 (Summer 1973): 56–76.

Moore, Barrington. *Soviet Politics: The Dilemma of Power*. Cambridge, Mass., 1950.

Newth, J. A. "The Communist Party of Uzbekistan, 1959." *Soviet Studies* 17 (April 1966): 484–89.

Nikolaeva-Tereshkova, Valentina. "Zhenskii vopros v sovremennoi obshchestvennoi zhizni." *Pravda*, February 4, 1975, pp. 2–3.

Ofer, Gur. *The Service Sector in Soviet Economic Growth: A Comparative Study*. Cambridge, Mass., 1973.

———. "Industrial Structure, Urbanization, and Growth Strategy of Socialist Countries." Research Report No. 53, Hebrew University of Jerusalem. Jerusalem, 1974.

Oppenheimer, Valerie. *The Female Labor Force in the United States: Demographic and Economic Factors Governing Its Growth and Changing Composition*. Population Monograph Series No. 5, Institute of International Studies, University of California. Berkeley, 1970.

———. "Demographic Influence on Female Employment." *American Journal of Sociology* 78 (1973): 946–61.

Osborn, Robert. *Soviet Social Policies: Welfare, Equality and Community*. Homewood, Ill., 1970.

Osipov, G. V., and Shchepan'skii, Ia., eds. *Sotsial'nye problemy truda i proizvodstva*.

Moscow, 1969.

Osmond, Marie Withers, and Martin, Patricia Yancey. "Sex and Sexism: A Comparison of Male and Female Sex-Role Attitudes." *Journal of Marriage and the Family* 37 (November 1975): 744–58.

Ostapenko, L. V. "Vliianie novoi proizvodstvennoi roli zhenshchiny na ee polozhenie v sem'e." *Sovetskaia etnografiia* No. 5 (1971): 95–102.

Papanek, Hanna. "Purdah: Separate Worlds and Symbolic Shelter." *Comparative Studies in Society and History* 15 (June 1973): 289–325.

Parsons, Talcott, and Bales, Robert, eds. *Family, Socialization, and the Interaction Process*. New York, 1955.

Partiinaia zhizn'. Selected issues, 1969–1974.

Patai, R., ed. *Women in the Modern World*. New York, 1967.

Patrushev, V. D. *Vremia kak ekonomicheskaia kategoriia*. Moscow, 1966.

Perevedentsev, V. "Problemy vosproizvodstva naseleniia." *Voprosy ekonomiki* 6 (June 1976): 127–33.

Perrie, Maureen. "The Social Composition and Structure of the Socialist-Revolutionary Party before 1917." *Soviet Studies* 24 (October 1972): 223–50.

Pethybridge, Roger. *The Social Prelude to Stalinism*. London, 1974.

Petrosian, G. S. *Vnerabochee vremia trudiashchikhsia v SSSR*. Moscow, 1965.

Pimenova, A. L. "Sem'ia i perspektivy razvitiia obshchestvennogo truda zhenshchin pri sotsializme." *Nauchnye doklady vysshei shkoly: filosofskie nauki* 3 (1966): 35–44.

―――. "Novyi byt i stanovlenie vnutrisemeinogo ravenstva." *Sotsial'nye issledovaniia* 7 (1971): 34–45.

Pirozhkov, S. I. *Demograficheskie protsessy i vozrastnaia struktura naseleniia*. Moscow, 1976.

Piskunov, V. P., and Steshenko, V. S., eds. *Demograficheskaia politika*. Moscow, 1974.

Pleck, Joseph. "Work and Family Roles: From Sex Patterned Segregation to Integration." University of Michigan, 1975. Mimeographed.

Plenum Ivanovskogo Obkoma KPSS. "Povyshat' politicheskuiu i proizvodstvennuiu aktivnost' zhenshchin," *Partiinaia zhizn'* 16 (August 1975): 39–45.

Porokhniuk, E. V., and Shepeleva, M. S. "O sovmeshchenii proizvodstvennykh i semeinykh funktsii zhenshchin-rabotnits." *Sotsiologicheskie issledovaniia* 4 (1975): 102–8.

Pravda. Selected issues, 1968–1976.

Prudenskii, G. A. *Problemy rabochego i vnerabochego vremeni*. Moscow, 1972.

Putnam, Robert. *The Comparative Study of Political Elites*. New York, 1976.

Rakowska-Harmstone, Teresa. *Russia and Nationalism in Central Asia: The Case of Tadzhikistan*. Baltimore, 1970.

Razin, I., ed. *Komsomol'skii byt*. Moscow-Leningrad, 1927.

Reich, Wilhelm. *The Sexual Revolution*. 4th ed. rev. Translated by Theodore P. Wolfe. New York, 1969.

Rigby, T. H. *Communist Party Membership in the USSR*. Princeton, 1968.

Rimlinger, Gaston. *Welfare Policy and Industrialization in Europe, America, and Russia*. New York, 1971.

Roby, Pamela, ed. *Child Care: Who Cares?* New York, 1973.

Rodman, Hyman. *Marital Power and the Theory of Resources in Cultural Context*. Detroit, 1970.

Rosaldo, Michelle, and Lamphere, Louise, eds. *Women, Culture and Society*. Stanford, 1974.

Rossi, Alice S. "Equality between the Sexes: An Immodest Proposal." *Daedalus* 93 (Spring 1964): 607–52.

———. "Sex Equality: The Beginning of an Ideology." *The Humanist*, September–October 1969.

———, ed. *John Stuart Mill and Harriet Taylor Mill: Essays on Sex Equality*. Chicago, 1970.

Rowbotham, Sheila. *Women, Resistance, and Revolution*. New York, 1972.

Rumiantseva, M. S., and Pergament, A. I. *Spravochnik zhenshchiny-rabotnitsy*. Moscow, 1975.

Rutkevich, M. N., ed. *The Career Plans of Youth*. White Plains, N. Y., 1969.

Sacks, Michael Paul. *Women's Work in Soviet Russia*. New York, 1976.

Sadvokasova, E. A. *Sotsial'no-gigienicheskie aspekty regulirovaniia razmerov sem'i*. Moscow, 1969.

Safilios-Rothschild, Constantina. "The Study of Family Power Structure: A Review 1960–1969." *Journal of Marriage and the Family* 32 (November 1970): 539–52.

———. "A Cross-Cultural Examination of Women's Marital, Educational, and Occupational Options." *Acta Sociologica* 14 (1971): 96–113.

Sakharova, N. A. *Optimal'nye vozmozhnosti ispol'zovaniia zhenskogo truda v sfere obshchestvennogo proizvodstva*. Kiev, 1973.

Salaff, Janet, and Merkle, Judith. "Women in Revolution: The Lessons of the Soviet Union and China." *Berkeley Journal of Sociology* 15 (1970): 166–91.

Schlesinger, Rudolph, comp. *Changing Attitudes in Soviet Russia: The Family in the USSR*. London, 1949.

Schwarz, Solomon. *Labor in the Soviet Union*. New York, 1931.

Scott, Joan W., and Tilly, Louise A. "Women's Work and the Family in 19th Century Europe." *Comparative Studies in Society and History* 17 (January 1975): 36–64.

Selivanova, Nina N. *Russia's Women*. New York, 1923.

Serebrennikov, G. N. *The Position of Women in the USSR*. London, 1937.

Sergeeva, G. "O professional'noi strukture rabotaiushchikh zhenshchin." *Planovoe khoziaistvo* 11 (November 1976): 37–46.

Shanin, Teodor. *The Awkward Class*. Oxford, 1972.

Shinn, William T. "The Law of the Russian Peasant Household." *Slavic Review* 20 (December 1961).

Shishkan, N. "Nepolnyi rabochii den' dlia zhenshchin v usloviiakh sotsializma." *Ekonomicheskie nauki* 8 (1971): 42–47.

———. *Trud zhenshchin v usloviiakh razvitogo sotsializma*. Kishinev, 1976.

Shkaratan, O. I. "Sotsial'naia struktura sovetskogo rabochego klassa." *Voprosy filosofii* 1 (1967): 28–39.

Shlindman, Sh., and Zvidrin'sh, P., *Izuchenie rozhdaemosti*. Moscow, 1973.

Shmelev, G. I. *Raspredelenie i ispol'zovanie truda v kolkhozakh*. Moscow, 1964.

Shorter, Edward. *The Making of the Modern Family*. New York, 1975.

Shubkin, V. N., and Kochetov, G. M. "Rukovoditel', kollega, podchinennyi." *Sotsial'nye issledovaniia* 2 (Moscow, 1968): 143–55.

Shukurova, Kh. S. *Sotsializm i zhenshchina Uzbekistana.* Tashkent, 1970.

Sifman, R. I. *Dinamika rozhdaemosti v SSSR.* Moscow, 1974.

———, and Darskii, L. E. "Indices of Rate of Marriage and Fertility of Women." *Soviet Sociology* 8 (Summer 1969): 95–109.

Silver, Brian. "Levels of Sociocultural Development among Soviet Nationalities: A Partial Test of the Equalization Hypothesis." *American Political Science Review* 68 (December 1974): 1618–37.

Skilling, H. Gordon, and Griffiths, Franklin, eds. *Interest Groups in Soviet Politics.* Princeton, 1971.

Skolnick, Arlene S., and Skolnick, Jerome. *Family in Transition.* Boston, 1971.

Slesarev, G. A. *Metodologiia sotsiologicheskogo issledovaniia problem narodonaseleniia SSSR.* Moscow, 1965.

Smelser, Neil. *Social Change in the Industrial Revolution.* Chicago, 1959.

Smith, Jessica. *Women in Soviet Russia.* New York, 1927.

Smuts, Robert W. *Women and Work in America.* New York, 1959.

Solov'ev, N.; Lazauskas, Iu.; and Iankova, A., eds. *Problemy byta, braka i sem'i.* Vilnius, 1970.

Sonin, M. "'Demograficheskii vzryv ili novye zakonomernosti." *Mirovaia ekonomika i mezhdunarodnye otnosheniia* 6 (1970): 131–35.

"Sotsial'no-filosofskie problemy demografii." *Voprosy istorii* 9 (1974): 84–97; 11 (1974): 83–96; 1 (1975): 57–78.

Sovetskaia Sotsiologicheskaia Assotsiatsiia, Institut konkretnykh sotsial'nykh issledovanii AN SSSR. *Dinamika izmeneniia poiozheniia zhenshchiny i sem'ia.* 3 vols. Moscow, 1972.

Soviet Review. Selected issues, 1968–1974.

Sperling, Gerald, and Zurick, Elia. "Social Composition of the Communist Parties of Central Asia." *Studies on the Soviet Union,* New Series 8 (1968): 30–45.

Stacey, Judith. "When Patriarchy Kowtows: The Significance of the Chinese Family Revolution for Feminist Theory." *Feminist Studies* 2 (1975): 76–112.

Stalin, J. V. *Sochineniia.* 13 vols. Moscow, 1946–1952.

Starodub, B. I. *Zhenshchina i obshchestvennyi trud.* Leningrad, 1975.

Stewart, Philip. *Political Power in the Soviet Union: A Study of Decision-Making in Stalingrad.* New York, 1965.

Stites, Richard. "M. L. Mikhailov and the Emergence of the Woman Question in Russia." *Canadian Slavic Studies* 3 (Summer 1969): 178–99.

———. "Women's Liberation Movements in Russia, 1900–1930." *Canadian-American Slavic Studies* 7 (Winter 1973): 460–74.

———. "Zhenotdel 1917–1930: Bolshevism and Women's Liberation." *Russian History,* in press.

Strumilin, S. G. *Izbrannye proizvedeniia.* Vol. 3. Moscow, 1964.

Stuart, Robert. "Structural Change and the Quality of Soviet Collective Farm Management, 1952–1966." In *The Soviet Rural Community,* edited by James Millar. Urbana, 1971.

Suleimanova, A. A. "Iz opyta raboty zhenotdelov po privlecheniiu zhenshchin Tadzhikistana k aktivnomu uchastiiu v obshchestvennoi zhizni v gody pervoi

360   Selected Bibliography

piatiletki."*Uchenye zapiski* 76 (1971).
Sullerot, Evelyne. *Woman, Society and Change*. London, 1971.
Supplement of the Bulletin of the Institute for the Study of the USSR. May 1971.
Szalai, Alexander. *The Use of Time: Daily Activities of Urban and Suburban Populations in 12 Countries*. The Hague, 1972.
Tatarinova, N. I. *Stroitel'stvo kommunizma i trud zhenshchin*. Moscow, 1964.
————. "Nauchno-tekhnicheskii progress i trud zhenshchin." *Voprosy ekonomiki* 11 (1973): 57–64.
Tiger, Lionel, and Shepher, Joseph. *Women in the Kibbutz*. New York, 1975.
Tikhomorov, L. *Russia, Political and Social*. Vol. 2. London, 1883.
Timasheff, Nicholas S. *The Great Retreat*. New York, 1946.
Tolkunova, V. N. *Pravo zhenshchin na trud i ego garantii*. Moscow, 1967.
————. "K voprosu o ravenstve zhenshchin v trude i bytu pri sotsializme." *Sovetskoe gosudarstvo i pravo* 10 (1969): 17–21.
———— *Sotsial'naia pomoshch' i trudovye l'goty zhenshchinam po materinstvu v SSSR*. Moscow, 1973.
————. *Trud zhenshchin*. Moscow, 1973.
————, ed. *Zakonodatel'stvo o pravakh zhenshchin v SSSR*. Moscow, 1975.
Trotskii, Leon. *Problems of Everyday Life*. New York, 1973.
————. *The Revolution Betrayed*. Translated by Max Eastman. New York, 1937.
————. *Women and the Family*. New York, 1970.
Tsentral'noe statisticheskoe upravlenie pri sovete ministrov SSSR. *Itogi vsesoiuznoi perepisi naseleniia 1970 goda: Tom 2: Pol, vozrast i sostoianie v brake naseleniia SSSR, soiuznykh i avtonomnykh respublik, kraev i oblastei*. Moscow, 1972.
————. *Itogi vsesoiuznoi perepisi naseleniia 1970 goda: Tom 3: Uroven' obrazovaniia naseleniia SSSR, soiuznykh i avtonomnykh respublik, kraev i oblastei*. Moscow, 1972.
————. *Itogi vsesoiuznoi perepisi naseleniia 1970 goda: Tom 4: Natsional'nyi sostav naseleniia SSSR, soiuznykh i avtonomnykh respublik, kraev i oblastei*. Moscow, 1973.
————. *Itogi vsesoiuznoi perepisi naseleniia 1970 goda: Tom 6: Raspredelenie naseleniia SSSR i soiuznykh respublik po zaniatiiam*. Moscow, 1973.
————. *Narodnoe khoziaistvo SSSR: 1922–1972*. Moscow, 1972.
————. *Narodnoe khoziaistvo SSSR v 1972 g*. Moscow, 1973.
————. *Narodnoe khoziaistvo SSSR v 1973 g*. Moscow, 1974.
————. *Narodnoe khoziaistvo SSSR v 1974 g*. Moscow, 1975.
————. *Narodnoe khoziaistvo SSSR v 1975 g*. Moscow, 1976.
————. *Narodnoe khoziaistvo SSSR za 60 let*. Moscow, 1977.
————. *Narodnoe obrazovanie, nauka i kul'tura v SSSR*. Moscow, 1971.
————. *Naselenie SSSR 1973: Statisticheskii sbornik*. Moscow, 1975.
————. *Zhenshchiny i deti v SSSR*. Moscow, 1969.
————. *Zhenshchiny v SSSR: Statisticheskii sbornik*. Moscow, 1975.
Tsentral'noe statisticheskoe upravlenie pri sovete ministrov Turkmenskoi SSR. *Narodnoe khoziaistvo TSSR v 1974 g*. Ashkhabad, 1976.
————. *Zhenshchiny sovetskogo Turkmenistana*. Ashkhabad, 1973.
Tucker, Robert. *Stalin as Revolutionary, 1879–1929*. New York, 1973.
Tyrkova-Williams, Ariadne. *Na putiakh k svobode*. New York, 1952.
Urlanis, B. Ts. *Problemy dinamiki naseleniia SSSR*. Moscow, 1974.

U. S. Congress Joint Economic Committee. *Soviet Economic Prospects for the Seventies.* Washington, D. C., 1973.

——. *Soviet Economy in a New Perspective.* Washington, D. C., 1976.

U. S. Department of Labor. *1975 Handbook on Women Workers.* Washington D.C., 1975.

Valentei, D. I., et al., eds. *Demograficheskii analiz rozhdaemosti.* Moscow, 1974.

——. *Demograficheskaia situatsiia v SSSR.* Moscow, 1976.

——. *Narodonaselenie: Naselenie i trudovye resursy.* Moscow, 1973.

Vanek, Joann. "Time Spent in Housework." *Scientific American* 231 (November 1974): 116–20.

Vermishev, K. "Stimulirovanie rosta naseleniia." *Planovoe khoziaistvo* 12 (December 1972): 102–7.

Vishnevskii, A. G. "Demograficheskie protsessy v SSSR." *Voprosy filosofii* 9 (1973): 115–27.

——. *Demograficheskaia revoliutsiia.* Moscow, 1976.

Voprosy vnutripartiinoi zhizhni. Moscow, 1974.

Vorozheikin, E. M. *Brak i sem'ia v SSSR.* Moscow, 1973.

Wadekin, Karl. *The Private Sector in Soviet Agriculture.* Berkeley, 1973.

Wilensky, Harold. "Women's Work: Economic Growth, Ideology, Structure." *Industrial Relations* 7 (May 1968): 235–48.

Winch, Robert F. *The Modern Family.* Rev. ed. New York, 1963.

Winter, Ella. *Red Virtue: Human Relationships in the New Russia.* New York, 1933.

Wolf, Margery, and Witke, Roxanne, eds. *Women in Chinese Society.* Stanford, 1975.

Woody, Thomas. *New Minds: New Men?* New York, 1932.

Yanowitch, Murray, and Dodge, Norton T. "The Social Evaluation of Occupations in the Soviet Union." *Slavic Review* 28 (December 1969): 619–43.

—— and Fisher, Wesley, eds. *Social Stratification and Mobility in the USSR.* White Plains, N. Y., 1973.

Young, Marilyn, ed. *Women in China: Studies in Social Change and Feminism.* Ann Arbor, 1973.

Zalkind, Aron. *Revoliutsiia i molodezh'.* Moscow, 1925.

Zaripova, N. "Zhenshchiny—aktivnye stroiteli kommunizma." *Kommunist* 12 (1965): 26–33.

Zdravomyslov, A. G.; Rozhin, V. P.; and Iadov, V. A. *Chelovek i ego rabota.* Moscow, 1967.

Zelditch, Morris. "Role Differentiation in the Nuclear Family." In *Family, Socialization, and Interaction Process*, edited by Talcott Parsons, Robert Bales, and others. New York, 1955.

Zetkin, Clara. *Reminiscences of Lenin.* London, 1929.

"Zhenshchiny v SSSR." *Vestnik statistiki* 1 (January 1977): 82–95.

Index

Abduction of women, in Central Asia, 61
Abortion, 121
  Decree on Legalization of Abortions
    (1920), 60n–61n
  number of, 299
  Soviet policy toward, 1960s, 239
  Stalin's attack on, 113–14
Academy of Sciences of USSR, 297–98
  women members of, 156 table, 189
Adams, Abigail, 20
Administration, 178 table, 179–80, 184
    table, 222 table. *See also*
    Occupations, vertical structure of;
    Political roles, female
Adultery, as cause of divorce, 255, 256
    table
Affection, loss of, as cause of divorce, 255,
    256 table
Affirmative action strategy, Soviet, 13,
    123–60
  educational opportunities, 135–60
  protective labor legislation, 124–28
  public child-care institutions, 128–35
Age
  age structure in Baltic and Slavic
    republics, 295
  of female *obkom* bureau members, at
    appointment, 224
  illegitimate births per 1000 women,
    Belorussia, 1959 and 1970, by age
    group, 259 table
  at marriage, in select republics, 260
  number of births per 1000 females by
    age of mother, 1926/27–1973/74, 294
    table
  number of males and females, married,
    by age group, 1959 and 1970, 252
    table
  number of males and females, married,
    by age group, in Uzbekistan and
    Lithuania, 1959 and 1970, 253 table
  time-allocation differential of males and
    females correlated with, 273
Agriculture. *See also* Collective farms; Labor
    force, agricultural, female
    participation in; Rural society
  collectivization of, 104
  and changing role of women, 96
  private sector share of, 105n
  vertical structure of occupations in,
    175–81

Agriculture (Continued)
  collective-farm workers, 176–77, 178
    table, 179
  low status of, 180–81
  mobility in, 176–77, 179
  private subsidiary workers, 176, 179
  state farm workers, 176–77, 178 table,
    179
  women employed in
    average monthly wages, 1975, 192 table
    in management positions, 178 table,
      179–80, 184 table, 222 table
    in prerevolutionary Russia, 164
    in socialized sector, 1940–74, 172 table
Alcoholism, 288
  as cause of divorce, 255, 256 table
Alimony
  in contemporary Soviet law, 240
  in 1922 Land Code, 92
All-Russian League for Women's Equality,
    32
Apoliticism, female, 199–200
Armand, Inessa, 40, 44, 47–48, 51–52, 63,
    88
Armenia, Soviet Socialist Republic of
  age of women at marriage, 260
  composition of deputies elected to local
    soviets, 1975, by sex, Party
    affiliation, and occupation, 206 table
  divorce rate, 255n
  family behavior trends, 262
  family size, 250, 261 table
  population growth rate, 1974, 296 table
  secondary school female dropout rate,
    140
  women as school directors, 187
Armenian nationality
  female-male education ratio, urban and
    rural, 1959 and 1970, 142 table
  literacy rate, by sex, 141
  women in higher education, 1960 and
    1970/71, 153 table
Arts, women in, and average monthly
    wages of, 1975, 192 table
Assimilationist orientation to sex roles,
    324–25, 333–34, 341–42, 344
Austria, female participation in labor force
    in, 162
Authority structure
  Bolshevik authoritarianism and women's
    political activity, 203

United States (Continued)
feminism, 17
proportion of women holding graduate
degrees, compared to Soviet Union,
158
view of family, 233
women as percentage of physicians, 188n
Urbanization
as consequence of First Five Year Plan,
100–102
and family behavior trends, 262
sexual equality and, 5
Urban society. *See also* Housing conditions
family size, 250, 261 table
female participation in soviets, 204
and industrialization under Stalin, 105–6
political mobilization of women in, 68
Uzbekistan, Soviet Socialist Republic of
age of women at marriage, 260
backlash effect of women's political
mobilization, 69–70
composition of deputies elected to local
soviets, 1975, by sex, Party
affiliation, and occupation, 206 table
divorce rate, 255n
family size, 261 table, 295
population growth rate, 1974, 296 table
proportion of married men and number
of men and women married, per
1000, 1959 and 1970, 253 table
women as percentage of all teachers, 187
Uzbek nationality
female-male education ratio, urban and
rural, 1959 and 1970, 142 table
women in higher education, 1960 and
1970/71, 153 table
Urlanis, Boris, 292, 310
on family allocation program and child
care, 306–7, 309, 315

Values. *See also* Legal engineering
alteration of social values in favor of large
families, 301–2
contemporary trend toward privatization
and assertion of family values, 86,
246–47
desired and actual, for sexual division of
labor, 274–75
femininity and nurturance as values
stressed in sexual-differentiation
orientation toward sex roles, 325–29
post-revolutionary transformation of,
54–57
Vel't, Nina, 90
Viriatino, 177
Vocational-technical schools. *See*
Education, technical-vocational

Wages and earnings. *See also* Income
average monthly wage, 1972, 170
bonuses for management, 194
decline in real wages during First Five
Year Plan, 102
distribution of women workers and
employees, and average monthly
earnings, by economic sector, 1975,
192 table
impact of occupational stratification,
190–94
level of, as determinant of large-scale
recruitment of women into labor
force, 169–70
male-female wage differentials, 127,
190–94
correlated with educational
background, 184–85, 186 table
due to occupational segregation,
163–64
Soviet wage structuure, economic and
political priorities of, 190
Wallace, Anthony, on goal culture, 55
Washing machines, 34
Welfare administration, women in, 220
Wollstonecraft, Mary, 20
Woman question in prerevolutionary
Russia, 17–53
Bolshevism and feminism, 44–53
emergence of Russian feminism, 26–34
Marxism and Leninism on, 40–44
Russian radicalism, 24–40
Women's affairs, administration of, women
in leadership positions, 222 table
Women's liberation
conditions necessary for, in Marxism,
42
emergence of issue in 1960s, 285
Soviet critique of American movement's
ideology, 322n–23n
Soviet policy contradictions on, 235–49
Work conditions
coordination of work and vacation
schedules of spouses, 301
reduction of work week and sexual
division of labor in family, 276–77
regulation of, 124–28
suggestions for improvement of, 319
Work day, reduction of, 60n, 319. *See also*
Part-time employment
Work roles. *See* Labor force, female
participation in; Occupational roles,
family roles and
World War I, political organization of
women and, 49–50
World War II
effect on female industrial labor force, 99